DECIPHERING ECONOMICS

DECIPHERING ECONOMICS

Timely Topics Explained

David E. O'Connor

 GREENWOOD

AN IMPRINT OF ABC-CLIO, LLC

Santa Barbara, California • Denver, Colorado • Oxford, England

Library of Congress Cataloging-in-Publication Data

O'Connor, David E. (David Edward)
  Deciphering economics : timely topics explained / David E. O'Connor.
    pages cm
  Includes bibliographical references and index.
  ISBN 978–1–4408–0410–6 (hard copy : alk. paper) — ISBN 978–1–4408–0411–3 (ebook) 1. Economics.
I. Title.
HB71.O273   2014
330—dc23   2013045850

ISBN: 978–1–4408–0410–6
EISBN: 978–1–4408–0411–3

18 17 16 15 14   1 2 3 4 5

This book is also available on the World Wide Web as an eBook.
Visit www.abc-clio.com for details.

Greenwood
An Imprint of ABC-CLIO, LLC

ABC-CLIO, LLC
130 Cremona Drive, P.O. Box 1911
Santa Barbara, California 93116-1911

This book is printed on acid-free paper ∞

Manufactured in the United States of America

Contents

List of Figures

List of Tables

Preface

Throughout history changes in the human condition have stimulated debate about how to best answer society's basic economic questions of what, how, and for whom to produce. Over the past two and a half centuries the economic debate matured. Professional economists formed and tested theories in the laboratory of everyday life. Some theories reinforced the status quo, while others fomented revolution. All attempted to explain or influence the economic behaviors of people.

Today the study of economics is highly scientific. Yet even with centuries of accumulated knowledge and the use of computer modeling techniques, economists are unable to untangle some of our most vexing economic mysteries. During the 1990s, for example, the U.S. economy reveled in its seeming conquest of inflation and unemployment. Optimism reigned as the confident nation experienced a decade of economic growth and prosperity. A modest economic downturn in the early 2000s dampened this confidence some. Truly humbling were the more recent financial crises and the Great Recession (2007–2009), which reminded us that there were still lessons to learn.

Changes in economic conditions tend to jostle people's worldview and serve as a springboard to new economic thinking, reforms, even revolution. The Great Depression of the 1930s, for instance, changed many Americans' view about limited government. In the blink of an eye, at least in the grand scheme of economic history, the time-honored laissez-faire doctrine was swept under the rug in favor of a more interventionist role for government—a role that made growth in national output, full employment, and price stability government responsibilities. And words penned by economists, such as John Maynard Keynes, were at the epicenter of this transition.

Deciphering Economics, as the book title implies, acknowledges that the study of economics is part art and part science. It seems the professional economists are still "deciphering"! It is true that the basic principles of economics are derived from thoughtful and ongoing experimentation and research. Yet the study of economics is grounded in the real world, a world that refuses to stand still and, at times, defies predictability. Changing conditions make the study of economics dynamic, fraught with wrangling, debate, even derision. These debates are far more than stuffy academic exercises, however. Instead, they influence local, national, and global policies and actions—and thus affect our own quality of life and the economic landscape of the planet. *Deciphering Economics* hopes to increase your knowledge base and comfort level in economics—and your willingness to join the conversation!

Acknowledgments

The author recognizes the following individuals for their contribution to this reference book: Raquel Reichard, freelance graphics specialist, for the production of the book's charts, graphs, and diagrams; Armand Saccomanno, teacher, for his assistance in the production of the book's tables; Brian Romer, acquisitions editor, for his assistance in drafting the original book proposal; Erin Ryan, preproduction and media editor, for her assistance with photograph and primary documents permissions; the core of teachers and academic, public, and corporate librarians who reviewed the initial book proposal; Nicole Azze, Production Coordinator; Suba Ramya Nambiaruran, Project Manager; Caroline Price, Media Resource Analyst; and Hilary D. Claggett, senior editor for business, economics and finance, for her patient guidance throughout the project.

The author recognizes the following professional organizations for their work on behalf of economic education in the United States. These include the National Council on Economic Education (NCEE) and the Foundation for Teaching Economics (FTE). Over the years their innovative programs for teachers and students and their instructional materials have advanced the cause of economic literacy at the elementary, middle, and high school levels. Appreciation is also extended to the National Council for the Social Studies (NCSS) for its continued support for economic education in the nation's schools.

The author recognizes the following government agencies and multilateral organizations for their efforts to collect, analyze, and report on the state of the U.S. and global economy. Significant contributions to this reference book were made by U.S. government agencies such as the Bureau of Labor Statistics, Bureau of Economic Analysis, International Trade Administration, Office of Management and Budget, Federal Reserve System, and U.S. Census Bureau. Similarly, special appreciation is extended to multilateral organizations for sharing global economic data and insights with the people of the world. Included are the International Labor Organization, International Monetary Fund, Organization for Economic Cooperation and Development, United Nations Conference on Trade and Development, United Nations Development Program, World Bank Group, and the World Trade Organization.

Using This Reference

Deciphering Economics: Timely Topics Explained explores the fundamentals of economics. In language that is clear and precise, this reference guide introduces and applies the basic economic concepts and principles, analyzes economic choices and decisions, examines competing theories, traces historical trends and movements, and explains the operation of the U.S. and global economy. The structure of this user-friendly reference guide enables students, teachers, researchers, and others to quickly access a wealth of timely information. The four main parts of the book create a logical flow to economic information from an introduction to economics (Chapters 1–3), to microeconomic topics (Chapters 4–7), to macroeconomic topics (Chapters 8–10), and finally to international economics (Chapters 11–13). The ease of access to specific information is also enhanced by the structure of each chapter. That is, information within chapters is organized under a series of major headings and subheadings. A chapter summary is found at the end of each chapter.

A number of strategies will help users of *Deciphering Economics* locate information. Readers seeking information on a general topic such as "economic systems," "business organizations," or "international trade" should begin their search by scanning the table of contents at the beginning of the book. The 13 chapter titles and the major headings beneath each title give clear indications about the subject of each chapter. For example, "economic systems" is covered in some detail in Chapter 3, "Economic History and Economic Systems." The four major headings in Chapter 3 include:

- Stages of Economic History
- Economic Systems: The Models
- Capitalism
- Other Economic Systems

The reader can further narrow the search by scanning the Chapter 3 subheadings. For example, under the major heading "Other Economic Systems" there are four subheadings. These subheadings divide the topic of other economic systems as follows:

- Socialism
- Communism

- Economies in Transition: Shock Therapy in The Russian Federation
- Economies in Transition: Gradualism in The People's Republic of China

Another way for readers to fine-tune their search for specific information is to scan the general index at the end of the book and other book features. The general index provides instant access, by page number, to additional information on a topic. The reader could use the general index to locate additional information on "Economies in Transition: Gradualism in the People's Republic of China" under the heading "China." Other book features also deal with China's economy. "Economics in History: The Case of Hong Kong and Economic Freedom"; Table 11.1, "Top Exporting and Importing Nations, 2012"; Table 12.3, "Largest U.S. Merchandise Trade Deficits and Surpluses, 2012"; and "A Timeline: Key Economic Events That Shaped the Modern Era, 1776 to 2014" all give additional detail about China's economic transition.

The breadth of information, and the meticulous attention to citing authoritative sources, makes the use of this reference book adaptable to many learning situations. It is an excellent print source for research papers, reports, or projects. It is a handy academic guide for students at the high school or undergraduate levels, or in teacher preparation programs. It is also a comprehensive citizen's guide for expanding people's understandings of many timely economic topics.

Consider the comprehensiveness of this reference guide. Part I, "An Introduction to Economics," consists of Chapters 1–3. These chapters provide a foundation for the study of economics. This part introduces the basic economic concepts, principles, and methodology of economics. It also traces the stages of economic history and the formation of economic systems. Part II, "Microeconomic Topics," consists of Chapters 4–7. These chapters examine in detail the roles of the individual decision makers in the economy—consumers, businesses, workers, and the government. Part III, "Macroeconomic Topics," consists of Chapters 8–10. Macroeconomics, which became a branch of economics during the late 1930s and 1940s, analyzes the performance of the overall economy. This part of the book focuses on economic growth and stability in the U.S. economy. Part IV, "International Economics," consists of Chapters 11–13. This part deals with the forces that support global economic connectivity, a process that economists typically refer to as globalization. It also deals with the prospects for sustainable economic development in our increasingly interdependent world.

Like other aspects of *Deciphering Economics,* the information that appears in the book's front matter and back matter facilitates access to general or specific topics. The *front matter* includes a list of figures, list of tables, guide to related topics, and "A Timeline: Key Economic Events that Shaped the Modern Era, 1776–2014." The lists of figures and tables identify by title and page number more than 80 tables, charts and graphs, diagrams, and formulas, that support and enrich the running narrative. The Guide to Related Topics shows how the five basic economic principles described in Chapter 1 apply to many topics in the study of economics. The Timeline puts the people and events of the modern era into a proper sequence, which creates historical perspective for the reader. Photographs reinforce and enrich the topics presented in the book. The *back matter* consists of several handy reference tools including a comprehensive glossary of selected terms, common abbreviations in economics, selected bibliography, key economic web sites, index to primary documents, index to economics in history, and a general index. Combined, these features also help the reader find specific topics within this reference book and topics from outside print and online sources.

Guide to Related Topics

Five basic economic principles are listed and explained in Chapter 1 of this reference book. These time-tested principles are underlying understandings about the functioning of economies. They explain economic situations, state relationships, and predict consequences to certain stimuli. These principles can be applied to a variety of situations in the U.S. economy and global economy.

The five basic economic principles are shown in **bold print** below. Listed beneath each basic principle is a set of related topics—applications of the basic principle found in this reference book. Subheadings from chapters were used to make the lists of related topics. Each subheading is followed by the appropriate chapter number, 1–13. Thus, to locate these applications of the five basic economic principles in the book, simply turn to the listed chapter and subheading.

PRINCIPLE 1: ECONOMIC CHOICES INVOLVE COSTS

Consumer choices
- Budget constraint: A model of consumer choice (2)
- Price system (2)
- Consumers in the U.S. economy (4)
- Consumer rights and responsibilities (4)
- Consumer credit and creditworthiness (4)
- Personal bankruptcy (4)
- Sustainable consumption (4)

Business choices
- Production possibilities frontier: A model of producer choice (2)
- Sole proprietorships (5)
- Partnerships (5)
- Corporations (5)
- Franchises (5)
- Other forms of business organization (5)
- Business costs, profits and losses (5)
- Business bankruptcy (5)
- Codes of business behavior (5)

- Worker behavior (6)
- The hiring decision (6)

Government choices
- Cost-benefit analysis (7)
- Federal budget process (7)
- Budget surpluses and deficits (7)
- National debt (7)
- The debt ceiling (7)

PRINCIPLE 2: INCENTIVES INFLUENCE PEOPLE'S DECISIONS

Consumers
- Product market (2)
- Demand (2)
- Changes in demand (2)
- Price elasticity of demand (2)
- Utility theory (4)
- Income effect of a price change (4)
- Substitution effect of a price change (4)
- Consumer surplus (4)
- Advertising (4)
- Personal bankruptcy (4)
- Consumer cooperatives (4)

Businesses
- Factor market (2)
- Supply (2)
- Changes in supply (2)
- Price elasticity of supply (2)

Entrepreneurs
- Sole proprietorships (4)
- Partnerships (4)
- Corporations (4)
- Franchises (4)
- Other forms of business organization (4)
- Entrepreneurship and entrepreneurs (5)
- Entrepreneurship and knowledge (8)
- Microfinance institutions (13)
- Marginalized informal economies (13)

Workers
- Worker behavior (6)
- Wage determination (6)
- The hiring decision (6)
- U.S. labor movement: The early years (6)
- U.S. labor movement: The modern era (6)

Savers and investors
- Types of savings accounts (9)
- Types of investment accounts (9)

- Stock markets (9)
- Bond markets (9)
- Mutual funds (9)
- Futures markets (9)
- Financial contagion and the East Asian financial crisis of 1997–1998 (9)
- The financial crisis of 2007–2008 (9)
- Foreign exchange markets (11)

Government
- Functions of taxes (7)
- Types of taxes (7)
- Tax fairness (7)
- Monetary policy tools (10)
- Quantitative easing (10)
- Fiscal policy tools (10)
- Different approaches to stabilization (10)

PRINCIPLE 3: COMPETITIVE MARKETS PROMOTE EFFICIENCY

Markets
- Product market (2)
- Factor market (2)
- Flows of products, resources, and money payments (2)
- Market clearing price (2)
- Price system (2)

Markets and economic systems
- Traditional economy (3)
- Command economy model (3)
- Market economy model (3)
- Origins of capitalism (3)
- Modern capitalism (3)
- Global capitalism (3)
- Economies in Transition: Shock Therapy in The Russian Federation (3)
- Economies in Transition: Gradualism in The People's Republic of China (3)

Market structure and competition
- Perfect competition (5)
- Monopolistic competition (5)
- Oligopoly (5)
- Monopoly (5)

Financial markets
- Commercial banks (9)
- Thrift institutions (9)
- Credit unions (9)
- Foreign exchange market (11)

Global market liberalization
- Absolute and comparative advantage (11)
- General Agreement on Tariffs and Trade (11)

- Regional trade agreements (11)
- Institutions of the global economy (12)
- Multilateral development institutions (13)

Financing government interventions
- Functions of taxes (7)
- Types of taxes (7)
- Tax fairness (7)
- Federal taxes (7)
- State and local taxes (7)
- The debt ceiling (7)

PRINCIPLE 5: SPECIALIZATION PROMOTES PRODUCTIVITY AND ECONOMIC INTERDEPENDENCE

Specialization (historical)
- Food gathering and hunting (3)
- Permanent agriculture and animal domestication (3)
- Industrial age (3)
- Information age (3)

Productivity
- Savings and investing: The virtuous cycle (8)
- Efficient use of the factors of production (8)
- Entrepreneurship and knowledge (8)
- Advanced economies (13)
- Emerging market and developing economies (13)
- The virtuous cycle (13)

Trade and interdependence
- Mercantilism (1)
- The classical school (1)
- Growth in international trade (11)
- Balance of trade: Deficits and surpluses (11)
- Absolute and comparative advantage (11)
- General Agreement on Tariffs and Trade (11)
- World Trade Organization (11)
- Terms of trade (11)

Globalization and interdependence
- Global capitalism (3)
- Waves of globalization (12)
- The globalization debate in brief (12)
- International trade (12)
- Foreign direct investment (12)
- Cross-border financial flows (12)

Timeline: Key Economic Events That Shaped the Modern Era, 1776–2014

1776 Adam Smith, the founder of modern economics, writes *An Inquiry into the Nature and Causes of the Wealth of Nations*, an anchor text for the classical school of economic thought.

1791 The United States establishes the First Bank of the United States, a central bank with a 20-year charter.

1798 Thomas Malthus writes *An Essay on the Principles of Population as It Affects the Future Improvement of Society*, causing some to label economics as the "dismal science".

1803 Jean Baptiste Say writes his *Treatise on Political Economy* and popularizes laissez-faire capitalism.

1816 The United States establishes the Second Bank of the United States, the nation's second central bank, with a 20-year charter.

1817 David Ricardo writes *Principles of Political Economy*, which uses the theory of comparative advantage to defend free trade in global markets.

1832 U.S. president Andrew Jackson vetoes legislation that would have extended the charter of the Second Bank of the United States for another 20 years.

1848 Karl Marx and Friedrich Engels write *The Communist Manifesto*, a foundation of the Marxist school of economic thought.

1867 Karl Marx writes the first of three volumes of *Das Capital*, a tome explaining the inevitability of scientific socialism.

1869 Uriah Stephens founds the Knights of Labor, a secret society of workers seeking improvements in the workplace.

1876 Thomas A. Edison creates the world's first private research laboratory, then called an invention factory, in Menlo Park, New Jersey.

1886 Samuel Gompers founds the American Federation of Labor, which soon replaces the Knights of Labor as America's top labor union.

1890 Alfred Marshall writes *Principles of Economics*, which becomes the world's most widely recognized economics textbook.

Congress passes the Sherman Antitrust Act to opposes the formation of monopolies and other restraints on competitive markets.

1896   Charles H. Dow creates the Dow Jones Industrial Average, an index of stock performance based on price changes of twelve leading stocks.

1899   The National Consumers League is founded as America's first national consumer organization.

1900   The term "economics" replaces "political economy" in common usage.

1903   Mary Harris (Mother) Jones lead the march of the mill children to bring national attention to the plight of child labor in America.

1905   The Industrial Workers of the World is founded under the slogan "One Big Union" to support workers' rights and oppose capitalism in the United States.

1913   The Federal Reserve Act establishes the Federal Reserve System, the first central bank in the United States since the 1830s.
The Ford Motor Company introduces the moving assembly line in the production of automobiles.
The Sixteenth Amendment to the U.S. Constitution establishes a national income tax.

1914   The Clayton Antitrust Act and Federal Trade Commission Act outlaw anti-competitive business practices in U.S. markets.
The first great wave of globalization ends when World War I erupts in Europe.

1917   Vladimir I. Lenin leads a successful communist revolution in Russia.

1919   The International Labor Organization is founded to advocate for labor's rights throughout the world.

1922   The Union of Soviet Socialist Republics is formally established as the world's first communist country.

1928   Joseph Stalin introduces the five-year plan in the Soviet Union and suppresses opposition to the Communist Party's rule in the country.

1929   The stock market crash at the New York Stock Exchange is the unofficial beginning of the Great Depression in the United States.

1933   U.S. president Franklin D. Roosevelt introduces elements of New Deal legislation designed to address the hardships caused by the Great Depression.
The Glass-Steagall Banking Act separates commercial and investment banking, and creates the Federal Deposit Insurance Corporation.
Frances Perkins is appointed secretary of labor, the first woman cabinet appointee in U.S. history.

1935   The Social Security Act is created to provide some income security for the elderly and other distressed groups.
The Wagner Act guarantees workers the right to form unions and bargain collectively with employers.

1936   John M. Keynes writes *The General Theory of Employment, Interest, and Money*, which launches the Keynesian school of economic thought.
The Consumers Union, which publishes *Consumer Reports*, is founded in the United States.

1938   The Fair Labor Standards Act creates the first national minimum wage of $0.25 per hour, a maximum work week of 44 hours, and overtime pay.

The Congress of Industrial Organizations is founded as an industrial union and a rival union to the American Federation of Labor.

1941   Simon Kuznets, the father of the gross national product, writes *National Income and Its Composition, 1919–1938*.

1942   Joseph A. Schumpeter writes *Capitalism, Socialism, and Democracy*, stressing the role of innovation and "creative destruction" in the functioning of a capitalist economy.

1944   The Bretton Woods Conference creates the World Bank and the International Monetary Fund.
The fixed exchange rate system is established to support international trade and other global exchanges.

1945   The United Nations is founded at the San Francisco Conference.
A second great age of globalization begins at the close of World War II.

1946   The invention of the electronic numerical integrator and calculator (ENIAC) launches the computer age.
The Employment Act of 1946 expands the U.S. government's role in promoting full employment, maximum output, and price stability.

1947   The General Agreement on Tariffs and Trade is created to support free trade.

1949   Mao Zedong leads a successful communist revolution in China, which leads to the founding of the People's Republic of China.

1955   The American Federation of Labor and the Congress of Industrial Organizations merge to form the AFL-CIO, the nation's largest labor union.

1960   The Organization of Petroleum Exporting Countries, a producer cartel, is founded.

1962   U.S. president John F. Kennedy identifies four basic consumer rights: the right to safety, to be informed, to choose, and to be heard.

1964   The Civil Rights Act of 1964 provides protections against job and wage discrimination based on race, color, religion, gender, or national origin.
U.S. president Lyndon B. Johnson initiates a series of Great Society programs to expand the social safety net for the needy.

1966   Cesar Chavez founds the United Farm Workers, a union representing agricultural and migrant farmworkers.

1967   Tanzanian president Julius Nyerere introduces *ujamaa*, a type of socialism based on traditional tribal communalism.

1969   ARPANET, the precursor of the Internet, is invented by the U.S. Department of Defense.

1970s Stagflation, the simultaneous occurrence of stagnant growth and inflation, complicates government stabilization policies.

1970   Paul Samuelson is the first American economist to win the Nobel Prize in Economic Science.

1971   Ralph Nader founds Public Citizen and is recognized as the chief spokesperson for the American consumer movement.

1973   The flexible exchange rate system replaces the fixed exchange rate system.
The United States dips into a severe recession.

1976   Mao Zedong dies, which opens discussions about the introduction of market-oriented economic reforms in China.

1977   Fiber optics technology vastly expands communications potential.

1978   Deng Xiaoping adopts a gradualist approach to initiating market-based economic reforms in China.

1980   The United States enters a severe "double-dip" recession, which lingers until 1982.

1981   U.S. president Ronald Reagan supports supply-side economics, often called Reaganomics, during his two terms as president.

1983   Muhammad Yunis founds the Grameen Bank, a microcredit institution in Bangladesh.

1985   Soviet premier Mikhail Gorbachev introduces market-oriented economic reforms under the banner of *perestroika*, and political reforms under *glasnost*.

1987   Alan Greenspan is appointed chairman of the Federal Reserve System, a position he holds until 2006.
The Montreal Protocol, a multilateral environmental treaty, targets ozone-depleting substances in the atmosphere.

1989   Tim Berners-Lee invents the World Wide Web.

1990   The United Nations Development Program introduces a Human Development Index to assess the progress countries make in improving people's quality of life.
The United States enters a mild recession, after a prolonged period of expansion during the 1980s.

1991   The Union of Soviet Socialist Republics formally dissolves, and the Commonwealth of Independent States is formed from 12 of the former Soviet republics.

1992   The Russian Federation and other transition countries begin an uneasy transition from communism toward capitalism and from totalitarianism toward democracy.

1993   The Maastricht Treaty creates the European Union.

1994   The North American Free Trade Agreement takes effect.
The Common Market of the South, or MERCOSUR, is formed.
The eighth and final GATT trade round concludes at Marrakesh, Morocco, with the creation of the World Trade Organization.

1995   The World Trade Organization formally replaces the General Agreement on Tariffs and Trade.

1996   The Temporary Assistance for Needy Families program replaces the unpopular Aid to Families with Dependent Children as the chief income assistance program for the poor.

1997   Hong Kong is transformed from a British colony to a Special Administrative Region of China.
The East Asian financial crisis destabilizes the global economy, illustrating the danger of financial contagion in the global economy.
The U.S. minimum wage is increased for the twentieth time since 1938, from an hourly wage rate of $4.75 to $5.15.

1998   The United States achieves the first of four federal budget surpluses during the presidency of Bill Clinton.

1999   The World Trade Organization's Millennium Round of trade negotiations flops in Seattle amid massive antiglobalization protests by civil society organizations.
The euro begins its phase-in as the European Union's common currency.

Congress repeals portions of the Glass-Steagall Act, an act that had separated commercial banking from riskier investment banking since the 1930s.

2000   The World Bank introduces a new measure of economic well-being, the gross national income (GNI) per capita.

The United Nations announces eight Millennium Development Goals to guide and measure progress toward sustainable economic development.

2001   The United States slips into a mild recession after a prolonged expansion during the 1990s.

Terrorist attacks on New York City and Washington, DC, slow international trade and foreign direct investment.

2002   The euro officially replaces the national currencies of 12 of the 15 EU member nations, thus creating the European Monetary Union (Eurozone).

2003   Officers of several large U.S. corporations, including Enron, are indicted for financial crimes.

The Jobs and Growth Tax Relief Reconciliation Act reduces income tax rates and tax obligations to stimulate economic growth.

2004   A European Union "enlargement" adds 10 countries to the EU.

2005   The United Nations proclaims 2005 as the International Year of Microcredit.

2006   A U.S. and global financial meltdown begins with the collapse of the U.S. real estate market and the uncertain value of derivatives, a widely used financial instrument.

Ben Bernanke is selected as the new chairman of the Federal Reserve System and serves two terms, ending in 2014.

2007   The Dow Jones Industrial Average peaks on October 9 at 14,165.

The U.S. housing bubble bursts, sending shock waves throughout the global economy.

The Great Recession begins in December and lasts until June 2009.

2008   U.S. president George W. Bush offers a tax rebate to stimulate growth in the U.S. economy.

Emergency stimulus spending and the Toxic Assets Relief Program pump more than a trillion dollars into the sputtering U.S. economy; governments in many other countries initiate similar policies to reverse the economic slide into global recession.

2009   The Dow Jones Industrial Average troughs on March 5 at 6,926.

The global recession reduces global output, international trade, and foreign direct investment.

The Great Recession officially ends in June, but unemployment tops 10 percent for a time.

The Federal Reserve System initiates the first phase of quantitative easing by purchasing $1.75 trillion in debt.

The U.S. federal budget deficit swells to more than $1 trillion, and annual budget deficits in excess of $1 trillion continue for four consecutive years.

2010   The Wall Street Reform and Consumer Protection Act is passed by Congress, tightening some restrictions on investment practices and strengthening some protections for the public.

The Federal Reserve System initiates a second phase of quantitative easing to stimulate borrowing and spending.

The Affordable Health Care Act is passed by Congress.

China surpasses Japan as the world's second largest economy behind the United States.

2011   Standard & Poor's downgrades the credit rating of the U.S. government from AAA to AA+ over concerns about spiraling federal deficits and other financial instability.

The U.S. GDP-to-debt ratio surpasses 100, which means that the U.S. national debt is larger than the nation's gross domestic product.

The Occupy Wall Street movement begins as a sign of discontent with the pace of the economic recovery, the growth of inequality, and abuses by the financial system.

The U.S. poverty rate remains at about 15 percent, or 46 million people (an all-time high).

2012   The tepid U.S. recovery continues to show some gains such as slow but positive growth in national output and slow but steady declines in the unemployment rate.

The Federal Reserve System announces a third phase of quantitative easing in September ($40 billion in bond and asset purchases) and soon thereafter an additional $45 billion per month in bond purchases, which increases Fed purchases to $85 billion per month through 2013.

2013   Sluggish or negative economic growth in Europe slows global growth, international trade, and foreign direct investment.

The U.S. federal budget sequester goes into effect in March, which makes automatic spending cuts in national defense and other discretionary programs.

The Dow Jones Industrial Average hits a series of record highs during the summer and fall signaling investor confidence in the U.S. economy.

The unemployment rate continues to fall, reaching 7.4 percent of the labor force during the summer months.

U.S. consumers show some resilience by increasing their purchases of major items such as automobiles and homes, while moderating other types of spending.

The U.S. national debt ($16.9 trillion) tops the gross domestic product ($15.8 trillion) by about $1 trillion.

2014   The U.S. Senate confirms Janet Yellen to a four year term as Fed chair, the first woman to lead the Federal Reserve System.

On the eve of the 2015 target date, several of the United Nations' Millennium Development Goals have been reached, and progress continues on others.

The World Bank's 2014 *World Development Report* focuses on the need to manage risks inherent in attaining sustainable economic development in the world's poorer regions.

Europe braces for additional financial stresses within the Eurozone with its European Stability Mechanism, which funds financial assistance to troubled member nations.

United Nations observances include dedications of 2014 as the International Year of Small Island Developing States, and the International Year of Family Farming.

Part I

AN INTRODUCTION TO ECONOMICS

1

The Basics of Economic Thinking

While people have made economic decisions since the beginning of humankind, the formal study of economics has only recently emerged. Its origins can be traced back to the sixteenth and seventeenth centuries as the fledgling nation-states of Europe grappled with the basic economic questions of what, how, and for whom to produce. This chapter explores the content and methodology of economic science, introduces key economic principles, and traces how different schools of economic thought have influenced the decisions of people and countries over time.

ECONOMIC SCIENCE

Scarcity is the universal economic problem. Scarcity exists because people have unlimited needs but limited resources to satisfy their material desires. Scarcity is called the universal economic problem because it affects all people in all societies and has done so throughout history. Even the wealthy who have sufficient resources to satisfy their basic needs cannot buy everything they may want. As long as resources are scarce, people will have to make choices about how to use their scarce resources.

Resources that are used to produce goods and services are called the factors of production. The three main factors of production are natural resources, or land; human resources, or labor; and capital goods, or capital. Natural resources are the gifts of nature such as rivers, sunlight, fish and animals, natural forests, and soil. Human resources are the people who are involved in production such as teachers, scientists, carpenters, farmers, and assembly line workers. Capital goods are items that are designed to produce other products. Capital goods include cement mixers, shopping malls, business computers, oil tankers, and factory buildings. Resources that have been processed but are designed for use in the production of another product are called intermediate goods. Lumber, for example, is an intermediate good because it is destined for use in the construction of houses or the manufacture of furniture. Some economists include entrepreneurship as a fourth factor of production. Entrepreneurship represents the risk taking and innovation of entrepreneurs—people who create new products, businesses, or production methods.

A wind turbine is a capital good, whereas the wind that powers the turbine is a natural resource. (Shutterstock.com)

Economics as a Social Science

Economics is the study of how people choose to use their scarce resources to satisfy their needs. Thus, economics deals with the production, distribution, and consumption of goods and services. The term "economics" comes from *oikonomikos*, which means "skilled in household management."[1] It wasn't until the early twentieth century that the term "economics" came into common usage, replacing the more familiar "political economy"—a term that was introduced in the early 1600s and popularized during the 1700s.

Economics is a social science because it systematically studies human relationships and behaviors of people. The economic choices and behaviors of households, businesses, and government are at the heart of economic science. Economics, like the other social sciences—anthropology, human geography, political science, psychology, and sociology—are not exact sciences, however. This is because the social sciences deal with human behaviors, and people sometimes behave in unpredictable ways. The social sciences also study human behaviors in the real world, not in a laboratory or other controlled environment. Thus, the social scientist is unable to isolate or account for all of the variables that affect the actions of individuals or groups. Today, the study of economics is often divided into two main branches, microeconomics and macroeconomics.

Microeconomics is the branch of economics that focuses on interactions among the individual decision-making units within an economy. Microeconomics is the older of the two branches of economics, occupying much of the attention of the early schools of economic thought. The most important participants in the microeconomy are households, business firms, and the government. The private sector, or nongovernmental sector of the economy, consists of households and firms. Households make decisions about consuming products, saving and investing money, and employment. Businesses, on the other hand, make production decisions related to output, product pricing, and hiring workers. Government decision making in the microeconomy deals with providing public goods, providing social programs, and regulating business activity.

Macroeconomics is the branch of economics that deals with the economic performance of the entire economy. Macroeconomics, as a broad field of study, arose during the twentieth century, largely in response to the global depression of the 1930s. Macroeconomics focuses on economic growth and economic stability in a nation. Economic growth is often measured by tracking a nation's real gross domestic product over time. The real gross domestic product (GDP) is the dollar value of all newly produced goods and services in an economy in a given year, adjusted for inflation. Economic stability refers to maintaining stable prices and a fully employed labor force. In sum, macroeconomics deals with aggregates such as national output, national income, national savings rates, and the national unemployment rate. It follows that macroeconomics also deals with government stabilization policies such as monetary policy and fiscal policy that influence these national aggregates.

The Scientific Method

Economic thinking *is* scientific thinking. Economists approach economics in much the same manner as chemists approach chemistry and physicists approach physics. The social and physical sciences share a common approach to organizing, analyzing, and explaining information. Economists often use an inductive or deductive approach to form generalizations, economic theories and laws, and solutions to problems.

The **inductive approach** begins by identifying a problem and then collecting and organizing relevant data. From this data, the economist forms one or more generalizations to note general tendencies about the problem or issue. A generalization may be prefaced with words such as "in most cases" or "rarely" to indicate that it is really a statement of probability and that there may be exceptions to the general rule. Generalizations must be tested in a real-world setting.

The **deductive approach**, on the other hand, begins the scientific inquiry by forming a hypothesis using just general observations or impressions about an economic issue or problem. The economist then collects, organizes, and analyzes data related to the topic. Before the hypothesis can be validated, it must withstand the scrutiny of testing in the real world.

A generalization or a hypothesis that survives repeated testing over time earns the title of **economic law**. For example, the most famous economic law, the law of demand, states that consumers buy more of a good when its price is low and lesser amounts of a good when its price is high. While the law of demand seems to be little more than a statement of common sense, it wasn't until the nineteenth century that economists were able to devise a demand curve to illustrate the relationship between price and the quantity demanded of a good. Economic laws state general tendencies about people's economic behaviors but are not perfect predictors of their actions. There are even exceptions to the famous law of demand. A higher price for certain luxury goods, such as name-brand watches or custom-built automobiles, actually increases the demand for these status products.

Fallacies in Reasoning

A **fallacy** occurs when an error is made in one's research or reasoning that, in turn, results in erroneous conclusions. There are several types of fallacies that plague the study of economics and the other social sciences.

A cause-effect fallacy occurs when an incorrect or incomplete relationship is drawn between one event and another. One type of cause-effect fallacy is the **single-cause fallacy**, which identifies just one cause or one solution to a complex problem when in reality there are multiple causes or solutions. The single-cause fallacy is often called *oversimplification* because the economist's reasoning excludes key variables related to the problem. A second type of cause-effect fallacy is the **post hoc fallacy**, which assumes that because one event happens before another event, the first must have caused the second to occur. A third type of cause-effect fallacy is the **correlation-as-cause fallacy**, which assumes that because two events occur at about the same time, one must have caused the other. In the study of economics, many events occur before, at the same time, or after other events. At times these events are related, even causal, and at other times they are not.

An **evidence fallacy** occurs when an economist's conclusions are based on insufficient, irrelevant, or inaccurate information. Evidence fallacies may be intentional (to promote a certain position or policy) or unintentional. In either case, the economist's conclusion is tainted by faulty evidence.

The **fallacy of composition** assumes that what is true or proper for a piece is true or proper for the whole. In the study of economics, what is good or appropriate behavior for an individual (the piece) is not necessarily the proper behavior for the entire society (the whole). For instance, it is commonly agreed that monthly household budgets for individuals should be balanced to ensure that all bills are paid. On the national level, however, budgetary deficits are sometimes viewed as necessary to moderate downturns in the economy, as was the case during the Great Depression of the 1930s and the Great Recession of 2007–2009.

Types of Economists

An **economist** is a social scientist concerned mainly with the collection and analysis of economic data. As social scientists, economists study the economic behaviors of people and institutions. They identify patterns of behavior, form generalizations and theories, discern economic trends, and make economic forecasts. Their specialized skills also influence economic decisions made by households, businesses, governments, global institutions, and others.

The U.S. Bureau of Labor Statistics (BLS) classifies economists as social scientists, a type of professional occupation. In 2010, there were 15,400 economists employed in the United States.[2] The *Occupational Outlook Handbook 2012–2013*, a publication of the U.S. Department of Labor, predicted slower than average job growth for economists from 2010 to 2020. As is the case for other occupations, the demand for economists is a derived demand. That is, the demand for economists is derived from the demand for the services they offer. Economists are valued for their quantitative skills, computer skills, research and critical thinking skills, and communications skills. These skills, in turn, make economists valuable human capital to businesses, academic institutions, and the government. In 2010 about half of all economists employed in the United States worked for the government at the federal, state, or local level. Job prospects for individuals with a master's degree or a doctorate in economics were considered good, far better than the prospects for job seekers with just a bachelor's degree. In 2010 the median annual wage for an economist in the United States was $89,450.[3]

Business economists are employed by private enterprises to analyze economic data and to help management make informed business decisions. According to the National

Association for Business Economics (NABE), the nation's leading professional association in the field of business economics, business economists share three common qualities. They are "shrewd observers of what goes on both inside and outside the firm; enlightened analysts who can formulate and test promising ideas in an objective way; and persuasive communicators to management and others on behalf of the firm."[4] Jobs for business economists expanded rapidly during the second half of the twentieth century as businesses redoubled their efforts to anticipate changes in national economic activity and reap the benefits of a more integrated global economy.

Academic economists are employed mainly by colleges and universities to teach, conduct scholarly research, and publish academic books and articles in the field of economics. Academic economists are also employed by private foundations, think tanks, and research institutes. In addition, they serve as consultants to businesses, government, and other organizations. Today many academic economists specialize in a defined field of study such as econometrics, economic history, industrial economics, international economics, labor economics, or public finance. One recent study showed that full professors at top universities that award doctorates in economics earned salaries in excess of $220,000 per year.[5]

Government economists are employed by the federal, state, or local government to collect and analyze data necessary to form public policy. The federal government hires government economists to work within its many departments such as Agriculture, Commerce, Health & Human Services, Labor, Transportation, and the Treasury. Many government economists are specialists. For instance, economists with strong backgrounds in money and banking are employed by the Federal Deposit Insurance Corporation (FDIC), Securities and Exchange Commission (SEC), Internal Revenue Service (IRS), and Federal Reserve System (Fed). Government economists are also employed at the state

U.S. Department of Agriculture and other federal departments employ economists. (U.S. Department of Agriculture)

ECONOMICS IN HISTORY: Government Economists Respond to Early Twentieth-Century Crises

The federal government employed the first government economists during the early twentieth century, an era of progressive reform in the United States. Shaken by the Panic of 1907, many reformers supported the hiring of professional economists to assist in the creation of public financial institutions and policies. During the Progressive Era, the Federal Reserve System (1913) was founded to stabilize the nation's financial system, Amendment 16 (1913) was approved to create a national income tax, and the Clayton Act (1914) was enacted to prevent monopolies from forming.

Another spurt in the hiring of federal economists occurred during the Great Depression of the 1930s. Economists helped President Franklin D. Roosevelt and Congress devise New Deal legislation, which reformed the banking system, supported family farms, created public works jobs, and initiated the Social Security system. Francis Perkins, a labor economist from New York, served as Secretary of Labor during the Depression years, the first woman to achieve cabinet rank.

Employment of government economists snowballed during and after World War II. During the war, economists were employed to mobilize the nation's resources and coordinate the nation's production and consumption policies to support the war effort. Economists were valued employees of the federal War Production Board, the Office of Price Administration, the War Labor Board, and others. Shortly after the war ended, the historic Employment Act of 1946 pledged government support for economic growth, full employment, and stable prices. This act also expanded the role of economists in public decision making by creating the influential Council of Economic Advisors (CEA). Today CEA is the inner circle of economic counselors who help the president develop and implement national economic policy.

and local levels to analyze data related to tax policy, regional economic development, urban planning, infrastructure, environmental protection, consumer advocacy, and so on.

Why Economists Disagree

Noneconomists may be perplexed as to why economists disagree about the causes or the solutions to economic problems. After all, economists tend to agree on the basic language of economics and share many common understandings about the methodology of this social science. So why do economists so often arrive at different conclusions?

One reason for disagreements among economists is that people's economic behaviors are difficult to predict. Economists, unlike their cousins in the physical sciences, cannot limit or control all of the variables in a laboratory setting. The economist's laboratory is the world of economic activity. In addition, disagreements among professional economists stem from economic modeling. The sheer volume and complexity of economic data requires that economists simplify reality. This is accomplished by constructing an **economic model**, which focuses attention on specific relationships among a limited set of variables. Even with the use of highly sophisticated mathematical models and computer technologies, a methodology referred to an **econometrics**, different economist can still draw different conclusions from data.

Finally, economists sometimes disagree because their professional views can be colored by their personal values or beliefs. Normally, there are fewer disagreements within the realm of positive economics than in normative economics. **Positive economics**, sometimes called descriptive economics, is concerned with "what is." That is, positive economics deals with economic statements that can be objectively tested with data. "The national debt had climbed to $16.4 trillion by March 2013" is a positive statement because this claim can be objectively tested with data provided by the federal government. In this case, the statement accurately states the size of the national debt in 2013. Positive statements can also be proven inaccurate using the same type of testing. **Normative economics**, sometimes called prescriptive economics, offers a viewpoint on an economic topic or issue. Normative statements are subjective and often propose or comment on policies, programs, or other actions that "should" or "should not" happen. "The United States should initiate policies to eliminate the national debt within a decade" is a normative statement. That is, it prescribes a course of action that can be debated endlessly.

FIVE BASIC ECONOMIC PRINCIPLES

Economic principles are time-tested understandings about how the economy functions. Economic principles represent understandings that are broader than economic laws. Like economic laws, however, these principles are generalizations that tend to be true in most cases. In essence, economic principles are statements that have a high probability of accurately explaining an economic situation, or predicting a response or reaction to certain stimuli. The five basic economic principles that follow provide a set of understandings that apply to numerous situations in the microeconomy and the macroeconomy.

Economic Choices Involve Costs

Economic choice is a conscious decision to use scarce resources in one manner rather than another. Scarcity forces people to make trade-offs because they simply cannot have everything they may want. Scarcity takes many forms. Scarce financial resources limit a consumer's ability to purchase products. Scarce natural resources limit a producer's ability to supply products. Scarce human or capital resources limit a nation's progress toward economic development. Students often experience a scarcity of time—for homework, athletics, jobs, and recreation. Because people live in a world of unlimited wants and finite resources, they must choose wisely among competing wants or needs. The study of economics helps people determine how to use their scarce resources.

The most basic understanding about economic choice is that all choices have a cost. Ordinarily, people equate the cost of a good with its price. That is, if the price of a cup of coffee is $1.50, most people express the "cost" of that cup of coffee in monetary terms—one dollar and fifty cents. Economists, however, tend to measure the true cost of the choices people make through a different lens. Economists see the real cost, or **opportunity cost**, of any choice in terms of what is foregone, or given up, if resources are used one way rather than another. To put it another way, the opportunity cost of a choice represents the second best use of scarce resources—the item the consumer did not buy, the good the business did not produce, or the program the government did not fund. Once again, consider the purchase of a $1.50 cup of coffee. If the buyer was both thirsty and hungry but had just $1.50 to spend, the opportunity cost of buying the coffee may well have been the lost opportunity to consume a $1.50 pastry.

Another key understanding about economic choice is that many of our decisions are made "at the margin." In the study of economics, the term "margin" refers to the *next* or *additional* unit. **Marginalism** is a type of analysis that weighs the additional costs of any decision against the additional benefits that might be derived. People are involved in many types of marginal decisions. Consumers, for example, consider the marginal utility, or additional satisfaction that they might receive from the purchase of a second or third cup of coffee before buying additional coffees. People tend to reject most "all or nothing" decisions, preferring the rationality of making decisions at the margin.

Incentives Influence People's Decisions

Incentives are factors that motivate people to pursue certain actions and discourage others. Incentives affect many types of decisions. For instance, there are fines for many types of traffic infractions. Hefty fines provide an incentive for drivers to follow established rules of the road. In a similar way, incentives influence people's economic decisions and actions.

Incentives signal to consumers, businesses, workers, savers and investors, and other marketplace participants how they should use their scare resources. Consumers, for example, respond to price incentives. When the price of a product falls, consumers tend to buy a greater quantity of the product. Conversely, when a product's price rises, consumers buy a lesser quantity. This predictable consumer response to a change in price is the foundation of the most famous law in economics—the law of demand. Similarly, businesses respond to profit incentives. Profit is the difference between the price of an item and the cost of producing the item. The lure of profit encourages businesses to seek the lowest cost inputs when producing a product. This desire for profit also motivates businesses to devote more resources to the production of goods for which there is a high demand. Conversely, the fear of business losses discourages the production of certain goods when input costs rise or the demand for these goods falls. Workers, savers, investors, and other marketplace participants also respond to a variety of invisible price signals to guide their decisions.

Competitive Markets Promote Efficiency

A **market** exists whenever people get together to make an exchange. A competitive market is one that brings large numbers of buyers and sellers together for purposes of exchange. *Buyers* in competitive markets, it is assumed, are rational decision makers. That is, these buyers carefully weigh the costs and benefits of their buying decisions. The cost in this case is the price of the product as well as the lost opportunity to purchase other items with the same money—that is, the opportunity cost. The benefit is the amount of satisfaction they expect to receive from the product. Similarly, it is assumed that *sellers*—often referred to as producers or business firms—also make rational decisions. From the seller's perspective, the ultimate goal of producing products is to earn profits, or, to be more precise, to maximize profits. Recall that no one forces buyers or sellers to make a market transaction. The decision to buy or to sell is voluntary and is based on the principle of mutual benefit—each side in the exchange expects to be better off as a result of the transaction.

Economists consider competitive markets to be the most efficient type of market structure. Generally speaking, **economic efficiency** is achieved when a society is able to produce goods and services that people want to buy, at the lowest possible costs of production. Allocative efficiency occurs when society's resources are channeled into enterprises where consumer demand is strong. It would be allocatively inefficient, however, to use society's resources to produce goods that nobody wants to buy. Technical efficiency occurs when a producer gets the highest possible output while using the fewest or the least costly mix of inputs—natural resources, human resources, and capital goods. Technical efficiency is enhanced by sophisticated capital goods, applied research and development, skilled human capital, and innovative entrepreneurs.

Investments in sophisticated equipment increase a country's capital stock and improve the productivity of its labor force. (Shutterstock.com)

Government Interventions Address Market Shortcomings

While competitive markets are the most efficient way to allocate society's scarce resources, competitive markets do not always produce socially desirable outcomes. Prior to the Great Depression of the 1930s, the concept of *limited government* severely restricted the role of government in the economy. This hands-off policy was referred to as the laissez-faire doctrine. The government provided some public goods such as schools and roads, and enforced certain rules that protected private property, patents and copyrights, and contracts. But the economic well-being of individuals was very much a personal responsibility, not the responsibility of the federal government.

Government interventions since the Great Depression have expanded to provide additional public goods, support economic security and equity for the vulnerable, regulate businesses, and stabilize the macroeconomy. Today, for example, the government provides a far broader range of public goods than it did a century ago. These public goods are deemed necessary for a well-ordered economy mainly because such projects would be underproduced by the private sector. Similarly, with government intervention, certain essential services for the poor, the sick, or the elderly would be underproduced. Finally, government interventions have also reined in the excesses of private enterprises, helping to improve the treatment of workers and the quality of the natural environment.

Specialization Promotes Productivity and Economic Interdependence

Specialization occurs when an individual, business, or region produces a specific product or narrow range of products. An individual artisan, for example, might specialize in the production of fine jewelry. A large business might specialize in the production of automobiles. An economic region might specialize in the production of a crop such as cocoa or bananas. Specialization, when applied to workers' tasks, is often referred to as the **division of labor**. The main goal of a division of labor is to increase the firm's productivity. The division of labor within a production facility often creates focused, defined tasks for workers that are matched to workers' abilities or talents. Specialization is often credited with increasing the productivity of individual business firms and entire regions or countries.

Specialization promotes business productivity by encouraging the most efficient use of available resources. **Productivity** occurs when a business firm is able to increase the amount of output *per unit of input*. The most common measure of productivity is the amount of output produced per unit of labor. One way producers increase the productivity of labor is by investing in their workers through work-related education or training. Producers also increase worker productivity through investments in real capital such as machinery and software.

Regional specialization occurs when firms in a certain geographic location develop one or a few key resources or products for commercial purposes. Naturally, these economic regions produce goods most suited to their local resources. For example, Saudi Arabia, Kuwait, and the United Arab Emirates specialize in the production of petroleum products because these countries sit on large reserves of crude oil. They produce enough petroleum to satisfy their own needs and to export surpluses to foreign buyers. The cross-border trade and investment opportunities for these and other countries create strong and mutually beneficial economic bonds among nations. In this way, regional specialization promotes an efficient use of the world's scarce resources, generates greater global output, and encourages economic interdependence in the global economy.

ECONOMIC SCHOOLS OF THOUGHT: AN HISTORICAL OVERVIEW

A **school of economic thought** consists of economists who share common ideas about how scarce resources should be used to achieve society's goals. Numerous schools of economic thought have arisen since the 1700s. Some schools of thought have stressed economic freedom and the value of private incentives to allocate society's resources. Others have advocated the abolition of private property and profits to create economic equity and justice. Competing schools of thought have evolved over time, have challenged well-established economic doctrines, and have instigated monumental changes in how societies answer the basic economic questions of what, how, and for whom to produce.

Mercantilism

Mercantilism is the belief that a country's wealth is derived from its ability to accumulate specie—mainly gold and silver. Mercantilism is not a school of economic thought in the traditional sense, mainly because there is no unified body of writing that mercantilists accept. Instead, the viewpoints expressed by the mercantilists represented the interests of the merchant and business classes during the sixteenth, seventeenth, and eighteenth centuries. The most eloquent mercantilist spokesman of the era was Thomas Mun (1571–1641), a merchant from London, England. The mercantilists generally agreed that accumulating bullion was vital to the survival the nation but stressed the value of international trade rather than conquest to acquire these riches.

The mercantilists encouraged the government to create trade policies that would result in a favorable balance of trade, a condition in which the value of a country's exports is greater than the value of its imports. A favorable balance of trade ensured that more wealth, including specie, flowed into the nation than flowed out. This prescription for prosperity was supported in Mun's *England's Treasure by Foreign Trade* (1664). In this treatise, Mun argued that England must "sell more to strangers yearly than we consume of theirs in value."[6] To achieve a favorable balance of trade, countries such as England, France, and Spain adopted mercantilist policies during the 1600s and 1700s. Central to the mercantilists was the creation of trade barriers such as import tariffs and quotas to discourage or prohibit certain foreign imports. Governments subsidized domestic industries and granted trade monopolies to leading shipping companies. Governments also built vast colonial empires, and restricted trade and business activity within these empires to favor the mother country.

History has shown that the mercantilists viewed the world through a selective lens that invariably catered to the narrow interests of the commercial class and the monarchy. The mercantilist approach to creating national wealth, which equated wealth with a specie-filled treasury, failed to give proper attention to other growth factors such as agricultural production, the quality of the labor force, or technological advances. The common people were often viewed as little more than a source of cheap labor, a market for industrial output, and an endless supply of soldiers to carry out the monarch's global ambitions. The mercantilists also embraced a narrow view of trade, seeing international exchanges in terms of winners and losers rather than as business transactions from which both parties could benefit.

The Physiocratic School

The **physiocratic school**, or physiocracy, is generally viewed by economists as the first true school of economic thought. This school focused on the dominance of agriculture, the agricultural class, and free markets to guide the use of society's resources. The physiocrats emerged in 1760s France, drawing their economic theories from Francois Quesnay, and their political clout from allies in the royal court of King Louis XIV and King Louis XV. Quesnay's *The Economic Table* laid the philosophical foundations of the physiocratic school.

In *The Economic Table*, Quesnay proclaimed the existence of a natural order in the economic life of nations, a natural order that stressed the primacy of agriculture and the agricultural class over the less productive classes of proprietors, craftsmen, industrialists, and merchants. To the physiocrats, agricultural land enabled farmers to produce enough output to satisfy domestic demand and have surpluses to sell in foreign markets. The central goal of economic activity was to increase the nation's net product, which was measured by the value of agricultural output above and beyond the costs of production. Given the physiocratic school's emphasis on a natural economic order, it is appropriate that this economic school of thought took its name from the term "physiocracy," or "rule of nature."

Laissez-faire was another important feature of the physiocrats' natural order. **Laissez-faire** is the belief that market forces should determine the use of society's scarce resources and that the government should not interfere in business activities. Laissez-faire was a direct attack on prevailing mercantilist doctrine, which favored many types of government intervention in business activity, including the use of trade barriers to restrict free trade, subsidies to protect weak businesses, and state monopolies to bolster business profits.

The rise of the physiocrats was an important step in the development of economic science. This early school of economic thought recognized that participants in an economy such as farmers, merchants, and manufacturers functioned in an interdependent system. These insights underpin today's circular flow model, which illustrates the exchanges of goods and resources for money payments in the product market and factor market. Despite its splash in academic circles and at the French royal court, the physiocratic school had little impact on government policies in France or elsewhere. Their preoccupation with agriculture led the physiocrats to vastly underestimate the role of merchants and manufacturers in building the country's wealth.

The Classical School

The **classical school** of economics emerged during the 1770s, and for more than a century influenced economic thinking and economic policies in Europe and the Americas. The origin of the classical school can be traced to Adam Smith, the founder of modern economics. In *The Inquiry into the Nature and Causes of the Wealth of Nations* (1776), Smith described the undercurrents of the classical school, including the conviction that free markets allocate resources in the fairest and most efficient manner, that government intervention in the economy obstructs prosperity, and that competition creates opportunities for enterprising businesses and individuals. Other key classical economists included Jean Baptiste Say, David Ricardo, Thomas Malthus, and John Stuart Mill.

The free market ideas of the classical economists put them in conflict with the mercantilists and their allies, who clung tenaciously the prevailing system of government preferences and regulations designed to benefit the wealthy classes. The American rebellion against the British crown in 1776, the same year that *The Wealth of Nations* was published, caused many people to question the wisdom of mercantilism and sparked interest in Smith's alternative route to national wealth.

The classical economists believed that establishing self-regulating markets, rather than government intervention, was the most rational path to national wealth. In *The Wealth of Nations*, Smith also argued that the pursuit of one's own self-interest was the best and surest path toward a prosperous economy. Smith observed, "It is not from the benevolence of the butcher, the brewer, or the baker, that we expect our dinner, but from their regard to their own interest. We address ourselves, not to their humanity but to their self-love, and never talk to them of our own necessities but of their advantages."[7] It is not surprising that the classical school adopted the laissez-faire doctrine from the physiocrats—a doctrine that opposed most forms of government interference in business activity and supported economic freedom in competitive markets.

Classical economists supported free trade in international markets. Free trade occurs when trade barriers such as tariffs and import quotas are eliminated. In addition, free trade requires the removal of government subsidies to domestic industries and the end of other assistance to domestic firms. The less coddling of firms by the government, the more productive they would necessarily become. In short, free trade sought to level the playing field for foreign and domestic producers to compete for consumers' dollar votes. Later, David Ricardo expanded on Smith's support of free trade by introducing the theory of comparative advantage. Ricardo argued that different countries were endowed with different resources and, thus, these countries should specialize in the production of goods best

---

PRIMARY DOCUMENT: Adam Smith Describes the Division of Labor

[I]n the way in which this business [the production of pins] is now carried on, not only the whole work is a peculiar trade, but it is divided into a number of branches, of which the greater part are likewise peculiar trades. One man draws out the wire, another straights it, a third cuts it, a fourth points it, a fifth grinds it at the top for receiving the head; to make the head requires two or three distinct operations; to put it on, is a peculiar business, to whiten the pins is another; it is even a trade by itself to put them into the paper; and the important business of making a pin is, in this manner, divided into about eighteen distinct operations, which, in some manufactories, are all performed by distinct hands. . . . I have seen a small manufactory of this kind where ten men only were employed. . . . Those ten persons . . . could make among them upwards of forty-eight thousand pins each day. . . . But if they had all wrought separately and independently, and without any of them having been educated to this peculiar business, they certainly could not each of them have made twenty, perhaps not one pin in a day.

In every other art and manufacture, the effects of the division of labour are similar to what they are in this very trifling one.

An Inquiry Into the Nature and Causes of the Wealth of Nations, Adam Smith

---

suited to their resources. He supported regional specialization to encourage the efficient use of resources and to develop cooperative trade relationships among countries.

Classical economists saw a direct connection between worker productivity and a rising standard of living for the people. Smith argued that higher worker productivity could be accomplished through a division of labor, particularly in manufacturing enterprises. A division of labor requires that the tasks workers perform be broken down into smaller, more specialized functions within a plant. It is also dependent on the use of advanced capital goods and the effective management of wage laborers. In *The Wealth of Nations*, Smith explained the benefits of a division of labor in the production of pins, as shown in the above passage.[8]

Some classical economists shunned Smith's optimism, and took a dimmer view of the world's economic future. Thomas Malthus, for example, argued that population growth would soon outpace economic growth and food production, a situation later economists referred to as the Malthusian trap. Malthus predicted a decline in the human condition marked by poverty and misery for the masses mainly because "the power of population is indefinitely greater than the power of the earth to produce subsistence for man."[9] It is no wonder that economics, in some quarters, was referred to as the dismal science! Later classical economists, such as John Stuart Mill, also questioned the fairness of free markets, particularly in the area of income distribution. By the mid-1800s, Mill and others observed the inhumanity of sweatshop working conditions for the growing urban working class and concluded that some government interventions might be required to correct economic injustices.

The Marginalist School

The **marginalist school** of economic thought was founded in the 1870s by William S. Jevons, Karl Menger, Leon Walras, and Knut Wicksell. By the turn of the century, the marginalists had more fully explored the process of rational decision making on both sides of the market—the demand side and the supply side. Economic decisions, the marginalists argued, were typically made at the margin. In economics, "margin" refers to the next unit or the additional unit. The groundbreaking work of the marginalists soon dominated supply and demand analyses, the theory of value, and other topics related to decision making by market participants.

On the *demand side* of the market, the marginalists developed the concept of utility and how changes in utility effect the price people are willing to pay for goods or services. Utility refers to the usefulness or satisfaction a consumer derives from the consumption of an item. In the early 1870s, marginalists developed the law of diminishing marginal utility. This economic law states that as a consumer purchases additional units of the same item in a given period of time, the marginal utility falls. This observation is core to rational consumer decision making and to pricing decisions by businesses.

On the *supply side* of the market, the marginalists built on earlier work by the classical economists to more fully examine the value of resources used in production. The supply side of the market deals with the behaviors and actions of the producer. In the 1890s, Swedish economist Knut Wicksell developed the marginal productivity theory. According to this theory, firms should employ additional resources in production only when the additional (marginal) revenues were equal to or greater than the additional (marginal) costs that they had to pay for these resources. After all, if the marginal costs were greater than the marginal revenues, the firm would lose money. Meanwhile in Austria, Karl Menger developed the concept of derived demand, which stated the demand for resources was derived from the demand for the goods that these resources produced. In other words, resources—including human labor—have value only when they can be used to produce goods that people are willing to buy.

Marxism

Marxism is a school of economic thought grounded in socialist principles, dedicated to the overthrow of capitalism, and committed to the creation of a perfected form of socialism called communism. Marxism originated in the mid-nineteenth century when German-born Karl Marx teamed with English businessman Friedrich Engels to write *The Communist Manifesto* (1848). In this brief treatise, Marx and Engels examined the nature of class conflict throughout history, concluding that communism would inevitably replace the oppressive capitalist system. Marxism has sometimes been called scientific socialism to reflect the depth of Marx's examination of capitalism, its weaknesses, and reasons for its eventual collapse. Much of the theory of the Marxist school of economic thought is presented in *The Communist Manifesto* and in several volumes of *Capital*.

Marxism is based on socialist principles. But Marxism carried socialist ideas to a new, more revolutionary level in several key respects. First, it called for the complete abolition of private property, which Marxists believed was the root cause of injustice, oppression, and class conflict. Second, it argued that all surplus value—the value of the worker's contribution to the production of a good—belonged to the worker and not the capitalist who owned the plant. In Marx's view, the excesses of nineteenth-century industrialism such as sweatshops and absence of labor power intensified class antagonism. Third, Marxism offered a theory of history based on the clash of conflicting classes, broadly defined as the oppressor class and the oppressed class. Past conflicts that had toppled old political and economic systems were a prelude to the decisive battle between oppressors and the oppressed during the capitalist stage of history. Marx observed that under capitalism society was "splitting up into two great hostile camps, into two great classes directly facing each other: *bourgeoisie* and *proletariat*."[10] The proletariat consisted of the industrial wage laborers, and the bourgeoisie consisted of the factory owners. The Marxists concluded that the inevitable clash between the proletariat and the bourgeoisie would likewise topple capitalism and result in a new and final stage of history, communism. Under communism, private property would disappear and the government would wither away.

Marxism drew its inspiration from the writings of Karl Marx, but the Marxist school of thought splintered into a number of directions soon after his death in 1883. One early debate within the Marxist camp concerned the inevitability of capitalism's demise and the triumph of socialism. This basic tenet of Marxism was challenged by Eduard Bernstein but was vigorously defended by those closest to Marx, including Friedrich Engels and Karl Kautsky.

During the twentieth century, Marxist views were adapted to address unforeseen situations. In the early 1900s, Russian revolutionary Vladimir Ilyich Lenin abandoned the Marxist notion that the proletarian revolution would necessarily begin in an industrialized country with a large urban proletariat, such as Germany or Great Britain. Lenin eventually led a successful communist revolution in largely agrarian Russia and, under the banner of Marxism-Leninism, established the Union of Soviet Socialist Republics in 1922. Similarly, Mao Zedong adapted Marxist ideas by tapping into the revolutionary fervor of China's rural peasantry, rather than an urban proletariat, to topple the Nationalist government of Chiang Kai-shek. In 1949 Mao established the People's Republic of China.

The Keynesian School

The **Keynesian school** of economic thought, also called the Keynesians, provided the theoretical foundations for greater government intervention to promote economic growth and stability. British economist John Maynard Keynes founded the Keynesian school in the 1930s. During the global depression of the 1930s, many of the world's advanced economies suffered from a drop in national output and investment as well as a dramatic rise in unemployment. In his landmark book—*The General Theory of Employment, Interest, and Money* (1936)—Keynes recommended that governments intervene in the economy to stimulate aggregate (total) demand, create jobs, and boost economic growth. Keynes's proposals were viewed as heresy by mainstream economists, many of whom were disciples of the classical laissez-faire doctrine. As the worldwide depression deepened during the 1930s, the influence of laissez-faire economists diminished.

Keynes focused on changing aggregate demand to promote economic growth and stability. Aggregate demand is the total demand for all goods in an economy. During the global depression of the 1930s, called the Great Depression in the United States, aggregate demand was low due to massive unemployment, an epidemic of bank failures, and low consumer confidence. Keynes believed that the federal government should increase aggregate demand by pumping more money into the economy.

To jump-start the U.S. and other stagnant economies, Keynes proposed an aggressive use of fiscal policy by the federal government. Specifically, he supported an expansionary fiscal policy, a policy that included tax reductions and increased government spending. Keynes noted that these fiscal policy actions would immediately put more money into the hands of individuals and businesses and, thus, cause a rebound in aggregate demand. Higher demand, in turn, would cause businesses to increase production, employ additional workers, and invest in new capital goods.

President Franklin D. Roosevelt, fireside chat, 1937. (Library of Congress)

Governments from around the world, including the administration of Franklin D. Roosevelt (FDR) in the United States, latched onto the Keynesian solution during the 1930s. In the United States, FDR and Congress approved an avalanche of new programs, collectively called the New Deal, to bolster consumer confidence and aggregate demand. During the dark days of the Great Depression, FDR also provided moral support to the shaken American people with regular radio addresses called fireside chats.

The Keynesians ushered in a new era in economic thinking, particularly with respect to expanded government responsibilities in the economy. The Keynesians opened new discussions and debate in the field of macroeconomics, especially problems related to economic growth, unemployment, and inflation. In the United States, the Employment Act of 1946, which made it national policy to "promote maximum employment, production, and purchasing power,"[11] formalized a new era of government responsibility in supporting the nation's macroeconomic goals.

CHAPTER 1 SUMMARY

Economic Science
- Economics is a social science that studies how people choose to use their scarce resources to satisfy their needs.
- Economists use the scientific method to form generalizations, economics theories and laws, and solutions to economic problems.

- Common fallacies in reasoning lead to erroneous generalizations, theories, or solutions.
- Economists play a key role in analyzing economic information and forming policies in a number of business, academic, and government settings.
- Economists often disagree with one another due to different modeling and forecasting techniques, and different values or beliefs.

Five Basic Economic Principles

- Because resources are scarce, people must choose between competing wants or needs; all economic choices involve costs.
- People's economic choices, decisions, or actions are influenced by market incentives such as prices or profits.
- Competitive markets promote allocative and technical efficiency.
- Government interventions in the economy address market shortcomings by providing public goods, social programs, and business regulations.
- Specialization by firms and by economic regions promotes productivity and economic interdependence.

Schools of Economic Thought: An Historical Overview

- Mercantilists favored the regulation of trade, and the use of business subsidies, to create a favorable balance of trade.
- Physiocrats favored the primacy of agriculture and laissez-faire principles to limit government interventions in the economy.
- Classical economists supported self-regulating competitive markets, including free trade, to promote prosperity.
- Marginalists argued that rational decision making requires people to consider the additional costs and the additional benefits of their decisions.
- Marxists supported a revolutionary form of socialism to end capitalism and its institutions such as private property and profit.
- Keynesians supported the aggressive use of fiscal policy tools to regulate aggregate demand and thereby promote economic growth and stability.

NOTES

1. Federal Reserve Bank of San Francisco, "Major Schools of Economic Theory," www.frbsf.org/publications/education/greateconomists/grtchls.html.

2. U.S. Department of Labor, Bureau of Labor Statistics, "Economists," *Occupational Outlook Handbook, 2012–2013*, 2012, www.bls.gov/ooh/life-physical-and-social-sciences/economists.htm

3. Ibid.

4. National Association for Business Economics (NABE), *Careers in Business Economics* (Washington, DC: NABE, 1997–2001), 3.

5. Charles E. Scott and John J. Siegfried, "American Economic Association Universal Academic Questionnaire Summary Statistics." *American Economic Review*, 101 (3), 664–667, www.aweaweb.org/articles.php?doi=10.1257/aer.101.3.664.

6. Thomas Mun, *England's Treasure by Foreign Trade* (1664 original electronic text held by the Department of Economics, McMaster University), Chapter 2, par. 1, www.socserv.mcmaster.ca/econ/ugcm/3113/mun/treasure.txt.

7. Adam Smith, *An Inquiry into the Nature and Causes of the Wealth of Nations* (Chicago; Henry Regnery Company, 1953), 25.

8. Ibid., 9–10.

9. Thomas Robert Malthus, *An Essay on the Principle of Population* (New York: W. W. Norton, 1976), 20.

10. Karl Marx and Friedrich Engels, *The Communist Manifesto* (New York: Washington Square Press, 1964), 58–59.

11. "The Employment Act of 1946," in *Documents in American History*, 7th ed., edited by Henry S. Commager (New York: Appleton-Century-Crofts, 1963), 514–15.

2

Basic Economic Concepts

The study of economics begins with the study of scarcity—the universal economic problem—and the choices people make to satisfy their needs. This chapter further examines this theme by examining two economic models, the production possibilities frontier and budget constraint, to illustrate specific opportunity costs that result from people's choices. Other models help explain how market economies function. The circular flow model illustrates the flow of products, resources, and money payments in a market economy. Demand and supply graphs illustrate how the market clearing price is determined.

SCARCITY, CHOICE, AND OPPORTUNITY COST

Economic choice is a conscious decision to use scarce resources in one manner rather than another. Because of scarcity, people simply cannot have everything they may want. Scarcity takes many forms. Scarce financial resources limit a consumer's ability to purchase products. Scarce natural resources limit a producer's ability to supply products. Scarce human or capital resources limit a nation's progress toward economic development. Students often experience a scarcity of time—for homework, athletics, jobs, and recreation. Because people live in a world of unlimited wants and finite resources, they must choose wisely among competing wants or needs. The study of economics helps people determine how to use their scarce resources.

Production Possibilities Frontier: A Model of Producer Choice

The most basic understanding about economic choice is that all choices have a cost. Economists see the real cost, or opportunity cost, of any decision in terms of what was foregone, or given up, if resources are used one way rather than another. The opportunity cost of a choice represents the second best use of scarce resources—the product that was *not* purchased by a consumer, the item that was *not* produced by the business, the public good or service that was *not* provided by the government.

Producers, including business firms and even entire countries, make choices about how to use scarce resources to meet people's needs. These production choices result in opportunity costs. A **production possibilities frontier** (PPF) is an economic model that shows the range of possible production choices for two products at a moment in time. It also shows the opportunity costs that a business or a country might incur at any point along its PPF. As an economic model, the PPF is a simplification of reality, a model that illustrates the opportunity costs that result from a production decision. The PPF model deals with production decisions that have been narrowed to just two products, such as wheat and corn, as shown in Figure 2.1.

Economists make two main assumptions when constructing a PPF. The first assumption is that all of the producer's resources are efficiently used at all points *on* the PPF. Thus, all points on the existing PPF represent technical efficiency. In the language of the economist, this means that all resources are fully employed. Society's decision to produce at a certain point on its PPF may or may not result in allocative efficiency, however. Allocative efficiency occurs only when there is a demand for all of the output produced by the producer. If a production decision does not mesh with society's wants or needs, lots of unwanted goods could sit unsold on store shelves. The second assumption is that the country's resources and technology are fixed at this moment in time.

The PPF shown in Figure 2.1 illustrates the range of production possibilities for Country X for two agricultural products, wheat and corn. The possible quantities of corn are shown on the horizontal axis, while the possible quantities of wheat are shown on the vertical axis. The PPF model shows two things—the amount of each good than can be produced at each point on the curve, and the opportunity cost of each possible production decision.

In Figure 2.1, all of Country X's resources are devoted to the production of wheat at point A. Thus, 50 million units of wheat are produced, and 0 units of corn are produced.

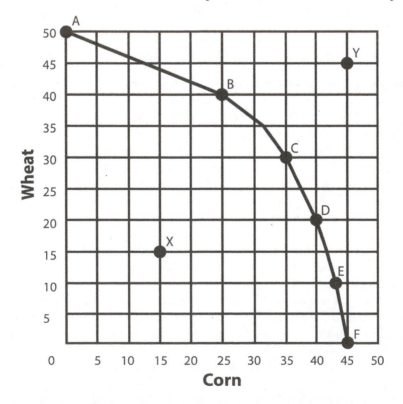

Figure 2.1   Production Possibilities Frontier for Country X (in millions of bushels)

The opportunity cost of production at point A is 45 million units of corn. This is because Country X sacrificed the 45 million units of corn so that all of its resources could be used to produce wheat. Point F represents the opposite extreme, where all of Country X's resources are devoted to the production of corn. Thus, at point F, 45 million units of corn are produced, and 0 units of wheat are produced. The specific opportunity cost at point F is the 50 million units of wheat that were not produced.

Rarely does a country produce at either of these extremes. Instead, countries typically produce at a point somewhere along the PPF. For example, if Country X chose to produce at point B, 40 million units of wheat and 25 million units of corn are produced. How could opportunity cost be expressed at point B? In terms of wheat, the opportunity cost of producing at point B is 10 million units (50 − 40 million = 10 million) because Country X chose to sacrifice these 10 million units of wheat to use some of its resources to produce corn. In terms of corn, the opportunity cost of producing at point B is 20 million units (45 − 25 million = 20 million) because Country X chose not to produce 20 million units of corn. PPFs visually represent a key understanding in economics—every decision involves a cost.

Consider points X and Y, also shown in Figure 2.1. Point X shows a production combination *inside* of the PPF, AF. Production at a point inside the existing PPF indicates that available resources are not being used efficiently. Instead, resources are available for use but at this moment in time are not being used. This underutilization of resources often takes the form of unemployment, underemployment, or idle factories. Production at point Y is not possible at this time. That is, no matter how the producer allocates available resources, there is no way to reach a production level at point Y. A producer may strive to reach point Y in the future, but to achieve this goal, the producer needs to use new technology or additional resources.

The PPF for any producer, whether it is a business or a country, is a snapshot of production possibilities at a specific moment. Over time, however, a PPF can shift in a positive direction (to the right) or in a negative direction (to the left). A *positive shift* of the PPF occurs if new technology or new resources are made available and the producer is able to produce a greater quantity of both products. A *negative shift* of the PPF occurs if productive resources are no longer available, perhaps destroyed by war or natural disaster. When fewer key resources are available, the PPF shifts inward to show that a lower quantity of both products is produced.

Budget Constraint: A Model of Consumer Choice

Consumer behavior deals with people's buying decisions in an economy. In the American mixed economy, consumers are free to choose which goods and services to purchase. This freedom of choice is best demonstrated when consumers cast their dollar votes for or against products. Naturally, consumers are not financially able to buy unlimited quantities of products. Instead, consumer choice is influenced by budget constraints. A **budget constraint** sets a limit on a person's consumption decisions based on income and the price of products.

Budget constraint, like a PPF, is illustrated with a model. The budget constraint model deals with the consumption choices of a buyer rather than with the production choices of a producer, however. As an economic model, the budget constraint shown in Figure 2.2 simplifies reality by narrowing a person's buying decision to just two items, in this case donuts and muffins. Suppose the buyer has a weekly allowance of $20 and that the price of a donut is $1 and the price of a muffin is $2. Also assume that the buyer is willing to spend the entire $20 on some combination of these two products.

The buying options for this person range from point A to point F. At point A, for example, 0 donuts are purchased, so the buyer can afford to buy 10 muffin ($2 × 10 muffins = $20). Remember, the $20 allowance is the maximum amount the buyer can spend each week. At the other extreme, point F, the buyer uses the entire $20 to purchase 20 donuts and has no money left to buy any muffins. Most likely, the buyer will want some donuts and some muffins during the week. At point B, for example, the buyer buys 4 donuts at $1 each (the buyer spends $4 on donuts), hence can afford by buy 8 muffins with the remaining $16 ($2 × 8 muffins = $16).

The budget constraint model not only shows the monetary cost of donuts and muffins, but also shows the opportunity costs of people's buying decisions. At point A, for example, the buyer spends the entire $20 to purchase 10 muffins, hence there is no money left to buy any donuts. Therefore, the opportunity cost at point A is what was not purchased,

Point	Number of Donuts	Number of Muffins	Spending on Donuts	Spending on Muffins	Weekly Spending
A	0	10	$0	$20	$20
B	4	8	$4	$16	$20
C	8	6	$8	$12	$20
D	12	4	$12	$8	$20
E	16	2	$16	$4	$20
F	20	0	$20	$0	$20

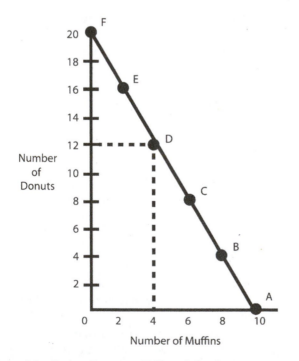

Figure 2.2   Budget Constraint Table and Graph

in this case the 20 donuts. At the other extreme, point F, the buyer spends the entire $20 to purchase 20 donuts, hence there is no money left to buy any muffins. The opportunity cost at point F is the 10 muffins that were not purchased. Suppose the buyer wants to consume some donuts and some muffins, say at point D. The opportunity cost at point D in terms of donuts is 8 donuts (20 − 12 = 8 donuts not consumed). The opportunity cost at point D in terms of muffins is 6 muffins (10 − 4 = 6 muffins not consumed).

The budget constraint for an individual or a household can change over time. Like the PPF for producers, the budget constraint curve can shift in a positive direction (to the right) or in a negative direction (to the left). A *positive shift* in a budget constraint occurs if the price of one or both items falls, or the person's income rises. Each of these situations normally allows the person to consume a greater quantity of each item. A *negative shift* in a budget constraint occurs if the price of one or both items rises, or the person's income falls. Each of these situations reduces the number of items the person can consume.

THE CIRCULAR FLOW MODEL

Economic activity in a market economy is based on the free flow of products and resources in free markets. A simplified **circular flow model** illustrates how goods and services are exchanged in free markets. Like any economic model, the circular flow model is a simplification of reality. The circular flow model shown in Figure 2.3 illustrates exchanges in two markets, the product market and the factor market. The primary actors in the circular flow model are households and business firms—the two main components of the private sector in the U.S. domestic economy. More detailed circular flow models sometimes include the role of government, financial institutions, and foreign firms in the conduct of business.

Product Market

The **product market** represents the purchases of finished goods and services in an economy. Households are the main buyers of goods and services in the product market, and businesses are the sellers of goods and services, as shown in the top half of Figure 2.3. From the circular flow model, it appears that the product market is a single physical location where products are bought and sold. But this is clearly not the case. Instead, the product market represents the millions of buy-sell transactions that are made every day in supermarkets, gas stations, convenience stores, department stores, bakeries, laundries, dentist and doctor offices, delis, and coffee shops.

The transactions that take place in the product market are based on the principle of voluntary exchange. That is, both the buyer (household) and the seller (business firm) believe

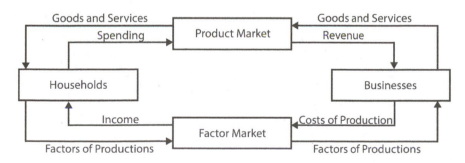

Figure 2.3 The Circular Flow Model

they will benefit from an exchange; otherwise, it will not take place. The spending by a household becomes revenue earned by a business. In an expanded version of the circular flow model, the government also appears as an important buyer of goods and services in the product market. For example, the government purchases military goods such as submarines and aircraft from private firms. Household and government spending become important sources of revenue for businesses.

In 2012 households purchased $11.1 trillion worth of goods and services in the U.S. product market. This staggering figure accounts for more than two-thirds of the country's gross domestic product—the total output of newly produced goods and services in the U.S. economy. Of this total, $3.8 trillion was spent on goods. *Goods* are tangible items. The two main categories of goods are durable goods and nondurable goods. Durable goods are items designed for long-term use, such as motor vehicles, household furnishings, and household appliances. Nondurable goods, on the other hand, are items produced for immediate consumption. Commonly consumed nondurable goods include clothing and footwear, food and beverages, and gasoline. The larger part of household spending was on services. *Services* are activities performed for a fee. In 2012 U.S. households spent $7.3 trillion on services in areas such as health care, transportation, recreation, and personal finance.[1] The dollar value of transactions between households and businesses in the U.S. product market is, by far, the largest in the world.

Factor Market

The **factor market**, sometimes called the resource market, represents the purchase of resources in an economy. In the factor market, households are the sellers of resources, and business firms are the buyers of resources, as shown in the bottom half of Figure 2.3.

A river market in Thailand illustrates many features of a free market economy. (Ninmon/ Shutterstock.com)

Again, the circular flow model makes it appear as though the factor market consists of a single location where resources are bought and sold. This model is a simplification of reality, however. In fact, every day millions of transactions take place throughout the United States in the factor market. How do factor market transactions taken place?

First, resources are owned by households and sold to businesses. These resources are called the **factors of production**—things that are used to make goods and services. The three main factors of production are natural resources, the gifts of nature; human resources, the human element in production; and capital goods, human-made items that are used to produce other items. Some economists also include entrepreneurship as a fourth factor of production. Entrepreneurship represents the innovative commercial ideas of entrepreneurs working on their own or within existing businesses. Resources have value because they are the main ingredients of production. That is, resources are transformed by businesses into items that households, government, and other businesses are willing to buy.

Second, the **costs of production** are the payments businesses make in exchange for the factors of production. Note from Figure 2.3 that the costs of production eventually make their way into the pockets of households, who own the factors of production. Some resources are owned directly by people in households. For instance, workers directly own their labor, and entrepreneurs own their special talents or skills. At other times, households own resources indirectly, mainly through their ownership of business enterprises—including the natural resources and capital goods that comprise the holdings of these business firms.

The main costs of production incurred by businesses are wages or salaries, which is the payment for human resources; rents, the payment for natural resources; interest, the payment for capital goods; and profits, the payment for entrepreneurship. The largest category of payments—and thus the largest source of household income—is wages and salaries. In 2012 private businesses paid American workers $5.7 trillion in exchange for their labor. Wages paid by government to public sector employees added another $1.2 trillion to household income. Individual proprietors earned $1.1 trillion from their own businesses.[2] While workers' pay consists of wages and salaries, entrepreneurs often expect entrepreneurial profits in exchange for their labor. The term "profits" in this context refers to financial "above normal" compensation—a type of financial incentive to reward entrepreneurs for business innovation and risk taking.

Flows of Products, Resources, and Money Payments

The circular flow model also shows the two other flows: the flow of products (goods and services) and resources on the outer circle, and the flow of money payments on the inner circle. The *outer* circle shows that households willingly supply resources—human resources, natural resources, capital goods, and entrepreneurship—to businesses in the factor market. Businesses, in turn, transform these resources into finished goods and services for sale in the product market. Thus, the outer circle shows the things that are purchased in the factor market and the product market.

The *inner* circle shows the flow of the money payments as these payments travel through the American economy. In the factor market, businesses make money payments to households in the form of wages and salaries, interest, rents, and entrepreneurial profits. These money payments, which are the costs of production for businesses, become sources of income for households. Households, in turn, use their income to buy finished goods and services in the product market. This household spending on goods and services becomes revenues for businesses. Business revenues enable firms to buy resources from households—

and so the money flow continues. In the American market economy, the flows in both the product market and the factor market are free from most types of government regulation.

DEMAND

A central feature of a market economy is the efficient operation of free markets. A **market** occurs whenever two or more parties freely exchange something of value. Recall from the circular flow model that there are two primary types of markets, a product market where households buy products from businesses and a factor market where businesses buy resources from households. There are countless exchanges that take place in the U.S. product market and factor market every day. But how are the prices for goods, services, and resources determined? In a market economy, the impersonal forces of demand and supply establish most prices and, in doing so, bring order to the seeming chaos of the marketplace.

Demand

Demand is the amount of a good, service, or resource that people are willing and able to buy at a series of prices at a moment in time. The demand for a product or resource is illustrated in tabular form by a demand schedule, or with a demand curve, as shown in Figure 2.4. The demand curve slopes downward, reflecting the most famous of all economic laws, the law of demand. According to the **law of demand**, there is an inverse relationship between price and quantity demanded. That is, if the price of a good increases, the quantity demanded will decrease. Conversely, if the price of a good decreases, the quantity demanded will increase.

To construct an initial demand curve for a product, economists employ the ceteris paribus assumption. Under the ceteris paribus assumption, all external factors that might affect the demand for the product, except price, are temporarily held constant. In the product market, the demand curve typically represents the viewpoint of the consumer, who buys final goods or services from businesses. In the factor market, the demand curve typically represents the viewpoint of the producer, who buys resources from households.

The demand curve shown in Figure 2.4 represents the demand for product X at a moment in time. Hence, a change in the price of product X causes a change in the *quantity demanded*, not a change in the overall *demand* for the product. Speaking precisely, economists say that a change in price causes a *movement* along an existing demand curve. In Figure 2.4, for example, if the price of product X decreases from $6 to $4, there is a downward movement along the existing demand curve. In this case, the $2 decrease in price caused the quantity demanded to increase from 6,000 items to 8,000 items but had no impact on the overall demand for product X. Note that a change in price does not cause the demand curve to shift to the right or to the left.

Changes in Demand

How does a change in the overall demand for a good occur? To change the demand for a good, the ceteris paribus assumption is lifted, allowing other factors, called determinants of demand, to enter the picture. A change in one or more of the determinants of demand causes buyers to want more or less of a good at each and every price. There are six main determinants of demand: people's tastes and preferences, income level, market size, price of substitute goods, price of complementary goods, and expectations.

Suppose, for example, that a successful television commercial favorably affects people's tastes and preferences for product X. The likely result is that buyers would purchase more of product X at each and every price. Perhaps at a price of $10, buyers would now be

Demand Schedule for Product X

Price	Quantity Demanded (in Thousands)
$10	2
$8	4
$6	6
$4	8
$2	10

Demand Curve for Product X

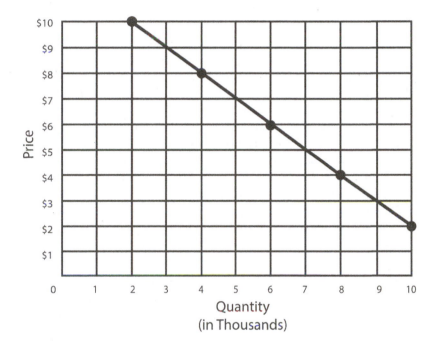

Figure 2.4   Illustrating the Demand for Product X

willing to purchase 4,000 items; at $8 they would buy 6,000 items; at $6 they would buy 8,000 items; at $4 they would buy 10,000 items; and at $2 they would buy 12,000 items. Hence, a change in tastes and preferences, a determinant of demand, causes the entire demand curve to *shift* to the right (a *positive shift*). The new demand curve represents the new reality of the marketplace, so the original demand curve disappears. Of course, people's tastes and preferences can also work against a product or service, as is often the case with fads or products that have become obsolete such as typewriters or horse-drawn wagons. A decline in people's tastes and preferences causes a shift of the entire demand curve to the left to show that people are willing to buy less of the product at each and every price. In addition to tastes and preferences, the other determinants of demand include:

- *Income level.* An increase in people's incomes causes the demand for most goods to increase; a decrease in income causes a decrease in demand for most products.

- *Market size.* An increase in market size (a larger number of potential buyers) causes the demand for most goods to increase; a decrease in market size causes a decrease in demand for most products.
- *Price of a substitute good.* An increase in the price of a substitute good causes an increase in the demand for the related product; a decrease in the price of a substitute good causes a decrease in the demand for the related product. (A **substitute good** is a product that can be used in place of a similar good.)
- *Price of a complementary good.* A decrease in the price of a complementary good causes an increase in demand for the related good; an increase in the price of a complementary good causes a decrease in the demand for the related good. (A **complementary good** is a product that is used in conjunction with another product.)
- *Expectations.* An optimistic view about personal or national prosperity causes an increase in the demand for most goods; a pessimistic view has the opposite effect.

Price Elasticity of Demand

The law of demand shows an inverse relationship between the price of a product and the quantity demanded—as the price increases, the quantity demanded decreases, and when the price decreases, the quantity demanded increases. What still needs to be determined is the degree to which a change in price affects the quantity demanded. This question, to the economist, concerns the price elasticity of demand.

The **price elasticity of demand** measures the impact of price changes on the quantity demanded of a good. The demand for a good is said to be *elastic* when even a relatively small change in the price of a good causes a larger change in the quantity demanded. In other words, people's demand for some goods is very flexible, or responsive to a change in the good's price. Conversely, the demand for a good is considered *inelastic* when even a relatively large change in a good's price causes a smaller change in the quantity demanded. That is, people's demand for the other good is inflexible, and people will be less willing to change their buying habits even when the price changes. Three main determinants explain the price elasticity of demand of a certain good or service: the availability of close substitutes, whether the good is a necessity or a luxury, and time, as shown in Table 2.1.

The demand for a good tends to be price *elastic*, or flexible, when there are close substitute goods available for purchase, when this good is viewed as a luxury, and when there is more time to make a buying decision. Consider the demand for a particular automobile. While an auto is a necessity for many people, the demand for a *particular* auto is elastic because there are many substitutes available in the automobile market—many different makes and models of autos from which to choose. In most cases, people who want to buy an auto also have sufficient time to visit a number of auto dealerships so that a rational buying decision can be made. The consumer may even decide to postpone the purchase of the auto for another year if the right deal cannot be reached.

Table 2.1   Determinants of Price Elasticity of Demand

Types of Elasticity	Determinants of Elasticity		
	Availability of Substitute Goods	*Necessity or Luxury Goods*	*Time Constraints*
Elastic demand	Many	Luxury	Longer time period
Inelastic demand	Few or none	Necessity	Shorter time period

Offshore oil platforms supplement onshore production of petroleum, one of the world's most important energy resources. (Shutterstock.com)

The demand for a good tends to be price *inelastic*, or inflexible, when there are no close substitutes available for purchase, when this good is viewed as a necessity, and when time constraints prevent a convenient switch to another product. Consider the demand for the gasoline that is used in the automobile. The demand for gasoline is price inelastic because there are few if any substitutes for this fuel, it is essential to the operation of the auto, and when the tank moves toward empty, more gasoline must be purchased. In recent years gasoline prices have been on a roller coaster, with rapid and significant price increases and decreases. Despite these price changes, gasoline consumption in the United States, by and large, has changed little.

SUPPLY

The demand side of a market represents the interests of buyers who, naturally, want to spend as little money as possible to purchase goods. The supply side of a market represents the interests of producers. Producers are businesses that make or distribute products to buyers. Producers, it is assumed, strive to earn maximum profits. Businesses earn a profit when the price they charge for a product is greater than the average cost of producing the item. Business profits are used to reward investors and to finance business modernization or expansion. Hence, businesses and consumers see markets through a very different lens.

Supply
Supply is the amount of a good, service, or resource that producers are willing and able to sell at a series of prices at a moment in time. The supply of a product or resource is

Supply Schedule for Product X

Price	Quantity Supplied (in Thousands)
$10	10
$8	8
$6	6
$4	4
$2	2

Supply Curve for Product X

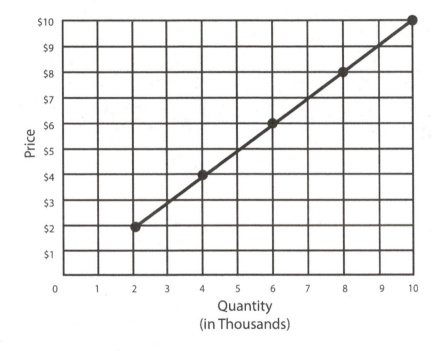

Figure 2.5   Illustrating the Supply of Product X

illustrated in tabular form by a supply schedule, or with a supply curve, as shown in Figure 2.5. The supply curve slopes upward, reflecting the law of supply. According to the law of supply, there is a direct relationship between the price of a good and the quantity supplied. That is, if the price of a good increases, the quantity supplied will also increase. Conversely, if the price of a good decreases, the quantity supplied will also decrease.

The ceteris paribus assumption is used to construct an initial supply curve, just as it was used when charting an original demand curve. In the product market, the supply curve typically represents the viewpoint of businesses, which produce or sell final goods or services to households. In the resource market, the supply curve represents the viewpoint of households, which sell their labor and other resources to businesses.

The supply curve shown in Figure 2.5 represents the initial supply of product X at a moment in time. A change in the price of product X causes a change in the *quantity supplied*, not a change in the overall *supply* of the product. Economists say that a change in price causes a *movement* along an existing supply curve. In Figure 2.5, if the price of product X increases from $2 to $4, there is an upward movement along the existing supply curve. In this situation, the $2 increase in price causes the quantity supplied to increase from 2,000 items to 4,000 items. This change in price had no impact on the overall supply of product X, however. Note that a change in price does not cause the supply curve to shift to the right or to the left.

Changes in Supply

The overall supply of a product changes when the ceteris paribus assumption is lifted and one or more of the determinants of supply changes. A change in a determinant of supply causes the producer to supply more or less of a good or resource at each and every price. There are five main determinants of supply: resource prices, technological advance, number of firms in an industry, taxes, and expectations.

Suppose there was a decrease in the price of natural resources used in the production of product X. Lower costs of production would likely cause producers to supply more of product X at each and every price. At a price of $2, for example, producers would be willing to supply 4,000 items; at $4 they would supply 6,000 items; at $6 they would supply 8,000 items; at $8 they would supply 10,000 items; and at $10 they would supply 12,000 items. Thus, a change in the price of a key resource, a determinant of supply, causes the entire supply curve to *shift* to the right (a *positive shift*). The new supply curve represents the new reality of the marketplace, so the original supply curve disappears. Conversely, an increase in the price of key resources used in the production of product X would raise the costs of production, which would cause producers to supply less at each and every price (a *negative shift*). In addition to resource prices, the four other determinants of supply are:

- *Technological advance.* Improvements in technology allow businesses to improve efficiency and cut production costs, thus encouraging firms to increase the supply of the product. Technological advances in one industry can also negatively affect production in a related industry. For example, technological advances in the computer industry made the typewriter obsolete.
- *Number of firms in an industry.* When additional firms enter an industry, the supply of the product tends to increase. Conversely, when firms exit an industry, the overall supply of the product tends to fall.
- *Taxes.* Lower taxes reduce production costs and encourage businesses to increase the supply of goods. Higher business taxes tend to increase business costs and thus cause businesses to reduce the supply of goods and services.
- *Expectations.* Optimistic expectations about future prosperity in the economy or about the prospects for high prices and healthy profits within an industry, cause businesses to increase the supply of goods. Pessimistic economic forecasts cause businesses to reduce the supply of goods.

Price Elasticity of Supply

The law of supply shows there is a direct or positive relationship between the price of a product and the quantity of that product supplied by producers. That is, when the price of a product increases, the quantity supplied by producers also increases. But when the price of a product falls, the quantity supplied also tends to fall.

The **price elasticity of supply** measures the impact of a price change on the quantity supplied of a product. The supply for the product is *elastic* when even a small change in the price of the product causes a larger change in the quantity supplied. Conversely, the supply of a product is *inelastic* when even a relatively large change in the product's price causes a smaller change in the quantity supplied. The price elasticity of supply is affected mainly by time.

The supply of a product tends to be *elastic* over a longer period of time or—to be more precise—in the long run. The long run is defined as the amount of time it takes for firms to change any resource used in production. In the long run firms are able to change the number of workers at the plant, the amount of raw materials or semifinished goods used in production, and even the size of the plant itself. Further, in the long run additional firms can enter into the industry or exit from the industry. Recall that the price elasticity of supply measures how responsive the quantity supplied of a product is to a change in its price. When a product's price increases, firms in the long run can devote more resources—workers, materials, capital goods, even a larger production facility—to the production of these products. Conversely, when the product's price falls, firms can decrease production by removing resources, closing plants, or exiting the industry. Thus, given enough time to adjust production levels, firms have the ability to respond to price changes.

The supply of a product tends to be *inelastic* for a shorter period of time, or the short run. In the short run, only certain resources can be changed, mainly the number of workers, the materials used to make the product, and some of the capital equipment within the plant. The plant size, however, cannot be changed in the short run. Moreover, in the short run additional firms are not able to enter the industry. What this means for firms is that they do not have sufficient time to adjust their level of output significantly. As a result, a change in the price of a product will have a smaller impact on the quantity supplied in the short run.

One special case is worth noting with regard to price elasticity of supply—products with a perfectly inelastic supply. A perfectly inelastic supply means that the supply is fixed or unchangeable regardless of a change in the price. While this may seem like an extreme situation, it is not all that uncommon. The number of beachfront properties along a certain stretch of sandy shoreline is perfectly inelastic. The number of seats available at a sports arena or stadium is perfectly inelastic. Individual works of art by Van Gogh, Rembrandt, or Picasso have a perfectly inelastic supply—there is just one original copy of each piece of artwork.

Items with a perfectly inelastic supply often command a high price when demand for the item is high. In 2012, for example, an Edvard Munch painting, *The Scream*, sold for a record $120 million at auction.[3] Many collectables also are in perfectly fixed supply. Collectibles include baseball cards, record albums, jewelry—even comic books! In 2010 a rare 1938 edition of Action Comics No. 1, which introduced Superman to the world, sold at auction for $1.5 million.[4]

MARKET EQUILIBRIUM

You just read that demand represents the interests of the consumer, while supply represents the interests of the producer. Consumers will buy a greater quantity of products at a low price, while producers will make a greater quantity of products at a high price. The reality of any market is that neither buyers nor sellers can get exactly the price they want. Instead, it is only through compromise between the interests of buyers and sellers that a market price and quantity can be reached.

During the eighteenth and nineteenth centuries, economists explored how the forces of demand and supply affected the functioning of markets. In 1890 prominent British

---

PRIMARY DOCUMENT: Alfred Marshall Describes the Importance of Demand and Supply

We might as reasonably dispute whether it is the upper or the under blade of a pair of scissors that cuts a piece of paper, as whether value [the price of an item] is governed by utility [the demand side of the market] or cost of production [the supply side of the market]. It is true that when one blade is held still, and the cutting is effected by moving the other, we may say with careless brevity that the cutting is done by the second; but the statement is not strictly accurate, and is to be excused only so long as it claims to be merely a popular and not a strictly scientific account of what happens.

In the same way, when a thing already made has to be sold, the price which people will be willing to pay for it will be governed by their desire to have it, together with the amount they can afford to spend on it. Their desire to have it depends partly on the chance that, if they do not buy it, they will be able to get another thing like it at as low a price: this depends on the causes that govern the supply of it, and this again upon the cost of production.

Principles of Economics, Alfred Marshall

---

economist and mathematician Alfred Marshall (1842–1924) published *Principles of Economics*, which expanded on the work of the earlier economists. Marshall brought earlier analyses of supply and demand together onto the same graph, noting that free markets balance the interests of suppliers of products and demanders of products at an equilibrium price and quantity. When asked whether supply or demand was the more dominant determinant of the good's price, Marshall compared supply and demand to the blades of scissors. Just as both blades are needed to cut a piece of paper, both supply and demand are needed to establish market equilibrium, as explained in the above passage.[5]

Market Clearing Price and Quantity

The **market equilibrium** for a product occurs at the point where the demand curve and supply curve intersect. Thus, the market equilibrium is the best compromise between the interests of consumers, represented by the demand curve, and producers, represented by the supply curve. At the market equilibrium, the product's price and quantity are determined. The market equilibrium is also called the market clearing price because at this compromise point, all of the output supplied by businesses is demanded by buyers. Figure 2.6 illustrates the demand and supply for product X. At a low price of $2, the quantity demanded is high, 10,000 items in this case. Producers, on the other hand, are only willing to produce 10,000 items if they can charge a high price of $10 per item.

The power of the free market is its ability to make the necessary compromises without decrees or coercion from the government. Figure 2.6 shows that at this moment in time, the equilibrium price for product X is $6 and its equilibrium quantity is 6,000 items. Note that the horizontal axis is now labeled "quantity," rather than "quantity demanded" or "quantity supplied," because both the demand curve and the supply curve are shown on the same graph.

Price Ceilings and Price Floors

While the forces of supply and demand are responsible for establishing most prices in the U.S. economy, the government sometimes overrides the compromises of the market

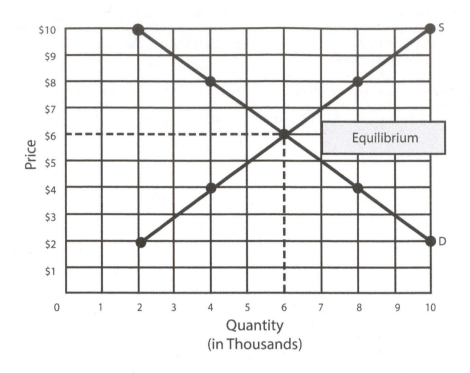

Figure 2.6   Market Equilibrium for Product X

to set the price for a product or a resource. This type of government intervention in the economy typically occurs when government, at any level, feels a price is unfairly high for consumers or unfairly low for producers. There are two types of government price controls, price ceilings and price floors.

A **price ceiling** is a government-imposed maximum price that a seller may charge for a good or service. The main goal of a price ceiling is to make a product more affordable to consumers. A rent control on apartment units is one common type of price ceiling used in the United States. Some local governments limit rents for apartment units at a price below the true market equilibrium. In Figure 2.7, for example, the true equilibrium price for a rental unit is $500 per month, and the equilibrium quantity is 40,000 rental units. The government-imposed price ceiling, however, dictates that the apartment owners cannot charge more than $400 in monthly rent to people renting these apartments. This $400 appears as a horizontal line to show that no matter how many apartments are demanded or supplied, the price (rent) stays constant at $400. At this lower controlled price, the *quantity demanded* of rental units increases to 50,000, shown at point B. An unintended consequence of the lower rents, however, is that the quantity supplied of rental units decreases to 30,000, shown at point A. The result is a *shortage* of rental units because the quantity demanded (50,000 rental units) is now greater than the quantity supplied (30,000 rental units).

Price ceilings have been used sparingly in the U.S. economy. For example, during World War II the federal government imposed price ceilings on certain consumer goods to hold inflation in check. The government also imposed price ceilings on domestically produced oil during the mid-1970s in response to skyrocketing oil prices in U.S. and global markets.

A **price floor** is a government-guaranteed minimum price for a product or a resource. In the product market, the main goal of a price floor is to provide higher revenues for suppliers

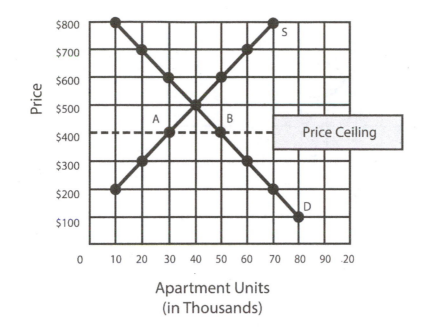

Figure 2.7   Price Ceilings and Shortages

of certain goods. For example, the U.S. government has instituted price floors on a number of agricultural products to boost revenues for the country's farmers. In the factor market, the federal government's price floor on wages, called the minimum wage, sets a minimum price for the services of workers. A minimum wage creates the lowest wage that an employer can offer an employee. The Fair Labor Standards Act created the country's first minimum wage of $0.25 per hour in 1938. In 2013 the federal minimum stood at $7.25.[6]

The impact of a minimum wage on some low-wage labor markets might resemble that shown in Figure 2.8. Note that the equilibrium wage in this labor market occurs where the supply curve and demand curve for labor intersect, in this case an hourly wage rate of $4 and a quantity of 5,000 employed workers. Suppose a minimum wage of $7 was applied to this labor market, as shown in Figure 2.8. This $7 per hour wage appears as a horizontal line to show that no matter how many workers are demanded or supplied, the price of labor (wage rate) stays constant at $7 per hour. The result is a drop in the number of workers that firms demand from 5,000 to just 2,000, as shown on the demand curve. At the same time, the number of workers willing to work at this higher wage rises from 5,000 to 8,000, as shown on the supply curve. Hence, a labor *surplus* of 6,000 workers is created because the quantity supplied (8,000) is greater than the quantity demanded (2,000) at the new government-imposed wage rate. This theoretical model overstates the job loss that would occur due to an increase in the minimum wage but illustrates the potential for unemployment when the government intervenes in certain markets.

Price System

A **market economy** is a type of economy that relies on the private sector—individuals and business firms—to answer the basic economic questions of what to produce, how to produce, and for whom to produce. In practice, this means that people can own and control private property and exercise a variety of freedoms in the marketplace.

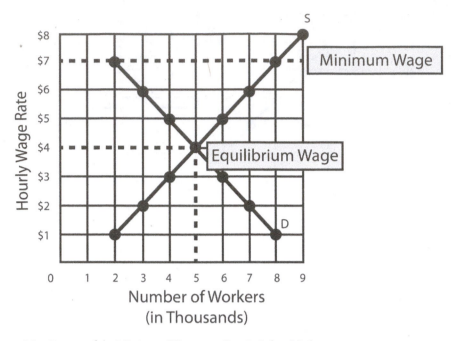

Figure 2.8   Impact of the Minimum Wage on a Certain Labor Market

The Hong Kong Special Administrative Region (SAR) is the freest economy in the world. (Shutterstock.com)

ECONOMICS IN HISTORY: The Case of Hong Kong and Economic Freedom

Over the past few decades the former British colony of Hong Kong has been among the freest market economies in the world. Established as a free port by the British in the early 1840s, Hong Kong attracted foreign trade and investment during the nineteenth and twentieth centuries. The influx of aspiring entrepreneurs and foreign capital accelerated during the early twentieth century as people fled the chaos of war and revolution in neighboring China, including the devastating civil war between the Nationalists and the Communists—a conflict that raged until the victorious Communists created the People's Republic of China in 1949.

British policies encouraged free markets and profit incentives in Hong Kong. By design, there were few government regulations on business activity. The British also invested heavily in the development of a modern infrastructure, including an electrified railroad, a subway system, and an international airport. In 1997 Hong Kong was made a special administrative region of the People's Republic of China. Today, this region is called the Hong Kong SAR. The present government of the Hong Kong SAR has a strong commitment to free markets and lives by the principle of "Big Market, Small Government."[7] It retains a privileged position within China, however. The Hong Kong SAR enjoyed the most economic freedom of any economy in the world in 2010, according to *Economic Freedom of the World: 2012 Annual Report*.[8]

The **price system** coordinates most production and consumption decisions in a market system, largely through invisible "signals" to market participants—consumers, producers, workers, and others. Many of these signals are price signals. Recall from Chapter 1 that one of the basic principles of economics is that people respond to price incentives. That is, price incentives, rather than government authorities, allocate resources.

What are some of these price signals? Consumers enjoy the *freedom of choice*—the ability to consider the prices of goods when they spend their money. First, a lower price on a certain item signals consumers to purchase more of the lower-priced item and less of the higher-priced substitute goods. Second, consumer spending signals producers about what goods and services to produce—producers produce only what consumers will buy.

Producers, in turn, have the *freedom of enterprise*, which allows firms to consider the price of resources when they produce goods. Producers shop around for low-priced resources to make goods and services. The use of less expensive resources enables producers to remain competitive with other firms and to earn higher profits. Economists summarize the functions of the price system as follows:

- *Allocation function.* the price system encourages firms to make efficient use of resources, to lower production costs, and to produce goods that people are willing to buy; and
- *Rationing function.* the price system signals which products people can or cannot afford to buy at a moment in time.

CHAPTER 2 SUMMARY

Scarcity, Choice, and Opportunity Cost
- A production possibilities frontier shows the range of possible production choices for two products and the opportunity cost of each production choice.
- Budget constraint shows how two factors, income and the price of goods, set a limit on people's consumption choices.

The Circular Flow Model
- Households and other buyers purchase goods and services from businesses in the product market.
- Businesses purchase resources (the factors of production) from households in the factor market.
- The circular flow model shows two additional flows, the flow of resources and products on an outer circle, and the flow of money payments for resources and products on the inner circle.

Demand
- Demand is the amount of a product people are willing and able to buy at a series of prices, and is illustrated with a downward sloping demand curve.
- The demand for products often changes in response to a change in one or more of the determinants of demand.
- The price elasticity of demand measures the impact of a price change on the quantity demanded of a product; the demand for a product can be price elastic or price inelastic.

Supply
- Supply is the amount of a product producers are willing and able to sell at a series of prices, and is illustrated with an upward sloping supply curve.
- The supply of products often changes in response to a change in one or more of the determinants of supply.
- The price elasticity of supply measures the impact of a price change on the quantity supplied of a product; the supply of a product can be price elastic or price inelastic.

Market Equilibrium
- At the market equilibrium for a product, the demand curve and the supply curve intersect, thus establishing a market price and quantity for the product.
- The government can intervene in markets to set a price ceiling, which is a maximum price for a product, or a price floor, which is a minimum price for a product.
- The price system coordinates most production and consumption decisions by sending signals to market participants about how to use their scarce resources.

NOTES

1. U.S. Department of Commerce (DOC), Bureau of Economic Analysis (BEA), "Table 3: Gross Domestic Product and Related Measures: Level and Change from Preceding Period," *BEA News Release*, February 28, 2013, www.bea.gov/newsreleases/national/gdp/2013/pdf/gdp12_2.pdf

2. DOC/BEA, "Table 2.6: Personal Income and Its Disposition (Years and Quarters)," March 1, 2013, www.bea.gov/newsreleases/national/pi/pinewsrelease.htm

3. Caleb Melby, "The Top 10 Art Auction Sales Ever, Including Record $120 Million for Munch's 'The Scream,'" *Forbes*, May 3, 2012, www.forbes.com/sites/calebmelby/2012/05/03

4. CNN, "Rare Comic of Superman Debut Fetches $1.5 Million," *CNN Entertainment*, March 30, 2010, http://articles.cnn.com/2010-03-30/entertainment/superman.comic_1_action-comic-book-superman-book?_S=PM:SHOWBIZ

5. Alfred Marshall, *Principles of Economics*. Abridged. Amherst, NY: Prometheus, 1997, Book V, Chapter III, Section 27–28.

6. U.S. Department of Labor (DOL), "History of Federal Minimum Wage Rates under the Fair Labor Standards Act, 1938–2009," www.dol.gov/whd/minwage/chart.htm; DOL, "Changes in Basic Minimum Wages in Non-Farm Employment under State Law: Selected Years, 1968 to 2013," www.dol.gov/whd/state/stateMinWageHis.htm

7. Hong Kong Special Administrative Region, *Hong Kong: The Facts* (Hong Kong, China: Information Services Department, Hong Kong SAR, January), 2012, www.gov.hk

8. James Gwartney, Robert A. Lawson, and Joshua C. Hall, "Exhibit 1.2: Summary Economic Freedom Ratings for 2010," *Economic Freedom of the World: 2012 Annual Report* (Canada: Fraser Institute), 2012, 10, www.freetheworld.com/2012/EFW2012-complete.pdf

3

Economic History and Economic Systems

Economic history can be divided many different ways. This chapter identifies the sweeping transformation through four stages of history, from primitive food gathering and hunting to the present information age. The chapter also contrasts the different models for economies—the market model and the command model. In the modern era societies have adapted these models to form the three main "isms," which include capitalism, socialism, and communism.

STAGES OF ECONOMIC HISTORY

Economic history is often divided into four stages: primitive food gathering and hunting, permanent agriculture and animal domestication, the industrial age, and the information age. The progression from one economic stage to the next has been irregular, occurring in different countries and world regions at different times. Even today, where information and communications technologies have opened pathways to nearly infinite amounts of information, there is still a significant portion of the world's population—mainly in the developing world—that lacks the technology to fully join the information age.

Food Gathering and Hunting

The earliest stage of economic history, primitive food gathering and hunting, took place during the Old Stone Age, or Paleolithic Age (500,000 BCE to 10,000 BCE). At this time small nomadic tribes met their survival needs by "following the food." These tribes were scattered throughout the world with concentrations in China, Southeast Asia, Europe, and East Africa.

Tribal organization featured a rigid division of labor determined mainly by gender and physical strength. Men typically made weapons of stone, bone, and wood and hunted animals for food. Women gathered food, collecting nuts, berries, seeds or wild grains, fruits, roots, shellfish and other foodstuffs available from the natural environment. Women often maintained the campsite, which might consist of caves or temporary shelters. Women also tended the tribe's fire and to the children's needs.

Over time, the food gathering and hunting societies developed additional skills and tools to cope with their environment. For example, they developed language, which enabled them to pass on knowledge from one generation to the next and to learn from other tribes. They also created more advanced survival tools such as weapons, cutting tools, and needles. These primitive forms of real capital were devised mainly to enhance the tribe's survival through food gathering and hunting. Tools and weapons were made from natural resources such as stone, wood, and animal bones.

Permanent Agriculture and Animal Domestication

The second stage of economic history, permanent agriculture and animal domestication, began during the New Stone Age, or Neolithic Age (10,000 BCE to 3500 BCE). The term "**agricultural revolution**" is used to describe the momentous shift from a nomadic lifestyle to a more sedentary lifestyle on farms and in permanent settlements. Agricultural societies and nomadic groups coexisted throughout the Neolithic Age and beyond. Some of the regions that were earliest to embrace the agricultural revolution were located in the Middle East, northeastern China, Central and South America, and eastern Africa.

The agricultural revolution affected economic development in a number of ways. First, it enabled the rise of permanent settlements such as villages, towns, and cities. Many early settlements were established on fertile territories near rivers, such as the Tigris and Euphrates in the Middle East, the Nile in northeastern Africa, the Indus in India, and the Yellow in China. Cultivation was enhanced by fertile soil, water from rivers, and domesticated animals. Second, the rise of permanent agriculture encouraged specialization. This is because food surpluses produced on the farms were used to support a more sophisticated division of labor in the growing cities. Freed from the toils of farm work artisans, merchants, artists, engineers, and other skilled workers built and maintained cities. Third, the production of surpluses expanded trade among peoples. Surpluses of food, luxury items, natural resources, and other items provided incentives for civilizations to aggressively seek out new markets for their output. Fourth, new contacts among peoples accelerated technological advances. Innovations such as the wheel and the sail revolutionized the transport of goods, people, and ideas among the ancients.

Another innovation of the period was the creation of money. **Money** is any item that is commonly accepted in payment for goods or services or in payment of other debts. The introduction of money progressed in fits and starts over thousands of years. Slowly, money came to replace **barter**, a system of exchange in which one good is exchanged for a second good. Ancient civilizations used different items for money. In the Americas, for example, the Maya and the Aztecs used cloth and cocoa beans as money. Some west African kingdoms used cowrie shells. A significant breakthrough in the development of money was the introduction of coins. Over a thousand years before the Common Era, the Chinese used spade coins to facilitate transactions. In the seventh century BCE, the Lydians minted the stater, a coin originally comprised of a gold and silver mixture. About a century later the Athenians introduced the tetradrachma, ushering in an era of coin use by the Greek city-states.[1]

Industrial Age

The third stage of economic history, the industrial age, resulted from **industrialization**— the economic transition from small-scale labor-intensive production to large-scale capital-intensive production in factories and mills. Industrialization did not occur in all regions of the world simultaneously. Instead, widespread industrialization, which would soon be called the Industrial Revolution, began in Great Britain in the 1700s and spread to other European countries and the United States during the 1800s.

Great Britain was the catalyst for the epic economic and social changes brought about by industrialization. Great Britain was blessed with a wide variety of domestic resources such as navigable rivers and deep harbors, minerals such as iron ore and coal, and an abundance of inexpensive labor. Other resources, such as timber and cotton, were imported at low cost from Britain's colonial possessions in North America, Africa, and Asia. In addition, Britain's government was stable and, in many respects, far-sighted. For example, Britain was quick to recognize the economic benefits of establishing profitable trade relationships and a colonial empire—and of creating a formidable navy to protect its commercial interests.

During the industrial age a new model for the mass production of goods, called the factory system, was established. Under the **factory system** the size of production facilities grew, and production came to rely on the efficient operation of heavy machinery by unskilled labor. The factory system required workers to specialize in a specific task within a larger production process. This rigid division of labor often dehumanized the production process, forcing men, women, and children to endure sweatshop conditions in the factories, mills, and mines. It also dismantled the traditional **domestic system**—a production system in which people worked from their homes to make cloth, shoes, and other items.

The development of new technologies underpinned the growth of the factory system during the industrial age. During the 1700s and 1800s complex machinery was invented to produce items such as yarn or cloth. Steam was harnessed to power factories and mills, steamships, and locomotives. By the late 1800s electricity was being used to support basic infrastructure such as telephone communications, lighting systems, tramways, and railways. New technologies also expanded mass production techniques into entirely new industries, such as steel and the automobile as the industrial age matured. These technological advances increased national output in advanced economies such as Great Britain, Germany, and the United States. The industrial age also laid the foundation for a gradual improvement in workers' standard of living in the industrialized societies.

Information Age

The fourth stage of economic history, the information age, relies on information and communications technologies in the production process. **Information and communications technologies** (ICTs) are the technological advances that increase people's ability to collect, store, retrieve, and share information. The information age began during the final quarter of the twentieth century, but its roots were firmly planted in the technologies of the industrial age such as electricity, the telephone, early computers, and software. What is radically new about recent ICTs is the pace of their development and the degree to which they are integrated into business activity throughout the global economy.

The information age is grounded in several key technologies. The first is computer technology, which has progressed with lightning speed since World War II. In 1946 the Electronic Numerical Integrator and Calculator (ENIAC), the world's first functional electronic computer, was invented in the United States. Since that time, technological advances have allowed the computer industry to evolve from the use of vacuum tubes, to transistors, to integrated circuits, to microprocessors. Technology also broadened the appeal of computers by expanding the market from large mainframe computers, which were used mainly by big businesses, the government, and universities, to user-friendly personal computers. Second, the production of sophisticated software has complemented advances in computer technology, encouraging computer applications in homes, schools, and smaller businesses. Third, communications technologies, such as wireless telephones and other wireless devices, have accelerated exponentially in recent years.

The invention of the Internet in 1969 by the U.S. Department of Defense jump-started the process of connecting computer networks. The use of the Internet, or "internetworking of networks," expanded during the 1970s and 1980s when a basic infrastructure was developed and conveniences such as email were added. The invention of the World Wide Web by Tim Berners-Lee in 1989 opened the floodgates to Internet use. Through the World Wide Web, the information age exploded as people were able to communicate and share information through a global network that was both easy to use and inexpensive. By 2013 an estimated 2.7 billion people around the world had ready access to the Internet.[2]

The information age, like the earlier industrial age, has progressed at a different pace for countries around the world. High-income developed countries are better able to integrate the latest ICTs into their economies, while lower-income developing countries tend to lag behind. These technological inequities have created a significant ICT gap between richer and poorer countries, often called the digital divide. As a result, the poorest countries are further marginalized and are denied access to some trade and investment opportunities. In recent years a surge in Internet use in the developing world has narrowed the digital divide for some countries. From 2005 to 2013, for example, the number of Internet users in the developing world climbed from 408 million people to 1.8 billion people. This represents nearly one-third of all people living in the developing world. During this same period of time, Internet use climbed in the developed countries from 616 million to 958 million people, which represents 77 percent of all people living in these richer countries. While Internet use increased in all world regions from 2005 to 2013, it continued to lag in Africa, where fewer than one in five people had access to the Internet.[3]

Microwave towers enhance communications and are an important feature of a country's economic infrastructure. (Shutterstock.com)

ICTs have transformed the conduct of business in today's fast-paced global economy, especially in the richer developed countries. Over the Internet, businesses scan the planet for low-cost resources, advertise, and sell their output to buyers. Business activity that takes place over the Internet reduces some of the brick and mortar costs associated with traditional production methods such as the construction of retail stores or other buildings. By the 2010s trillions of dollars of business-to-business (B2B) and business-to-consumer (B2C) electronic commerce took place annually in the global economy. In the United States alone the U.S. Census Bureau reported $4.1 trillion in ecommerce in 2010, of which about 90 percent were B2B transactions and the remaining 10 percent B2C transactions.[4]

ECONOMIC SYSTEMS: THE MODELS

Scarcity forces people to make economic choices about how to use their resources. Throughout history people working alone, or in groups, have come to grips with this reality by forming economic systems. An **economic system** is the sum total of all economic activity that takes place within a society. That is, economic systems are comprised not only of the tangible economic institutions such as business firms, banks, and stock exchanges, but also the more subtle nuances that underlie business activity such as values, practices, customs, and traditions.

Economic systems also answer the three **basic economic questions**. What goods and services should be produced and in what quantity? How should these products be produced? For whom should these products be produced? Responses to the basic economic questions help distinguish between different types of economic systems: traditional economies, command economies, and market economies. In reality, virtually all economies today are mixed economies—economies that adopt features mainly from the command and market models.

Traditional Economy

A **traditional economy** is a type of economic system that relies on custom or tradition to answer the basic economic questions. That is, society's blueprint for economic activity is written by previous generations. Historically, traditional economies produced goods that satisfied basic survival needs for food, clothing, and shelter. These isolated peoples produced few surpluses and, as a result, there was little trade. Production methods, which relied on the use of primitive capital goods and a rigid division of labor, varied little from one generation to the next. Primitive communalism, based on community needs and kinship ties, helped determine who shared in the economy's output. Today there are few traditional economies. Small enclaves of people living in remote regions of Africa, Asia, Latin America, and the Arctic regions have many characteristics of traditional economies. Examples include the Mbuti Pygmies of central Africa, the Kavango tribes of Namibia, the Nigritos of the Philippines, and the Saharias of central India.

The Mbuti Pygmies have lived in the Ituri Forest for thousands of years. The Ituri is a rainforest in the present-day Democratic Republic of Congo (formerly Zaire), but Pygmy bands also inhabit regions that straddle neighboring Congo Republic and Cameroon. The Mbuti live in small bands or groups, are nomadic, and are well acquainted with the bounty of the forest, which provides them with food, clothing, and shelter. The Mbuti, who number 70,000 to 80,000 people, are mainly hunters and gatherers. The simple division of labor that has been passed from generation to generation is determined mainly by gender and age. Men lead the hunts using primitive capital such as the bow and arrow. Women have primary responsibility for cooking and maintaining the temporary campsites. Both men and women gather edible plants, such as fruits, mushrooms, and roots. The entire Mbuti community takes part in fishing, which typically involves corralling fish into nets. Hence, the needs of the community are met through collective action.

Today the Mbuti have some economic contact with the outside world. For instance, they trade with nearby Bantu tribes. Other contacts have not been as beneficial. Government outreach programs to teach farming techniques to the Mbuti have proven largely unsuccessful. Aggressive timbering and other development projects have also casts a shadow on the Mbuti lifestyle.

Command Economy Model

A **command economy** is a type of economic system in which the government dictates the answers to the basic economic questions. That is, economic decision making is highly centralized in the hands of the government. Command economies were the norm in different parts of the world for thousands of years. In northern Africa, the Old Kingdom in Egypt (2660 BCE to 2180 BCE) had a command economy headed by a pharaoh. The pharaoh owned all land, collected taxes from peasant farmers, and required peasants to work on public projects such as temples, canals, and pyramids. In Asia, the Chou Dynasty in China (1122 BCE to 256 BCE) established a complex feudal economy. Under Chinese feudalism, the emperor owned the land but allowed trusted nobles to govern large portions of the empire in exchange for their allegiance and tribute payments. A similar feudal system was established in Europe as early at the eighth century CE.

During the twentieth century the communist countries of eastern and central Europe and East Asia created command economies. In these countries the Communist Party and an elite corps of central planners devised and implemented five-year plans to dictate the use of society's resources. Central planning dominated economic activity in the Soviet Union by the late 1920s, in the Eastern bloc countries (Bulgaria, Czechoslovakia, East Germany, Hungary, Poland, and Romania) by the mid-1940s, and in the People's Republic of China by the 1950s. By owning and controlling all of the factors of production, the cumbersome communist planning bureaucracies discouraged entrepreneurship, individual initiative, and product innovation. The collapse of communism in most of the world during the late 1980s and early 1990s dismantled much of the state planning apparatus in these economies.

While there are no pure command economies in the world today, the basic features of a command economy can still be found in some countries. In the Republic of Cuba, for example, communist dictator Fidel Castro introduced Soviet-style central planning to control Cuba's economy after the existing government was toppled in the late 1950s. The Castro regime expropriated many businesses and reorganized agriculture into large state-owned farms. Business activity, including the wages of labor and the prices of products, was directed by Cuba's Central Panning Board. It was not until the collapse of its most important benefactor, the Soviet Union, in the early 1990s that Cuba began to institute limited market-oriented economic reforms. While these reforms recognized the value of private incentives, the vast majority of Cuba's human, capital, and natural resources remained firmly under the government's thumb during the early 2000s. Even after the reins of power were transferred from Fidel Castro to his brother Raul in 2006, the

Labor-intensive agricultural production in Cuba, processing tobacco. (Peter Manzelli/U.S. Department of Agriculture)

communists retained a monopoly on political power and exerted considerable control over economic activity.

Market Economy Model

A **market economy** is a type of economy that relies on the private sector—individuals and business firms—to answer the basic economic questions, and to own and control the factors of production. In a market economy decentralized decision making by individuals and firms determines what, how, and for whom to produce. At the heart of a market economy are private property and the economic freedoms of the marketplace. An invisible price system, rather than the government or customs, allocates resources in market economies.

The most basic freedoms in a market economy are the freedom of choice and the freedom of enterprise. Consumers enjoy the freedom of choice, which allows people to spend their money as they wish. By casting their "dollar votes" either for or against certain products, consumers answer the basic question of what to produce. Producers, in turn, have the freedom of enterprise, which encourages firms to use scarce resources in the most profitable ways. The market mechanism, which Adam Smith called the invisible hand, permits the forces of supply and demand to determine prices and allocate resources in free and competitive markets. The prices of goods, coupled with people's incomes, answer the third basic economic question of for whom to produce. Stated simply, a person's share of what is produced is determined by that person's ability to pay.

There are no pure market economies in the world. Yet in recent years a number of market-oriented economies around the world have been viewed as "free" based on criteria such as the amount of government regulation in the economy, the rule of law and private property rights, the size of government and tax burden, the ability to freely trade with other countries, and other conditions that generally support the basic freedoms of the marketplace. One widely recognized measure of economic freedom is found in *Economic Freedom of the World* (*EFW*), an annual report published by a consortium of economic think tanks such as the Fraser Institute in Canada and the Cato Institute in the United States. In the 2011 edition of *EFW*, the Hong Kong Special Administrative Region (SAR) topped the ranking as the most-free economy in the world, followed by Singapore, New Zealand, Switzerland, and Australia.[5] A second recognized measure of economic freedom is the *Index of Economic Freedom*, which is published annually by the Heritage Foundation and the *Wall Street Journal*. The *2012 Index of Economic Freedom* also ranked the Hong Kong SAR as the world's freest economy, followed by Singapore, Australia, New Zealand, and Switzerland.[6]

Mixed Economy

A **mixed economy** combines features from both the market model and the command model. In common usage, the term "mixed economy" refers to economies that are primarily market oriented, or capitalist, but that accept certain government interventions in the economy. Mixed economies stress decentralized private sector economic decision making, where individuals and firms own and control most of the factors of production and are responsible for answering the basic economic questions of what, how, and for whom to produce. Mixed economies borrow features from the command model, especially in the realms of business regulation, the provision of social programs, and stabilization policy. Technically, all economies are mixed economies, most leaning toward the market model and a few leaning toward the command model.

CAPITALISM

Capitalism is a type of economic system based on the private ownership and control of the factors of production—natural resources, human resources, capital goods, and entrepreneurship. In a capitalist economy the private sector, individuals and firms, are mainly responsible for answering the basic economic questions of what, how, and for whom to produce. Over the past several centuries the institutions and practices of capitalism have evolved. Capitalism is often referred to as the free enterprise system to emphasize the importance of marketplace freedoms.

Origins of Capitalism

The roots of capitalism date back to the twelfth and thirteenth centuries when European trading cities such as Florence and Ghent spearheaded lively trade in the Mediterranean region—the first serious challenge to Europe's parochial feudal system, a type of command economy. Over the next few centuries capitalism gradually expanded to regions in western and northern Europe, fed by the growth of international trade, industrialization, and changes in people's views.

The dramatic increase in international trade began with the rise of a merchant class in trading cities such as Venice and Florence in Italy, Bruges and Antwerp in Flanders, and London in England during the twelfth and thirteenth centuries. From the sixteenth century to the eighteenth century, the mercantilists gained a foothold in some powerful European countries, and had forged alliances with monarchs. These alliances resulted in an aggressive competition among the great powers to exploit profitable overseas markets and expand colonial empires. The economic goal was to achieve a favorable balance of trade and treasuries full of specie—gold and silver. At the same time these actions strengthened certain pillars of capitalism such as private property rights, profit incentives, and competitive markets.

A second factor that supported a rise in capitalism was the Industrial Revolution. The Industrial Revolution favored mechanized production over hand labor in the eighteenth and nineteenth centuries. The Industrial Revolution was born in England during the 1700s and soon spread to Germany, the United States, and other countries. The Industrial Revolution encouraged the rise of large corporations in the industrialized countries. These corporations, which were owned by stockholders, developed new technologies and created business opportunities for aspiring entrepreneurs. The industrialists also forged alliances with monarchs and received guarantees that basic capitalist principles would be protected—especially legal protections for private property and profits.

A third support for capitalism was a change in some people's worldview. One important change was rooted in the Protestant Reformation, which swept across large segments of northern and western Europe during the sixteenth and seventeen centuries. Embedded in this change were the economic virtues of hard work, individual initiative, thrift, productive enterprise, and economic rewards. Another shift in worldview occurred with the publication of Adam Smith's landmark book, *An Inquiry into the Nature and Causes of the Wealth of Nations* (1776). In *The Wealth of Nations* Smith extolled the benefits of a free market economy based on private sector decision making and the pursuit of one's own "self-interest." These views popularized the concept of laissez-faire capitalism, which rejected most types of government intervention in the economy.

Modern Capitalism

Laissez-faire capitalism, which seemed so secure during the 1800s and early 1900s, came to an abrupt end during the global depression of the 1930s. During this global depression, called the Great Depression in the United States, the weaknesses inherent in laissez-faire capitalism were exposed when businesses failed, unemployment rose, national output plummeted, and despair reigned. The prolonged global depression of the 1930s intensified the call for a more activist role for government in the economy. In the United States, Democrat Franklin D. Roosevelt (FDR) unseated the incumbent Republican president Herbert Hoover in the presidential election of 1932. FDR promised a "new deal" for the American people. Immediately after FDR's election to the presidency, an avalanche of New Deal programs were created to stem the tide of bank failures, home foreclosures, business bankruptcies, and lost jobs. During the 1930s the government became a prominent player in the national economy.

Despite these changes, capitalism proved to be a resilient economic system. While the concept of limited government in the U.S. economy has expanded, it has done so without abandoning the essential features of American capitalism. These features included the sanctity of private property, freedom of contract, profit incentives, freedom

ECONOMICS IN HISTORY: Partitioning the Planet: Capitalism and Imperialism

By the early 1900s the triumph of laissez-faire capitalism had created domestic markets largely unfettered by government regulations. It had also resulted in international markets where free trade, exuberant foreign direct investment, and investment in capital markets had stitched together a highly interdependent global economy. Capitalism's ascendancy was hastened by the imperialist policies of the world's major powers.

Imperialism is a process by which one country wrestles political power away from the existing leadership in another country, kingdom, tribe, or other political entity. It brought many of the poorer regions of the world under the control of the industrialized nations, mainly the major European powers. The scramble to expand colonial empires, and thereby control key resources and markets, intensified during the late 1800s and early 1900s. By the turn of the century, about 30 percent of the world's population lived under colonial rule, and an additional 37 percent lived under the thumb of absolute monarchs—some within the sprawling European empires.[7]

By the outbreak of World War I in 1914, much of Africa and Asia had been absorbed into colonial empires. Leading the charge to partition the planet were Great Britain, which controlled significant territories in the Middle East, southern and eastern Africa, western Asia (including India) and eastern Asia; the Netherlands in the Dutch East Indies (Indonesia); Japan in Korea and some Pacific islands such as Formosa (Taiwan); and France in northern and western Africa, and Indochina. On the eve of World War I, much of the world was marching to the beat of a capitalist drum, a circumstance that was viewed by the advanced countries as both desirable and irreversible.

---

of choice, freedom of enterprise, and competitive markets. The United States emerged from World War II in 1945 as the world's dominant capitalist nation, a position it still holds today.

American capitalism in the twenty-first century is embedded with different types of government interventions. These interventions are felt most keenly when the government provides public goods, offers social programs, regulates businesses, or influences macroeconomic conditions. The government provides public goods to support people's general well-being. Public goods include features of the nation's infrastructure (roads, bridges, seaports, airports), a criminal justice system (police, courts, prisons), educational system (public schools, universities), and national defense. Social programs, a type of safety net for the needy, redistribute some of society's wealth through a system of transfer payments. In 2013 the federal government spent $1.6 trillion on its three largest transfer programs—Social Security, Medicare, and Medicaid.[8] Business regulations protect competitive markets in the U.S. economy. They also protect people from market failures such as pollution, inadequate or misleading information, or other violations of the public trust. The Environmental Protection Agency (EPA), Occupational Safety and Health Administration (OSHA), and Securities and Exchange Commission (SEC) are examples of regulatory agencies. Macroeconomic stabilization occurs when the government uses fiscal policy, monetary policy, or other actions to promote full employment, economic growth, and price stability.

Global Capitalism

Global economic conditions present additional opportunities and significant challenges to capitalism, the world's dominant economic system. The direction of global capitalism during the twenty-first century will likely be influenced by many factors, especially the pace of technological advance, the degree of globalization, and the functioning of multilateral organizations.

Technological advance tends to support global capitalism. For example, new technologies introduced during the Industrial Revolution encouraged global economic connections between European manufacturers and resource producers around the world. More recently, information and communications technologies (ICTs) have transformed economies at an even quicker pace. ICTs offer almost limitless business opportunities for existing firms and aspiring entrepreneurs. ICTs, along with advances in transportation, have freed businesses from traditional geographic constraints by enabling ideas and information, goods and services, money, and people to effortlessly traverse the globe in search of profits. The main challenge is to determine how economic opportunities generated by ICTs and other technologies can be made available to all countries in the global economy.

Globalization provides additional support for global capitalism. Globalization occurs when individuals, businesses, multilateral organizations, and governments encourage cross-border flows of goods and services, people, real capital, and money. Globalization creates a more integrated and interdependent world economy based on free markets. It expands economic opportunities in three main areas: international trade, foreign direct investment (FDI), and cross-border financial investments. Yet the potential pitfalls of economic globalization cannot be ignored, especially with regard to how to create equitable trade and investment environments for all stakeholders.

Multilateral organizations offer a third support system for global capitalism. A **multilateral organization** is a formal group or institution designed to address global issues through collective action. Some multilateral organizations establish and enforce the rules for businesses to follow in the global economy. Examples include the United Nations, which supports economic well-being and sustainable economic development; the World Bank Group, which finances development projects; the International Monetary Fund, which promotes financial stability; the World Trade Organization, which promotes freer trade; and regional development banks, which finance sustainable development projects in Africa, Asia, eastern Europe, and Latin America. On a more grassroots level the conduct of business in the global arena is also influenced by **nongovernmental organizations** (NGOs), which gather and share information and instigate reforms. NGOs, and other broad-based civil society organizations (CSOs), are society's gadflies. They magnify the voices of ordinary citizens and pressure governments, transnational corporations, and multilateral organizations to re-examine economic and social policies that affect the quality of people's lives.

OTHER ECONOMIC SYSTEMS

Like capitalism, two other "isms" offer ways to organize economic activity: socialism and communism. The older of the two, socialism, dates back to the early nineteenth century. Different socialist groups often disagreed about specific policies to address the excesses of capitalism and the new industrial age but were linked by their support for a more equitable distribution of society's income and wealth. The second, communism, was born with the publication of *The Communist Manifesto* in 1848. During the twentieth century, communist revolutionaries sought to hasten capitalism's collapse through violent revolutions and the creation of communist states.

Socialism

Socialism is a type of economic system based on public ownership and control of key factors of production, mainly natural and capital resources. Under socialism the government owns key natural resources such as coal and oil, and capital resources such as large factories and mines. Socialism, in its many forms, also stresses the rights of labor, which include fair compensation and favorable working conditions for workers and a safety net of social programs for the needy.

Modern socialism first appeared in western Europe in the early 1800s, with many of the most influential socialist thinkers hailing from France and Britain. The French philosopher Comte Henri de Saint-Simon (1760–1825), the founder of French socialism, believed that capitalism's reliance on individual self-interest encouraged social disorganization, injustice, and exploitation. As an alternative to capitalism, Saint-Simon favored the creation of a society administered by experts such as scientists, engineers, artists, and industrialists. In Great Britain, Robert Owen (1771–1858) pioneered production methods at his New Lanark Mills that humanized people's workplace and community. Shortly thereafter other British socialists formed the Fabian Society to oppose gross disparities in income and wealth and to challenge other forms of capitalist oppression. In *The Decay of Capitalist Civilization* (1923), two leading Fabians, Beatrice and Sidney Webb, decried "[t]he outrageous disparity in capitalist countries between one man and another, and between one class and another."[9]

Socialism in the economically advanced countries adopted a distinctively non-Marxist and gradualist tenor during the post–World War II era. Its stronghold was in Scandinavia, western Europe, and several regions of the British Commonwealth such as Australia, Canada, and New Zealand. Since the late 1940s European socialism has often been referred to as **democratic socialism**—a type of socialism that embraces limited government ownership and control of the means of production, indicative planning, comprehensive social welfare programs, and democratic political institutions.

Democratic socialists favor limited government ownership and control of productive enterprises through nationalization. **Nationalization** occurs when the government assumes ownership or control over of an important firm or an entire industry but compensates the previous owners. Most nationalized businesses were structured as public corporations run by a government-appointed board of directors. During the 1950s and 1960s European governments nationalized key industries such as coal, steel, banking, railways, docks and harbors, some public utilities, and health care. By the late 1970s and 1980s, however, many governments moved toward privatization—the sale of state-owned enterprises (SOEs) to private individuals or firms. Since the 1970s privatization has generally helped to restore competitive markets, reduce burdensome government subsidies to SOEs, and put about $2 trillion in new revenues into governments' pockets.[10]

Indicative planning, a second feature of democratic socialism, is an inclusive economic planning process that sets national performance targets for economic growth, investment, inflation and unemployment, government spending, and international trade. This planning involves representatives from the public and private sectors, mainly government officials, business leaders, academicians, and workers. The overriding goal is to improve the standard of living for the people rather than meddle in the business operations of private firms. Most European countries had adopted some form of economic planning by the 1960s. Economic planning diminished in importance during the 1990s and 2000s as countries generally moved away from socialist ideas and toward free market principles.

The third and most visible feature of democratic socialism was the creation of the welfare state. In a **welfare state** the government plays a major role in ensuring at least a minimal standard of living for the people. To achieve this goal, the state invests heavily in public education, guarantees equal opportunities for success, and provides "cradle to grave" security for its people through a vast array of social programs. Soon after World War II ended, many western European countries embraced the welfare state, with Sweden leading the pack. By the 1990s and early 2000s, however, the pendulum in most European countries had swung decisively against the welfare state and toward the free market.

A second main strand of socialism, **third world socialism**, also developed after World War II. The road to socialism in the developing world was pitted with a variety of economic and political potholes, however, not least of which were dire poverty, inadequate financial and technical resources, and underdeveloped economic and political institutions. Internal conflicts based on ethnic, racial, or religious differences, and a profound distrust of foreigners who had only recently been their colonial overlords, layered additional burdens on early socialist regimes.

Third world socialism typically involved land reform, the nationalization or expropriation of private businesses, and central economic planning. Land reform involved a change in ownership and control of farmland from a landed aristocracy to village groups. In the 1960s, for example, Tanzanian president Julius Nyerere initiated *ujamaa*, a bold but largely unsuccessful program to create community-based farming collectives. Third world socialists also seized key industries, sometimes through nationalization and at other times through expropriation. **Expropriation** occurs when the government seizes property without compensating the previous owners. India's aggressive nationalization policies during the late 1940s and 1950s brought mining, heavy industries, transportation, communications, and financial services under the government's control. Finally, third world socialists relied on central economic planning to speed economic development and equity. The scope and rigidity of economic plans varied, sometimes resembling the indicative planning of the western European democracies and sometimes resembling the more authoritarian planning of the communists.

Socialist economies in the developing world struggled from the 1940s to the 1980s with predictable problems, including poor work incentives, distorted price signals, and a myriad of social, economic, and political ills that plague poorer countries. In short, socialist regimes could not meet the rising expectations of their people. By the 1980s most experiments in third world socialism had petered out in favor of market-driven approaches to economic development.

Communism

Communism is a type of command economy in which the government owns and controls the great majority of factories, farms, and other businesses. Public ownership and control over the means of production permits the government to dictate society's answers to the basic economic questions of what, how, and for whom to produce. Theoretical communism is grounded in the writings of Karl Marx and Friedrich Engels, who co-authored *The Communist Manifesto* in 1848.[11] In 1867 Marx published *Capital*, the first of a three-volume set of books. This trilogy more fully described his economic interpretation of history, which is often referred to as scientific socialism. Scientific socialism took different forms in different countries during the twentieth century.

The Union of Soviet Socialist Republics (USSR), or Soviet Union, was the world's first communist country. Its brand of communism was shaped by early leaders such as Vladimir I. Lenin and Joseph Stalin. During Stalin's tyrannical reign over the Soviet Union, which stretched from 1927 to 1953, the Soviets built a command economy. The Marxist foundations of this command economy were public ownership of the means of production, and

PRIMARY DOCUMENT: Karl Marx and Friedrich Engels Argue against Private Property

The immediate aim of the Communists is the same as that of all other proletarian parties: formation of the proletariat into a class, overthrow of the bourgeois supremacy, conquest of political power by the proletariat. . . .

The distinguishing feature of communism is not the abolition of property generally, but the abolition of bourgeois property. But modern bourgeois private property is the final and most complete expression of the system of producing and appropriating products that is based on class antagonisms, on the exploitation of the many by the few.

In this sense, the theory of the Communists may be summed up in a single phrase: Abolition of private property.

The Communist Manifesto, Karl Marx and Friedrich Engels

centralized decision making by Gosplan—the powerful state planning agency. Stalin stamped out the remnants of private incentives and private enterprise in the countryside by collectivizing agriculture. Entire villages were absorbed into massive state-owned farms. In the cities businesses were expropriated and converted into state-owned enterprises (SOEs). Under Gosplan, rigid five-year plans emphasized the production of military and capital goods at the expense of consumer goods.

In the mid-1980s Soviet premier Mikhail Gorbachev attempted to rescue the faltering Soviet economy with a series of economic and political reforms. Economic reforms, called *perestroika,* restructured the Soviet economy to include market-oriented incentives to promote economic growth and modernization. Perestroika encouraged some private enterprise, lifted many wage and price controls, reduced subsidies to SOEs, expanded global commercial contacts, and empowered plant managers to make their own production decisions. Gorbachev also introduced national campaigns to reduce corruption, alcoholism, and other drags on the fragile economy. Despite these economic reforms and a series of political reforms called *glasnost,* the Soviet economy continued its economic tailspin. In 1991 the Soviet Union dissolved, and the 15 republics that had comprised the USSR soon became independent countries.

China became a communist country in 1949 after a prolonged civil war. Under the leadership of Mao Zedong, Chinese communism, often referred to as Maoism, wavered between the pragmatic and the dogmatic. Under Maoism, the Chinese Communist Party (CCP) had a monopoly on political and economic power. Agriculture was collectivized into "people's communes." Most aspects of village life were scrutinized by the CCP to weed out counterrevolutionary activity, particularly activity that supported private incentives or profit. China's industrial sector endured a similar conversion with a systematic dismantling of private enterprises and the creation of state-owned enterprises (SOEs). By the mid-1970s China's economy was reeling from political turmoil and inefficient central planning. Shortly after Mao's death in 1976, however, a more reform-minded CCP leadership embraced certain market solutions to the nation's economic woes.

Economies in Transition: Shock Therapy in the Russian Federation

The inherent weaknesses of communism in the Soviet Union, China, and elsewhere were evident by the final quarter of the twentieth century. These economies quaked under the pressure of sluggish economic growth, stifling bureaucracies, low productivity, and a host of other economic problems. In addition, the people's standard of living in the communist nations continued to lag further behind that of the Western capitalist countries. In response, most communist countries sought a new path to economic prosperity, one that emphasized certain free market principles rather than Marxist doctrine. National strategies to achieve a transition toward free market economies differed, however. The Russian Federation adopted shock therapy in the early 1990s to jump-start its transition to capitalism.

The dissolution of the Soviet Union in December 1991 signaled the collapse of communism in central and eastern Europe and central Asia. It also signaled the beginning of an epic transition in the region as 28 countries sought to institute market reforms into their economic systems, and democratic principles into their political systems. Collectively, these 28 countries were called the transition economies, or transition countries. Twelve of the 15 former Soviet republics, now independent countries, also joined together into a loose confederation called the Commonwealth of Independent States (CIS) to ease the transition.

Since the early 1990s Russia's shock therapy approach to economic transition has generated mixed results. In the realm of economic reform, shock therapy relied on the implementation of aggressive government policies to rid the country of communist-era baggage and to institute new practices based on market principles. These reforms began under the leadership of Boris Yeltsin, who served as president from 1992 to 1999. Later reforms were instituted by Vladimir Putin, who served as Russia's president from 2000 to 2008, prime minister from to 2008 to 2012, and president again from 2012 to the present. The four cornerstones of Russia's shock therapy were mass privatization, limited government, competitive markets, and global connections.

Mass privatization transferred many state-owned properties such as farms, factories, mines, and retail stores to the private sector. Privatization occurred through the distribution of ownership vouchers, the sale of stocks, public auctions, and other means. Privatization was most successful in small and medium-sized enterprises (SMEs), mainly in light industries, services, construction, and retail trade. More problematic was privatization of large state-owned enterprises (SOEs) and the collective farms, each stuck in the mire of outdated capital, mismanagement, and endless subsidies that rewarded inefficiency. During the early 2000s reversals occurred as some privatized industries, such as the airlines and arms industries, came under the government's control. Unresolved was what to do with thousands of large, inefficient SOEs that dotted the Russian landscape.

Limited government removed many government restrictions on private sector business activity. Gosplan, the state planning agency, was disbanded. Reforms targeted the building of a legal framework to guide and protect private property rights, profits, and business activity—including policies to ensure compliance with contracts, clarify bankruptcy codes, adopt standardized accounting procedures, deregulate industries, reduce licensing restrictions on businesses, and reduce business subsidies. In the early 2000s a new land code permitted private ownership of land in the cities, while a new labor code expanded firms' freedom to hire and fire workers.

Competitive markets required individuals and firms to recognize and respond to the invisible signals of the price system. To reduce distorted prices in the economy, reforms eliminated most government controls on prices in the early 1990s. The predictable short-term result was hyperinflation, as the inflation rate soared to nearly 2000 percent in 1992 and 900 percent in 1993.[12] As the economy adjusted to market-determined prices, inflationary pressures eased, and in 2012 consumer prices rose by just 6.5 percent.[13] Russia also deregulated and liberalized business activity, and privatized thousands of small and medium-sized firms to promote competition.

Efforts to rejoin the global economy, the final cornerstone in Russia's transition, have progressed since the early 1990s. During the late 1990s and 2000s, government stabilization policies and market-oriented reforms made Russia's business climate more hospitable for international trade and long-term foreign direct investment (FDI). As a result, Russia recorded consistent trade surpluses during the 2000s. In 2011 its trade surplus in goods and services hit $163 billion, a surplus that was built largely on oil exports.[14] In addition, Russia attracted an average of $53 billion per year in FDI from 2007 to 2011, more than 10 times the FDI it attracted during the unsteady early years of its transition.[15] Another achievement was Russia's admission into the World Trade Organization (WTO) in 2012. Membership in the WTO required Russia to significantly reduce import quotas and tariffs and liberalize foreign investment regulations in key areas such as banking, insurance, telecommunications, transportation, and retail and wholesale trade.[16]

Economies in Transition: Gradualism in the People's Republic of China

In the late 1970s the Chinese Communist Party (CCP) came to view market reforms as essential to China's modernization. Under the leadership of Deng Xiaoping, a policy of gradualism was adopted to methodically explore market-oriented alternatives to central planning and government control over the economy. Deng referred to this gradualist approach as "crossing the river by feeling for the stones."[17] Gradualism produced a dual-track economic system. One track, considered the economic mainstream during the late 1970s and 1980s, consisted of China's existing planned economy, also called the state sector. The second track consisted of a series of market-oriented experiments.

The household responsibility system was the most significant of these early market-based reforms. This system encouraged peasants to lease agricultural land from the government, work the land, and sell some of their output to the state at a fixed price. Peasants were free to sell the remainder of their crops on the open market for a profit. These market incentives increased the productivity of labor and encouraged the CCP to proceed to the next stone, the expansion of township and village enterprises (TVEs). TVEs are profit-making firms in rural regions that are owned or financed mainly by local governments. After an initial flurry of TVE activity in the late 1970s and early 1980s, interest in TVEs waned during the 1990s and 2000s.[18]

Market reforms also enabled China to become a major player in the global economy. During the 1980s, for example, the Chinese government created free trade zones (FTZs) in a number of China's eastern cities. Goods assembled or otherwise processed within these special zones could be exported duty free to other countries. Other reforms reduced government regulations on private firms, which encouraged the creation of joint ventures (JVs) between Chinese and foreign firms and the founding of wholly owned foreign enterprises (WOFEs). Promarket reforms soon made China the top recipient of FDI in the developing world. In 2011 alone inflows of FDI to China hit $124 billion. In that same year China overtook the United States as the world's top exporter of goods and services. China exported $2.2 trillion in goods and services compared to $2.1 trillion by the United States. In addition, China's gross domestic product (GDP) measured in current U.S. dollars hit $7.3 trillion in 2011, second only to that of the United States ($15 trillion).[19]

Market-oriented reforms in China increased agricultural output and promoted economic growth in recent decades. (Hung Chung Chih/Shutterstock.com)

Significant obstacles to China's economic transition remain as this economic giant guides its dual-track economy into the twenty-first century. One challenge is the country's uneven development, which has traditionally favored eastern China over western China and urban areas over rural interests in the countryside. Second, China's safety net of social programs is inadequate to meet the people's needs, especially in rural areas and among the large "floating population" of migrant workers. Third, inefficient SOEs dominate major industries such as energy, a situation that requires costly government subsidies to these public firms. Fourth, while China can expand the supply of goods it creates, it cannot control the demand for its output in domestic or global markets. Recent economic slowdowns in China and in the global economy have pinched consumer demand for goods in major industries such as real estate and automobiles. Finally, the Chinese Communist Party's monopoly on political power sometimes creates an unfair and inefficient environment for business activity, including risky loans from China's state-controlled banks. The CCP's stranglehold on political power also poses an unsettling question—can an economic system striving to become more open and free co-exist with a one-party political system?

CHAPTER 3 SUMMARY

Stages of Economic History
- The earliest stage of economic history, primitive food gathering and hunting, was characterized by nomadic lifestyles and a rigid division of labor.
- The second stage of economic history, permanent agriculture and animal domestication, was characterized by the rise of settlements, specialization, and trade.

- The third stage of economic history, the industrial age, was characterized by industrialization and the supremacy of the factory system.
- The fourth stage of economic history, the information age, is characterized by the use of information and communications technologies (ICTs) to produce and distribute products.

Economic Systems: The Models

- A traditional economy relies on customs or traditions to answer the basic economic questions of what, how, and for whom to produce.
- A command economy relies on the government to answer the basic economic questions.
- A market economy relies on the private sector to answer the basic economic questions.
- A mixed economy combines features from the command and the market models to answer the basic economic questions. Most mixed economies lean toward the market model.

Capitalism

- The roots of capitalism are grounded in economic events in Europe, including the expansion of international trade and industrialization, and changes in people's worldview.
- Modern capitalism favors an expanded role for government in the national economy.
- Global capitalism is supported by new technologies and multilateral institutions, yet challenges remain for traditionally marginalized peoples.

Other Economic Systems

- Socialism favors some government ownership and control over certain key industries and policies to promote economic equity.
- Communism favors government ownership and control over most business enterprise, including the factors of production used in production.
- Economies transitioning toward capitalism have instituted reforms consistent with market principles.

NOTES

1. Federal Reserve Bank of Minneapolis, "The History of Money," www.minneapolisfed.org/community _education/teacher/history.org; *Moneys of the World* (New York: Chase National Bank Museum of Moneys of the World, 1953), 15-17.

2. International Telecommunications Union, "Key ICT Indicators for Developed and Developing Countries and the World," February 22, 2013, www.itu.int/ITU-D/ict/statistics/at_glance/keytelecom .html;World Bank, "Internet Users per 100 People," *World Development Indicators* (Statistical Annex), http://data.worldbank.org/indicator/IT.NET.USER

3. Ibid.

4. U.S. Bureau of the Census, U.S. Department of Commerce, "U.S. Shipments, Sales, Revenues and E-Commerce: 2010 and 2009," *E-Stats*, May 10, 2012, 2, www.census.gov/estats

5. James Gwartney, Robert A. Lawson, and Joshua C. Hall, "Exhibit 1.2: Summary Economic Freedom Ratings for 2010," *Economic Freedom of the World: 2012 Annual Report* (Vancouver, Canada: Fraser Institute), 2012, 10, www.freetheworld.com/2012/EFW2012-complete.pdf

6. Heritage Foundation and the *Wall Street Journal*, "Country Rankings," *2012 Index of Economic Freedom*, www.heritage.org/Index/about

7. Freedom House, *Democracy's Century: A Survey of Global Political Change in the 20th Century* (New York: Freedom House, 1999), 1-4.

8. Office of Management and Budget (OMB), "Table S-5: Proposed Budget by Category" (Summary Tables), *The Budget of the United States Government, Fiscal Year 2014* (Washington, DC: U.S. Government Printing Office, 2013), 189-190.

9. Sidney Webb and Beatrice Webb, *The Decay of Capitalist Civilization* (New York: Harcourt, Brace and Company, 1923), 17-18.

10. Sunita Kikeri and Matthew Perault, "Privatization Trends," *Viewpoint* 322 (May 2010): 1-2; Organization for Economic Cooperation and Development (OECD), *Privatization in the 21st Century: Recent Experiences of OECD Countries* (Paris: OECD, January 2009), 7; Sergei Guriev and William Megginson, "Privatization: What Have We Learned?" http://sitesources.worldbank.org/DEC/Resources

11. Karl Marx and Friedrich Englels, *The Communist Manifesto* (New York: Pocket Books, 1964), 81-82.

12. International Monetary Fund (IMF), "Table 13: Countries in Transition; Consumer Prices," *World Economic Outlook, May 2000* (Washington, DC: IMF Publications, 2000), 215.

13. IMF, "Table A7: Emerging Market and Developing Countries; Consumer Prices," *World Economic Outlook: April 2013* (Washington, DC: IMF Publication Services, 2013), 158.

14. World Trade Organization (WTO), "Table 1.7: Leading Exporters and Importers of World Merchandise Trade, 2011," and "Table 1.9: Leading Exporters and Importers in World Trade in Commercial Services, 2011," *International Trade Statistics, 2012*, 26, 28, www.wto.org/statistics

15. United Nations Conference on Trade and Development (UNCTAD), "Annex Table 1.1: FDI Flows, by Region and Economy, 2006–2011,"*World Investment Report 2012* (New York: UNCTAD, 2012), 172; World Bank, "What Can Transition Economies Learn from the First Ten Years? A New World Bank Report," *Transition Newsletter* 13, no. 1 (January–February 2002): 14, (www.worldbank.org/ transitionnewsletter).

16. WTO, "Working Party Seals the Deal on Russia's Membership Negotiations," *WTO: 2011 News Items*, November 10, 2011, www.wto.org/english/news_e/news11_e/acc_rus_10nov11_w.htm; WTO, "Ministerial Conference Approves Russia's WTO Membership," *WTO: 2011 News Items*, December 16, 2011, www.www.wto.org/english/news_e/news11_e/acc_rus_16dec11_e.htm

17. H. E. Liu Xiaoming, "Crossing the River by Feeling for the Stones," Ministry of Foreign Affairs of the People's Republic of China (Beijing, China), www.fmprc.en/eng/wjb/zwjg/zwbd/t812426.htm

18. International Labour Organization (ILO), "Development of Township and Village Enterprises," *China: Promoting Safety and Health in Township and Village Enterprises* (Bangkok, Thailand: ILO Regional Office for Asia and the Pacific, 1998), 6-8; Richard Hirschler, "China's Experience with Transition: What Is Behind Its Stunning Success?" *Transition Newsletter* 13, no. 3 (May–June, 2002): 5-7, (www.worldbank.org/transitionnewsletter); Embassy of the People's Republic of China in the United Kingdom, "The Development of China's Agriculture," www.chinese-embassy.org.uk/eng/ 14053.html

19. WTO, "Table 1.7: Leading Exporters and Importers of World Merchandise Trade, 2011," and "Table 1.9: Leading Exporters and Importers in World Trade in Commercial Services, 2011," *International Trade Statistics, 2012*, 26, 28, www.wto.org/statistics; UNCTAD, "Annex Table 1.1: FDI Flows, by Region and Economy, 2006–2011," *World Investment Report 2012* (New York: UNCTAD, 2012), 172; World Bank, "Data: GDP (current US$)," *World Development Indicators, 2012*, http://data .worldbank.org/indicator

Part II

MICROECONOMIC TOPICS

4

Consumer Power and Behavior

Consumers represent the basic consumption unit in the economy. In 2013 there were 316 million consumers in the United States. Over time consumers have struggled for their rights. Consumerists at the local, national, and international levels work to improve the conditions under which consumers make consumption choices. Significant support for consumer rights also comes from the government and international organizations. Consumers' buying decisions are influenced by many factors, including the perceived utility of goods, personal income, the availability of substitutes, and other measures of consumer well-being. Issues related to consumer behavior include the responsible use of credit, participation in consumer cooperatives, and the value of sustainable consumption.

CONSUMER RIGHTS AND PROTECTIONS

Consumers buy goods and services to satisfy personal wants or needs. Consumers are sometimes referred to as households. Consumers represent the demand side of a market. **Producers**, on the other hand, make or sell goods and services to earn profits. Producers are often called businesses or firms. Producers represent the supply side of a market. Combined, consumers and producers comprise the private sector of the economy. Decentralized private sector decision making by consumers and producers is a foundation of the American economy.

Consumers in the U.S. Economy

People's consumption of goods and services is directly related to their household income. In 2012, $13.4 trillion in income poured into American households. This income represents income from all sources, minus the mandatory payroll taxes for various social insurances. Income is divided into two broad categories: earned income and transfer payments. *Earned income* is the money generated by individuals in exchange for their work effort or their investments. Most earned income in the American economy is derived from wages and salaries, interest and dividend payments, and proprietors' profits. *Transfer payments*, on the other hand, are payments of money, goods, or services that are financed with tax dollars and distributed to groups that do not offer productive services in return. The largest government transfer program in the American economy is Social Security, a social

Table 4.1   Sources of Household Income, 2012

Income Sources*	Income ($ billions)	Income (%)
Wages and salaries	8,566	59.7
Proprietors' income	1,202	8.4
Rental income	463	3.2
Interest and dividends	1,750	12.2
Transfer payments	2,375	16.5

Source: U.S. Department of Commerce, Bureau of Economic Analysis, "Table 2: Personal Income and Its Disposition," *News Release*, March 29, 2013.

*Income prior to deductions for social insurances; wages include employer contributions for pensions and social insurances.

insurance program mainly for the nation's elderly. Other transfer payments offer income or other assistance to the poor, the unemployed, and others in need. Table 4.1 shows the sources of income before social insurance payments are deducted.[1]

Households often have multiple sources of income, perhaps a wage or salary collected from a job, interest from a savings account, and dividends from stocks. Even after taxes and social insurance contributions were deducted from household income, Americans' total disposable personal income in 2012 was $11.9 trillion, of which 96.1 percent was spent and 3.9 percent was saved.[2]

Consumer spending drives most economic activity in the American economy. During the 12 month period between July 2011 and June 2012 the average American household spent $50,631 on consumer goods and services. Over the years housing has been the largest category of consumer spending. Housing includes mortgage or rent payments, utilities, furniture and appliances, and other household needs. In 2011–2012 housing accounted for about one-third of consumer spending. Other major categories of consumer spending included transportation, food, and insurances and pensions. Table 4.2 shows the average consumer expenditures for a typical household in 2011–2012.[3]

Consumer spending on final goods and services is the largest component of spending in the U.S. gross domestic product (GDP). The GDP is the nation's most reliable measurement of total output of goods and services in a given year. The GDP is calculated by adding spending on consumer goods, investment goods, and government goods, and then adjusting this total by the value of net exports. In 2012 the U.S. GDP stood at $15.7 trillion after these adjustments were made. In this same year consumers spent more than $11 trillion

Table 4.2   Annual Consumption Expenditures for a Typical Household, 2011–2012

Categories of Spending	Household Spending	
	Dollar Amount	Percentage of Total Spending
Insurance and pensions	5,565	11.0
Food	6,532	12.9
Transportation	8,505	16.8
Housing	16,940	33.5
Other	13,089	25.8

Source: U.S. Department of Labor, Bureau of Labor Statistics, "Table A: Consumer Expenditures Midyear Update, July 2011 through June 2012 Average," *News Release*, March 27, 2013.

on goods and services, which accounted for more than two-thirds of the GDP. Nearly one-third of all U.S. spending was on investment goods and government goods.[4]

Because consumer spending represents more than two-thirds of all expenditures in the American economy, consumers' willingness and ability to purchase products is vital to the nation's economic health. When people's income rises, and people feel more confident about spending money, aggregate demand tends to rise. **Aggregate demand** is the total demand for goods and services in an economy. An increase in aggregate demand stimulates economic activity and thus contributes to prosperity. When people's income and confidence fall, however, aggregate demand likewise falls. Sagging consumer demand discourages production and investment, and contributes to economic downturns.

Consumer behavior in the American economy is influenced by present economic conditions and by expectations of future economic conditions. One of the most recognized gauges of consumer confidence is the Consumer Confidence Index (CCI). The Conference Board, a respected nonprofit economic research organization, publishes the CCI every month. The CCI reports on consumers' attitudes and buying intentions, which, in turn, influences business decisions concerning production, hiring, and so on. A second recognized gauge of consumer confidence, the University of Michigan's Consumer Sentiment Index, also shows the ups and downs of consumer confidence in the U.S. economy.

Consumer confidence can swing rapidly in the American economy in response to national or international events. For instance, in 2007–2009 the U.S. economy dipped into a serious recession. Economic conditions during this recession included a significant number of business failures, a decline in GDP, a rapid increase in the unemployment rate, and the specter of financial collapse. These dismal economic conditions caused a steep

Consumer spending is influenced by positive or negative economic conditions. (Shutterstock.com)

decline in the CCI from 112.6 in July 2007 to just 25.3 in February 2009. Four years later, in March 2013, the CCI had rebounded some to 59.7. This modest rebound was buoyed by improvements in the performance of the U.S. economy, which included positive growth in the GDP and a drop in the unemployment rate. The CCI was still low by historical standards, however, reflecting some consumer apprehension about economic conditions. For instance, the CCI in 2013 was just 59.7 compared to the CCI in the base year (1985), when it was set at 100.[5] The University of Michigan's Consumer Sentiment Index noted similar declines in consumer confidence during 2008 and 2009 and a slow, irregular assent from despair since this time.[6]

Consumer Rights and Responsibilities

Consumerists, at times working alone and at times working within consumer organizations, have sought to define and then protect the rights of consumers in the United States. This consumerist mission progressed in fits and starts throughout the twentieth century. The goal of defining consumer rights gained some traction in 1962, when President John F. Kennedy delivered his Special Message to the Congress on Protecting the Consumer Interest. In this historic message Kennedy identified four basic consumer rights, which soon were being called the Consumer Bill of Rights for Americans. These rights are shown in the following passage.[7]

Since the 1960s the topic of consumerism and consumer rights has spread to the global economy. Forward-looking consumerists, such as Esther Peterson, worked for universal consumer protection guidelines applicable to all peoples in the world. From 1983 to

---

PRIMARY DOCUMENT: President John F. Kennedy Proposes a Consumer Bill of Rights

Consumers, by definition, include us all. They are the largest economic group in the economy, affecting and affected by almost every public and private economic decision. Two-thirds of all spending in the economy is by consumers. But they are the only important group in the economy who are not effectively organized, whose views are often not heard.

Additional legislative and administrative action is required ... if the Federal Government is to meet its responsibility to consumers in the exercise of their rights. These rights include:

(1) The right to safety—to be protected against the marketing of goods which are hazardous to health or life.
(2) The right to be informed—to be protected against fraudulent, deceitful, or grossly misleading information, advertising, labeling, or other practices, and to be given the facts he needs to make an informed choice.
(3) The right to choose—to be assured, wherever possible, access to a variety of products and services at competitive prices; and in those industries in which competition is not workable and Government regulation is substituted, an assurance of satisfactory quality and service at fair prices.
(4) The right to be heard—to be assured that consumer interests will receive full and sympathetic consideration in the formulation of government policy, and fair and expeditious treatment in its administrative tribunals.

Special Message to the Congress on Protecting the Consumer Interest, John F. Kennedy

1993 Peterson represented the International Organization of Consumers Unions, now called Consumers International (CI), at the United Nations (UN). In 1985 the UN General Assembly adopted the *United Nations Guidelines for Consumer Protection*. The United Nations' consumer guidelines supported Kennedy's original statement of consumer rights and added four other rights to support people's basic needs, permit the creation of consumer organizations, eliminate abusive business practices, and expand international cooperation. In 1999 the United Nations added sustainable consumption to the list of consumer rights.[8]

With consumer rights come consumer responsibilities. First, consumers have a responsibility to make informed buying decisions. That is, consumers should comparison shop, distinguish wants from needs, consider personal budget constraints, obtain product information from a variety of sources, resist hard-sell techniques, and read and comprehend instructional manuals and warrantees. Consumers should keep sales receipts, warrantees, and other product information to help resolve disputes. Second, consumers should respectfully challenge business abuses by retailers and manufacturers. Abusive business practices include the use of deceptive advertising, the use of illegal sales techniques such as the bait and switch, the marketing of dangerous or defective products, and the failure to fulfill service contracts. Third, consumers should take steps to protect personal and financial information from identity thieves. Identity theft occurs when a person uses someone else's name, Social Security number, credit card number, or other piece of personal information without permission for fraud or other purposes.[9] Unfortunately, identity theft victimizes millions of people every year. The *2011 Identity Fraud Survey Report* noted that from 2003 to 2010 an average of 9 million people had their identities stolen *each year*, at an average annual cost of about $55 billion.[10]

Consumer Protection

Consumer protection in the United States is viewed as a shared responsibility involving federal agencies, local authorities, consumer organizations, the business community, and consumers themselves. Over the years a substantial body of consumer law has been enacted to support basic consumer rights, especially the rights to safety, to choose, to be informed, to be heard, and to redress grievances.

At the national level the chief consumer watchdog is the Federal Trade Commission (FTC). The FTC, founded in 1914, enforces many of the nation's consumer protection and antitrust laws. The FTC prevents unethical and deceptive business practices, protects competitive markets, and otherwise deters criminal activity. The FTC enforces existing laws and regulations in the realms of advertising, lending practices, credit, domestic and international marketing, and other areas of consumer concern. The FTC, along with the Antitrust Division of the U.S. Department of Justice, enforces antitrust legislation such as the Sherman Act (1890), Clayton Act (1914), and Celler-Kevauver Act (1950). These acts prevent anticompetitive mergers and business practices. In recent years the FTC has also intensified its efforts to "deter, detect, and defend" against identity theft.[11]

Other federal agencies, such as the Consumer Production Safety Commission (CPSC) and the Food and Drug Administration (FDA), provide additional safeguards for consumers. The CPSC, founded in 1972, is a federal regulatory agency that protects consumers "against unreasonable risks of injuries associated with consumer products."[12] The CPSC investigates complaints involving product safety and can order recalls to remove unsafe items from store shelves and showrooms. In 2011 the CPSC recalled 405 different products such as toys, clothing, and household items.[13] The FDA traces is roots to the passage of the Pure Food and Drug Act of 1906, although the agency's current name—Food and Drug Administration—was not formalized until 1930. The FDA is mainly concerned with protecting consumers from unsafe foods, medicines, and medical procedures. In 2012, for example, an FDA mandate required cigarette makers to add to all cigarette packaging significant new warnings about the health hazards of smoking.

Federal consumer law covers a wide variety of protections for U.S. consumers. Some legislation deals with product safety such the Flammable Fabrics Act (1953) and Hazardous Substances Labeling Act (1960). Other legislation protects people from unfair or unethical practices when they buy goods, borrow money, or use credit. For example, the Fair Housing Credit Act (1968) and the Equal Credit Opportunity Act (1974) prohibit discrimination in credit transactions based on race, national origin, gender, age, or marital status. The Truth in Lending Act (1968), the Consumer Leasing Act (1976), the Fair Credit and Charge Card Disclosure Act (1988), and the Truth in Savings Act (1991) ensure that sufficient financial information is made available to savers and borrowers. The more recent Credit Card Accountability, Responsibility, and Disclosure Act (2009) ensures that credit card holders understand the terms and costs of credit, and prevents unfair rate hikes and hidden fees.

In the private sector of the economy, business organizations and professional associations also support consumer interests. Local nonprofit Better Business Bureaus (BBBs) often provide information about area businesses and help reconcile consumer complaints made against local businesses. Similarly, professional associations, which represent people who work in a profession, monitor the quality of goods or services in certain markets. The American Medical Association (AMA) and the American Advertising Federation (AAF) are professional associations.

CONSUMER MOVEMENTS

Consumer power is the ability of people to influence their own economic well-being. At times individuals, working alone, have advanced consumer power by swaying public opinion and instigating consumer legislation. More commonly, consumer power is advanced through the collective actions of consumer groups.

Consumerism

Consumerism refers to the protection of consumer interests. There are many subsets to this definition. For instance, consumerism is directly concerned with protecting consumers' freedom of choice. That is, consumers have the right to buy products that are safe and that meet promised quality standards. Consumerism is also related to limiting firms' freedom of enterprise by regulating or prohibiting certain unethical, deceptive, or otherwise harmful business practices. In its broadest context, consumerism delves into matters of social justice, including issues related to the redistribution of society's wealth, sustainable consumption, environmental protection, and other quality of life concerns.

People who actively support the goals of consumerism are called **consumerists**. Consumerists work on behalf of consumer interests individually and as members of organizations or agencies in the private or public sectors. For more than a century, *private sector* consumerists have formed a loosely coordinated consumer movement in the United States. More recently, consumerism has gained momentum in the global community.

The **consumer movement** is the embodiment of the actions, programs, and other forms of activism by individual consumerists and private consumerist organizations. The movement welcomes the support of public officials, government agencies, and businesses on behalf of consumers but does not recognize the government or businesses as participants in the consumer movement.

State and Local Consumer Movement

The consumer movement at the state and local levels dates back to the late nineteenth century. State "consumer leagues," which were founded as early as the 1890s, advocated for the poor. These leagues targeted employers who subjected workers, including women and children, to sweatshop conditions in factories and mills. Early consumer leagues also strengthened the consumer's voice to ensure product safety, including the safety of the food supply. To expand the scope and the influence of the consumer's voice, state consumer leagues established the nation's first national consumer organization, the National Consumers League (NCL), in 1899.

During the twentieth century state and local consumer groups provided grassroots support for consumer-oriented legislation. In doing so, they complemented the work of national consumer organizations such as Consumers' Research, the Consumers Union, and the Consumer Federation of America. During the 1960s state and local consumer groups blossomed. Since the 1960s many state and local consumer groups have been established to address consumer issues in areas related to public utilities, housing, health care, energy, and personal finance.

Today state and local consumer groups generally share a number of characteristics. First, state and local consumer groups often focus on specific local issues such as inadequate local health care or housing. Larger issues, such as climate change and global poverty, are generally left to national consumer organizations. Second, state and local consumer groups normally conduct their operations independently. They establish their own goals, raise funds, and instigate reforms using local talent—often consisting of volunteers. Third, state and local consumer groups work within existing political institutions. Hence, their voices are heard at town council meetings, state legislatures, and other public forums.

Most consumer complaints at the state level center on everyday consumer problems. In its *2010 Consumer Complaint Survey Report*, the Consumer Federation of America identified the top areas of consumer dissatisfaction. Topping the consumer complaint list in 2010 were disputes related to auto sales and maintenance, credit and lending practices, home improvement and construction, retail sales, and the billing and services of utility companies.[14]

U.S. Consumer Movement

In the early 1900s the American consumer movement addressed two overriding issues: the human misery caused by poverty and the prevailing *caveat emptor* attitude. Consumerists' concerns for the poor focused on substandard living conditions for people in overcrowded cities, a problem that was aggravated by successive waves of immigration and large migrations of people from farms to cities during the period. At the same time caveat emptor, or "let the buyer beware," implied that producers were blameless for products that were unsafe or failed to meet performance standards. Substandard and injurious products such as unsafe food and medicines routinely victimized consumers. These issues caused people to become wary of businesses and prompted consumers to organize.

Early consumerist voices included the muckrakers, aggressive investigative news report-
ers and authors who researched unfair business practices, unsafe products, and other viola-
tions of the public trust. During the early twentieth century the muckrakers often
published their findings in magazines such as *McClure's* and *Puck*. Other muckrakers,
including Upton Sinclair, authored novels such as *The Jungle* (1906). *The Jungle* exposed
the horrific living conditions of immigrants and the nauseating production techniques
employed by Chicago's meat packing industry. *The Jungle* enraged the public—including
President Teddy Roosevelt—and pushed Congress to approve the Pure Food and Drug
Act of 1906, also called the Wiley Act. At about the same time, America's first national
consumer organization, the National Consumers League (1899), was formed. It advocated
for improved working and living conditions for the urban poor. Over time, other national
consumer organizations were formed, including Consumers' Research (1928), Consumers
Union (1936), Consumers International (1960), Consumer Federation of America (1967),
and Public Citizen (1971).

As the consumer movement matured, it became a recognized force for change in the
U.S. economy. During the 1950s and 1960s major national organizations such as the
Consumers Union and Consumers' Research expanded their product research capabilities
and became influential voices in shaping public opinion and public policy. Consumer

Children stuff sausages in a Chicago meatpacking house, 1893. (Library of Congress)

organizations pressured the government to enact consumer laws and regulations. They also nurtured the rise of a consumer consciousness, an attitude in which people rejected caveat emptor and insisted on honesty and fairness in marketplace transactions.

The consumer movement also gained momentum during the 1960s and 1970s through the efforts of individuals. In 1962 President John F. Kennedy's Consumer Bill of Rights for Americans defined consumer rights as the right to product safety, to be informed, to choose, and to be heard. Shortly thereafter consumerist Ralph Nader burst into the national limelight with his book *Unsafe at Any Speed* (1965). This hard-hitting book prompted reform legislation in the area of auto safety.

Since the 1960s the U.S. consumer movement has woven the concept of consumer rights into the economic mainstream. It has also broadened its mission. Today many specialized consumer groups advocate for improvements in health care, product and food safety, nutrition and nutrition labeling, truth in advertising, financial services, telemarketing, and environmental protection. The consumer movement has gained considerable clout. The movement's influence increased as it became more professional, better funded, and supported by both public opinion and by law. Today some consumer groups employ researchers, scientists, engineers, and other experts, which adds to their legitimacy. Professional lobbyists and lawyers are also employed by consumer groups to support consumers' interests through legislation and litigation.

International Consumer Movement

Consumers International (CI) coordinates the global consumer movement. CI is an independent, nonprofit organization of consumer groups and nongovernmental organizations (NGOs). CI, originally called the International Organization of Consumers Unions, was founded in 1960 to unify the voices of consumers worldwide. CI helped devise, and currently supports, the implementation of the *United Nations Guidelines for Consumer Protection*, which was adopted by the United Nations in 1985. These UN

ECONOMICS IN HISTORY: Ralph Nader and the American Consumer Movement

Ralph Nader is an American lawyer, social critic, and consumer advocate. Nader earned his bachelor's degree from Princeton in 1955 and three years later earned his law degree from Harvard Law School. In 1965 Nader published *Unsafe at Any Speed*, a book that attacked the U.S. auto industry for its emphasis on stylish design rather than safety. Largely in response to Nader's book, Congress passed the National Traffic and Motor Vehicle Safety Act (1966) to strengthen auto safety standards.

Nader soon became the most recognized voice in the U.S. consumer movement. As a consumer activist, Nader advocated for consumers' basic rights to safety, to choose, to be informed, and to be heard. In 1969 he established his first research organization, the Center for Study of Responsive Law. This center was the focal point for Nader's early consumer crusades and the work of a large cadre of supportive college students, who were soon dubbed Nader's Raiders. Under Nader's guidance, student-led Public Interest Research Groups (PIRGs) sprung up on college campuses across the nation to press for consumer rights. In 1971 Nader founded Public Citizen, an organization that would eventually spawn Congress Watch, Health Research Group, Critical Mass Energy Project, Global Trade Watch, and the Litigation Group.

Nader ran for president five times from 1992 to 2008. While none of these bids for the presidency earned him a permanent residence at the White House, his campaigns put a spotlight on topics such as consumer rights, environmental protection, and social and economic justice.

guidelines expanded on the four consumer rights named by President John F. Kennedy in his 1962 Consumer Bill of Rights for Americans. By the early 2010s CI membership included over 240 organizations spread across 120 countries. In its 2010 annual report CI reaffirmed its mission "to build a powerful international consumer movement to help protect and empower consumers everywhere."[15]

CI champions a variety of consumer concerns, many of which are connected with economic changes occurring in the global economy. Recent CI initiatives include food safety, availability of basic services, health care, environmental protection, consumer education, sustainable consumption, and corporate social responsibility. To these ends CI assisted member organizations reform national consumer policies. CI sponsors high-profile annual events such as World Consumer Rights Day, which in 2013 focused on consumer justice.[16] CI also participates in the decision making of global institutions such as the United Nations and in regional organizations such as the Economic Community for West African States (ECOWAS) and the Association of Southeast Asian Nations (ASEAN).

CONSUMER BEHAVIOR

The topic of consumer behavior is most concerned with how people make their buying decisions in an economy. In the American mixed economy consumers are free to choose which goods and services to purchase. This freedom of choice is best demonstrated when consumers cast their dollar votes for or against products. Naturally, consumers are not financially able to buy unlimited quantities of products. Instead, consumers must make choices, and these choices are influenced by many factors.

One important factor that influences consumer choice is the budget constraint that confronts every household. Recall from Chapter 2 that a household's **budget constraint** is determined by two factors: household income and the price of products. That is, people are able to buy more goods and services if their income increases or the price of goods decreases. Conversely, people are able to buy fewer products if their income decreases or the price of goods increases. In addition to budget constraint, four other factors affect consumer behavior: the perceived utility of a good, the income effect of a price change, the substitution effect of a price change, and consumer surplus. An understanding of these factors enables businesses, among others, to predict certain consumer behaviors.

Utility Theory

Utility reflects the amount of satisfaction a person receives from the consumption of a good or service. Economists measure the utility of a purchase in "utils," or units of satisfaction. In reality, people's tastes and preferences for products vary and therefore, a precise comparison of the utility of one product against a second product is impossible. Yet as a general principle, people tend to buy goods and services that offer them the highest utility, or satisfaction, per dollar spent. Pivotal to consumers' buying decisions is the **law of diminishing marginal utility**, which states that as additional units of the same product are consumed in a given period of time, the amount of additional satisfaction, the *marginal* utility, will decline.

Consider the utility for slices of pizza shown in Figure 4.1. In this hypothetical situation, Liam derives the greatest utility, 15 utils, from the first piece of pizza. *Total* utility rises when the second and third pieces of pizza are consumed because each slice results in some additional satisfaction. Note, however, that the *marginal* utility falls as additional slices are consumed, from 15 utils for the first slice, to 10 utils for the second slice, to 5 utils for the third slice. This diminishing marginal utility reflects the incremental reduction in satisfaction for slices of pizza consumed in a certain time period. In fact, by stuffing himself with the fourth and fifth slices of pizza, Liam encounters zero and then negative marginal utility. A graphic depiction of the downward sloping marginal utility curve is also shown in Figure 4.1.

An understanding of diminishing marginal utility offers important insights into consumer behavior. Foremost, it helps explain why a consumer might be willing to pay a high price for the first unit of a product that is consumed but a lower price for additional units. Liam may be willing to pay a high price, say $3, for the first pizza slice because it offers him such a high degree of satisfaction (15 utils). But he may not be willing to pay the same $3 per slice for the second (10 utils), third (5 utils), or fourth (0 utils) pizza slices because these

Number of Slices of Pizza	Total Utility (In Utils)	Marginal Utility (In Utils)
0	0	0
1	15	+15
2	25	+10
3	30	+5
4	30	0
5	25	-5

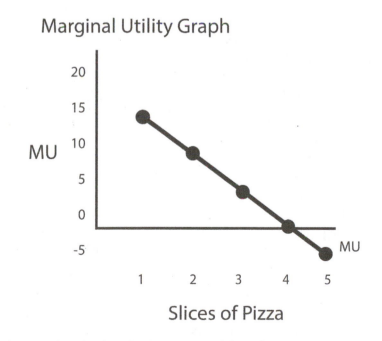

Figure 4.1   Liam's Utility from the Consumption of Slices of Pizza

later slices offer less and less satisfaction. Businesses also understand the law of diminishing marginal utility. For example, businesses often advertise the first item at the regular price and the second identical item at a reduced price. This sales technique helps increase the quantity demanded of many consumer goods ranging from toothpaste and deodorant to sweatshirts and shoes—and pizza slices.

Income Effect of a Price Change

The **income effect of a price change** states that as the price of a product falls, consumers are financially better off, and when the price of a product rises, consumers are financially worse off. Note that the income effect does not deal with a change in a household's *income*. Instead, the income effect deals with how a change in a product's *price* affects the amount of a good or service people are able to purchase.

To illustrate the income effect of a price change, suppose the Jones household typically buys 10 gallons of milk each month at a price of $4 per gallon. Thus, the Jones household's monthly expenditure for milk is $40. If the price of milk fell to $3 per gallon, the household's monthly expenditure for 10 gallons of milk would fall to $30. The Jones household is financially better off due to the drop in the price of milk because the extra $10 can be spent on additional gallons of milk or on other products. If, on the other hand, the price of milk increased from $4 per gallon to $5 per gallon, the Jones household would be financially worse off because it would have to reduce its consumption of milk or some other good or service.

Substitution Effect of a Price Change

The **substitution effect of a price change** states that if the price of a product falls, consumers will buy more of that product and buy less of a higher-priced substitute good. Conversely, if the price of a product rises, consumers will buy less of it and buy more of a lower-priced substitute.

Consider the Jones household's monthly milk expenditures once again. According to the substitution effect of a price change, a decrease in the price of milk from $4 per gallon to $3 per gallon would likely result in the purchase of additional gallons of milk and the purchase of fewer units of substitute goods such as soft drinks or bottled water. If, on the other hand, the price of milk jumped from $4 per gallon to $5 per gallon, the Jones household would likely respond by purchasing fewer gallons of milk and more units of substitutes such as soft drinks or bottled water.

Consumer Surplus

Consumer surplus is the difference between the price a consumer is willing to pay for an item minus the actual price of the item. Consumer surplus is often viewed as a measure of consumer well-being—the larger the consumer surplus, the greater the consumer's feeling of well-being. When firms such as an auto dealership or department store put merchandise "on sale," they are, in effect, trying to increase the buyer's consumer surplus and sense of well-being.

Consumer surplus is best illustrated using the demand curve for a product. Consider the demand curve for movie tickets at a local theater, as shown in Figure 4.2. According to this demand curve, at the market price of $10 the movie theater can sell 200 tickets per show. This means that all 200 customers are willing to pay at least $10 for a movie ticket. Yet the

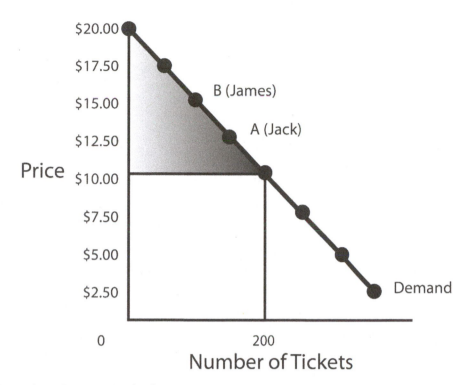

Figure 4.2   Consumer Surplus for Movie Tickets

downward sloping demand curve tells us that some of these customers would be willing to pay more than $10 per ticket. Jack, for example, shown at point A on the demand curve, is willing to pay $12.50 for the movie ticket, while James, shown at point B on the demand curve, is willing to pay $15 for the movie ticket. Both Jack and James have to pay only $10 per ticket, however. Hence, by purchasing the $10 movie ticket, Jack enjoys a consumer surplus of $2.50 ($12.50 − $10), and James enjoys a consumer surplus of $5 ($15 − $10).

The shaded area in Figure 4.2 shows the total consumer surplus for buyers of movie tickets in this market. Each ticket buyer in the shaded area, including Jack and James, is willing to pay more than $10 for a ticket.

Advertising

Advertising is a paid announcement by a business designed to inform consumers about a good or service and to persuade them to buy the product. Advertising by business firms strives to differentiate between competing goods, accenting unique features or benefits of the advertised product. The *features* of a product represent its composition, design, ingredients, components, or other physical attributes. The *benefits* highlight what the product can do for the buyer, including ways to improve one's health, appearance, performance, comfort, and so on.

Advertising can be local, national, or international in scope. Manufacturers, retailers, and other businesses hire advertising agencies to create advertising campaigns to increase the demand for certain goods and services. Ad agencies use a number of advertising appeals and techniques to get the consumer's attention, create brand loyalties, and shape tastes and preferences. An advertising appeal represents the general direction of an advertisement or

Table 4.3   U.S. Advertising Spending, 2012 (measured media spending)

Rank	Industry	Spending ($ bil.)	Rank	Business Firm	Spending ($ bil.)
1	Retail	16.35	1	Procter & Gamble	2.81
2	Auto	14.84	2	Comcast	1.71
3	Local Services	8.98	3	General Motors	1.64
4	Telecom	8.66	4	AT&T	1.57
5	Financial Services	7.89	5	L'Oreal	1.46

Source: Kantar Media, "Kantar Media Reports U.S. Advertising Expenditures Increased by 3 Percent In 2012," *Intelligence*, March 11, 2013, 4, 6.

an ad campaign. Leading ad appeals include humor, sex appeal, rational appeal, and a variety of emotional appeals. Frequently used ad techniques include bandwagon, which asks consumers to join the crowd by purchasing a product; card stacking, which lists the positive features or benefits of a product; product comparison, which shows the superiority of one product over a substitute; and testimonial, which relies on a personal endorsement of a product.

Over the past century the growth of America's consumer society and the growth of advertising proceeded hand in hand. In 2012 U.S. advertising spending on different measured media was $140 billion. Traditionally, most measured media ad spending was on television and print media such as magazines and newspapers. Other categories of media include the Internet, radio, and outdoor ads. Billions more in ad spending was on unmeasured media such as telemarketing, catalog advertising, direct mailings, and other product promotion. Predictably, fierce competition among businesses in industries that produce consumer goods generated the most significant advertising spending, as shown in Table 4.3. About one-third of all advertising spending in the world occurred in the United States.[17]

There is still some debate about the degree to which advertisers are able to influence consumer buying decisions in the American economy. The theory of *producer sovereignty*, which was popularized in the 1950s and 1960s by economist John Kenneth Galbraith (*The Affluent Society*) and sociologist Vance Packard (*The Hidden Persuaders*), argued that producers skillfully manipulated consumer demand through advertising and marketing campaigns. Today, however, the theory of *consumer sovereignty* represents mainstream economic thought. This theory states that knowledgeable, discerning consumers have sufficient information to exercise their freedom of choice and to make rational buying decisions. In other words, consumers are aware of producers' sales strategies and will cast their dollar votes for products that best meet their needs. Proponents of consumer sovereignty also note that Adam Smith, the founder of modern economics, confidently proclaimed that self interest would steer people to make informed buying decisions. Finally, consumers are shielded from business abuses, such as false or misleading product claims, by consumer protection laws, government regulatory agencies, and private consumer organizations.

CONSUMER ISSUES

Consumers have an important role in the U.S. economy. The widespread use of credit by consumers in recent decades has helped fuel the growth of the U.S. economy. The burden of debt has also driven millions of consumers into personal bankruptcy. Some consumers have enhanced their buying power in concrete ways, including the creation of consumer cooperatives. Others have re-examined their attitudes and buying preferences to support the goals of sustainable consumption.

Consumer Credit and Creditworthiness

Credit is a type of voluntary transaction or agreement between a borrower and a lender. Under a credit arrangement the borrower receives something of value, usually a sum of money, from a lender. The borrower agrees to repay this sum of money to the lender at some point in the future. In most cases, the borrower also agrees to pay the lender an agreed upon interest payment—a fee for the borrower's use of the money. There are many types of lenders in the U.S. economy such as banks, credit unions, and finance companies. The use of credit by consumers has a long history in the United States. During the 1920s the introduction of installment credit for major purchases such as an automobile instilled a "buy now pay later" mentality in many Americans. Over the past century, the use of credit in the American economy has expanded greatly.

The convenience of credit encourages consumer spending on goods and services in the U.S. economy. In 2012 there was $2.6 trillion in outstanding consumer credit in the U.S. economy.[18] Consumer credit includes credit purchases by people but excludes money borrowed for home mortgages. In fact, mortgage credit, the largest type of consumer borrowing, dwarfs consumer credit in the U.S. economy. In 2012 banks and other lending institutions held over $13 trillion in mortgage debt.[19] Three common ways for consumers to use credit today are to purchase items with credit cards, charge cards, and installment credit agreements.

Credit cards and charge cards are often called *plastic money* because these credit instruments add convenience to financial transactions. Yet economists do not consider credit and charge cards to be money mainly because these cards do not serve as a unit of accounting or as a store of value. Instead, credit and charge cards represent a type of loan made by the institution that issued the card to the cardholder. The use of a credit card or a charge card allows a consumer to buy now. The cardholder is expected to finalize the transaction each month by paying the issuing company all or a portion of the amount borrowed plus interest. Payments are usually made by check or by automatic withdrawals from the cardholder's checking account. Credit cards and charge cards share some common features, but there are some notable differences.

A **credit card** is payment card allows the cardholder to purchase goods at a variety of venues such as department stores, restaurants, grocery stores, and gas stations. In addition, credit cards permit the rollover of unpaid balances from one billing cycle to the next. Credit cards are issued by banks, thrift institutions, credit card companies, or other businesses. The three dominant credit cards in the United States are Visa, MasterCard, and American Express. Credit card companies charge relatively high interest on unpaid balances. In 2012 the average interest rate charged to cardholders was 12 percent. Some issuing companies also charge annual fees and fees for cash advances.[20]

A **charge card** is a payment card that allows the cardholder to purchase goods at a specific business. Charge cards usually require full payment for transactions at the end of each billing cycle. Charge cards are issued by a variety of retailers such as Sears, Macy's, Abercrombie & Fitch, and the Gap. Some charge cards carry an annual fee, but there are seldom interest charges because cardholders do not usually have rollover privileges. Some businesses also provide installment credit for major purchases. **Installment credit** requires buyers to repay the principal plus interest in monthly installments over a period of months or years. This practice is common in businesses that produce and sell larger items such as furniture, major appliances, home entertainment systems, and automobiles.

Most adult consumers have access to credit cards, charge cards, and installment credit because they are creditworthy. The single most important determinant of a person's credit-worthiness is a favorable credit score. Consumers earn a favorable credit score by using credit responsibly. The most recognized credit score for consumers in the United States is the FICO score. FICO is an abbreviation of Fair Issac and Company, the firm that developed the software that credit bureaus use to process credit information. Credit bureaus collect personal financial data and calculate individual FICO scores for consumers. Each credit bureau calls this FICO score by a different name. The highest possible FICO score is 850, and the lowest is 300. A high FICO score results in a favorable credit rating, which tells the potential lender such as a bank or a department store that this is a low-risk consumer. Typically, a consumer with a high FICO score will receive credit or other loans, and at a lower interest rate. A low FICO score, on the other hand, tells the lender that this consumer poses a higher risk; thus, the consumer is less likely to receive credit or other loans.[21]

The three credit bureaus—Experian, Equifax, and Transunion—collect data related to consumers' past use of credit. The FICO software enables the credit bureaus to evaluate the degree of risk lenders face if they extend credit to a certain individual. Relevant financial data includes information on the person's credit history, such as the size of the person's outstanding debts, the timeliness of past debt repayments, and whether debt collection agencies were needed to collect on past debts. An individual's FICO score is severely damaged if the person files for personal bankruptcy.

Personal Bankruptcy

The use of credit, and the accumulation of debt, is common in the U.S. economy. At times, personal debt overwhelms an individual or a household due to job loss, divorce, unanticipated medical expenses, credit abuse, or other financial difficulty. In many cases consumers who have fallen into serious debt can be guided out of their financial quagmire with assistance from a state consumer credit counseling service or, perhaps, a nonprofit debt consolidation firm. At other times, personal bankruptcy is the only viable solution to unsustainable personal debt.

Bankruptcy is a formal acknowledgement that an individual or business firm cannot repay its creditors. Personal bankruptcy is considered an action of last resort because it often results in the liquidation of personal assets, the loss of future credit, or other limits on the individual's freedom of choice. The Administrative Office of the U.S. Courts announced the filing of 1.2 million bankruptcies in 2012. Of this total, 96.7 percent were nonbusiness or personal bankruptcies, and the remaining 3.3 percent were business bankruptcies, as shown in Table 4.4.[22]

Most personal bankruptcies are filed under Chapter 7 or Chapter 13 of the U.S. bankruptcy code. In 2012, nearly 70 percent of all bankruptcies were filed under Chapter 7 of the code. Chapter 7 bankruptcies permit the courts to sell off most of the person's belongings in an effort to repay a portion of the individual's debts. Taxes owed to the government are paid off first. Typically, there is little money remaining to satisfy other creditors. Some financial obligations cannot be cancelled under Chapter 7, such as child support payments to a former spouse or student loans. The Bankruptcy Abuse Prevention and Consumer Protection

Table 4.4   Personal and Business Bankruptcy Filings, 2008–2012

| Year | Bankruptcies | | |
	Personal	Business	Total
2008	1,074,108	43,533	1,117,641
2009	1,412,838	60,837	1,473,675
2010	1,536,799	56,282	1,593,081
2011	1,362,847	47,806	1,410,653
2012	1,181,016	40,075	1,221,091

Source: Administrative Office of the U.S. Courts, *News Release*, February 4, 2013.

Act of 2005 made filing under Chapter 7 of the code more difficult. This 2005 law required some people with higher incomes—incomes higher than the median income in the filer's state—to file under Chapter 13 of the code instead. Bankruptcy applicants must also undergo credit counseling as a condition of filing for bankruptcy.[23]

Chapter 13 bankruptcy, also called the wage earner's plan, represented 30 percent of all bankruptcy filings in 2012. Chapter 13 bankruptcy offers some benefits to both the creditor and the debtor. Creditors benefit because they are repaid, in full or in part, in installments spanning three to five years. A court-assigned trustee collects money from the debtor each month and disperses debt payments to creditors in accordance with the terms outlined in the bankruptcy. Debtors, in turn, are protected from creditors. Creditors cannot contact or harass the debtor or lay claim to the debtor's assets such as house or car. Of course, any bankruptcy damages the debtor's credit score and creditworthiness.[24]

Consumer Cooperatives

The National Cooperative Business Association (NCBA) defines **cooperatives** as "independent, self-help organizations, owned and controlled by their members for the benefit of the members."[25] Cooperatives, also called co-ops, share certain values and beliefs. Chief among these beliefs is that co-op membership is voluntary and its structure democratic. Co-ops also value their own autonomy and support the work of other cooperatives. Co-ops are deeply concerned about the well-being of local peoples and local communities. Co-ops show this concern in many ways as they provide valuable and affordable services and goods to members, create employment opportunities, and render charitable assistance when possible.

There are several major types of cooperatives operating in the U.S. and global economy. Three leading co-op types include consumer co-ops, producer co-ops, and worker co-ops. A **consumer cooperative** is a nonprofit, member-owned business designed to provide services or goods to co-op members. A **producer co-op** is a firm that brings producers together, mainly in the agricultural sector of the economy, to store and market their output at more favorable prices. A **worker co-op** is a firm owned and operated by its employees. On the global level, cooperatives employ more than 100 million workers and have in excess of 800 million members.[26]

During the early 2010s a total of 30,000 co-ops operated in the U.S. economy, serving the needs of 100 million Americans. Of this total, 27,000 were consumer co-ops, with lesser numbers of producer co-ops, worker co-ops, and other types of co-ops.[27] Consumer cooperatives expand consumer power in the economy by creating more competitive markets and offering goods at reasonable prices. Profits earned by a consumer co-op are typically distributed to co-op members or shared with local communities.

Consumer co-ops in the United States provide services in many different industries. According to the Consumer Federation of America (CFA), consumer co-ops are especially important in providing financial services, electricity, and telecommunications services—including Internet access—to members. Consumer co-ops also supply food, housing, pre-school education and childcare, health care, insurance, college book and food services, and funeral arrangements.[28] Some consumer co-ops are large businesses that serve millions of members. For instance, the largest credit union in the United States, Navy Federal, is a consumer co-op. It has 3.9 million members and $47 billion in assets. Navy Federal accepts deposits, makes consumer loans, offers checking-type accounts, and provides a variety of other financial services to members.[29]

In the global economy, consumer and producer cooperatives have become highly effective enterprises "that put people at the center of their business and not capital."[30] In the global economy co-ops conduct business activity in virtually every major industry, ranging from agriculture and fisheries, to banking and insurance, to tourism and transportation. These co-ops support economic development in poorer world regions, while their core principles advance democracy. The International Co-operative Alliance (ICA), the world's largest nongovernmental organization (NGO), supports co-ops through lobbying, education and training, and technical assistance. The ICA represents 265 member organizations from 96 countries and defends the right of co-ops to serve nearly 1 billion people.[31] The United Nations proclaimed 2012 as the International Year of Cooperatives to accent the positive role of co-ops in achieving sustainable economic development, higher living standards, and democracy.[32]

Sustainable Consumption

Sustainable consumption is the ability to satisfy people's present consumption needs without undermining the world's capacity to meet the consumption needs of future generations. Sustainable consumption applies to the purchase or use of resources such as water or petroleum, as well as final goods such as food, household appliances, and motor vehicles. It also applies to the decisions made by all consumption units, including households, businesses, and governments.

Sustainable consumption in the global economy is supported by a number of international agreements. The landmark *Agenda 21*, which was adopted by the Rio Earth Summit in 1992, made a compelling link between unsustainable consumption and irresponsible production methods on the one hand, and global poverty and environmental degradation on the other. *Agenda 21* recommended a global shift in lifestyles and consumption patterns, particularly in industrialized countries. It called for more efficient and "green" production methods, the use of new and renewable energy resources, the development and sharing of green technologies, the creation of recycling and waste reduction programs, and the dissemination of information about ethical consumption through education, public awareness programs, advertising, and other means.

Sustainable consumption was formally added to the *United Nations Guidelines for Consumer Protection* in 1999. Consumers International (CI), a nonprofit federation of consumer groups and nongovernmental organizations (NGOs), was instrumental in framing the sustainable consumption addendum to the UN guidelines. The revised UN guidelines asked governments to introduce sustainable consumption practices into their own

One goal of sustainable consumption is to reduce waste, particularly in the industrialized countries. (Shutterstock.com)

operations, finance green research and development (R&D), end subsidies to inefficient producers, and require businesses to pay for external production costs such as pollution.

In the early 2000s the United Nations Environment Program (UNEP) reported slow progress in implementing the sustainable consumption recommendations outlined in the UN guidelines. A UNEP survey cited high compliance with sustainable consumption guidelines in Australia, Belgium, Brazil, the Czech Republic, Denmark, Estonia, Finland, Hungary, the Republic of Korea, Mexico, Nicaragua, Sri Lanka, and Sweden. Lower compliance with the UN guidelines was recorded in Bulgaria, Burundi, Costa Rica, Cote d'Ivoire, Cyprus, Ecuador, Haiti, Kenya, and Zambia.[33]

CHAPTER 4 SUMMARY

Consumer Rights and Protections
- Consumer spending represents the largest portion of the U.S. gross domestic product.
- American consumers enjoy a number of basic consumer rights but also must accept certain responsibilities for their decisions and behaviors.
- Consumer protection in the United States is a shared responsibility among federal agencies, local authorities, consumer organizations, businesses, and consumers.

Consumer Movements
- The local consumer movement works mainly on local consumer issues.
- The national consumer movement increases consumer power through national consumer organizations and individual initiatives.
- The international consumer movement addresses many quality of life issues in the global economy.

Consumer Behavior

- Utility theory helps explain consumer behavior by examining how incremental changes in satisfaction affect people's buying decisions.
- The income and substitution effects note how a price change affects people's buying decisions.
- Consumer surplus measures well-being by comparing the price a consumer is willing to spend for a product with the market price.
- Advertising is a paid announcement by a firm designed to increase the demand for a product.

Consumer Issues

- Credit, when used responsibly, adds convenience to a consumer's buying decisions.
- Bankruptcy is a last-resort measure that reduces or eliminates unsustainable debt.
- Consumer cooperatives are nonprofit, member-owned businesses that provide products, jobs, or other benefits to members.
- Sustainable consumption protects future generations' consumption.

NOTES

1. U.S. Department of Commerce (DOC), Bureau of Economic Analysis (BEA), "Table 2.1: Personal Income and Its Disposition," *News Release*, March 29, 2013, www.bea.doc.gov/newsreleases/national/pi/2013/pdf/pi0213.pdf

2. Ibid.

3. U.S. Department of Labor (DOL), Bureau of Labor Statistics (BLS), "Table A: Average Expenditures and Characteristics of All Consumer Units and Percent Changes, 2010 through June 2012," *News Release, Consumer Expenditures Midyear Update, July 2011 through June 2012 Average*, March 27, 2013, www.bls.gov/news.release/pdf/cesmy.pdf

4. DOC/BEA, "Table 3: Gross Domestic Product and Related Measures; Level Changes from Preceding Period," *News Release*, March 28, 2013, www.bea.gov/newsreleases/national/gdp/2013/pdf/gdp4q12_3rd.pdf

5. Conference Board, "The Conference Board Consumer Confidence Index Declines in March," *News Release*, March 26, 2013, www.conference-board.org/data/consumerconfidence.cfm

6. Thomson Reuters and the University of Michigan, "Consumer Confidence Higher Due to Job Gains," *Survey of Consumers*, January 27, 2012, 1.

7. John F. Kennedy, "Special Message to the Congress on Protecting the Consumer Interest," March 15, 1962, *The Public Papers of President John F. Kennedy, 1962*, www.jfklink.com/speeches/jfk/publicpapers/1962/jfk_contents_paper1962.html

8. United Nations Department of Economic and Social Affairs, *United Nations Guidelines for Consumer Protection*, as expanded in 1999 (New York: United Nations, 2003), 1-11. www.un.org/esa/sustdev/publications/consumption_en.pdf

9. Federal Trade Commission (FTC), "Identity Crisis . . . What to Do If Your Identity is Stolen," *FTC Facts for Consumers: Focus on Credit* (Washington, DC: FTC, August 2005), 1; FTC, *Fighting Back against Identity Theft*, May 2010, www.ftc.gov/idtheft

10. Javelin Strategy & Research, "Identity Fraud Fell 28 Percent According to New Javelin Strategy & Research Report," February 8, 2011, www.javelinstrategy.com

11. FTC, "Identity Crisis . . . What to Do If Your Identity is Stolen," *FTC Facts for Consumers: Focus on Credit* (Washington, DC: FTC, August 2005), 1; FTC, *Fighting Back against Identity Theft*, May 2010, www.ftc.gov/idtheft

12. U.S. Consumer Product Safety Commission (CPSC), "Frequently Asked Questions," www.cpsc.gov/about/faq.html

13. Consumer Product Safety Commission (CPSC), *2011 Performance and Accountability Report* (USCPSC), November 2011, 7, www.cpsc.gov/cpscpub/pubs/reports/2011par.pdf

14. Consumer Federation of America (CFA) et al., "Top Ten Complaints in 2010," *2010 Consumer Complaint Survey Report*, July 27, 2011, 5.

15. Consumers International (CI), *Annual Report and Financial Statement 2010* (London: Consumers International, December 31, 2010), 5-7, www.consumersinternational.org; CI, "The Global Voice for Consumers," www.consumersinternational.org

16. CI, "The Global Voice for Consumers: World Consumer Rights Day 2013; Consumer Justice Now," www.consumersinternational.org/our-work/wcrd/wcrd-2013

17. Kantar Media, "Kantar Media Reports U.S. Advertising Expenditures Increased 3 Percent in 2012," *Intelligence*, March 11, 2013, 1-6, http://kantarmediana.com/intelligence/press/us-advertising-expenditures-increased-3-percent-in-2012

18. Board of Governors of the Federal Reserve System, "G.19: Consumer Credit, January 2013," *Current Release*, March 7, 2013, www.federalreserve.gov/releases/g19/Current

19. Board of Governors of the Federal Reserve System, "Mortgage Debt Outstanding, March, 2013," www.federalreserve.gov/econresdata/releases/mortoutstand/current.htm

20. Board of Governors of the Federal Reserve System, "G.19: Consumer Credit, January 2013," *Current Release*, 7 March, 2013, www.federalreserve.gov/releases/g19/Current

21. "Credit Basics," www.myfico.com/CreditEducation/CreditScores.aspx

22. Administrative Office of the U.S. Courts, "Bankruptcy Filings Decline in Calendar Year 2012," *News Release*, February 4, 2013, Washington, DC: U.S. Courts, www.uscourts.gov/bankruptcy-filings-decline-calendar-year-2012

23. U.S. Department of Justice, "Bankruptcy Reform," Washington, DC: Department of Justice, November 3, 2011, www.justice.gov/ust/eo/bapcpa/index.htm; Administrative Office of the U.S. Courts, "Chapter 7: Liquidation Under the Bankruptcy Code," www.uscourts.gov/FederalCourts/Bankruptcy/BankruptcyBasics/Chapter7.aspx

24. Administrative Office of the U.S. Courts, "Bankruptcy Filings Decline in Calendar Year 2012," *News Release*, Washington, DC: U.S. Courts, February 4, 2013, www.uscourts.gov/bankruptcy-filings-decline-calendar-year-2012; Administrative Office of the U.S. Courts, "Chapter 13: Individual Debt Adjustment," www.uscourts.gov/FederalCourts/Bankruptcy/BankruptcyBasics/Chapter13.aspx

25. National Cooperative Business Association (NCBA), "About Co-Ops," 2011, http://co-opsusa.coop/about-co-ops-cooperatives

26. International Co-Operative Alliance (ICA), "What Is a Co-Operative?" June 16, 2010, www.ica.coop/coop/index.html

27. National Cooperative Business Association (NCBA), "Consumer Cooperatives," www.ncba.coop/ncba/about-co-ops/co-op-types/consumer-cooperatives

28. Consumer Federation of America (CFA), *The Cooperative Difference: Consumers Helping Themselves to Meet Needs and Save Money*, Washington, DC: CFA.

29. Ibid.; Navy Federal, "Operating Statistics, 4th Quarter, 2011," About Navy Federal, www.navyfederal.org/about/about.php

30. International Co-operative Alliance (ICA), "Co-operative identity, values & principles," http://en/what-co-op/co-operative-identity-values-principles

31. Ibid.

32. United Nations, "United Nations, International Year of Cooperatives 2012," http://social.un.org/coopsyear/about-iyc.html

33. United Nations Environment Program (UNEP) and Consumers International (CI), *Tracking Progress: Implementing Sustainable Consumption Policies*, 2nd ed. (New York: United Nations Publication, 2004), 64.

5

Businesses: The Basic Production Unit

Most business activity in the U.S. economy is conducted by private firms within two broad economic sectors: the services-producing sector and the goods-producing sector. The three main types of firms are sole proprietorships, partnerships, and corporations. Firms generally seek to maximize profits and operate in different types of competitive environments, or market structures. These market structures include perfect competition, monopolistic competition, oligopoly, and monopoly. Today business practices are monitored by the government, private organizations, and by businesses themselves.

BUSINESS BASICS

For-profit businesses produce the great majority of goods and services in the U.S. economy. In 2012 private business firms produced 87 percent of all final goods and services counted in the nation's gross domestic product (GDP). Government at the federal, state, and local levels accounted for the remaining 13 percent of GDP.[1] Households, businesses, and government consume trillions of dollars in goods and services each year. Three basic ways to categorize business firms is by industry, by size, and by economic sector.

Firms and Industries

A **firm** is a business entity that produces a good or service. A firm is often called a business or a company. In 2010 nearly 28 million private firms operated in the U.S. economy.[2] Most American businesses are **nonemployer firms**—firms that are owned by one person; earn at least $1,000 per year in revenues; and do not hire additional employees. In 2010 there were 22.1 million nonemployer firms in the U.S. economy. Despite the large number of nonemployer firms, they account for only a tiny percentage of total U.S. business receipts. In fact, business receipts of these nonemployer firms are so small that this financial data is excluded from most U.S. Census business statistics.[3] Another 5.7 million U.S. businesses are **employer firms**—firms that hire employees. The great majority of all employer firms are classified as small businesses and the remainder large businesses. Employer firms account for almost all business receipts in the U.S. economy.[4]

Firms use the factors of production—natural resources, human resources, and capital goods—to produce outputs. Entrepreneurship is often considered a fourth factor of production. Outputs are typically categorized by the degree of processing that has gone into the product. For example, the output of a logging firm is cut trees. Economists view unprocessed trees as a natural resource. The output of a sawmill is board lumber, a semifinished or intermediate good. The output of a furniture manufacturer might be a wooden table, a final good.

Some firms specialize in the production of one type of good or service, while others diversify to produce different types of products. Examples of firms that produce one type of product are General Motors, which produces motor vehicles; Nike, which produces athletic footwear and apparel; and H& R Block, which prepares people's tax forms. Highly diversified firms such as Procter & Gamble and Unilever produce many types of household and personal care products, beauty products, health and nutrition products, and more.

One way to classify firms is by industry. An **industry** represents all of the firms that produce a similar product. For example, General Mills, Kellogg, Post, and Quaker Oats, are *firms* that operate in the breakfast cereal *industry*. Similarly, General Motors, Ford Motor, and Chrysler are major firms in the U.S. auto industry. At times the term "industry" is more broadly defined, as is the case with the limited-service restaurant or fast food industry. Consider the variety of restaurants that might reasonably be placed in the fast food industry, including firms that specialize in hamburgers, tacos, chicken, pizza, sandwiches and subs, and so on. Industries that produce tangible products are categorized as goods-producing industries. Industries that produce services are categorized as services-producing industries. In the U.S. economy the vast majority of all firms, workers, and output are associated with the services-producing industries.

Small Businesses and Large Businesses

A second way to classify business firms is by their size. The government distinguishes a small business from a large business by number of employees and total business receipts. Using these two criteria, 99.9 percent of all firms in the U.S. economy—nonemployer and employer firms—are classified as small businesses. The U.S. Small Business Administration (SBA), an agency within the federal government, is a key advocate for small businesses in the United States. A primary goal of the SBA is to create a "level playing field" so that small businesses can compete with large business enterprises. To this end, SBA programs help small businesses obtain loans, grants, and other assistance. In addition, certain government contracts are reserved for small businesses.[5]

Small businesses accounted for more than 99 percent of the 5.7 million U.S. *employer* firms in 2010. Small businesses share several characteristics. First, a small business is a for-profit firm that does not dominate the production of a good or service in a certain market. Second, a small business cannot exceed the size standards prescribed by the government. For many industries, this means that the firm must have fewer than 500 employees and not have annual business receipts that exceed a specified dollar limit. These dollar limits vary from industry to industry. Firms involved in heavy construction, for example, cannot earn annual receipts greater than $33.5 million, while firms operating in retail trade cannot have receipts greater than $7 million. Third, a small business must be independently owned and operated. Fourth, a small business must operate mainly in the United States or contribute to the U.S economy through the payment of taxes or use of U.S. resources.[6] In 2010 small businesses employed about 55 million workers, produced nearly half of the U.S. gross domestic product (GDP), and paid $2.1 trillion in wages to

Table 5.1   Largest U.S. Businesses, 2012

Rank	Company	Revenues ($ billions)	Profits ($ billions)
1	Walmart	469	17.0
2	ExxonMobil	450	44.9
3	Chevron	234	26.2
4	Phillips66	170	4.1
5	Berkshire Hathaway	162	14.8

Source: "Largest U.S. Corporations," *Fortune*, May 20, 2013, F-1, F-2.

workers.[7] Small businesses also created nearly two-thirds of all new jobs between 1993 and 2009.[8]

A large business is a for-profit firm that exceeds the number of employees or annual receipts prescribed for small businesses. For the most part, this means that a large business employs 500 or more workers and earns annual receipts greater than the dollar limit set for its industry. The U.S. Census Bureau reported that in 2010 just 17,236 large businesses operated in the U.S. economy. Hence, large businesses accounted for about one-tenth of one percent of all firms. Yet this tiny number of large businesses employed 57 million workers, produced more than half of the U.S. GDP, and paid $2.8 trillion in wages to workers. Large business also created about one-third of all new jobs between 1993 and 2009.[9] In 2010 eight of the world's 20 largest businesses were American firms. The five largest U.S. businesses in 2012, ranked by total revenues, are shown in Table 5.1.[10]

Services-Producing Sector and Goods-Producing Sector

A third way to classify firms is by economic sector. An economic sector represents a broad production category. Many economies around the world divide national output into three general production categories, or economic sectors, including the agricultural, industrial, and service sectors. Today U.S. producers are generally lumped into one of two economic sectors: the services-producing sector or the goods-producing sector.

The **services-producing sector** consists of firms that supply productive activities in the economy. *Private* sector services-producing industries operate in areas such as utilities, transportation and communications, wholesale and retail trade, finance and insurance, real estate, information, and a wide variety of services related to business operations, health care, education, and social welfare. In its broadest context, *public* services of the federal, state, and local levels of government can also be included in the services-producing sector.

In the highly advanced economies most jobs and national output come from the services-producing sector. In 2012 services accounted for 114 million jobs, or 81.5 percent of all employed persons in the United States.[11] The services-producing sector also produced the lion's share of national output. National output is often measured in two ways: the gross domestic product (GDP) and gross output. The GDP measures value of *final* products produced each year. In 2012 private firms in the United States produced $10.8 trillion worth of services, which accounted for 79 percent of all final output produced by these firms.[12] The nation's gross output, on the other hand, counts the value of final products, semifinished products, and other resources in various stages of production. In 2012 the gross output of services in the U.S. economy was about $16.5 trillion. This meant that services accounted for nearly 70 percent of the nation's gross output.[13]

A stone quarry is a type of goods-producing enterprise. (Stanko07/Dreamstime.com)

The **goods-producing sector** consists of firms that supply tangible items. The goods-producing sector consists of industries within the general areas of agriculture, manufacturing, construction, and mining. In an advanced economy such as the United States, the goods-producing sector is capital intensive. *Capital-intensive* production relies heavily on the use of sophisticated capital goods, which, in turn, increases the productivity of labor. In 2012 firms in the goods-producing sector employed 26 million workers, or 18.5 percent of employed workers in the U.S. civilian labor force.[14] Meanwhile, private U.S. firms in the goods-producing sector accounted for 21 percent of the GDP and about 30 percent of the gross output of the U.S. economy.[15]

Firms in the world's advanced economies rely on sophisticated production methods, emphasizing capital over labor. In developing countries, however, firms tend to use *labor-intensive* production methods—methods that rely on physical labor rather than capital goods. The lack of capital goods helps explain why national output and the productivity of labor are relatively low in many poorer regions of the world. It also helps explain why such a large percentage of the labor force in poorer countries is devoted to agriculture, as shown in Table 5.2.[16] By contrast, just 1.5 percent of all workers in the United States are employed in agriculture.

BUSINESS ORGANIZATION

Yet another classification of firms is based on business organization. The three basic types of business organization are sole proprietorship, partnership, and corporation. In addition, business franchises enable some corporations to expand by creating and supporting satellite firms. Other forms of business organization include limited liability companies, joint ventures, producer cooperatives, and nonprofit organizations.

Table 5.2   Economic Sectors for Selected Developing Countries: Output and Employment, 2011

Country	Percentage of GDP (by sector)			Percentage of Labor Force (by sector)		
	Agric	Ind	Serv	Agric	Ind	Serv
Ethiopia	49	11	39	85	5	10
Haiti	25	16	59	38	12	50
Nigeria	35	34	31	70	10	20
Vietnam	20	41	39	54	20	26

Source: Central Intelligence Agency, *The World Factbook* (Washington, DC: CIA), 2011.

Sole Proprietorships

A **sole proprietorship** is an unincorporated firm that is owned by one person, the proprietor. In some instances the proprietor is the only paid worker employed in the business. In other cases the proprietor hires employees to help run the business. Sole proprietorships are the most common form of business organization, accounting for 22.6 million firms, or 71.5 percent of all firms in the U.S. economy. In 2008 sole proprietorships earned $1.3 trillion in business receipts, or 3.9 percent of all business receipts in the U.S. economy, as shown in Table 5.3.[17] Proprietors often operate businesses in areas such as retail shops, restaurants and food services, personal and health care services, consulting services, and construction.

There are a number of advantages of sole proprietorships. One advantage is the ease of forming and dissolving the firm. While a proprietor must abide by local zoning regulations, obtain necessary permits or licenses, and comply with health and safety standards, there are no significant obstacles to starting the firm. Similarly, the proprietor is able to dissolve or sell the business at his or her own discretion, without the hassle of consulting partners, stockholders, or other stakeholders in the company. Second, the proprietor is the boss. Thus, the proprietor is free to make all decisions necessary to the operation of the business, including production and hiring decisions. As the sole decision maker the proprietor also enjoys psychological rewards, such as pride and prestige, associated with running a successful firm. Finally, the proprietor is entitled to all profits generated by the firm. The proprietor's profits are taxed only once as personal income, thus avoiding the double taxation that plagues corporations.

There are also disadvantages of sole proprietorships. First, the decision making of the proprietor is the least expert of any form of business organization. This is because the proprietor is personally responsible for a myriad of business decisions connected with the

Table 5.3   Main Types of Business Organization, 2008

Type of Firm	Number of Firms (millions)	Percentage of All Firms	Business Receipts ($ bil.)	Business Receipts (%)	Profits ($ bil.)
Proprietorship	22.6	71.5	1,317	3.9	265
Partnership	3.1	10.0	4,963	14.8	458
Corporation	5.8	18.5	27,266	81.3	984

Source: U.S. Bureau of the Census, "Table 744," *Statistical Abstract of the United States: 2012* (Washington, DC: U.S. Government Printing Office), 2012, 491.

production, marketing, and distribution of the firm's output. Second, proprietors have unlimited liability for all business debts. This means that the proprietor's personal assets could be tapped to pay debts incurred by the firm. Finally, financial institutions view proprietorships as less creditworthy than other forms of business organization mainly because they are smaller, lack collateral, and rely on the business skills of a single individual—the proprietor. Proprietors are often obliged to dip into personal savings or to tap into the resources of family or friends to finance business expenses.

Partnerships

A **partnership** is an unincorporated firm that is owned by two or more people, called partners, each of whom has a financial interest in the company. Like sole proprietorships, most partnerships are small businesses. The two main types of partnerships include general partnerships and limited partnerships. In a general partnership the partners operate the business together, sharing decision making and other responsibilities. In a limited partnership, some partners run the business while others simply invest money in the firm—mainly to finance start-up costs. A silent partner invests money in the partnership but does not get involved in the day-to-day operation of the business. There are fewer partnerships in the U.S. economy than any other type of business organization. In 2008 the 3.1 million partnerships accounted for 10 percent of all firms and 14.8 percent of all business receipts in the U.S. economy, as shown in Table 5.3.[18] Partnerships are common in services-producing fields such as law, medicine, real estate, insurance, and engineering, and in the skilled trades such as construction and home repair.

The advantages of operating a partnership are similar to those of a sole proprietorship. First, partnerships are fairly easy to organize. Like sole proprietorships, partnerships comply with local zoning and licensing regulations. In addition, partners often draft a partnership contract to define each partner's role in the firm, determine how profits should be distributed, and state a process for dissolving the firm should the need arise. Second, decision making in partnerships is more specialized and, therefore, more expert than in sole proprietorships. Third, the quality of the service provided by the firm is improved through consultations and peer evaluations. Fourth, psychological rewards such as pride and self-esteem often accompany business success. Fifth, business profits are a direct affirmation of partners' business success. Sixth, like the proprietor's profits, the profits of partners are taxed just once as personal income.

There are also disadvantages of partnerships. First, shared decision making among partners is sometimes a source of conflict, which can be time consuming, costly, and demoralizing. Second, general partners have unlimited liability for business losses, obligations, or debts incurred by any of the partners. Thus, a poor business decision, an expensive legal suit, a product recall, or other business error can sap the personal assets of each general partner. Silent partners, however, have limited liability and, thus, their potential loss is capped at the dollar amount they invest in the firm. Third, access to credit is often limited. Like sole proprietorships, partnerships generally rely on the talents and health of a few people and often lack the collateral to back large loans from banks.

Corporations

A **corporation** is a firm that is a legal entity in itself and incorporated under state laws. A corporation is able to conduct business in its own name in much the same way an individual does. The owners of a corporation are its shareholders, who purchase certificates of ownership called shares or stocks. The management of a corporation, on the other hand, consists of hired professionals. Corporate management often is headed by a chief executive officer (CEO), chief financial officer (CFO), a president, a number of vice presidents, and other officers. The company's management is selected by a corporate board of directors, which also makes important policies and sets goals for the firm. In 2008 there were 5.8 million corporations operating in the U.S. economy, which represented about 18.5 percent of all business firms. Corporations generated $27.3 trillion in business receipts, or 81.3 percent of the total business receipts in the economy.[19] Measured by level of business activity, corporations are the dominant form of business organization in the U.S. economy.

Corporations are classified as public corporations or closed corporations. Most well-known corporations are **public corporations**, or corporations in which stock is widely traded on a stock exchange. Examples of well-known public corporations traded on the New York Stock Exchange include AT&T, Coca-Cola, Home Depot, IBM, Microsoft, and Walt Disney. Many other nationally known public corporations are widely traded over the counter on the NASDAQ stock exchange, including Amazon, Denny's, Mattel, Staple's, Starbuck's, and TiVo. **Closed corporations**, on the other hand, restrict stock ownership to a small group, perhaps family members or company employees. Examples of closed corporations, also called private companies, are Koch Industries, Mars, Enterprise Rent-a-Car, Levi Strauss, and Hallmark Cards.

There are several advantages of the corporate business structure. First, the shareholders of a corporation have limited liability, so the maximum amount of money an individual shareholder could lose is the amount invested in the corporation. Second, corporations have the most specialized and expert management of any type of business organization. Third, corporations are the most stable form of business organization. This is because a change in ownership, which occurs through the sale or other transfer of stock, does not interrupt business activity. Fourth, only corporations can raise money for their business by selling bonds and stocks to investors. **Bonds** represent corporate debt, rather than ownership in a corporation. Investors buy bonds to earn annual interest payments for the life of this debt. **Stocks** represent partial ownership in the corporation. Investors gain two types of returns from investments in stocks—dividends and capital gains. Dividends, the regular payments by the firm to stockholders, are distributed from corporate profits quarterly, semiannually, or annually. Capital gains occur when the investor sells a stock for an amount greater than its original purchase price.

Disadvantages of corporations also exist. First, the division between the owners and managers of a corporation could cause conflicts over the distribution of profits, business practices, or other concerns. Second, specialized decision making is time consuming, and decisions might be delayed as they travel through a complex chain of command. Third, corporations are the most difficult type of business to form. The rules of forming corporations vary, but most states adhere to the provisions outlined in the Model Business Corporation Act. Fourth, corporations are subject to double taxation of corporate profits. Double taxation begins with the corporate income tax, which taxes corporate profits. Next, the federal personal income tax takes another bite out of these same profits when dividends are distributed to shareholders. During the Republican administration of President George W. Bush, the Jobs and Growth Tax Relief Reconciliation Act of 2003 was passed to reduce this disadvantage by placing a 15 percent tax cap on dividend income and on capital gains. During the Democratic administration of President Barack Obama, the

Table 5.4   Top 5 Franchises, 2013

Rank	Franchise Name	Product Line
1	Hampton Hotels	Mid-priced hotels
2	Subway	Sandwiches and salads
3	Jiffy Lube, Int'l	Fast oil change
4	7-Eleven	Convenience stores
5	Supercuts	Hair salons

Source: "Entrepreneur 2013 Franchise 500," *Entrepreneur*, Entrepreneur Media, Inc., 2013.

2010 Tax Relief Act extended the 15 percent tax rate for dividends and capital gains through 2012.

Franchises

Some major corporations expand production and sales through franchising. A **franchise** is a business that consists of a parent company, called a franchiser, and satellite firms called franchisees. A franchise contract, which defines the business relationship between franchiser and franchisee, typically outlines the franchiser's responsibilities in training local managers and employees, connecting its franchisees with suppliers or distributors, and arranging for credit or other financial assistance to defray the franchisee's start-up costs. The contract also lists the franchisee's responsibilities, which often include assurances of quality standards and financial remunerations to the parent company for the use of its brand name, national advertising, and other assistance. Entrepreneurs who become franchisees enjoy many of the psychological and monetary rewards of sole proprietors but operate under the guidance and supervision of a parent company.

Franchise start-up costs vary widely. Some expensive franchise start-ups include hotels such as Hampton Hotels and Days Inns, and fast food restaurants such as McDonald's and Taco Bell. Lower start-up costs are typically found in service franchises such as fitness and commercial cleaning. Franchises are ranked each year using criteria such as financial strength, size, growth rate, and stability over time. Table 5.4 shows the top five franchises in 2013.[20]

Other Forms of Business Organization

Some businesses do not fit neatly under the traditional headings of sole proprietorships, partnerships, or corporations. Several of the most important adaptations of the traditional forms of business organization include limited liability companies, joint ventures, producer cooperatives, and nonprofit organizations.

A **limited liability company** (LLC) is a hybrid business organization that combines features from corporations, partnerships, and sole proprietorships. Like a corporation, a LLC registers with the state by filing an articles of organization. These articles identify the LLC owner, its location, and business name. Many LLCs also create an operating agreement to outline the decision making process, profit distribution, and a dissolution procedure. LLC owners enjoy limited liability, which resembles that of corporate shareholders. Also, the LLC is not subject to double taxation. Instead, LLC business profits are taxed just once as the owner's personal income. Today LLCs are a popular type of business organization for small businesses.[21]

A **joint venture** is a temporary business agreement between two or more companies to produce or sell a good or service. Any type of business organization can enter into a joint venture. In joint ventures each company contributes certain physical or financial assets and expertise to the business. Each firm also expects to earn profits from this temporary alliance. In some cases, joint ventures are formed between a foreign firm and a domestic firm for mutual benefit, such as access to new markets, technologies, management techniques, or production techniques. In 2011, for example, General Motors had 11 active joint ventures with automakers in China. One of these joint ventures was the Shanghai General Motors Co, Ltd., also called Shanghai GM, which brought GM and Shanghai Automotive Industry Corporation together in 1997. In 2011 the Shanghai GM joint venture produced 1.2 million cars in China.[22]

A **producer cooperative** is a not-for-profit business owned by member firms that produce a similar good or service. Producer co-ops are formed mainly to reduce the costs of production for member firms and thereby improve these firms' competitiveness in certain markets. For example, producer co-ops might reduce costs by using common storage facilities, marketing campaigns, and distributors. Producer co-ops usually select a board of directors and a manager, and hire employees. Co-op profits are typically distributed to member firms in the form of patronage refunds, also called patronage dividends.[23] Many producer co-ops operate in U.S. agriculture. Examples include Florida's Natural, Land O'Lakes, Sunkist, Ocean Spray, and Welch's.

A **nonprofit organization** exists to provide goods, services, or other assistance to people but not to earn profits for shareholders, employees, or other stakeholders. Many nonprofit organizations are organized as nonprofit corporations, also called nonstock corporations. Other nonprofit organizations are organized as unincorporated associations, partnerships, and foundations. Nonprofit organizations raise money to finance their activities mainly by soliciting contributions from individuals, firms, or the government. These funds, in turn, are used to support a variety of charitable, humanitarian, educational, scientific, or community programs and services. According to the National Center for Charitable Statistics (NCCS), there were about 1.6 million nonprofit organizations operating in the United States in 2009.[24] Examples include the Red Cross, the Boy Scouts and Girl Scouts of America, Veterans of Foreign Wars, the Sierra Club Foundation, the American Civil Liberties Union, and the United Way.

MARKET STRUCTURES

U.S. business firms operate within different competitive environments, or **market structures**. The four market structures are perfect competition, monopolistic competition, oligopoly, and monopoly. Market structures are compared and contrasted by number of firms, type of product, amount of nonprice competition, ease of entry or exit, and degree of market power held by firms.

Perfect Competition

Perfect competition is a type of market structure in which thousands of firms, operating independently, produce an identical or homogeneous product. Mainly because competitive firms produce an identical product, nonprice competition such as advertising is unnecessary. Firms are able to enter or exit perfectly competitive industries easily because there are few, if any, **barriers to entry**—factors that discourage or prevent firms from joining or leaving an industry. In addition, perfectly competitive firms have no market power. That is, individual firms have no control over the price they charge for their output.

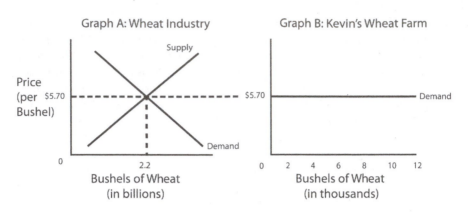

Figure 5.1   Perfectly Competitive Wheat *Industry* and Wheat *Firm*

Instead, firms are obliged to accept the market price for the identical product they all produce. Economists call competitive firms price takers to emphasize that the forces of supply and demand in the entire market, rather than the pricing decisions of individual firms, determine the price of output.

In the U.S. economy perfect competition is best illustrated by business activity in certain agricultural industries, such as wheat and corn, where thousands of firms produce an identical product for sale in domestic and international markets. A perfectly competitive *industry* and a perfectly competitive *firm* within this industry are illustrated in Figure 5.1.

Graph A, shown to the left in Figure 5.1, shows the perfectly competitive wheat *industry*, also called the wheat *market*. The upward sloping market supply curve represents the amount of wheat that thousands of wheat farmers are willing and able to produce at a series of prices. The downward sloping market demand curve, on the other hand, represents the quantity of wheat that buyers are willing and able to purchase at a series of prices. The buyers, in this case, are mainly firms that use wheat in their production of other products such as bread and breakfast cereals. Graph A shows the interaction of the sellers of wheat and the buyers of wheat. The interplay of supply and demand created an average equilibrium price of $5.70 per bushel for the 2.2 billion bushels of wheat produced in 2010.[25]

Graph B, shown to the right in Figure 5.1, shows the perfectly competitive wheat *firm*. Kevin, an individual wheat farmer, is a price taker who has no market power to increase the price of his wheat. Kevin must accept the market price of $5.70 per bushel. Note that the demand curve for Kevin's wheat is a horizontal line. This shows that at the market price of $5.70, there is a demand for any quantity of wheat Kevin is willing to produce. If Kevin tried to sell his wheat for a price higher than the market price, say, $5.80 per bushel, there are no buyers. Why would a buyer pay $5.80 for each bushel of Kevin's wheat if wheat could be purchased for just $5.70 per bushel from thousands of other farmers? If Kevin insisted on charging this higher $5.80 price, his sales and revenue would fall to zero. Conversely, Kevin would not lower the price of his wheat to $5.60 per bushel because he can already sell all of his wheat at the higher market price of $5.70. Kevin has zero market power due to the tiny portion of the nation's wheat crop his farm produces. In our hypothetical case, Kevin could produce up to 12,000 bushels of wheat in 2010. This might sound like a lot of wheat, but in relation to the 2.2 billion bushels produced by U.S. wheat farmers in 2010 it is statistically insignificant.

The market structure for competitive firms has a significant effect on business profits. **Profit** occurs when a firm's total revenues are greater than its total costs. When perfectly competitive firms earn profits this encourages other farmers to enter the industry. This is because profits are a type of signal, or incentive, for other firms to shift resources into industries where they can make money. If Kevin's farm, and thousands of other farms in the wheat industry, earn profits in 2010 it is reasonable to predict the entry of additional farmers into the wheat industry the following year. Recall that there are no significant barriers to entry in a perfectly competitive industry.

The entry of new firms increases the total supply of wheat. Higher wheat supplies, in turn, cause the price of wheat to fall. Additional farmers will continue to enter the wheat industry only as long as profits can be made. When industry profits dry up and farmers are at a break-even point, this signals farmers to plant fewer acres of wheat or to exit the wheat industry completely in favor of a more profitable crop. Economists refer to this break-even point as zero economic profit, or normal profit.

Monopolistic Competition

Monopolistic competition is a type of market structure in which there is a significant number of firms—perhaps 20, 50, or more—that produce similar but differentiated products. It is relatively easy for firms to enter or exit monopolistically competitive industries due to low barriers to entry. In monopolistically competitive industries, the economic rivalry among competing firms is often intense. Table 5.5 shows several industries that operate under conditions of monopolistic competition. Note that a significant portion of the industry's output is produced by the top 20 or 50 firms in the industry.[26] Still, compared to oligopolies and monopolies, these concentration ratios—typically measured by the percentage of the industry's output produced by the top four firms in the industry—are considered relatively low.

Product differentiation is important to firms operating under conditions of monopolistic competition. Often firms use nonprice competition to distinguish their product from other similar products. One way to do this is to create brand loyalty through advertising. A second way to distinguish between competing products is to improve the product's quality, thereby building a positive business reputation. A third way to distinguish one product from another is by offering related services such as a knowledgeable sales staff or free service calls to customers. Finally, firms might offer conveniences such as a "no questions asked"

Table 5.5   Concentration Ratios for Selected Monopolistically Competitive Industries

Industry	*Percentage of Industry Output by Number of Firms*			
	Top 4	*Top 8*	*Top 20*	*Top 50*
Manufacturing				
Auto parts	19	28	42	56
Furniture	21	27	37	49
Retail				
Convenience stores	16	20	23	26
Hardware stores	20	23	27	30
Limited-service restaurants	8	11	17	21

Source: U.S. Bureau of the Census/American FactFinder, "Concentration Ratios: Share of Shipments Accounted for by the 4, 8, 20, and 50 Largest Companies for Industries: 2007," *2007 Economic Census*.

return policy or conveniently situated stores, factory outlets, or service centers. Product differentiation gives these firms some market power and thus, some control over the product's price.

The traditional textbook model states that monopolistically competitive firms earn zero economic profits in the long run mainly because competitors are free to enter this type of industry and drive prices down. Yet this model assumes that these firms produce the same tired products with the same production methods as in the past. Firms in monopolistically competitive industries can innovate, however, and reinvent themselves by developing new and better products, expanding product lines, and lowering production costs. Consider recent innovations made by profitable limited-service restaurants such as health-conscious menu items, drive-through windows, and delivery services. Through innovation, monopolistically competitive firms can maintain healthy profits for a very long time.

Oligopoly

Oligopoly is a type of market structure in which several firms—perhaps three, six, or a dozen—dominate production in an industry. Some economists argue that an oligopoly exists when the top four firms control at least 40 percent of the industry's total output. High barriers to entry discourage new firms from entering or exiting the industry. Barriers could include high costs for real capital, research, and national advertising. Barriers could be derived from exclusive rights to certain patent-protected technologies or government rules prohibiting competition, as is the case with state-run liquor stores. Even brand names and brand loyalties, which are strong in certain oligopolies, discourage the entry of new firms into an industry. High barriers to entry help oligopolists maintain high concentration ratios, as shown in Table 5.6.[27]

There are two forms of oligopoly: differentiated and pure. Firms operating in **differentiated oligopolies** produce similar but not identical products. For example, General Motors, Ford Motor, and Chrysler comprise a differentiated oligopoly because they dominate domestic production of different makes and models of automobiles in the U.S. auto

Table 5.6   Concentration Ratios for Selected Oligopolies

Industry	Percentage of Industry Output by Number of Firms	
	Top 4	Top 8
Manufacturing		
Differentiated Oligopolies		
Automobile	68	91
Breakfast cereal	80	92
Soft drinks	58	71
Pure Oligopolies		
Aluminum	77	95
Flat glass	69	98
Iron and steel	52	67
Retail		
Athletic footwear	68	77
Discount department stores	97	100
Home centers	93	93

Source: U.S. Bureau of the Census/American FactFinder, "Concentration Ratios: Share of Shipments Accounted for by the 4, 8, 20, and 50 Largest Companies for Industries: 2007," *2007 Economic Census*.

industry. Similarly General Mills, Kellogg, Post, and Quaker Oats dominate the breakfast cereal industry. Firms operating in **pure oligopolies**, on the other hand, produce a homogeneous or identical product. Most pure oligopolies produce industrial goods such as aluminum, plate glass, or steel. For example, major steel companies include U.S. Steel, Bethlehem Steel, and LTV, while major aluminum producers are Alcoa, Alumax, and Reynolds Metals.

Oligopolies are characterized by interdependent pricing, as competing firms necessarily respond to the price changes of rivals. In some cases interdependent pricing takes the form of price leadership. In this legal pricing strategy one oligopolist typically raises a product's price, hoping its rivals will follow suit. In other cases, oligopolists cut their prices, which could lead to a price war. A price war is a downward price spiral, each firm undercutting its rival's price to maintain a certain share of the market. Price wars, for example, have occurred in the U.S. airline industry. These price wars have offered temporary benefits to travelers but have hurt airline profits.

Monopoly

Monopoly is a type of market structure in which one firm is the sole producer of a good or service in an industry. In other words, the firm *is* the industry. Entry into and exit from monopolies is very difficult due to high barriers to entry such as the high costs of capital, patented technology, or exclusive access to an essential natural resource. Monopolies have the highest concentration ratio because all or nearly all of the industry's output is produced by just one firm. Because there are no significant competitors, the monopolist's output is considered unique. Practically speaking, this means that there are no close substitute goods available for consumers to buy. To limit the monopolist's market power, the government often regulates the product's price, quality, or availability.

A **natural monopoly** exists when a single larger firm is able to produce a product more efficiently than could a larger number of smaller competing firms. The natural monopoly benefits from the **economies of scale**, which occurs when the average cost of producing a product declines as more units are produced. For example, American Telephone and Telegraph (AT&T) was a natural monopoly in the long-distance telephone industry from the 1920s to early 1980s. It was simply more efficient to consolidate the U.S. telecommunications industry under a single roof during this period of time. Later new mobile and cellular technologies successfully challenged the AT&T monopoly, and new companies made telecommunications more competitive. Today many state and local governments allow natural monopolies to supply local goods and services such as cable television, electrical power, and trash collection.

A **technological monopoly** exists when a firm develops a new technology that it alone can use to produce a product. Such technologies are protected by patents, which are granted by the U.S. Patent and Trademark Office (PTO). In 2010 there were 520,000 patent applications filed with the PTO, and 244,000 patents were granted.[28] Americans also filed 45,000 patents with the World Intellectual Property Organization (WIPO) in 2010 to protect their technologies.[29]

A **government monopoly** exists when any level of government becomes the sole producer of a good or service. On the local level towns and cities are often the sole producers of some basic services, such as water and sewerage services. Typically these types of services would not ordinarily be supplied in sufficient quantity, or at a reasonable price, by smaller competitive firms in the private sector. The largest government monopoly at the national

Protecting intellectual property from piracy is a cornerstone of an orderly global economy. (Shutterstock .com)

level is the U.S. Postal Service (USPS), which maintains its monopoly on "first-class" mail delivery. The USPS employed 557,000 workers in 2011 and competes with private mail delivery firms in other markets, such as overnight delivery service.[30]

A **geographic monopoly** exists when one producer is the exclusive provider of a good or service to a geographic region. Geographic monopolies generally appear in remote locations that, at most, can support just one supplier. For instance, a general store in a small community may be able to survive if this is the only shop providing essential goods.

BUSINESS BEHAVIOR

Business behaviors are shaped in part by self-interest as firms seek to earn profits. Business behaviors are also influenced by certain rules and regulations imposed by governments, organizations, or the companies themselves.

Entrepreneurship and Entrepreneurs

An **entrepreneur** is a person who starts a new business, develops a new product, or devises a better way to produce a product. Entrepreneurs tend to be innovative thinkers and risk takers. The Small Business Administration (SBA) describes entrepreneurs as creative, goal-oriented, confident, independent, self-motivated, resilient, and organized. In short, entrepreneurs see business opportunities and accept the challenge of turning these opportunities into profitable business ventures.

It is often said that entrepreneurship is what entrepreneurs do. It follows that **entrepreneurship** occurs when someone creates or otherwise advances a business venture independently or within the supportive environment of an existing business. When entrepreneurial

---

ECONOMICS IN HISTORY: A Snapshot of U.S. Antitrust Legislation

The *Sherman Act of 1890* outlawed trusts and other business combinations that attempted to limit competition or restrain interstate commerce. Restraints on trade included price fixing by rival firms and agreements to divide market share among competing firms.

The *Clayton Antitrust Act of 1914* strengthened and expanded the scope of the Sherman Act by outlawing certain anticompetitive business practices such as tying agreements and interlocking directorates. A **tying agreement** stipulates that to purchase one item, the buyer must also purchase other goods, usually complementary goods, exclusively from the same seller. In an **interlocking directorate**, some of the same people sit on the board of directors for rival corporations.

The *Federal Trade Commission Act of 1914* created the Federal Trade Commission (FTC) to enforce the Clayton Act. Later the FTC took a leadership role in monitoring truth in advertising. The FTC is empowered to halt anticompetitive practices such as **collusion**—a type of illegal communication among rival firms to set prices, market share, or profits. Today the FTC is also the leading federal consumer protection agency.

The *Robinson-Patman Act of 1936* prevented discriminatory pricing, especially pricing schemes to benefit large buyers over smaller ones.

The *Wheeler-Lea Act of 1938* prohibited business deception, including false or misleading advertising. The act also created an antitrust agency within the U.S. Department of Justice, which shares responsibility for the enforcement of antitrust laws with the FTC.

The *Celler-Kefauver Antimerger Act of 1950* prohibited firms from buying the *assets* of another firm if the result was to substantially reduce competition in an industry.

The *Antitrust Procedures and Penalties Act* of 1974 stiffened the penalties on corporations and individuals involved in anticompetitive business practices such as price fixing.

---

activity results in the creation of a new business, it is called **venture initiation**. From 2001 to 2009 venture initiation in the U.S. economy accounted for the birth of an average of 623,000 new firms each year. During this same time period an average of 590,000 firms closed their doors each year, mostly due to owner choice rather than business bankruptcy. Predictably, these business "births" and "deaths" followed the ups and downs in the U.S. business cycle. Business births outnumbered deaths by 77,000 per year during the expansion phase of the business cycle (2003–2007). During the darker days of the Great Recession in 2008 and 2009, however, business deaths outnumbered births by 38,000 and 108,000 respectively.[31]

Entrepreneurial activity might also occur within existing businesses, often in large corporations. Corporate scientists, engineers, researchers, and others have created new products and instigated changes in the production, marketing, or distribution of goods. Since its founding in 1976, for example, Apple has supported entrepreneurial activity from within the corporation. Apple's product innovations have changed the technological landscape of the planet. Early innovations during the 1970s and 1980s ushered in the era of the personal computer, or PC. More recently, new generations of iPhones, iPods, and iPads have revolutionized telecommunications and data storage and retrieval. Not surprisingly, Apple's entrepreneurial co-founder Steven Jobs was named CEO of the Decade by *Fortune* magazine in 2009.

Business Costs, Profits, and Losses

Economists assume that the main goal of firms is to maximize profits. Firms earn profits when total revenues are greater than total costs. Hence, reducing the firm's costs of production is one way to become a more profitable business enterprise. The costs of production are payments made by firms for the factors of production. For most firms the largest cost of production is wages and salaries, which are payments for workers' labor. Other costs of production include rents, the payment for natural resources; interest, the payment for the money borrowed to purchase capital goods; and entrepreneurial profits, the payment for the risk-taking and innovation of entrepreneurs.

Firms divide their costs into two main categories: fixed costs and variable costs. **Fixed costs** (FCs) are business costs that do not change with a change in the firm's rate of output. That is, whether a firm produces 1,000 items or 10,000 items in a given time period, the FCs remain constant. Typical fixed costs include monthly rents on property, long-term leases on plant or equipment, insurance premiums on a facility, local property taxes, and interest payments to creditors. **Variable costs** (VCs), on the other hand, are business costs that change with a change in the rate of output. That is, VCs increase when production rises and decrease when production falls. The two main VCs are wages and the payments for raw materials and intermediate goods used in production. After all, to produce more goods firms need additional workers and materials. A firm's **total cost** (TC) is the sum of its FCs and VCs. In a market economy firms that are able to earn consistent profits survive, while firms that incur consistent losses tend to fail.

Business Bankruptcy

Bankruptcy is the legal recognition that a business, an individual, or even an entire city, cannot repay its debts. In the U.S. economy a bankruptcy code identifies the requirements and procedures for declaring bankruptcy. The Administrative Office of the U.S. Courts reported 1.2 million business and nonbusiness bankruptcy filings in 2012, a marked decline from the 1.6 million bankruptcy filings in 2010. In 2012 just 40,075 of the 1.2 million bankruptcy filings were business bankruptcies. Thus, business bankruptcies represented 3.3 percent of the bankruptcy filings in 2012, while the remaining 96.7 percent were personal bankruptcies.[32]

Many firms opt to file under Chapter 11 of the bankruptcy code. In 2012 about one-quarter of all business bankruptcy filings were under Chapter 11. Chapter 11 protects a struggling firm from creditors, in some cases for years, while the firm restructures its operations. The goal of a Chapter 11 filing is to give the firm time to return to profitability and to make good on some or all of its past debts—a process closely monitored by the courts.[33]

Chapter 11 bankruptcies have a mixed record of success in reviving struggling companies. For example, after filing for Chapter 11 bankruptcy in June 2009, U.S. auto giant General Motors (GM) emerged as a profitable firm in 2010. Under the terms of the bankruptcy, GM was able to sell assets, close certain assembly plants, cancel some contracts with auto dealerships and suppliers, renegotiate labor contracts, and restructure its debts. GM's business turnaround was also helped by billions of dollars in loans from the U.S. government. On the flip side Borders, a leading distributor of books and music, filed for Chapter 11bankruptcy in 2011. Unable to find a solution to the firm's economic woes, the Borders filing was changed to Chapter 7, the firm was dissolved, and its assets were sold off to repay some creditors.

In 2013 the largest municipal bankruptcy in U.S. history was filed by the city of Detroit, Michigan. Detroit's filing satisfied the main criteria established under Chapter 9 of the U.S. bankruptcy code, namely, that the city was drowning in debt and was unable to pay its bills. The city's bankruptcy filing was viewed as the opening salvo in a long legal struggle to determine how to equitably apportion the inevitable financial pain among creditors, city employees and pensioners, and others.

Business Mergers and Acquisitions

Business firms expand their operations in two ways. One way to expand is by building new production facilities, such as a factory, office building, shopping mall, or farm. A second way is through mergers and acquisitions (M&As). A **merger** occurs when two or more firms combine their assets, or equity, to form a single larger firm. Typically, mergers also result in a larger ownership base because investors from each company now share in the ownership of the new company. The merger between Exxon and Mobil to form the ExxonMobil Corporation in 1999 illustrates this process.

Acquisitions occur when one firm buys some or all of the ownership in a second firm. In many cases one firm can acquire a second firm by purchasing a portion of its stock or through other negotiated financial transfers. For example, pharmaceutical giant Pfizer negotiated a number of multibillion-dollar deals during the 2000s to acquire Warner-Lambert (2000), Pharmacia Corporation (2003), and Wyeth (2009). Today Pfizer is the world's largest pharmaceutical company.[34]

The primary motive for negotiating M&As is to generate additional business profits. There are a number of ways this goal might be achieved. First, M&As can reduce production costs. Through corporate downsizing redundant employees are laid off, and less efficient production facilities are closed. Second, an acquiring firm's output expands immediately because a seamless transfer of ownership does not interrupt production. Third, M&As provide instant access to the research and technology, patents and copyrights, brand names, and managerial expertise of the acquired firm. Fourth, M&As reduce production bottlenecks by bringing different phases of a larger production process under the control of a single management. Fifth, M&As provide access to new domestic or international markets. A cross-border M&A, for example, allows a multinational corporation to build on the acquired firm's business relationships, customer base, and channels of distribution. From 2005 to 2010 the value of cross-border M&As averaged more than half a trillion dollars per year.[35]

The three main types of mergers and acquisitions reflect different corporate strategies to increase the size and profitability of a firm. A **horizontal merger** combines competitors that sell similar products in the same market. The aggressive combination of oil refineries by John Rockefeller in the late 1800s created the Standard Oil monopoly. This combination of firms dominated one phase in the production—the refining of petroleum. A **vertical merger** combines firms that produce items needed in different phases of production. The combination of about 180 firms to create the U.S. Steel Corporation in 1901 was based on gaining control of production facilities at each phase in the production of steel, from the mining of iron ore to the manufacture and distribution of finished steel. A **conglomerate merger** combines unrelated firms from different industries into a single business enterprise. In its heyday during the 1960s and 1970s, International Telephone and Telegraph (ITT) combined about 350 diverse companies under its corporate umbrella, including the Hartford Insurance Company, Avis Rent-a-Car, and Sheraton Hotels.

Codes of Business Behavior

Nongovernmental organizations (NGOs), multilateral organizations, and corporations themselves have worked to improve corporate citizenship over the past few decades.

Under the banner of **corporate social responsibility** (CSR), various groups have defined the responsibilities that corporations, including transnational corporations (TNCs), have to workers and their families, consumers, investors, host governments, and indigenous peoples. The heart of CSR is that ethical business conduct benefits all stakeholders in an economy. By the 1970s corporations and other organizations had devised voluntary codes to guide the behaviors of businesses in domestic and global markets.

One type of code is the corporate code of conduct. A corporate code of conduct is written and implemented by a corporation. Under a corporate code of conduct, the firm establishes ethical standards to govern its treatment of workers, its dealings with indigenous peoples, and its use of the natural environment. One concern about a corporate code of conduct is that the corporation itself enforces the code. A second concern is that major corporations cannot always dictate business practices to their subcontractors. Subcontractors are firms hired to do a portion of the work in the production of a good, often in far-away low-wage countries.

A second type of code is the code of conduct for multinationals. Organizations outside of the corporation devise this type of code. One of the most recognized codes is the *OECD Guidelines for Multinational Enterprises.* This code was originally produced by the Organization for Economic Cooperation and Development (OECD) in 1976, and has been updated regularly, most recently in 2011. The guidelines oppose business practices that result in environmental degradation, child and forced labor, workplace discrimination, and bribery and other forms of corruption. They support human rights, transparency, honesty in advertising and marketing, consumer safety and privacy, technology transfers, effective worker associations, and respect for local laws and cultures.[36] Similar goals are found in the *Tripartite Declaration of Principles Concerning Multinational Enterprises and Social Policy*, a document produced by the International Labor Organization (ILO),[37] and the United Nation's *Global Compact*, as shown in the following passage.[38]

"Next!" Standard Oil's power over private businesses and the government, 1904. (Library of Congress)

PRIMARY DOCUMENT: The United Nations Proposes Ten Principles to Guide Business Behaviors

HUMAN RIGHTS

1. Businesses should support and respect the protection of internationally proclaimed human rights; and
2. make sure that they are not complicit in human rights abuses.

LABOR

3. Businesses should uphold the freedom of association and the effective recognition of the right to collective bargaining;
4. the elimination of all forms of forced and compulsory labor;
5. the effective abolition of child labor; and
6. the elimination of discrimination in respect of employment and occupation.

ENVIRONMENT

7. Businesses should support a precautionary approach to environmental challenges;
8. undertake initiatives to promote greater environmental responsibility; and
9. encourage the development and diffusion of environmentally friendly technologies.

ANTI-CORRUPTION

10. Businesses should work against corruption in all its forms, including extortion and bribery.

UN Global Compact, United Nations

CHAPTER 5 SUMMARY

Business Basics

- A firm is a business entity that produces products, while an industry consists of all firms that produce a similar product.
- Most firms are small businesses based on their annual revenues or on number of employees, but more that half of all jobs and wages are derived from large businesses.
- In the U.S. and other advanced economies, most output is produced by firms in the services-producing sector rather than the goods-producing sector.

Business Organization

- Sole proprietorships are firms owned by an individual and account for about 4 percent of all business receipts.
- Partnerships are firms owned by two or more people and account for nearly 15 percent of all business receipts.

- Corporations are firms owned by stockholders and run by professional managers. Corporations account for about 81 percent of all business receipts.
- Franchises consist of a parent company and related satellite companies.
- Other profit and nonprofit organizations produce products in the U.S. economy.

Market Structures

- Under perfect competition many independent firms produce a homogeneous product, but these firms have no market power.
- Under monopolistic competition 20 or more firms produce a differentiated product, and these firms have some market power.
- Under oligopoly a few firms produce differentiated or homogeneous products, and these firms have significant market power.
- Under monopoly a single firm produces a unique product, and this firm has the most market power.

Business Behavior

- Entrepreneurs are motivated by the lure of profits to start new businesses, develop new products, or devise better ways to produce products.
- Firms exist to earn profits, but sometimes business losses force firms into bankruptcy.
- Business mergers or acquisitions enable firms to expand their production of a product or diversify their product line.
- Codes of conduct are devised by nongovernmental organizations, multilateral institutions, and corporations to promote corporate social responsibility.

NOTES

1. U.S. Department of Commerce (DOC), Bureau of Economic Analysis (BEA), "Table 5. Value Added by Industry Group as a Percentage of GDP," *News Release*, April 25, 2013, www.bea.gov/iTable/print.cfm

2. U.S. Bureau of the Census, "Number of Firms, Number of Establishments, Employment, and Annual Payroll by Small Enterprise Employment Sizes for the United States, NAICS Sectors: 2010," *Statistics of U.S. Businesses*, October 2012; U.S. Small Business Administration (SBA), "Non-Employer Firms and Receipts by State, 1992, 1997–2010," www.sba.gov/advocacy/849/12162

3. U.S. Bureau of the Census, "Nonemployer Statistics," www.census.gov/econ/nonemployer

4. U.S. Bureau of the Census, "Number of Firms, Number of Establishments, Employment, and Annual Payroll by Small Enterprise Employment Sizes for the United States, NAICS Sectors: 2010," *Statistics of U.S. Businesses*, October 2012; U.S. Small Business Administration (SBA), "Non-Employer Firms and Receipts by State, 1992, 1997–2010," www.sba.gov/advocacy/849/12162

5. SBA/Office of Advocacy, "What Is a Small Business?" www.sba.gov/advo

6. SBA, "Small Business Size Regulations," www.sba.gov/content/small-business-size-regulations; SBA, "Summary of Size Standards by Industry," www.sba.gov/content/summary-size-standards-industry; SBA, "Am I a Small Business Concern?" www.sba.gov/content/am-i-small-business

7. U.S. Bureau of the Census, "Number of Firms, Number of Establishments, Employment, and Annual Payroll by Small Enterprise Employment Sizes for the United States, NAICS Sectors: 2010," *Statistics of U.S. Businesses*, October 2012.

8. SBA/Office of Advocacy, "What Is a Small Business?" www.sba.gov/advo

9. U.S. Bureau of the Census, "Number of Firms, Number of Establishments, Employment, and Annual Payroll by Small Enterprise Employment Sizes for the United States, NAICS Sectors: 2010," *Statistics of U.S. Businesses*, October 2012; U.S. Small Business Administration, "Non-Employer Firms and Receipts by State, 1992, 1997–2010," www.sba.gov/advocacy/849/12162; SBA/Office of Advocacy, "What Is a Small Business?" www.sba.gov/advo

10. "Largest U.S. Corporations," *Fortune*, May 20, 2013, F-1, F-2.

11. U.S. Department of Labor (DOL), Bureau of Labor Statistics (BLS), "Table A-21: Employed Persons by Industry and Occupation," www.bls.gov/web/empsit/cpseea21.pdf

12. DOC/BEA, "Industry Data: Value Added by Industry, 2004–2012," April 25, 2013, www.bea.gov

13. DOC/BEA, "Gross Output by Industry," November 13, 2012, www.bea.gov

14. DOL/BLS, "Table A-21: Employed Persons by Industry and Occupation," www.bls.gov/web/empsit/cpseea21.pdf

15. BEA, "Industry Data: Value Added by Industry, 2004–2012," www.bea.gov; DOC/BEA, "Gross Output by Industry," November 13, 2012, www.bea.gov

16. Central Intelligence Agency (CIA), *The World Factbook* (Washington, DC: CIA), 2011, www.cia.gov/library/publishers/the-world-factbook.geos/et.html

17. U.S. Bureau of the Census, "Table 744: Number of Tax Returns, Receipts, and Net Income by Type of Business, 1990 to 2008," *Statistical Abstract of the United States: 2012* (Washington, DC: U.S. Government Printing Office), 2011, 491.

18. Ibid.

19. Ibid.

20. "Entrepreneur 2013 Franchise 500," *Entrepreneur*, Entrepreneur Media, Inc., 2013, www.entrepreneur.com/franchises/index.html

21. Internal Revenue Service (IRS), "Limited Liability Company," www.irs.gov/business/small/article/0,,id=98277,00.html

22. General Motors, "General Motors China: Backgrounder," 1-2. http://media.GM.com/content/media

23. National Cooperative Business Association (NCBA), "Producer Cooperatives," www.ncba.coop/ncba/about-co-ops/co-op-types/producer-cooperatives

24. National Center for Charitable Statistics (NCCS)/Urban Institute, "Number of Nonprofit Organizations in the United States, 1999–2009," http://nccsdataweb.urban.org/PubApps/profile1.php

25. U.S. Department of Agriculture, *Crop Production Annual Summary*, January 2011, cited in "Table 861: Wheat; Acreage, Production, and Value by Leading States, 2008 to 2010," *Statistical Abstract of the United States, 2012* (Washington, DC: U.S. Government Printing Office), 2011, 551.

26. U.S. Bureau of the Census and American FactFinder, "Concentration Ratios: Share of Shipments Accounted for by the 4, 8, 20, and 50 Largest Companies for Industries: 2007," *2007* Economic Census, http://factfinder2.census.gov/faces/tableservices/jsf/pages/productview.html?fpt+document

27. Ibid.

28. U.S. Patent and Trademark Office (PTO), "U.S. Patent Statistics, Calendar Years 1963–2011," www.uspto.gov/web/offices/ac/idol/oeip/taf/us_stat.pdf

29. World Intellectual Property Organization (WIPO), "International Patent Filings Set New Record in 2011: Annex 1," *Press Release* (Geneva, Switzerland: WIPO), March 5, 2012, www.wipo.int/pressroom/articles/2012/article_0001.html

30. Ibid.

31. U.S. Bureau of the Census, "Table 765: Firm Births and Deaths by Employment Size of Enterprise, 1990–2007," *Statistical Abstract of the United States: 2012* (Washington, DC: U.S. Government Printing Office), 2011, 506; SBA/Office of Advocacy, "Frequently Asked Questions," January 2011.

32. Administrative Office of the U.S. Courts, "Bankruptcy Filings Decline in Calendar Year 2012," *News Item*, February 4, 2013 (Washington, DC: Administrative Office of the U.S. Courts), 1, www.news.uscourts.gov/bankruptcy-filings-decline-calendar-year-2012

33. Ibid.; Administrative Office of the U.S. Courts, "Reorganization Under the Bankruptcy Code," www.uscourts.gov/Federal Courts/Bankruptcy/Bankruptcy Basics/Chapter11.aspx

34. Pfizer, "Pfizer Inc: Exploring Our History, 2000-Present," www.pfizer.com/about/history/2000_present.jsp)

35. United Nations Conference on Trade and Development (UNCTAD), "Annex Table 1.3: Value of Cross-border M&As, by Region/Economy of Seller/Purchaser, 2005–May 2011," *World Investment Report: 2011* (New York: UNCTAD), 2011, 195.

36. Organization of Economic Cooperation and Development (OECD), "II. General Principles," *OECD Guidelines for Multinational Enterprises*, 2011 ed. (OECD Publishing, 2011).

37. International Labor Organization (ILO), *Tripartite Declaration of Principles Concerning Multinational Enterprises and Social Policy*, 4th ed. (Geneva, Switzerland: International Labor Office), 2006, 1-29.

38. United Nations, "The Ten Principles," *The UN Global Compact*, www.unglobalcompact.org/AboutTheGC/TheTenPrinciples/index.html

6

Workers and Worker Power

In the spring of 2013 the civilian labor force in the United States was comprised of 155.2 million workers.[1] The economic behaviors of workers are influenced by incentives such as wages and salaries. In the American economy the forces of supply and demand determine the wages for most workers. Laws and other government regulations also influence some wages. Over time labor power in the United States grew significantly due to labor activism, prolabor legislation, and changing attitudes among employers about their responsibilities to employees. In recent years right to work laws and the offshoring of some production have affected worker power in some labor markets.

WORKERS AND WORKER BEHAVIOR

Labor, or human resources, represents the human input in production. Labor is generally considered the most important input, or factor, of production. Without labor other factors of production, such as capital goods and natural resources, would remain idle and nonproductive. Some labor is mainly manual, including many types of jobs in construction, manufacturing, mining, and agriculture. Other labor is mainly intellectual, including many jobs in education, law, medicine, and engineering. The labor of entrepreneurs is instrumental in the creation of new businesses, the wellspring of jobs for many workers. Economists sometimes view entrepreneurship as a fourth factor of production. From an economic perspective, labor mobilizes the other inputs and in exchange expects monetary compensation, usually in the form of a wage or salary.

U.S. Labor Force

The **labor force** in the United States consists of individuals who are 16 years of age or older and who are either employed or actively seeking a job. In the spring of 2013 the civilian labor force numbered 155.2 million workers, of which 143.6 million were employed and 11.6 million were unemployed. The **employment rate**, or percentage of the labor force that had a job, was 92.5 percent. The **unemployment rate**, or percentage of the labor force without a job, was 7.5 percent.[2] The U.S. labor force experienced phenomenal growth over the past century, climbing from 28.5 million in 1900 to 155 million in 2013.[3] Table 6.1 shows the dramatic growth of the U.S. civilian labor force, by decade,

New technologies have created more flexible work environments, including opportunities to work from home. (Mudplucker/Dreamstime.com)

since 1950. It also shows the labor force participation rate, or percentage of the working age population in the labor force, during the same period.[4] Note that the U.S. population roughly doubled during this 60-year period, and the labor force increased by more than 90 million workers.

To create a profile of the American labor force, economists often categorize workers by job type, gender, educational background, or other characteristic. One characteristic of the U.S. labor force is the dominant position of service sector jobs. In 2012 the nonfarm services-providing industries employed about 82 percent of all workers in the private sector of the economy. Important job categories within the services-providing sector include

Table 6.1   U.S. Population and Labor Force, 1950–2010

Year	U.S. Population (millions)	Adult Population (millions)	Labor Force (millions)	Labor Force Participation Rate
1950	151	107	62	58.3
1960	179	117	70	59.4
1970	203	137	83	60.4
1980	227	168	107	63.8
1990	249	189	126	66.5
2000	281	210	141	67.2
2010	309	238	154	64.7

Source: U.S. Bureau of the Census, "No. 1," No. 560," "No. 561," *Statistical Abstract of the United States: 2002* (Washington, DC: U.S. Government Printing Office), 2001, 8, 367; U.S. Bureau of the Census, "Table 1," "Table 586," *Statistical Abstract of the United States: 2012*, 8, 377; Ben J. Wattenberg, *Statistical History of the United States: From Colonial Times to the Present*, Series D11-25 (New York: Basic Books), 1976, 127–128.

Employment of the U.S. Labor Force: 1900

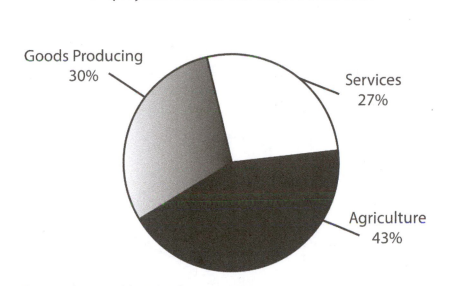

Figure 6.1   Employment of the U.S. Labor Force, 1900
Source: U.S. Bureau of the Census, *The Statistical History of the United States: From Colonial Times to the Present*, 139.

transportation and public utilities, wholesale and retail trade, finance and insurance, real estate, and a wide variety of other services in the realms of health, entertainment, business maintenance, law, education, auto repair, and others. In addition, most public sector, or government jobs also provided services such as mail delivery, education, and law enforcement.

The goods-producing sector accounted for 16 percent of all nonfarm private sector jobs in 2012. The main goods-producing industries are associated with manufacturing, construction, and mining. The agricultural sector employed the remaining 2 percent of jobs in the farming, dairying, fishing, and forestry industries in 2012. Today, some economists categorize agriculture as a subset of the goods-producing sector.

The Labor Department predicts that 20.5 million new jobs will be created between 2010 and 2020—18 million in the services-providing industries and the remainder in goods-producing and agricultural industries. This distribution of jobs in 2012 is contrasted with U.S. employment patterns during the early twentieth century in Figure 6.1 and Figure 6.2.[5]

A second feature of the U.S. labor force is the growing importance of women workers in American labor markets. The expanding role for women in the labor force is best illustrated by comparing the labor force participation rate for men and women over time. For example, in early 2013 the overall labor force participation rate for all working age people was 63.3 percent, which meant that nearly two-thirds of all working age Americans were in the labor force. Reported by gender, the participation rate for men was about 70 percent and for women about 57 percent. The participation rate was far wider between men and women in the past, however, as shown in Table 6.2.[6]

A third feature of the U.S. labor force is the high educational level of American workers. The educational attainment of American workers increased dramatically over the past

Employment of the U.S. Labor Force: 2012

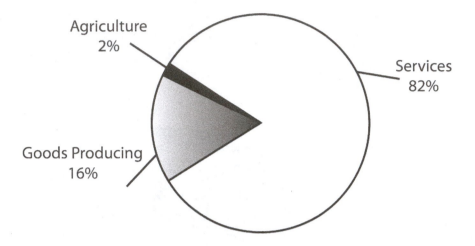

Figure 6.2   Employment of the U.S. Labor Force, 2012
Source: U.S. Department of Labor/Bureau of Labor Statistics, "The Employment Situation—April 2012, Table A-8," May 4, 2012.

century. For example, in 1900 just 6 percent of the general population had earned a high school diploma. By 2010, 87 percent of all Americans were at least high school graduates, and 30 percent of the adult population had earned a four-year college degree or more.[7] Similarly, the educational attainment by the U.S. labor force increased steadily during the past century. By 2013 about 91.7 percent of all employed workers aged 25 years or older had earned at least a high school diploma, and more than one-third of these workers had earned a bachelor's degree or higher. Economists view education as a key factor in developing a society's human capital—the acquired skills or competencies held by workers. Table 6.3 shows the educational attainment of American workers in 2013.[8] Note that workers with higher levels of education are more likely to find employment than lesser educated workers.

A fourth feature of the American labor force is its growing flexibility. In recent years workers have had greater choice in determining the time and location of their employment. For example, the number of full-time workers on flexible schedules more than doubled from 1985 to 2004, climbing from 12.4 million workers to 27 million during this period.

Table 6.2   U.S. Labor Force Participation Rate by Gender, 1900–2013

Year	*Women*		*Men*	
	Number (1000s)	*Participation Rate*	*Number (1000s)*	*Participation Rate*
1900	5,319	18.8	30,092	80.0
1950	18,389	33.9	43,819	83.7
2013	72,617	57.2	82,621	69.8

Source: U.S. Department of Labor/Bureau of Labor Statistics, "Table A-1," *The Employment Situation—April 2013*, May 3, 2013; Ben J. Wattenberg, *Statistical History of the United States: From Colonial Times to the Present*, Series D11-25 (New York: Basic Books), 1976, 127–128.

Table 6.3   Educational Attainment and Employment Status, April 2013

Educational Attainment	Number in Civilian Labor Force (1000s)	Percentage of Labor Force	Unemployment Rate
Less than high school diploma	11,072	8.3	11.4
High school graduate, no college	36,224	27.0	7.2
Some college or an associate degree	37,058	27.7	6.0
Bachelor's degree and higher	49,663	37.0	3.6

Source: U.S. Department of Labor, Bureau of Labor Statistics, "Table A-4: Educational Status of the Civilian Population 25 Years and over by Educational Attainment," *News Release*, May 3, 2013.

Flexible schedules typically allow workers to start and end their workdays at nonstandard times. By the early 2000s the highest concentrations of workers that benefited from flexible work schedules were employed in private sector managerial and professional occupations or in public sector jobs at the federal or state levels. In addition, in the early 2000s about 20 million workers opted to perform at least some of their regular work at their homes rather than the factory, office, or other workplace. New technology supported this trend toward work in the home. By the early 2000s about 80 percent of those who did some work at home used a computer, and most also used email or the Internet while working at home.[9]

Worker Behavior

Workers respond to market incentives in much the same way that consumers, savers, and other groups do. That is, workers exercise their freedom of choice in the labor markets. In the American economy workers are free to choose an occupation, free to train for alternative employment, and free to set a career path that best satisfies their financial and psychological needs. Workers are also free to make choices about how much time they devote to work and leisure. From an economic perspective, **work** is time spent in paid productive activity. **Leisure** represents all other uses of time such as recreational activities, household chores, shopping, and even sleep. All workers make trade-offs between work time and leisure time. A *trade-off* occurs when people choose to use a resource, in this case time, in one way rather than another. A worker's final decision about how much time should be spent on the job, or spent in leisure activities, is influenced by a number of factors, including the substitution effect and the income effect of a change in wages.

The **substitution effect of a wage increase** states that as the wage rate increases, workers will work more hours. In other words, there is a positive relationship between the wage rate and hours worked, as shown in Figure 6.3. In this example an increase in the wage rate from $4 per hour to $6 per hour causes the worker to trade off five hours of leisure to work five additional hours. As the wage rate continues to increase, additional hours of leisure are foregone so that the worker can work still more hours. The traditional labor supply curve illustrates this positive relationship between wage increases and the corresponding increases in the quantity of labor supplied. Where the substitution effect of a wage increase dominates, the labor supply curve is upward sloping to the northeast.

The **income effect of a wage increase** states that as the wage rate increases, workers will work fewer hours. In other words, there is an inverse relationship between the higher wage rate and the number of hours a person is willing to work. The income effect seems to contradict the substitution effect. But consider the financial position of a popular entertainer, a skilled brain surgeon, or a top rock star. In each of these occupations the worker is able to

Labor Supply Schedule: The Substitution Effect

Wage Rate (per hour)	Number of Hours Worked (per week)
$4.00	5
$6.00	10
$8.00	15
$10.00	20
$12.00	25

Labor Supply Curve: The Substitution Effect

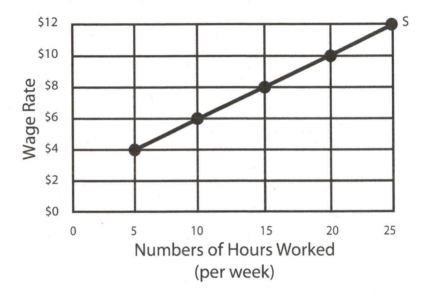

Figure 6.3   The Substitution Effect of a Wage Increase

command a high wage for each performance and, over time, each earns a high income. Under these conditions the entertainer, surgeon, or rock star may choose to reduce the number of performances, in effect trading off work to have more leisure time. The inverse relationship between wages and the quantity of labor supplied is shown in Figure 6.4. Note that the supply curve of labor tends to travel "backward" to the northwest. In this example the worker's compensation per performance increases from $2 million, to $4 million, and so on, which enables this worker to reduce time spent on the job.

Wage Determination

The forces of supply and demand determine the wages for workers in most labor markets in the U.S. economy. Labor is exchanged for wages in the nation's factor market. In the factor market households supply labor resources, and business firms and other employers demand labor resources.

Labor Supply Schedule: The Income Effect

Wage Rate (per performance)	Number of Performances (per month)
$2,000,000	5
$4,000,000	4
$6,000,000	3
$8,000,000	2
$10,000,000	1

Labor Supply Curve for a Popular Entertainer (wage rate per performance in $ millions)

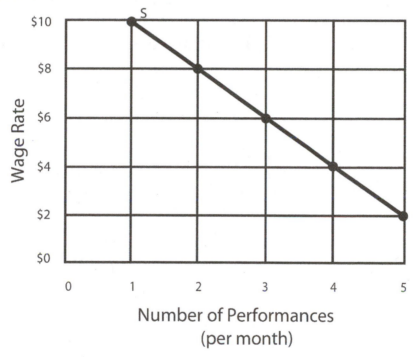

Figure 6.4   The Income Effect of a Wage Increase

On the *supply side* of the labor market, there is a direct relationship between the wage rate and the quantity of labor workers are willing to supply. That is, an increase in the wage rate typically results in an increase in the quantity of labor supplied, while a decrease in the wage rate causes a decrease in the quantity of labor supplied. This direct relationship between wages and the quantity supplied of labor is illustrated by the upward sloping labor supply curve shown in Figure 6.5. At a relatively low wage rate of $6 per hour, for example, just 2,000 laborers are willing to work. At a relatively high wage rate of $14 per hour, however, 10,000 laborers are willing to work.

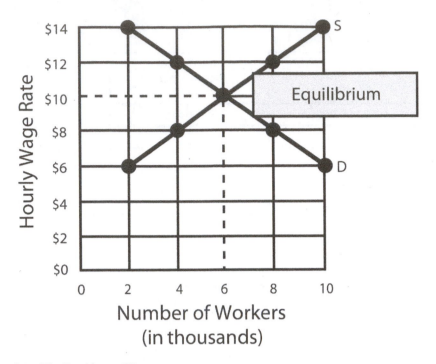

Figure 6.5   The Equilibrium Wage

On the *demand side* of the market, there is an inverse relationship between the wage rate and the quantity of labor firms are willing to hire. That is, an increase in the wage rate decreases the quantity of labor demanded by firms, while a decrease in the wage rate causes an increase in the quantity of labor demanded by firms. This inverse relationship between wages and the quantity of labor demanded is illustrated by the downward sloping labor demand curve shown in Figure 6.5. At a relatively high wage rate of $14 per hour, for example, employers are willing to hire just 2,000 workers. At a relatively low wage rate of $6 per hour, however, employers are willing to hire 10,000 workers.

An **equilibrium wage** occurs at the point of intersection between the labor supply curve and the labor demand curve, also shown in Figure 6.5. In essence, the equilibrium wage and quantity is the best compromise between the interests of the workers and the firms. Note that the equilibrium wage is $10 per hour. At this hourly wage rate the quantity of workers supplied is equal to the quantity of workers demanded, in this case 6,000 workers.

So why do some occupations command a high wage or salary, while other occupations offer lesser compensation? Supply factors and demand factors help explain differences in workers' wages. The supply side of a labor market may be influenced by the amount of education or training required in an occupation, or by the location or workplace conditions in certain occupations. For example, there are relatively few brain surgeons because of the intensity of their study and the cost of higher education. As a result, these surgeons are in short supply, and they command a high wage. Like brain surgeons, other highly educated professionals such as physicians, lawyers, and engineers earn higher wages, on average, than lesser-educated workers, as shown in Figure 6.6.[10] Occupations that are located in remote regions, or that have unpleasant or dangerous workplace conditions also tend to command

Figure 6.6   Education and Wage Income, 2013
Source: U.S. Department of Labor/Bureau of Labor statistics, "Table 5," *News Release*, April 18, 2013.

higher wages. This is because it is more difficult to find qualified workers to accept jobs in remote or dangerous workplaces.

The demand for labor is a **derived demand**. That is, the demand for a certain type of worker is *derived* from the demand for the output produced by that worker. The U.S. Department of Labor recently predicted a significant increase in the demand for workers in computer and information technology (IT), health care, personal care, social services, and construction between 2010 and 2020. Hence, experts anticipate significant growth in the number of jobs that produce these services such as IT specialists, registered nurses, home health care and medical aides, physical therapists, carpenters, and plumbers. Conversely, the Department of Labor predicted slower growth or even declines in certain production and agricultural fields from 2010 to 2020. Job losses are expected in occupations such as shoe machine and sewing machine operators, mail sorters, telephone operators, and agricultural workers.[11]

Government and Wages

The government influences wage rates for some workers in the U.S. economy through federal legislation or economic policies. Most federal laws related to wage rates and the conditions of employment promote equal opportunity and equity in the American workplace. For example, the Equal Pay Act of 1963 requires employers to pay the same wage rate to workers performing identical jobs, regardless of the worker's gender. This act allows differences in pay if the differential is based on seniority, worker productivity, or merit incentives, however.

Similarly, under Title VII of the Civil Rights Act of 1964, it became unlawful for employers "to fail or refuse to hire or to discharge any individual, or otherwise discriminate against any individual with respect to his compensation, terms, conditions, or privileges of employment, because of such individual's race, color, religion, sex, or national origin."[12] The Civil Rights Act of 1964 created a new federal agency, the Equal Employment Opportunity Commission (EEOC), to ensure compliance with antidiscrimination laws. Since the mid-1960s other landmark legislation has been enacted by Congress to promote equality of opportunity in the workplace, including the Age Discrimination in Employment Act of 1967 and the Americans with Disabilities Act of 1990.

Governments, mainly at the state level, also grapple with the issue of pay equity. One controversial approach to dealing with pay equity is to enact comparable worth legislation. **Comparable worth** refers to the equalization of pay rates between different jobs in a workplace, jobs that require essentially the same types of skills and that have about the same value to the employer. Supporters of comparable worth legislation argue that laws are needed to reduce wage rate discrepancies between jobs traditionally held by women and those held by men. The fact that median salaries of women were just 81.2 percent of those earned by men in 2013 fueled demands by some advocacy groups and legislators to support comparable worth laws.[13] Opponents counter that such government intervention disrupts the efficiency of labor markets, which rely on the forces of supply and demand to establish an equilibrium wage. Further, opponents argue that there are legitimate reasons for wage discrepancies between jobs, including differences in education or training, productivity, seniority, and personal choices related to job selection and family responsibilities. During the 2000s a number of state legislatures considered bills compatible with the goals of comparable worth.

The most direct way the government affects wages is through the **minimum wage**, a government-imposed price floor on the hourly wage an employer can offer to an employee. The first national minimum wage was established in 1938 by the Fair Labor Standards Act (FLSA). Since 1938 the federal minimum wage has been raised 23 times, from the original $0.25 per hour to $7.25 per hour, where it has rested since 2009. The FLSA defined the maximum workweek, which was originally 44 hours and today is 40 hours of work per week. A wage rate of at least time and a half for the hours employees work beyond the maximum workweek is required in most jobs. In addition, by 2013 nineteen state governments and the District of Columbia had established their own minimum wages above the federal rate of $7.25. Some states make annual cost-of-living adjustments to their state minimum wage rate to account for inflation.[14] The timing and size of increases in the minimum wage have been debated since the late 1930s.

Supporters of a higher minimum wage argue that an hourly wage rate of $7.25 cannot provide for a minimum standard of living in the United States. For example, a full-time minimum wage employee who worked 40 hours per week for 52 weeks in 2012 would earn an annual income of just $15,080. If this employee headed a family of four, the household's income would fall $8,601 *below* the poverty line of $23,681.[15] In addition, the federal minimum wage is not adjusted annually for inflation. As a result, the minimum wage automatically declines in value as inflation eats away at the purchasing power of the dollar.

Opponents of a higher minimum wage argue that higher wages increase business costs and may cause employers to cut jobs in some lower-skilled labor markets. They also note that only a small percentage of the U.S. labor force earns the minimum wage and that the wage rate for many of these workers quickly rises above the minimum standard. In 2012 there were 3.6 million workers—about 4.7 percent of all hourly paid employees in the United States—earning an hourly of wage $7.25 or less.[16] In addition, opponents of a higher minimum wage argue that many minimum wage workers hold part-time jobs and are not the primary breadwinners in the household.

The Hiring Decision
The hiring decision deals with whether a firm should hire workers, fire workers, or maintain its current workforce. The desire to maximize profits helps firms determine the

Table 6.4   The Hiring Decision at Dan's Deli

1 Number of Workers	2 Deli's Total Output	3 Marginal Product (MP)	4 Marginal Revenue Product (MRP)	5 Marginal Factor Cost (MFC)	6 Profit or Loss
0	0	0	0	0	0
1	50	50	$250	$75	$175
2	110	60	$300	$75	$225
3	130	20	$100	$75	$25
4	145	15	$75	$75	0
5	150	5	$25	$75	−$50

number of workers to employ. The core hiring principle for a profit-maximizing business is that the firm will employ an additional worker only if the additional revenue generated by this worker is greater than or equal to the additional cost of the worker, namely, the worker's wage. In the language of the economist, a firm will hire a worker if the marginal revenue product (MRP) is greater than or equal to the marginal factor cost (MFC). Consider the hiring decision for Dan's Deli, as shown in Table 6.4. For this case, assume that the price of a sandwich produced at the deli is $5 and that the daily wage of $75 per worker is the only cost of production.

Table 6.4 shows that Dan's Deli could hire from one to five workers. If the firm hires one worker (column 1), the deli produces 50 sandwiches (column 2). The additional output, called the marginal product (MP), is also 50 sandwiches (column 3) because production jumped from 0 to 50 as a result of hiring the first worker. Recall that the word "marginal" means additional, or the next. Hence, the marginal product is the additional output that results from hiring each worker. The marginal revenue product (MRP) is the additional revenue earned by the firm because of this first worker, in this case $250 (column 4). This is because 50 sandwiches are sold at a price of $5 per sandwich. The marginal factor cost (MFC) is the daily $75 wage for each worker (column 5). The MFC represents the additional cost for each factor of production (each worker) hired by the firm. When the first worker is hired, Dan's Deli earns a profit of $175 (column 6). This is because the marginal revenue product ($250) generated by the first worker is greater than the marginal factor cost ($75) of this worker.

Table 6.4 shows that Dan's Deli earns additional profits when the first (+$175), second (+$225), and third workers (+$25) are hired. Thus, to maximize profits Dan's Deli would certainly hire the first three workers. The fourth worker's MRP of $75 is equal to this worker's MFC of $75. Should this fourth worker be hired? Economists support the hiring of the fourth worker, even though the firm earns zero profit from this worker. The hiring of the fourth worker sends an invisible signal to the firm to stop hiring at this point, however. The fifth worker shown in Table 6.4 should not be hired because this fifth worker generates just $25 in additional revenue but costs the firm $75 in wages—a net loss of $50 per day. Economists conclude that the profit-maximizing firm should hire additional workers up to and including the point where the MRP = MFC.

Some hiring decisions have stirred controversy in recent years. For example, some people wonder why chief executive officers (CEOs) for major corporations collect multimillion-dollar wage and bonus packages even when their corporations suffer losses. Others marvel at the yearly wage and bonus packages of highly paid professional athletes and entertainers.

Questions about what constitutes fair compensation for our modern-day captains of industry and other celebrities help illustrate the difficulties of applying the hiring decision to certain occupations.

LABOR UNIONS AND WORKER POWER

The U.S. labor movement represents the collective actions of workers to improve their wages and working conditions. The driving force behind the U.S. labor movement has traditionally been labor unions. A **labor union** is a formal association of workers designed to improve the condition of labor in the workplace. The main power of a labor union is collective bargaining. **Collective bargaining** empowers union representatives to negotiate on behalf of the entire membership, in effect increasing the market power of workers in negotiations with the firm's management. Traditionally, the wage and benefit packages negotiated under a union banner have outpaced wages and benefits negotiated in comparable nonunion workplaces. Labor unions have also influenced labor reforms and labor legislation at the state and national levels. Labor unions became a countervailing power to the growth of large and powerful manufacturers during America's industrialization process.

U.S. Labor Movement: The Early Years

The origins of the American labor movement can be traced to the first glimmers of worker consciousness, which occurred more than 200 years ago. In the late 1700s, long before the Industrial Revolution took root in the United States, conflicts between employers and their workers were already taking place in certain trades.

By the mid-1800s the first national unions in the United States were formed. One short-lived union was the National Trades Union (1834–1837), or NTU, which was founded in New York City. The NTU recruited members from local crafts unions, mainly from eastern cities located between Boston, Massachusetts, and Baltimore, Maryland. The union supported bread-and-butter reforms such as the 10-hour workday and equal pay for equal work.

Shortly thereafter, William H. Sylvis organized the National Labor Union (1866–1872), or NLU. The NLU was a loose confederation of skilled and unskilled unions. Sylvis believed that union power was best achieved through mass membership. The NLU supported the eight-hour workday, immigration restrictions, the creation of a federal department of labor, and improved working conditions for women. Neither the NTU nor NLU made much progress in achieving their goals.

The American labor movement was bolstered by the creation of the Noble and Holy Order of the Knights of Labor by Uriah H. Stephens in 1869. At first the Philadelphia-based Knights was organized as a secret society of wage earners. Secrecy was necessary to avoid reprisals, such as blacklisting, by employers. In 1879 Terence V. Powderly assumed leadership of the Knights. He removed the veil of secrecy from the organization. His vision was to create a mass union for nearly all workers—skilled and unskilled, black and white, men and women. By 1886 membership in the Knights, now renamed the Knights of Labor, swelled to more than 700,000 workers. The Knights demanded the eight-hour workday, equal wages for women, and prohibitions against child labor, convict labor, and contract labor. On a broader scale, the Knights also sought reforms to promote a more equitable distribution of wealth and the introduction of a federal progressive income tax. A series of unauthorized and unsuccessful strikes, and violence at a union-sponsored rally

Sweatshop in a New York City tenement, 1889. Photograph by Jacob Riis. (Library of Congress)

in Chicago in 1886, crippled the reputation of the Knights. During the 1890s the Knights of Labor faded into obscurity.

The American Federation of Labor (AFL) was founded in 1886 by Samuel Gompers as a federation of skilled craft unions. Within a few years the AFL replaced the Knights of Labor as the chief voice of the American labor movement. As a **craft union,** the AFL restricted membership to unions comprised of skilled workers such as carpenters, masons, or printers. Unskilled workers, African Americans, and women were systematically excluded from the AFL. Gompers and the AFL supported "pure and simple" unionism to improve workers' wages, working hours, and working conditions. AFL membership topped 4 million in 1920, which accounted for about 80 percent of all unionized workers. By the mid-1920s unionized workers' average wages had outpaced nonunionized workers in similar occupations. In addition, the average workweek was shorter for unionized than nonunionized workers.[17] The AFL struggled to maintain membership levels during the 1920s and 1930s due to a generally unsympathetic political environment, internal squabbles, and the ravages of the Great Depression.

In 1935 an industrial union originally called the Committee for Industrial Organization was founded as an alternative to the crafts-dominated AFL. Three years later, in 1938, this union's name was changed to the Congress of Industrial Organizations (CIO). As an **industrial union**, the CIO recruited all workers within an industry regardless of their skills, gender, or race. John L. Lewis, the CIO's first president, saw great potential for industrial unions as a means to expand worker power in the United States, particularly in the growing mass-production industries such as automobiles, textiles, rubber, and steel. Despite some labor unrest during the Great Depression and the bitter rift between the newly formed CIO and its rival, the AFL, union membership grew rapidly from the

Table 6.5 Union Membership in the United States, 1910–2010

| | Union Membership in the United States | | | | |
Year	Total Number (1000s)	Percentage of Labor Force	AFL (1000s)	CIO (1000s)	Indep. Unions (1000s)
1910	2,116	8.2	1,562	–	554
1930	3,632	11.6	2,961	–	671
1950	14,823	31.5	8,494	3,713	2,616
1970	20,752	27.4	AFL-CIO	15,978	4,773
1990	16,740	16.1	AFL-CIO	13,933	2,807
2010	14,715	11.9	AFL-CIO	12,200	2,515

Source: Ben J. Wattenberg, *Statistical History of the United States: From Colonial Times to the Present* (New York: Basic Books), 1976, 127, 176–177; U.S. Bureau of the Census, "No. 628," *Statistical Abstract of the United States: 2002* (Washington, DC: U.S. Government Printing Office), 2001, 411; U.S. Bureau of the Census, "Table 644," *Statistical Abstract of the United States: 2012* (Washington, DC: U.S. Government Printing Office), 2011, 429.

1940s to the 1960s, as shown in Table 6.5.[18] In 1955 a merger between the AFL and CIO created the AFL-CIO, an action that restored some unity to the American labor movement.

Pro-labor legislation during the presidency of Franklin D. Roosevelt (1933–1945) gave crucial support to the American labor movement. The National Labor Relations Act (1935), more commonly called the Wagner Act, secured workers' right to form unions and to bargain collectively with employers. This act also created the National Labor Relations Board (NLRB) to prevent unfair labor practices by employers or by labor unions. In addition, the Fair Labor Standards Act (1938) established a minimum wage of $0.25 per hour for some workers, a maximum workweek of 44 hours, and overtime pay for hours worked beyond this maximum.

ECONOMICS IN HISTORY: The Mollies and the Wobblies: The Radical Fringe of the Labor Movement

Labor radicalism occurred mainly at the fringes of the American labor movement. Two of the most militant of these fringe groups were the Molly Maguires and the Industrial Workers of the World (IWW).

The Molly Maguires, often called the Mollies, was a secret society comprised of Irish immigrants. The Mollies had a long and stormy history marked by violence against the British and the propertied classes in Ireland. The first Mollies arrived in United States in the mid-1840s, and many congregated in the coal mining regions of Pennsylvania. Here they worked in company towns—towns owned and operated by the mine owners. Low wages, dangerous working conditions, and abusive bosses mobilized the Mollies, who resorted to sabotage and physical violence against mine owners. In the early 1870s dozens of Mollies were tried and convicted for their crimes, but little was done to alleviate the horrific working conditions in the mines.

The Industrial Workers of the World (IWW), or Wobblies, was a revolutionary labor organization founded in Chicago in 1905. The Wobblies grew in strength during the early 1900s under the leadership of William (Big Bill) Haywood. The Wobblies directly challenged the capitalist economic system, including private property rights and the practice of wage labor. Under the slogan "One Big Union," the Wobblies supported an extreme version of industrial unionism and scored some labor victories in the mining and lumbering regions of the Pacific Northwest. The Wobblies' influence soon faded due to internal disputes, government opposition, their opposition to American participation in World War I, and the antiunion climate of the 1920s.

U.S. Labor Movement: The Modern Era

The merger of the AFL and CIO in 1955 created a new union, the AFL-CIO. With a membership of 16 million workers from 139 local affiliates, the great majority of unionized workers in the United States belonged to the AFL-CIO. The 1950s and early 1960s also represented the heyday of organized labor in the United States, when over 30 percent of the civilian labor force was unionized. Since that time the **union membership rate**—the percentage of U.S. workers who belong to a union—has declined steadily. In 2012 the union membership rate was 11.3 percent, which accounted for 14.4 million American workers.[19] Table 6.6 summarizes the state of union membership in the United States.[20]

The decline in union membership over the past half-century is rooted in some fundamental economic changes in the American economy. First, an improved standard of living for most Americans made workers less inclined to form or join unions. Second, federal legislation addressed some important workplace issues. For example, the Occupational Safety and Health Administration (1970) established safety regulations in the workplace. Third, the shift from a manufacturing to a services-producing economy drained workers from traditional union strongholds such as auto manufacturing plants and textile mills. Fourth, forces associated with globalization, including an avalanche of new global competitors and new offshoring opportunities to low-wage countries, reduced union power. Fifth, unions suffered from negative public opinion due, in part, to costly labor contracts and union involvement in political campaigns.

Some government policies also reduced the power of unions. At the federal level the Taft-Hartley Act (1947) banned the **closed shop**, an arrangement that required employers to hire only labor union members. This act also broadened the authority of government to block certain strikes through injunctions. The Landrum-Griffin Act (1959), which was enacted after union corruption was exposed in the 1950s, set rules for the selection of union leaders and for the conduct of union business.

Table 6.6   Characteristics of U.S. Union Membership, 2012

Characteristics	*Union Membership*	*Data*
Public sector	Union members (number)	7.3 mil.
	Union membership (rate)	35.9%
Private sector	Union members (number)	7.0 mil.
	Union membership (rate)	6.6%
Gender	Men	12.0%
	Women	10.5%
Race/ethnicity	African American	13.4%
	Asian	9.6%
	Hispanic	9.8%
	White	11.1%
Weekly earnings	Union workers	$943
	Nonunion workers	$742
High membership	Teachers, police officers, firefighters, transportation, utilities, construction workers	
Low membership	Retail sales, agriculture, financial services, food preparation	

Source: U.S. Department of Labor, Bureau of Labor Statistics, "Union Membership Summary (2012)," *Economic News Release*, January 23, 2013.

Despite the decline in the union membership rate since the 1960s, today's labor movement shows signs of vitality. The AFL-CIO, the flagship organization in the U.S. labor movement, continues its commitment "to improving the lives of working families, to bringing fairness and dignity to the workplace and securing social equity in the Nation."[21] In 2012 the AFL-CIO represented more than 12 million workers from 57 associated national and international labor unions. Its membership includes workers from the services-producing and goods-producing sectors and from all socio-economic groups. Its mission reflects the need to mobilize the power of workers and give voice to their concerns at the local, national, and international levels.

There are some encouraging signs for organized labor in the United States. For example, the number and percentage of public sector employees enrolled under a union banner increased significantly in recent decades. In 2012, 35.9 percent of all government employees belonged to unions. And while just 6.6 percent of all private sector workers were union members, many of the nation's leading industries were heavily unionized, such as construction, utilities, transportation, and telecommunications. Union leaders also point to significantly higher pay for union labor, as the median weekly wage for union workers is 27 percent higher than the wage of nonunion workers.[22]

The Labor Movement in the Global Economy

Since its founding in 1919, the International Labor Organization (ILO) has advocated for the rights of labor on a global level by coordinating and strengthening the efforts of national labor unions. In 1946 the ILO became a specialized agency within the United

---

PRIMARY DOCUMENT: The International Labor Organization Establishes Fundamental Rights for Workers

The International Labor Conference

1. Recalls:
    (a) that in freely joining the ILO, all Members have endorsed the principles and rights set out in its Constitution and in the Declaration of Philadelphia, and have undertaken to work towards attaining the overall objectives of the Organization to the best of their resources . . .
    (b) that these principles and rights have been expressed and developed in the form of specific rights and obligations in Conventions recognized both inside and outside the Organization.

2. Declares that all Members, even if they have not ratified the Convention in question, have an obligation arising from the very fact of membership in the Organization to respect, to promote and to realize, in good faith and in accordance with the Constitution, the principles concerning the fundamental rights which are the subject of those Conventions, namely:
    (a) freedom of association and the effective recognition of the right to collective bargaining;
    (b) the elimination of all forms of forced or compulsory labor;
    (c) the effective abolition of child labor; and
    (d) the elimination of discrimination in respect of employment and occupation.

Declaration on Fundamental Principles and Rights at Work, International Labor Organization

Nations system. The ILO is not a labor union, however. Instead, it is an international organization of 185 countries designed to promote cooperation among labor groups, business interests, and governments.[23] In 1998 the ILO adopted the *Declaration on Fundamental Principles and Rights at Work*.[24] Today this document is one of the most widely recognized statements of labor rights in the global economy. The four basic principles of this declaration are shown on page 122. More recently the *ILO Declaration on Social Justice for a Fair Globalization* (2008) expanded its push to protect the rights of labor in an era of globalization.[25] Other major documents that protect workers' rights include the United Nations' *Global Compact* and the Reverend Leon H. Sullivan's *Global Sullivan Principles of Corporate Social Responsibility*.

The International Trade Union Confederation (ITUC) has emerged as another major player in the global labor movement. Founded in 2006, the ITUC brought a number of international labor groups under one umbrella organization to "better the conditions of work and life of working women and men and their families, and to strive for human rights, social justice, gender equity, peace, freedom and democracy."[26] In 2012 the ITUC represented 175 million workers in 153 countries through 308 national affiliates. In addition, the ITUC pledged continued support for the work of the International Labor Organization (ILO), and cooperation with other trade unions and civil society organizations to end child labor, forced labor, discrimination and racism, and other forms of worker abuse in the global economy.[27]

LABOR ISSUES

Workers and worker unions have achieved significant victories in the past. Yet challenges persist in the United States and in the wider global economy. The decline in union

Protecting the rights of labor is a cornerstone of a just global economy. (Eskinder Debebe/UN Photo)

membership, for example, raises some concerns about the viability of labor unions to counterbalance the enormous power of major corporations. Right to work laws, offshoring, and other behaviors of transnational corporations pose challenges to the well-being of workers locally and globally.

Right to Work Laws

Right to work laws allow workers at a unionized firm to reject union membership and the payment of union dues. At the same time, these nonunion workers are entitled to the same wages, fringe benefits, legal protections, or other benefits that appear in the union-negotiated contract with the employer. By 2013, twenty-four state legislatures had passed right to work laws. Most right to work states are located in the south and midwestern regions of the United States.[28] Right to work legislation has been controversial since its origins in the 1940s.

Supporters argue that right to work laws create a probusiness climate in a state by giving businesses greater discretion in hiring and compensating workers. That is, firms' freedom of enterprise is enhanced. In addition, supporters argue that right to work laws increase workers' freedom of choice, in this case the freedom to join or not join an existing union at a workplace. Supporters generally conclude that these marketplace freedoms stimulate job creation, business investment, economic growth, and a higher standard of living for people.

Opponents argue that right to work laws have a negative impact on workers and on the economy. Opponents generally view right to work laws as an assault on organized labor and on the collective bargaining process guaranteed under the Wagner Act of 1935. This is because right to work laws enable workers at unionized plants to opt out of union membership while at the same time being covered by the wage and benefit package negotiated by the union. In 2011, for example, about 1.5 million workers in right to work states rejected union membership at their workplace but benefitted from a union-negotiated contract.[29] Opponents view these nonunion workers as free riders because they do not pay union dues but benefit from the union-negotiated contract. Opponents conclude that wages, job security, and living standards suffer when right to work laws deplete union membership.

The debate over right to work laws came to a head in 2011 when the National Labor Relations Board (NLRB), which was created under the Wagner Act, announced its opposition to the production of a new Boeing aircraft in South Carolina—a right to work state—rather than in the state of Washington. The NLRB case sided with the machinists' union at Boeing's Puget Sound, Washington, facility. The NLRB case immediately came under fire by some in Congress and by right to work supporters. Later in 2011 the machinists' union at the Boeing plant in Washington negotiated a favorable contract and, at the urging of the machinists' union, the NLRB dropped its case against Boeing.[30]

Offshoring

Offshoring occurs when a producer from one country outsources production to another country. The two types of offshoring are captive offshoring and offshore outsourcing. *Captive offshoring*, also called intrafirm offshoring, occurs when a producer in one country transfers production to one of its affiliates in a second country. *Offshore outsourcing* occurs when a producer in one country transfers production to an unaffiliated local company in the second country. Not all outsourcing is connected with offshoring. In fact, most outsourcing occurs between companies in the same country. For example, U.S. corporations often outsource peripheral services to outside accountants, tax preparers, lawyers, and others. Liberalized trade and investment regimes, and advanced information and communications technologies (ICTs), have accelerated offshoring in recent years.

Offshoring is a political hot potato in the United States. Heated debate rages about offshoring, especially as it relates to the "export of U.S. jobs" to low-wage countries. Offshoring during the 1990s mainly affected manufacturing in industries such as textiles and clothing, motor vehicles and auto parts, and electronics. By the 2000s many services-producing industries were also offshored. Low-skill offshored services included call centers and data entry services; medium-skill services included accounting, basic computer programming, and bill collecting; and high-skill services included architectural, engineering, and medical services. U.S. firms offshored manufacturing facilities to Mexico, China, and other low-wage countries in Latin America and Asia. In the 2000s popular offshoring destinations for the services-producing industries were Ireland, India, Canada, and Israel.

Offshoring provides a variety of benefits to home and host economies. The ability to lower production costs is the main reason firms offshore some production. Lower wages and favorable tax regimes are two common types of cost savings. In some cases outsourced production also results in improved product quality, lower consumer prices, and higher corporate profits. Benefits to host countries include job creation, capital formation, technology transfers, and expanded global connectivity—key factors in the process of sustainable economic development.

Home and recipient countries also experience offshoring-related costs. Home countries risk job loss in manufacturing and service industries, and downward pressure on wages in some labor markets. Offshoring also causes cross-border plant relocations, which reduces tax revenues and public services in local communities. Recipient countries face adjustment issues related to employment, industrial production, and the environment. Today the ease of cross-border relocations of firms, especially as firms seek ever-greener pastures for their investments, raises some concerns about the sustainability of economic gains from offshoring.

CHAPTER 6 SUMMARY

Workers and Worker Behavior
- The U.S. labor force has grown significantly over the past century.
- Workers in the U.S. labor force respond in predictable ways to incentives such as wages or salaries.
- Most wages in the U.S. economy are determined by the interplay of supply and demand in labor markets.
- Wages in the U.S economy are also influenced by certain government interventions, including the minimum wage.
- Profit maximizing firms hire workers as long as the marginal revenue product of each worker is great than or equal to the marginal factor cost.

Labor Unions and Worker Power
- Early U.S. labor unions were typically organized either as craft unions or industrial unions.
- The union membership rate in the United States rate grew during the first half of the twentieth century but declined thereafter.
- Organizations such as the International Labor Organization and the International Trade Union Confederation have worked to strengthen workers' power in today's global economy.

Labor Issues

- Right to work laws affect the power of unions and labor rights.
- Offshoring can improve corporate efficiencies and profits but can also create some job and labor union insecurity.

NOTES

1. U.S. Department of Labor (DOL), Bureau of Labor Statistics (BLS), "The Employment Situation, April 2013, Table A-1: Employment Status of the Civilian Population by Sex and Age," *News Release*, May 3, 2013, www.bls.gov/news.release/pdf/empsit.pdf

2. Ibid.

3. Ben J. Wattenberg, "Series D 1-10: Labor Force and Its Components, 1900 to 1947," *Statistical History of the United States: From Colonial Times to the Present* (New York: Basic Books, 1976), 126; DOL, *Occupational Outlook Handbook: 2012–2013 Edition*, 2012, www.bls.gov/ooh/About/Projections-Overview.htm

4. U.S. Bureau of the Census, "No. 1: Population and Area, 1790 to 2000," "No. 560: Employment Status of the Civilian Population, 1960 to 2001," "No. 561: Civilian Labor Force Participation Rates, with Projections, 1980 to 2010," *Statistical Abstract of the United States: 2002* (Washington, DC: United States Government Printing Office), 2001, 8, 367; Ben J. Wattenberg, "Series D 11-25: Labor Force Status of the Population, 1870 to 1970," *Statistical History of the United States: From Colonial Times to the Present* (New York: Basic Books, 1976), 127-128; U.S. Bureau of the Census, *Statistical Abstract of the United States: 2012* (Washington, DC: U.S. Government Printing Office), "Table 586: Civilian Population: Employment Status, 1970 to 2010," "Table 1: Population and Area, 1790 to 2010," 377, 8.

5. Ben J. Wattenberg, *Statistical History of the United States: From Colonial Times to the Present* (New York: Basic Books, 1976), 139; DOL, *Occupational Outlook Handbook: 2012–2013 Edition*, www.bls.gov/ooh/About/Projections-Overview.htm; DOL/BLS, "The Employment Situation, March 2012, Table B-1: Employees on Nonfarm Payrolls by Industry Sector and Selected Detail," April 6, 2012; DOL, "The Employment Situation, April 2012, Table A-8: Employed Persons by Class of Worker and Part-Time Status," *News Release*, May 4, 2012, www.bls.gov/news.release/pdf/empsit.pdf

6. DOL/BLS, "The Employment Situation, April 2013, Table A-1: Employment Status of the Civilian Population by Sex and Age," *News Release*, May 3, 2013, www.bls.gov/news.releases/pdf/empsit/pdf; Ben J. Wattenberg, "Series D 11-25: Labor Force Status of the Population, 1870 to 1970," *Statistical History of the United States: From Colonial Times to the Present* (New York: Basic Books, 1976), 126-127.

7. Ben J. Wattenberg, "Series H 598-601: High School Graduates, by Sex, 1870 to 1970," *Statistical History of the United States: From Colonial Times to the Present* (New York: Basic Books, 1976), 379; U.S. Census Bureau, "Table 229: Educational Attainment by Race and Hispanic Origin, 1970 to 2010," *Statistical Abstract of the United States: 2012* (Washington, DC: U.S. Government Printing Office), 151.

8. U.S. Department of Labor, Bureau of Labor Statistics, "Table A-4: Educational Status of the Civilian Population 25 Years and over by Educational Attainment," *Economic News Release*, May 3, 2013, www.bls.gov/news.release/empsit.t04.htm

9. DOL/BLS, "Workers on Flexible and Shift Schedules in 2001 Summary," *BLS News*, April 18, 2002, www.bls.gov/news.release/flex.nr0.htm; DOL/BLS, "Work at Home in 2001," *BLS News*, March 1, 2002, www.bls.gov/news.release/homey.nr.0.htm; DOL/BLS, "Workers on Flexible and Shift Schedules in May 2004," *News*, July 1, 2005, www.bls.gov/news.release/pdf/flex.pdf

10. DOL/BLS, "Table 5: Quartiles and Selected Deciles of Usual Weekly Earnings of Full-Time Wage and Salary Workers by Selected Characteristics" (first quarter 2013), *News Release*, April 18, 2013, www.bls.gov/rews.release/pdf/wkyeng.pdf.

11. DOL, *Occupational Outlook Handbook: 2012–2013 Edition*, "Overview of the 2010–20 Projections," www.bls.gov/ooh/About/Projections-Overview.htm

12. The U.S. Equal Employment Opportunity Commission (EEOC), citing Title VII of the Civil Rights Act of 1964, (Pub. L. 88-352, Sec. 2000e-2), *United States Code*, Vol. 42, www.eeoc.gov/laws/vii.html

13. DOL/BLS, "Table 2: Median Usual Weekly Earnings of Full-Time Wage and Salary Workers by Selected Characteristics, Quarterly Averages, Not Seasonally Adjusted," *News Release*, April 18, 2013, www.bls.gov/news.release/pdf/wkyeng.pdf

14. DOL, "History of Federal Minimum Wage Rates under the Fair Labor Standards Act, 1938–2009," www.dol.gov/whd/minwage/chart.htm; DOL, "Minimum Wage Laws in the States, January 1, 2013," www.dol.gov/whd/minwage/america.htm

15. U.S. Bureau of the Census, "Poverty Thresholds for 2012 by Size of Family and Number of Related Children under 18 Years,, www.census.gov/hhes/www/poverty/data/threshld

16. U.S. Bureau of the Census, "Table 653: Workers Paid Hourly Rates by Selected Characteristics, 2012," *Statistical Abstract of the United States: 2012* (Washington, DC: U.S. Government Printing Office), 423.

17. Ben J. Wattenberg, "Series D 765-778: Average Hours and Average Earnings in Manufacturing, in Selected Nonmanufacturing Industries and for 'Lower-Skilled' Labor 1890 to 1926," *Statistical History of the United States: From Colonial Times to the Present* (New York: Basic Books, 1976), 168.

18. Ben J. Wattenberg, "Series D 11-25: Labor Force Status of the Population, 1870 to 1970," "Series D 927-939: Labor Union Membership, by Affiliation, 1935 to 1970," "Series D 940-945: Labor Union Membership, by Affiliation, 1897 to 1934," "Series D 946-951: Labor Union Membership and Membership as Percent of Total Labor Force and of Nonagricultural Employment, 1930 to 1970," *Statistical History of the United States: From Colonial Times to the Present* (New York: Basic Books, 1976), 127, 176-178; U.S. Bureau of the Census, "No. 628: Labor Union Membership by Sector, 1983 to 2001," *Statistical Abstract of the United States: 2002* (Washington, DC: U.S. Government Printing Office), 411. U.S. Bureau of the Census, "Table 664. Labor Union Membership by Sector: 1985 to 2010," Statistical Abstract of the United States: 2012 (Washington, DC: U.S. Government Printing Office), 2011, 429.

19. Ben J. Wattenberg, "Series D 927-939: Labor Union Membership, by Affiliation, 1935 to 1970," *Statistical History of the United States: From Colonial Times to the Present* (New York: Basic Books, 1976), 176; DOL/BLS, "Union Members Summary (2012), Tables 1–4," *Economic News Release*, January 23, 2013, www.bls.gov/news.release/union2/nr0.htm

20. DOL/BLS, "Union Members Summary (2012), Tables 1–4," *Economic News Release*, January 23, 2013, www.bls.gov/news.release/union2/nr0.htm

21. American Federation of Labor–Congress of Industrial Organizations (AFL-CIO), "Our Mission and Vision," 2013, www.aflcio.org/About/Our-Mission-and-Vision; AFL-CIO, "What the AFL-CIO Does," www.aflcio.org/About/What-the-AFL-CIO-Does

22. DOL/BLS, "Union Members Summary (2012), Tables 1–4," *Economic News Release*, January 23, 2013, www.bls.gov/news.release/union2/nr0.htm

23. International Labor Organization (ILO), "Alphabetical List of ILO Member Countries (185)," www.ilo.org/public/english/standards/relm/country.htm

24. ILO, *Declaration on Fundamental Principles and Rights at Work*, www.ilo.org/public/english/standards/decl/declaration/faq/index.htm

25. ILO (Office of the Legal Advisor), *ILO Declarations*, September 27, 2011, www.ilo.org/public/english/bureau/leg/declarations.htm

26. International Trade Union Confederation (ITUC), ITUC *Constitution & Standing Orders* (amended, June 2010), (Brussels, Belgium: ITUC), 6.

27. Ibid., 6–8.

28. National Right to Work Legal Defense Foundation," "Right to Work States," www.nrtw.org/rtws.htm

29. DOL/BLS, "Union Members 2011," *News Release*, January 27, 2012, www.bls.gov/news.release/pdf/union2/pdf

30. Steven Greenhouse, "Labor Board Drops Case against Boeing after Union Reaches Accord," *New York Times*, December 9, 2011, www.nytimes.com/2011/12/10

7

Governments Raise and Spend Money

Governments at the federal, state, and local levels raise and spend money. Governments raise money mainly through taxation. Today most federal tax dollars are spent in five major areas: national defense, Social Security, Medicare, Medicaid, and interest payments on the nation's public debt. Most state and local tax dollars are spent on education, health care, infrastructure, and a variety of social services. Governments at all levels have struggled to pay their bills. In recent years federal budget deficits have vastly increased the size of the national debt.

GOVERNMENT REVENUES

A **tax** is a mandatory payment by an individual or a business firm to any level of government—national, state, or local. All societies rely on tax revenues to support essential government programs. Taxes are also used to influence the behaviors of individuals and firms. The federal government's power to tax the people is granted in the *Constitution of the United States* (Article I, Section 8), which states: "The Congress shall have Power To lay and collect Taxes, Duties, Impost and Excises, to pay the debts and provide for the common Defense and general Welfare of the United States."[1] At the federal level the bulk of the government's tax revenues are generated through the personal income tax, social insurance payroll taxes such as the Social Security and Medicare taxes, and the corporate income tax. At the state and local levels, other taxes dominate such as the sales tax, state income tax, and property tax.

Functions of Taxes

The first function of taxes is to raise needed revenues to pay for the public goods and services provided by government. Taxes represent the largest source of revenue for the government. Governments, especially at the state and local levels, also collect revenues from license fees (motor vehicles, fishing, hunting) and charges for local services. Some government programs or services, such as national defense, are financed mainly by the federal government. Others, such as public education, are financed by state and local governments. The provision of certain public goods or services is sometimes considered a *shared responsibility* of different levels of government—federal, state, and local. Shared responsibility often applies to infrastructure projects such as interstate highways and to the provision of certain public transfer programs such as Medicaid.

In addition to raising needed funds for the government, taxes also influence people's economic behaviors. That is, taxes can serve as an incentive to encourage certain behaviors by individuals or firms, or a disincentive to discourage other behaviors. The tax credit offered to first-time home buyers during 2008–2010 illustrates the incentive function of taxes. Under this first-time home owner tax credit, a person who purchased a home was eligible for a one-time tax credit of 10 percent of the purchase price—up to $8,000. This popular tax credit encouraged people to buy houses and, in the process, revive the sluggish U.S. housing market.[2] Similarly, the Energy Improvement and Extension Act of 2008 offered a 30 percent tax credit to encourage the installation and use of solar power in certain facilities. An excise tax, on the other hand, is a disincentive for people to buy certain items.[3] An **excise tax** is a tax on a specific product such as gasoline, alcohol, and cigarettes. High excise taxes make certain products more expensive and therefore discourage consumers from purchasing these products. Excise taxes are sometimes referred to as sin taxes because they generally discourage the use of goods that could harm people's health or well-being.

Types of Taxes

The three types of taxes—progressive, proportional, and regressive—assign different tax burdens to different income groups. A **progressive tax** takes a larger percentage of income in taxes from high-income households than from low-income households. The federal personal income tax is a progressive tax. Some state income taxes are also mildly progressive. The Jobs and Growth Tax Relief Reconciliation Act of 2003, which lowered federal income tax rates for many Americans, established six income tax rates of 10 percent, 15 percent, 25 percent, 28 percent, 33 percent, and 35 percent. In 2013 a seventh tax rate of 39.6 percent was added. Low-income households pay a lower percent of their income in taxes, while high-income households pay incrementally higher percentages on different portions of their taxable income.

A **proportional tax** takes the same percentage of income in taxes from all households— low-income, middle-income, and high-income households. The Social Security tax, a social insurance payroll tax, is an example of a proportional tax—at least up to a government-determined cap. In 2011 and 2012 wage earners paid just 4.2 percent of their wage in the form of Social Security tax, rather than the normal 6.2 percent. This temporary reduction in the Social Security tax was designed to stimulate the sluggish U.S. economy. The 4.2 percent payroll tax applied only to wages up to a certain amount, called a cap. In 2012 this cap was $110,100. In 2013 the Social Security tax returned to 6.2 percent, and the cap was raised to $113,700. The Medicare tax, another social insurance payroll tax, takes 1.45 percent of a wage earner's pay. Unlike Social Security tax, however, there is no cap on Medicare. Hence, the Medicare tax is a proportional tax, taking the same percentage of all wage earners' income.

A **regressive tax** takes a larger percentage of income in taxes from low-income than from high-income households. A state sales tax is a good example of a regressive tax. At first glance a state sales tax may appear to be a proportional tax because all people pay the same percentage on their purchases. But consider how much of a poorer household's income must be spent on taxable items compared to that of a richer household. Low-income households typically spend all of their income to satisfy basic needs, and many of these basic needs are subject to the sales tax. High-income households, on the other hand, tend to put significant portions of their incomes into savings, investments, retirement plans, college tuition payments, mortgage payments, and other uses that are not subject to the sales tax. As a result, low-income households tend to pay a larger *percentage* of their income in sales taxes than do high-income households. Many states soften the regressive nature of the sales tax by exempting certain necessities such as food, medicine, and some clothing.

Tax Fairness

The subject of tax fairness strays into the realm of normative economics. Recall that normative economics deals with "what ought to be," while positive economics deals with "what is." There are many opinions about how taxes ought to be levied and who ought to pay more or less to the government in the form of taxes. Hence, the answer to the question of what is a fair tax is elusive. You just read about one measure of tax fairness based on the type of tax. That is, progressive, proportional, and regressive taxes affect different income groups in different ways. Progressive taxes, for example, tend to lean most heavily on the rich. Regressive taxes, on the other hand, tend to put the greatest burden on the poor. Which is the fairest type of tax? Answers to this question will vary. The U.S. tax system, which consists of all three types of taxes, attempts to balance the tax burdens of different stakeholders in the economy.

Periodically, the Congressional Budget Office (CBO) estimates the share of the federal tax burden by different income groups in the United States. The CBO data includes the amount of money households pay for the four largest federal taxes: the individual income tax, social insurance payroll taxes, corporate income taxes, and excise taxes. Table 7.1 shows the share of federal taxes paid by five income groups, called quintiles. Each quintile represents a 20 percent segment of U.S. households. The lowest quintile, for example, represents the poorest 20 percent of U.S. households, while the highest quintile represents the richest 20 percent of U.S. households. In 2009 the poorest quintile paid less than 1 percent of the tax revenues collected by the federal government, the second quintile paid 3.8 percent, the middle quintile paid 9.4 percent, the fourth quintile paid 18.3 percent, and the richest quintile paid 67.9 percent. In recent decades the percentage of federal taxes paid by the first four quintiles has generally decreased while the amount paid by the richest quintile has increased.[4]

The most commonly used principles of tax fairness in the U.S. economy are the benefit-received principle and ability-to-pay principle. The **benefit-received principle** states that people should be taxed in proportion to the benefit they receive from government goods

Table 7.1   Shares of Federal Tax Liabilities for All Households, 1980–2009

Year	Lowest Quintile	Second Quintile	Middle Quintile	Fourth Quintile	Highest Quintile
1980	2.0	7.0	13.3	21.3	56.3
1990	1.9	6.8	12.6	20.7	57.9
2000	1.1	4.8	9.8	17.5	66.6
2009	0.3	3.8	9.4	18.3	67.9

Source: Congressional Budget Office, "Table 2: Shares of Federal Tax Liabilities for All Households, by Before-Tax Income Group, 1979–2009."

such as schools, roads, or libraries. Highway tolls are sometimes based on the benefit-received principle. This is because revenues gained from highway tolls are often used for highway construction and repair. Hence, drivers of automobiles, trucks, or other vehicles directly contribute to the upkeep of the highways. Similarly, revenues gained from the excise tax on gasoline are often earmarked to build or maintain roads, bridges, and other features of the transportation infrastructure. Supporters of the benefit-received principle argue that this is a fair arrangement because it resembles the functioning of free markets. That is, people are free to choose which public goods to use and then pay for these goods by paying tolls or excise taxes. Critics of the benefit-received principle counter that it is impossible to determine each person's actual benefit from many public goods or services. For instance, how could society calculate each person's benefit from local police or fire protection?

The **ability-to-pay principle** states that people with more income or wealth should pay more in taxes because they have a greater capacity to pay. The ability-to-pay principle is often divided into two categories: ability-to-pay based on *income* and ability-to-pay based on *wealth*. The federal personal income tax is based on ability-to-pay based on *income*. Recall that the federal income tax is a progressive tax. Hence, high-income people not only pay a larger dollar amount in taxes, but also a larger percentage of their income in taxes than do low-income groups. The local property tax, on the other hand, is based on the ability-to-pay based on *wealth* principle. Wealth is an asset owned by a person, rather than the income earned by a person. The largest asset most people own is a house. A person's house is subject to a local property tax, which must be paid every year. The more valuable the house, the more money the homeowner must pay in property tax to the local government.

There are supporters and critics of the ability-to-pay principle of taxation. Supporters of the ability-to-pay principle argue that people with larger incomes, or with greater wealth, are in a better position to pay taxes than poorer people. This argument stresses that richer individuals can easily attend to their necessities and that taxes only eat into their consumption of nonessential or luxury goods. Conversely, taxes paid by poorer households reduce their ability to buy food, clothing, shelter, and other basic necessities. Critics of the ability-to-pay principle, on the other hand, argue that society should not penalize people for being successful—for earning higher incomes or acquiring more wealth. In addition, some groups, such as the elderly, may have significant wealth but very little income after they retire. Is it fair for local governments to impose high property taxes on retirees who lived on fixed incomes?

Federal Taxes

All levels of government collect taxes to finance public goods and services. The most important taxes at the federal level are the personal income tax, social insurance taxes, corporate income tax, and excise taxes, as shown in Table 7.2. In 2013 the federal government collected $2.7 trillion in taxes from individuals and business firms.[5] In many government publications federal revenues are called government *receipts*.

The **personal income tax** is a federal tax on a person's taxable income. In 2013 the federal government collected $1.2 trillion in income taxes, as shown in Table 7.2. Income derived from wages and salaries, interest and dividend payments, and other sources is subject to the personal income tax. *Taxable income* is the income that remains once all deductions are made from a person's gross income, including deductions for dependent

Table 7.2   Federal Tax Receipts, 2013

Federal Taxes	Tax Receipts ($ billions)	Tax Receipts (% of total)
Personal income tax	1,234	45.5
Social insurance taxes	951	35.1
Corporation income tax	288	10.6
Excise taxes	85	3.1
Other receipts	154	5.7
Total federal receipts	2,712	100.0

Source: Office of Management and Budget, "Table S-5," *Budget of the U.S. Government: Fiscal Year 2014*, 189–190.

children, interest on mortgage payments, local property taxes, contributions to religious and charitable organizations, and contributions to tax-sheltered retirement plans.

The **personal income tax** is a progressive tax. This means that as a person's income increases, there is an incremental increase in the percentage taken by the government. These incremental steps are called tax rates. In 2013 here were seven tax rates ranging from a low of 10 percent to a high of 39.6 percent, as shown in Table 7.3. The first tax rate of 10 percent, for example, applies to a person's taxable income between $0 and $8,925. In other words, all income up to $8,925 is taxed at the lowest tax rate. If a person's taxable income was higher than $8,925, this taxpayer would pay a larger percentage only on income above $8,925. Table 7.3 shows the tax rates for each of the seven tax brackets.[6]

Suppose Christopher's filing status was "unmarried individual" in 2013 and that he had a taxable income of $90,000. How much would Christopher owe to the government in personal income taxes? Using the tax rates shown in Table 7.3 and Table 7.4 the first $8,500 would be taxed at the lowest tax rate of 10 percent. Thus, on this first slice of his taxable income, or income in the first tax bracket, Christopher owes $892.50 (0.10 x $8,925 = $892.50). The second tax bracket consists of all income between $8,926 and $36,250, or $27,324. Christopher pays the next highest tax rate of 15 percent on this $27,324, which amounts to an additional tax of $4,098.60 (0.15 x $27,324 = $4,098.60), as shown in Table 7.4. Note the remaining slices of Christopher's income are taxed at the 25 percent tax rate and the 28 percent tax rate. Christopher's total personal income tax payment is the sum of what he owes on income within each tax bracket, in this case $18,492.85, as shown in Table 7.4. In addition to the unmarried individual filing status, there are three others: married filing jointly, married filing separately, and head of household.

Table 7.3   Income Tax Rate Schedule, 2013 (Unmarried Individual Filing Status)

Taxable Income	Tax Rate
$0 to $8,925	10%
$8,926 to $36,250	15%
$36,251 to $87,850	25%
$87,851 to $183,250	28%
$183,251 to $398,350	33%
$398,351 to $400,000	35%
$400,001 and above	39.6%

Source: U.S. Department of the Treasury, Internal Revenue Service, "Table 3," *Revenue Procedures 2013–15*, 4.

Table 7.4   Christopher's Personal Income Tax Payment in 2013

Tax Bracket	Income in Each Tax Bracket		Tax Rate		Amount Owed in Taxes on Each Slice of Income
First tax bracket	$8,925	×	0.10	=	$892.50
Second tax bracket	$27,324	×	0.15	=	$4,098.60
Third tax bracket	$51,599	×	0.25	=	$12,899.75
Fourth tax bracket	$2,150	×	0.28	=	$602.00
Christopher's total income tax payment				=	$18,492.85

Social insurance payroll taxes are a second important source of revenue for the federal government. The largest social insurance taxes are the Social Security tax and the Medicare tax, which together are often referred to as the FICA taxes. FICA stands for the Federal Insurance Contributions Act. Today 94 percent of all workers pay into the Social Security System. In 2013 government revenues generated directly or indirectly from social insurance payroll taxes amounted to $951 billion.[7]

Under the Federal Insurance Contributions Act, the federal government collects a Social Security tax of 6.2 percent of a worker's pay from the employee and an equal amount from the employer each pay period. Thus, the government collects an amount equal to 12.4 percent of the worker's pay each pay period. This money is deposited at the U.S. Treasury. The government also collects the Medicare tax, which takes another 1.45 percent of the worker's pay from the both the employee and employer—2.9 percent in all. Medicare tax receipts are also sent to the U.S. Treasury. Thus, the FICA taxes claim an amount equal to 15.3 percent of a typical worker's pay each pay period, half paid by the employee and

Most U.S. workers and their employers pay into the Social Security and Medicare systems. (Shutterstock.com)

half paid by the employer. This 15.3 percent FICA payment also applies to the self-employed.

The Social Security tax claims 6.2 percent of a worker's wage up to a cap. No Social Security tax is collected on a worker's wage above this cap. The government has increased the cap many times since the Social Security system was created in the 1930s. The original cap of $3,000 applied to workers' wages from 1937 to 1950. Since the early 1970s the cap has increased almost every year. In 2013 the cap stood at $113,700. In 2011 and 2012 wage earners paid just 4.2 percent of their wage in the form of Social Security tax, rather than the normal 6.2 percent. This temporary reduction from 6.2 percent to 4.2 percent was authorized under the Tax Relief, Unemployment Insurance Reauthorization, and Job Creation Act of 2010. Under this act employers continued to pay the full 6.2 percent, however. The Medicare tax remained at 1.45 percent for employee and employer alike.[8] Thus, in 2013 a worker with a $100,000 income would pay a Social Security tax of $6,200 (0.062 × $100,000 = $6,200), plus a Medicare tax of $1,450 (0.0145 × $100,000 = $1,450), for a total contribution of $7,650. The employer would also pay $7,650 to the Treasury.

The **corporation income tax**, also called the corporate income tax, is a third important source of federal revenues. The corporate income tax is a tax on corporate profits. In 2013 the corporate income tax generated $288 billion for the federal tax coffers. The corporate income tax is similar to the personal income tax. As with the personal income tax, corporations are allowed to make certain deductions before paying their income tax to the government. These deductions usually include some business expenses, charitable contributions, tax credits for investment, and deductions for wear and tear on the corporation's capital goods. In 2012 corporate income tax rates ranged from 15 percent to as high as 39 percent.[9] The corporate income tax is a controversial tax. Some people argue that corporations, like individuals, should shoulder some tax responsibilities when they earn profits. Others argue that high U.S. business taxes are a disincentive for American firms to invest within the United States. Instead, critics insist, high business taxes encourage American firms to offshore production facilities to other countries and discourage foreign investment in the United States.

State and Local Taxes

State and local governments also collect taxes to finance essential public goods and services. In 2008 state and local governments collected $1.3 trillion in tax receipts. State and local governments also collected large sums of money from nontax sources. In fact, only about one-half of the revenues collected by state governments came from taxes, and only about one-third of all local revenues came directly from taxes. The two largest sources of nontax revenues for state and local governments are charges for certain services such as hospital care and higher education, and from grants or other intergovernmental financial transfers. Table 7.5 compares the revenue sources for state governments with those of local governments.[10]

State taxes represent nearly one-half of all state government revenues collected each year. In 2008 state governments collected about $1.6 trillion in total revenues: $782 billion in tax revenues and $837 billion in nontax revenues. Most *tax* revenues at the state level came from the sales tax and state individual income tax. A **sales tax** is a tax placed on many types of goods and services that people purchase. In 2008, for example, total state sales tax receipts were $241 billion. To reduce the burden on low-income households, most state

Table 7.5   Revenue Sources for State and Local Governments

Revenue Sources	State Governments (%)	Local Governments (%)
Tax revenues	48.3	35.9
Intergovernmental revenues	27.5	34.3
Charges and miscellaneous	17.7	21.4
Other revenues	6.5	8.4
Total from all revenue sources	100.0	100.0

Source: U.S. Bureau of the Census, "Table 451," "Table 455," *Statistical Abstract of the United States: 2012* (Washington, DC: U.S. Government Printing Office), 2011, 292, 293.

sales taxes include exemptions for food and prescription drugs. In 2012 there was a sales tax in 45 out of the 50 states.[11]

State individual income taxes raised an additional $278 billion for state governments in 2008. The **individual income tax** is a tax on people's income. Most state individual income taxes were mildly progressive. This means that high-income households were taxed at a higher rate than low-income households in most states. In 2012, there were 43 states with an income tax. Of those states with an income tax, 36 had a progressive income tax and seven had a flat rate, a type of proportional tax in which all households are taxed at the same tax rate regardless of household income. Other taxes generating revenue for states included excise taxes, corporate income taxes, property taxes, death and gift taxes, and severance taxes.[12]

Tax revenues account for about one-third of all local government revenues collected each year. In 2008 local governments collected about $1.5 trillion in total revenues: $549 billion in local tax revenues, and $982 billion in nontax revenues. Most of the *tax* revenues at the local level were generated by the local property tax. A **property tax** is a tax on personal property such as a house, building, undeveloped property, or even a car. In 2008, $397 billion was collected in local property taxes—more than 70 percent of all tax receipts by local governments.[13] The property tax is based on the assessed value of a property. Typically, the amount owed in property taxes is determined by a mill rate. A mill rate tells the property owner how many dollars are owed for each $1,000 in property the taxpayer owns. To figure a person's property tax bill each year, simply multiply the mill rate times the number of thousands at which the property is valued. Suppose a town has a mill rate of 30. If Derek owned a house assessed at $100,000 he would owe the town $3,000 in property taxes. This is because there are 100 thousands in $100,000 (100,000/1,000 = 100). If the mill rate increased to 32 the following year, Derek would owe the town $3,200 (32 x 100 = $3,200) in local property taxes.

GOVERNMENT SPENDING

Government spending increased significantly over the past century at the federal, state, and local levels. One reason for the growth in government spending is population growth. The U.S. population increased from 76 million in 1900 to 316 million in 2013.[14] A larger population increases the demand for public goods and services. Second, people's expectations of government have changed over time. During the twentieth century, for example, a myriad of social programs such as Social Security, Medicare, and Medicaid were created to meet the needs of Americans. Third, government has assumed a greater role in reversing

Spending on national defense, orchestrated primarily through the Pentagon, accounts for about half of all federal outlays for appropriated programs. (Library of Congress)

economic crises. Expensive New Deal programs pumped money into a depressed U.S. economy during the 1930s to stimulate economic growth and job creation. Stimulus money was also spent to reverse job loss and economic stagnation during more recent economic downturns, including the Great Recession of 2007–2009. Finally, the United States' role as a global superpower has carried a high price tag in terms of human and financial costs. Massive government spending was required to fight two world wars, regional conflicts in Korea and Vietnam, and more recent conflicts in Afghanistan (2001–2014) and Iraq (2003–2010).

Federal Spending

Measured in *constant dollars* the federal government's spending showed an increase of nearly 400 percent between 1960 and 2010—from $629 billion to $3,067 billion. **Constant dollars** are dollars that have been adjusted for inflation. This adjustment for inflation permits a more accurate comparison of government spending over time. Figure 7.1 shows the real growth of federal spending from 1960 to 2010 as measured in constant 2005 dollars.[15] In many government publications federal spending is called government *outlays*.

Government outlays are often divided into three main categories: appropriated (discretionary) programs, mandatory programs, and net interest. In 2013 federal spending, measured in **current dollars**—dollars not adjusted for inflation—was nearly $3.7 trillion.[16] Note that this $3.7 trillion is measured in *current* dollars rather than constant dollars. The use of current dollars is useful when people, such as taxpayers and policy makers, want to know the precise amount of money needed to fund current programs.

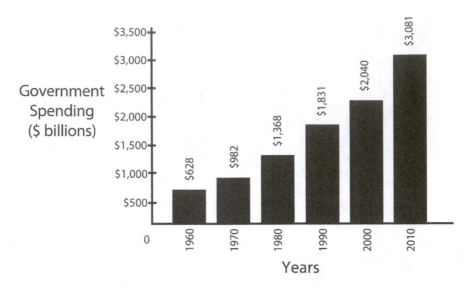

Figure 7.1   Federal Government Outlays, 1960–2010 (in constant 2005 dollars)
Source: Office of Management and Budget, "Table 1.3," *Historical Tables: Budget of the U.S. Government: Fiscal Year 2013,* 26-27.

Federal outlays for **appropriated programs**, also called discretionary spending, are determined each year by Congress. That is, members of the House of Representatives and the Senate pass specific bills into law to support spending on government programs. The two main categories of appropriated programs are expenditures for national defense and for nondefense programs. In 2013 appropriated programs accounted for $1.3 trillion in federal spending, which represents 34 percent of all federal spending. Of this total, $651 billion was spent on defense, and the remaining $606 billion was spent on nondefense programs. In recent years defense spending has risen significantly, especially in the aftermath of the September 11, 2001, terrorist attacks on the United States. Nondefense spending has also increased in recent years. Traditional nondefense spending includes grants to state and local governments, and spending on energy, the environment, and other programs.[17]

Federal spending on mandatory programs is a second important category of federal outlays. Spending on **mandatory programs** occurs automatically each year and thus does not require congressional legislation to authorize the spending. In 2013 mandatory programs accounted for $2.2 trillion in federal spending, which represented 60 percent of all federal spending. The big three mandatory programs are Social Security ($813 billion), Medicare ($504 billion), and Medicaid ($267 billion). Combined, these three programs accounted for about $1.6 trillion in federal spending. The remaining $620 billion spent on mandatory programs included outlays for unemployment insurance, deposit insurance, Supplemental Security Income, Supplemental Nutrition Assistance Program (SNAP), and a host of other programs for the needy.[18]

Net interest is the third major category of federal outlays. **Net interest** is the amount of money the federal government pays in interest on the national debt minus the interest payments and fees it receives from other agencies within the U.S. government. The government borrows money when tax revenues are not sufficient to cover government expenditures. The government borrows money by selling U.S. government securities to investors such as banks, investment funds, foreign governments, and trust funds within the U.S. government—such as the Social Security Trust Fund. Naturally, these investors expect to earn a fair rate of return, called interest, on their investments. In 2013 net interest payments hit $223 billion, which accounted for roughly 6 percent of federal spending. Historic low interest rates helped keep net interest payments fairly constant during the 2000s.[19]

State and Local Spending

There are approximately 90,000 state and local governments operating in the United States. State and local governments tend to spend tax receipts and other revenues on local needs. Table 7.6 shows several major categories of spending by state and local governments in 2008.[20]

The 50 state governments spent $1.5 trillion in 2008. The largest single category of state government spending was for intergovernmental transfers, which accounted for nearly one-third of all state spending. *Intergovernmental transfer* refers to money that state governments distribute to local governments. In recent years the lion's share of these financial transfers has been used by local governments to fund public education. State governments also spent heavily on public welfare, education, health and hospitals, and highways. Combined, these five categories accounted for 83 percent of all state spending, as shown in Table 7.6. The remaining 17 percent of state spending paid for other important services such as housing and community development, the general operation of government, and interest on state debt.[21]

Local governments spent about $1.6 trillion on local services and goods in 2008. The largest categories of local government spending were education, health and hospitals, and police and corrections. Spending on these three categories accounted for about one-half of all local spending, as shown in Table 7.6. Local governments also spent money on public goods such as highways and waste disposal systems, public welfare programs, parks and recreation programs, the administration of local governments, and interest on local government debt.[22]

Table 7.6 Spending by State and Local Governments, 2008

State Government Spending	Percentage of State Spending
Intergovernmental transfers	31.8
Public welfare	23.6
Education	15.5
Health and hospitals	6.1
Highways	6.0
Other	17.0
Local Government Spending	Percentage of Local Spending
Education	37.3
Health and hospitals	7.3
Police and corrections	6.5
Other	48.9

Source: U.S. Bureau of the Census, "Table 456," *Statistical Abstract of the United States: 2012*, 294.

Cost-Benefit Analysis

Government at the federal, state, and local levels provides trillions of dollars in public goods, services, and other assistance to people each year. With this level of spending it would seem as though the government could provide unlimited assistance to people. Yet this is not the case. The government has limited resources and must choose between alternative wants and needs. One way governments decide which public goods, services, and programs to provide is through a cost-benefit analysis.

A **cost-benefit analysis** is a process by which the costs of providing certain public goods are weighed against the likely benefits these goods will provide to society. Like most economic decisions the provision of public goods or services is rarely an all-or-nothing proposition. Instead, decisions in the public sector, like decisions made in the private sector, are typically made at the margin. That is, a cost-benefit analysis helps determine whether the government should provide the next or additional unit of a good.

Consider a hypothetical cost-benefit analysis. Microtown seeks to improve its traffic flow by building additional roads and wants to make a rational spending decision on this road-building project. Microtown determines that each additional mile of road would cost the town $1 million. In the language of the economist, each mile of new road represents the marginal social cost (MSC) to the town, in this case $1 million per mile. The MSC is shown in Column 1 of Table 7.7. Note that the first, second, third, fourth, and fifth mile of new road would each cost Microtown $1 million. Microtown also determines that each additional mile of road would contribute some additional benefit to society, ranging from $1.5 million in additional benefit from the first new mile of road to just $500,000 in additional benefit from the fifth mile of road. Economists call the additional benefit gained from each new mile of road the marginal social benefit (MSB), as shown in Column 2 of Table 7.7.

How many miles of road should Microtown build? The quick answer to this question is three miles of road. Assuming Microland has the financial resources to build roads, the first and second miles of new road would be built. This is because the additional benefit each mile of new road is greater than the additional cost to the town. The first new mile of road contributes $1.5 million in additional benefits but costs the town only $1 million to build. Similarly, the second new mile of road contributes $1.25 million in additional benefits but costs the town only $1 million to build. In other words, the town's *cost-benefit analysis* indicates that the benefits derived from the first and second miles of road outweigh the costs.

But should the third, fourth, and fifth miles of road be built? For the third mile of road, the MSC ($1 million) and MSB ($1 million) are equal. Economists generally agree that this mile of road should be built as long as the additional benefits match the additional

Table 7.7   A Cost-Benefit Analysis for Microtown

Miles of Road	Column 1 Marginal Social Cost (MSC)	Column 2 Marginal Social Benefit (MSB)
0	None	None
1	$1,000,000	$1,500,000
2	$1,000,000	$1,250,000
3	$1,000,000	$1,000,000
4	$1,000,000	$750,000
5	$1,000,000	$500,000

costs. The fourth and fifth miles of road, on the other hand, would not be built because in each case the MSC is greater than the MSB. The bottom line is that rational public sector decision makers will provide a public good or service if the MSB is greater than or equal to the MSC but will not provide a public good or service if the MSC is greater than the MSB.

THE FEDERAL BUDGET

Each year the federal government is charged with formulating and approving a **federal budget**, a document that outlines how the government plans to raise and spend money during the upcoming fiscal year (FY). The FY for the federal government begins on October 1 and ends on September 30 of the following year. Hence, the federal budget for FY2014 runs from October 1, 2013 to September 30, 2014. Unlike most state budgets, the federal budget does not have to be a balanced budget. Instead, a federal budget could have a built-in surplus or deficit. The Constitution of the United States does not stipulate specific guidelines for the creation of the federal budget. Instead, laws such as the Budget and Accounting Act of 1921 and the Congressional Budget and Impoundment Control Act of 1974 have been enacted to provide such guidelines.

Federal Budget Process

The original budget proposal is drafted by the Office of Management of Budget (OMB) and is often called the president's budget because it reflects the president's views on tax policy and spending priorities. The president's budget is transmitted to Congress by the first Monday in February, where it is studied, debated, and amended on a timeline that permits implementation by October 1—the first day of the new fiscal year. Key elements in this budget timeline include agreement on a concurrent budget resolution by April 15. Soon thereafter, the House Appropriations Committee begins its work to allocate funds to cover expenses in 13 broad categories of discretionary spending such as national defense, homeland security, agriculture, energy, education, and general governmental operations. The timeline calls for Congress to pass these appropriations bills by the end of June. While this timeline establishes a tidy blueprint to create a federal budget, Congress rarely meets these target dates. In fact, the last time Congress was able to pass all 13 appropriations bills before the start of the next FY (October 1) was in 1997.

If one or more of the 13 appropriations bills are not passed by Congress before October 1, a *continuing resolution* (CR) is approved by Congress and signed by the president to temporarily fund the affected government programs and agencies at current levels. CRs can last for different lengths of time, for as little as a single day or for months. At times a series of CRs are necessary when congressional gridlock makes it impossible to pass appropriations bills.[23]

In more extreme cases, the president can order a government shutdown to pressure Congress to compromise on appropriations bills. In November 1995, for example, President Bill Clinton ordered a government shutdown that sent 800,000 nonessential federal employees home until Congress could agree on certain budget compromises. The one-week government shutdown was unpopular among the idle federal workers and the many Americans who were denied entry into national parks, museums, and other federal venues. In October 2013 an equally unpopular partial government shutdown lasted for 16 days. Much of the congressional haggling involved whether to fund the Affordable

---

PRIMARY DOCUMENT: Proposing a Balanced Budget Amendment to the U.S. Constitution

[Sections 1-3. January 5, 2011]

Section 1. Total outlays for any fiscal year shall not exceed total receipts for that fiscal year, unless three-fifths of the whole number of each House of Congress shall provide by law for a specific excess of outlays over receipts by a rollcall vote.

Section 2. The limit on the debt of the United States held by the public shall not be increased, unless three-fifths of the whole number of each House shall provide by law for such an increase by a rollcall vote.

Section 3. Prior to each fiscal year, the President shall transmit to the Congress a proposed budget for the United States Government for that fiscal year in which total outlays do not exceed total receipts.

112th Congress (2011-2012), H.J. RES.2.IH

Care Act, more commonly known as ObamaCare. Government shutdowns typically draw the ire of voters and pressure congressional leaders back to the bargaining table.

Budget Surpluses and Deficits

A federal budget might be balanced, in surplus, or in deficit. A **balanced budget** is a budget in which receipts are equal to expenditures. A **budget surplus** occurs when receipts are greater than expenditures. A **budget deficit** occurs when receipts are less than expenditures. From the start of the Great Depression in 1929 until 2013, the federal budget has been in deficit 71 times and in surplus 14 times. Over the past couple of decades, the United States has been in surplus just four times, from FY1998 to FY2001, as shown in Table 7.8.[24] Periodically, Congress has debated ways to balance the federal budget. In 2011, for example, the House of Representatives debated, and then rejected, a balanced budget amendment, as shown in the above passage.[25]

Over time, many factors contributed to America's budget deficits. First, national emergencies such as World War II (1941–1945), and wars in Korea (1950–1953), Vietnam (1950s–1975), the Persian Gulf (1991), Afghanistan (2001–2014), and Iraq (2003–2010) increased budget deficits by requiring massive military spending by the federal government. Second, economic crises such as the Great Depression of the 1930s and the

Table 7.8   U.S. Budget Surpluses and Deficits, 1994–2013

Year	Surplus or Deficit ($ billions)	Year	Surplus or Deficit ($ billions)	Year	Surplus or Deficit ($ billions)
1994	−203	2001	+128	2008	−459
1995	−164	2002	−158	2009	−1,413
1996	−107	2003	−378	2010	−1,293
1997	−22	2004	−413	2011	−1,300
1998	+69	2005	−318	2012	−1,087
1999	+126	2006	−248	2013	−973
2000	+236	2007	−161		

Source: Office of Management and Budget, "Table 1.1," *Historical Tables: Budget of the U.S. Government, Fiscal Year 2014*, 23–25; OMB estimate for 2013.

Great Recession of 2007–2009 slowed tax receipts and increased government spending to jump-start the economy. Recent economic relief efforts included tax rebates, stimulus spending, bailouts of troubled financial institutions, and expanded financial support for the unemployed and the needy. Third, the rapid growth of some social programs, including Social Security and Medicare, resulted in large increases in federal spending. In 1966, for example, the $21 billion spent on Social Security and Medicare represented about 15 percent of the federal budget. In 2013 spending on these two programs had jumped to $1.3 trillion, more than one-third of all federal expenditures.[26]

Budget deficits over the past few decades have grown steeper. During the 1970s the average annual budget deficit was about $37 billion, in the 1980s about $157 billion, in the 1990s about $192 billion, in the 2000s about $443 billion, and in the early 2010s more than $1 trillion per year. Table 7.8 shows U.S. government budget surpluses and deficits from 1994 to 2013.[27]

National Debt

The **national debt**, also called the federal debt, is the accumulated debt of the federal government over time. In 2012 the national debt hit $16.1 trillion. The national debt is divided into two categories: debt held by the public and intragovernmental holdings. The *debt held by the public* is the money the federal government has borrowed from individuals, companies, state and local governments, and foreign investors—including foreign governments. In 2012 the debt held by the public was $11.3 trillion, which was 70 percent of the total national debt. The government borrows from the public through the sale of government securities such as Treasury bills, notes, inflation-protected securities, and savings bonds. Government borrowing is necessary to cover annual budget shortfalls in revenues, or budget deficits. *Intragovernmental holdings*, on the other hand, represent debts that the government owes to itself. For example, agencies within the federal government regularly borrow money from the Old-Age and Survivors Insurance Trust Fund (also called the Social Security Trust Fund), the federal employees retirement funds, and others. In 2012 the intragovernmental debt was $4.8 trillion, or 30 percent of the total U.S. national debt.[28]

In 1982 the national debt topped the $1 trillion mark for the first time, a sum that represented 35 percent of the nation's gross domestic product (GDP). Since that time, the national debt has grown in terms of total dollars and as a percentage of the nation's GDP. In 2012 the $16.1 trillion national debt was 103 percent of GDP. This means that the national debt is larger than the total output of all final goods and services produced in the U.S. economy. It is also the highest amount of debt relative to GDP since the World War II era. By 2013 the U.S. national debt had grown to about $53,000 per person.[29]

There are several concerns about the growing national debt. One troubling effect of the growing national debt is the cost of debt servicing. *Debt servicing* refers to the government's obligation to pay interest on the government securities it issued over time—interest on the Treasury bills, notes, and so on. In 2012 the government owed $445 billion in interest payments to the public and its own trust funds, such as the Social Security Trust Fund. Note that the net interest of $223 billion paid by the U.S. government in 2012 was only about half this $445 billion figure. This is because the U.S. government also receives interest and fees from other agencies within the federal government and deducts these revenues from the $445 billion it owes.[30] Debt servicing costs hundreds of billions of dollars every year, and much of this money flows to creditors outside of the United States. Debt

ECONOMICS IN HISTORY: A Balanced Budget Amendment in Historical Perspective

Americans have long voiced concerns about budget deficits and the growth of the national debt. In the 1790s Thomas Jefferson decried the debts incurred by President John Adams and called for restraints on government spending. More recently, attempts to place legal limits on federal budgets through legislation and through the amendment process have gained some traction at the national level. A number of proposals for a balanced budget amendment have been forwarded to Congress in recent decades. The strongest executive support for such amendments came from President Ronald Reagan and President George H. W. Bush during the 1980s and early 1990s.

A balanced budget amendment requires federal receipts and federal spending to be in balance each fiscal year. Recall that an amendment is an addition to the Constitution itself, rather than simply an act of Congress or law. To propose an amendment to the Constitution, a two-thirds majority vote is needed in both houses of Congress—the House of Representatives and the Senate. In addition, three-quarters of all state legislatures—a total of 38 states—must approve the amendment within a certain period of time.

Different versions of a balanced budget amendment have been debated in Congress, most of which have provided some leeway for deficit spending to attend to national crises such as war or economic downturns. The first proposal supporting a balance budget amendment occurred in 1936, largely in response to growing federal deficits during Franklin D. Roosevelt's administration. The closest the United States ever came to gaining the required two-thirds vote in the House and Senate occurred in 1995 when a balanced budget amendment proposal was approved by the House but rejected in the Senate by a single vote. The most recent attempt to add a balanced budget amendment to the Constitution was in 2011, but the amendment proposal was rejected by the House of Representatives.

servicing also necessitates trade-offs because money spent on interest payments cannot be spent on other important federal programs such as national defense or social programs.

A broader problem with out-of-control growth in the national debt is its possible long-term impacts on economic growth and stability. Massive government borrowing eventually weakens the U.S. dollar and worsens the nation's credit rating. Sensing greater risk in U.S. securities, cautious investors in the United States and abroad will eventually demand higher interest rates on U.S. government securities. In fact, the Congressional Budget Office has already predicted a sharp increase in debt service payments when interest rates rise to normal levels.[31] Further, the ripple effect of higher interest rates on government securities could spill over into the private sector of the economy, forcing businesses and households to pay higher interest on credit and loans. Economic growth and job creation depend on robust consumer demand and business investment, each of which suffers when interest rates are high.

The Debt Ceiling

The **debt ceiling**, also called the debt limit, sets a limit on the total amount of debt the U.S. Department of the Treasury can issue to the public and to other agencies within the federal government. The government issues debt by selling Treasury securities, such as Treasury bills and notes, to investors. The debt held by the *public* is mainly government securities purchased by financial institutions, local or state governments, foreign investors, and the Federal Reserve System. The debt held by other *federal agencies*, sometimes called intragovernmental holdings, represents the government securities purchased by the Social Security Trust Fund, Medicare, and other federal retirement funds.[32]

The first statutory limit on the U.S. government's total debt was created by the Second Liberty Bond Act of 1917. This legislation not only set limits on certain categories of U.S. government debt, but also increased the government's ability to issue long-term Liberty Bonds to finance U.S. participation in World War I. Since 1917 Congress has changed the debt ceiling many times. For example, Congress increased the debt ceiling repeatedly during national crises such as the Great Depression in the 1930s and World War II (1941-1945), and decreased the debt ceiling after World War II ended.[33] Between 1960 and 2013 Congress increased or extended the debt ceiling 82 times, most recently by the Continuing Appropriations Act of 2014. Under this legislation the debt ceiling was temporarily suspended from October 17, 2013 through February 7, 2014. This meant that additional federal debt could be added onto the previous debt ceiling of $16.7 trillion for nearly four months. By the close of 2013 the debt ceiling had already topped $17 trillion.[34]

The debt ceiling is often confused with the federal budget process, but in reality they are two distinct topics. The debt ceiling represents a type of cap on the total debt the federal government can accumulate. It is not connected to the annual congressional fiscal policy debates over taxes or spending programs. The federal budget process, on the other hand, is intimately connected with congressional tax policies and spending initiatives each fiscal year. When these budget decisions result in a budget deficit, as is frequently the case, the government must borrow money to pay its bills. Hence, federal budget deficits push the nation's total debt closer to the debt ceiling—the legal limit on the government's borrowing. Massive budget deficits, especially since the Great Recession of 2007-2009, have required frequent and substantial increases in the debt ceiling. But increases in the debt ceiling do not cause budget deficits. Instead, an increase in the debt ceiling simply enables the government to pay the bills already authorized by Congress.[35]

Economists generally agree that raising the debt ceiling to enable the Treasury to pay its bills is a necessary and proper action. In fact, over the past half century most increases in the U.S. debt ceiling have occurred without much fanfare. In recent years, however, congressional haggling has politicized changes in the debt ceiling. Some of the opposition to raising the debt ceiling was a continuation of earlier congressional disagreements about federal spending and budget deficits. By the early 2010s political maneuverings in Congress had tied support for an increase in the debt ceiling to future concessions, including spending cuts. The Budget Control Act of 2011 was one such deal. In exchange for a higher debt ceiling Congress was required to make significant cuts in federal spending or face automatic across-the-board spending cuts—a process called budget sequestration. A congressional impasse on the required budget cuts set budget sequestration into motion on March 1, 2013.[36]

The main consequence of failing to raise the debt ceiling to cover existing obligations is government default. **Default** occurs when a government, a business, or an individual is not willing or able to pay its bills. Default by the government is often called sovereign default. The U.S. government has never defaulted on its financial obligations. What would a default look like? Likely results of a U.S. government default would include disruptions in the distribution of Social Security, Medicare, and other benefits to the needy; delays in tax refunds; furloughs or job loss for government workers and the military; and deterioration of other public services. A default would also weaken the government's credit-worthiness at home and abroad. This is because risk-averse investors are hesitant to buy securities from a government that has reneged on past debts. The U.S. Treasury would likely increase interest rates on its securities to attract investors. Higher interest rates in the public and private sectors discourage productive business investment and consumer buying, thus slowing an already tepid economic recovery. A default in the world's largest economy would also raise the specter of financial crises in the United States and in other countries around the world. Default erodes confidence in an economy, a particularly troubling situation when this economy is the bedrock of the global financial system.[37]

CHAPTER 7 SUMMARY

Government Revenues
- The government levies taxes to raise revenues and influence people's economic behaviors.
- The three main types of taxes are progressive, proportional, and regressive taxes.
- Tax fairness is often based on the benefit-received principle or the ability-to-pay principle.
- Most federal tax receipts come from the personal income tax, social insurance taxes, and the corporation income tax.
- Most state and local tax receipts come from the sales tax, state income tax, and property tax.

Government Spending
- Federal spending on appropriated (discretionary) and mandatory programs has increased dramatically in recent decades.
- State and local government spending attends to local needs such as public welfare, education, health care, and infrastructure.
- Rational government decision making involves a cost-benefit analysis.

The Federal Budget
- The federal budget shows anticipated receipts and spending each fiscal year.
- In most years the federal budget is in deficit, that is, government spending exceeds government receipts.
- The national debt, which grows with each budget deficit, imposes costs on society.
- The debt ceiling sets a limit on the total amount of debt the U.S. Department of the Treasury can issue to the public and to other federal agencies.

NOTES

1. National Archives, The Constitution of the United States, www.archives.gov/exhibits/charters/constitution_trnascript.html

2. Internal Revenue Service (IRS), "First-Time Homebuyer Credit," www.irs.gov/newsroom/article/0,,id=204671,00.html

3. Comptroller of the Currency, U.S. Department of the Treasury, "Solar Energy Investment Tax Credits and Grants," (Office of the Comptroller of the Currency, September 2011), 1.

4. Congressional Budget Office (CBO), "Table 2: Shares of Federal Tax Liabilities for All Households, by Before-Tax Income Group, 1979–2009," ...www.cbo.gov/sites/default/files/.../43373-Supplemental_Tables_Final.xls

5. Office of Management and Budget (OMB), "Table S-5: Proposed Budget by Category," *Budget of the U.S. Government: Fiscal Year 2014* (Washington, DC: U.S. Government Printing Office), 2013, 189-190.

6. U.S. Department of the Treasury, IRS, "Table 3, Section 1(c): Unmarried Individuals," *Revenue Procedures 2013-15*, 4, www.irs.gov/pub/irs-drop/rp-13-15.pdf

7. Social Security Administration (SSA), "Factsheet: Social Security" (Baltimore: SSA Press Office, 2012), 1; OMB, "Table S-5: Proposed Budget by Category," *Budget of the U.S. Government: Fiscal Year 2014* (Washington, DC: U.S. Government Printing Office), 2013, 189-190.

8. SSA, "Benefits Planner: Maximum Taxable Earnings, 1937–2012," www.socialsecurity.gov/planners/maxtax.htm; SSA, "Factsheet: Social Security," 1.

9. U.S. Department of the Treasury, IRS, "Tax Rate Schedule," *Instructions for Form 1120*, 17, www.irs.gov/pub/irs-pdf/i1120.pdf

10. U.S. Bureau of the Census, "Table 451: State Governments, Summary of Finances, 1990 to 2008," "Table 455: Local Governments, Revenue by State, 2008," *Statistical Abstract of the United States: 2012* (Washington, DC: U.S. Government Printing Office), 2011, 286, 292-293.

11. Federation of Tax Administrators (FTA), "State Sales Tax Rates and Food & Drug Exemptions," January 1, 2012, www.taxadmin.org/fta/rate/sales.pdf; U.S. Census Bureau, "Table 451: State Governments, Summary of Finances, 1990 to 2008," *Statistical Abstract of the United States: 2012* (Washington, DC: U.S. Government Printing Office), 2011, 286; Telles, Rudy, Sheila O'Sullivan, and Jesse Willhide, *State Government Tax Collections Summary Report: 2011* (Washington, DC: U.S. Department of Commerce), April 12, 2012, 1-4. U.S. Bureau of the Census, "Table 455. Local Governments—Revenue by State: 2008," *Statistical Abstract of the United States: 2012* (Washington, DC: U.S. Government Printing Office), 2011, 292-293.

12. FTA, "State Individual Income Taxes," January 1, 2012, www.taxadmin.org/fta/rate/ind_inc.pdf; U.S. Bureau of the Census, "Table 451. State Governments—Summary of Finances: 1990 to 2008," *Statistical Abstract of the United States: 2012* (Washington, DC: U.S. Government Printing Office), 2011, 286; and Rudy Telles, Sheila O'Sullivan, and Jesse Willhide, *State Government Tax Collections Summary Report: 2011* (Washington, DC: U.S. Department of Commerce), April 12, 2012, 1–4.

13. U.S. Bureau of the Census, "Table 455: Local Governments, Revenue by State, 2008," *Statistical Abstract of the United States: 2012* (Washington, DC: U.S. Government Printing Office), 2011, 292-293.

14. U.S. Bureau of the Census, "Table 1: Population and Area, 1790 to 2012," *Statistical Abstract of the United States: 2012*, 8; U.S. Bureau of the Census, "U.S. POPClock Projection," April 1, 2013, www.census.gov/population/www/popclockus.html

15. OMB, "Table 1.3: Summary of Receipts, Outlays, and Surpluses or Deficits in Current Dollars, Constant (FY 2005) Dollars, and as Percentages of GDP, 1940–2017," *Historical Tables: Budget of the U.S. Government, Fiscal Year 2013*, 26-27.

16. OMB, "Table S-5: Proposed Budget by Category," *Budget of the U.S. Government: Fiscal Year 2014* (Washington, DC: U.S. Government Printing Office), 2013, 189-190.

17. Ibid.

18. Ibid.

19. OMB, "Table S-5," *Budget of the U.S. Government: Fiscal Year 2014* (Washington, DC: U.S. Government Printing Office), 2013, 189-190.

20. U.S. Bureau of the Census, U.S. Department of Commerce, *State and Local Government Finances Summary: 2009* (prepared by Jeffrey L. Barnett), October 2011, 1–4; U.S. Bureau of the Census, "Table 454: State Governments, Expenditures and Debt by State, 2008," "Table 456: Local Governments, Expenditures and Debt by State, 2008," *Statistical Abstract of the United States: 2012* (Washington, DC: U.S. Government Printing Office), 2011, 290-291, 294-295.

21. Ibid

22. Ibid

23. James V. Saturno, "The Congressional Budget Process: A Brief Overview," *CRS Report for Congress* (Congressional Research Service/Library of Congress, January 28, 2004), 1-5.

24. OMB, "Table 1.1: Summary of Receipts, Outlays, and Surpluses or Deficits, 1789–2017," *Historical Tables: Budget of the U.S .Government, Fiscal Year 2013*, 21-23.

25. Library of Congress, "Bill Text, 112th Congress (2011–2012), H.R.RES.2.IH," January 5, 2011, www.thomas.loc.gov/cgi-bin/query/z?112:H.J.RES.2

26. OMB, "Table S-5," *Budget of the U.S. Government: Fiscal Year 2014*, 187.

27. OMB, "Table 1.1: Summary of Receipts, Outlays, and Surpluses or Deficits, 1789–2018," *Historical Tables: Budget of the U.S .Government, Fiscal Year 2014*, 23-25.

28. OMB, "Table 7.1: Federal Debt at the End of the Year, 1940–2018," *Historical Tables: Budget of the U.S. Government, Fiscal Year 2014*, 143-144; U.S. Department of the Treasury, Financial

Management Service, "Table FD-3: Government Accounts Series," 24, www.fms.treas.gov/bulletin/index.html

29. OMB, "Table 7.1: Federal Debt at the End of the Year, 1940–2018," *Historical Tables: Budget of the U.S. Government, Fiscal Year 2014*, 143-144; "U.S. National Debt Clock," June 22, 2013, www.brillig.com/debt_clock

30. Congressional Budget Office (CBO), "Table 3-7: Federal Interest Outlays Projects in CBO's Baseline," *The Budget and Economic Outlook: Fiscal Years 2012 to 2022*, January 2012, 77; OMB "Table S-5," *Budget of the U.S. Government, Fiscal Year 2014*, 189.

31. CBO, *The Budget and Economic Outlook: Fiscal Years 2013 to 2023*, February 2013, 25; OMB, "Table S-5," *Budget of the U.S. Government: Fiscal Year 2014*, 189.

32. Congressional Budget Office (CBO), "Federal Debt and the Statutory Limit, November 2013," 2013, 1-4.

33. D. Andrew Austin, "The Debt Limit: History and Recent Increases," CRS Report for Congress (Washington, DC: Congressional Research Service), April 29, 2008, 2-4.

34. CBO, "Federal Debt and the Statutory Limit, November 2013," 2013, 1-4; U.S. Department of the Treasury. "Debt Limit: Myth v. Fact," May 2011, 1-3.

35. *Ibid.*

36. Richard Kogan, "The Pending Automatic Budget Cuts: How the Two "Sequestrations" Would Work," Center on Budget and Policy Priorities, February 26, 2013, www.cbpp.org/cms/index.cfm; "The Sequester," 2013, www.whitehouse.gov/issues/sequester

37. CBO, "Federal Debt and the Statutory Limit, November 2013," 2013, 1-4; U.S. Department of the Treasury. "Debt Limit: Myth v. Fact," May 2011, 1-3.

Part III

MACROECONOMIC TOPICS

8

Growing the Economy

The most widely recognized measurements of economic growth are the real gross domestic product (GDP) and GDP per capita. Prospects for economic growth are enhanced by saving and investment, the efficient use of resources, entrepreneurship, technological advances, and a stable economic and political environment. Economic growth creates long-run prosperity for many people. Yet there are often unintended consequences of economic growth including income and wealth disparities and stresses on the natural environment.

THE GROSS DOMESTIC PRODUCT

The gross domestic product, or GDP, is an important macroeconomic concept because it relates to the aggregate (total) output of goods and services produced in an economy. Today the ups and downs in the GDP are a widely used barometer of a country's economic health. It was not until the depths of the Great Depression of the 1930s that economists started to look seriously at macroeconomic data, mainly to explain and correct economic downturns. During this time of distress economists developed a measurement of aggregate output, which they dubbed the gross national product (GNP). In more recent decades the gross domestic product has replaced the GNP as the primary gauge of an economy's performance.

GDP Defined

The **gross domestic product** is the total market value of final goods and services produced in a nation each year. This definition sets conditions about the types of goods and services that are counted in the GDP. First, GDP includes only final goods and services. *Final goods* are products produced and sold for direct consumption by consumers, producers, or the government. Excluded from the GDP are *intermediate goods*, or goods that will be further processed or used in the production of another good. For example, an automobile is a final good, while a windshield is an intermediate good. The exclusion of intermediate goods avoids the problem of double counting, that is, counting the same item twice in the GDP. Second, GDP includes only those products produced within the borders of a nation. Thus, the U.S. GDP includes the final output of all firms operating in the United States, whether domestic or foreign owned. Third, GDP includes only newly produced output in a given year. GDP excludes all transactions of used, or secondhand, items. Fourth, GDP excludes all paper transactions that do not result in new output, including the value of stock or bond transactions, mergers and acquisitions of existing firms, Social Security and other transfer payments, and the resale of existing residential properties.

The GDP and gross national product (GNP) are similar measurements of national output. Yet there is a key difference between the two measurements. The **gross national product** (GNP) calculates the total market value of final goods produced by a country's firms within the domestic economy and abroad. Thus, the U.S. GNP includes the market value of output produced by American firms that operate within the United States and by American transnational corporations, independent contractors, and other U.S.-based producers that operate in other countries. Simon Kuznets, an American economist and founder of the GNP, introduced this method of national income and product accounting in the 1930s. Today there is little difference between the size of the GDP and GNP in most countries. In 2012, for example, the U.S. GDP was $15,685 billion, and the GNP was $15,928 billion.[1]

The **real GDP** adjusts the current GDP, also called the nominal GDP, for inflation each year. Real GDP is a more accurate measurement of total national output than nominal GDP because it enables annual growth comparisons based on constant, inflation-adjusted dollars. The GDP price deflator, a price index derived by the government, is used to convert the nominal GDP to the real GDP. The formula for the conversion to real GDP is nominal GDP divided by the price deflator, times 100, as shown in Figure 8.1. In 2012 the nominal GDP of the United States was $15,685 billion, and the GDP deflator was 115.39. In this calculation current dollars are adjusted to the dollar's value in 2005. Figure 8.1 shows how a $15.7 trillion *nominal* GDP is converted into a $13.6 trillion *real* GDP.[2]

The **GDP per capita** states the value of total national output *per person* in a country. The terms "GDP per capita" and "GNP per capita" are often used interchangeably with the term "per capita income." The GDP per capita is calculated by dividing the GDP by the total population of a country. In 2011 the GDP per capita in the United States was $48,112, the eleventh highest per capita GDP among the world's advanced economies. The top five advanced economies ranked by per capita GDP are shown in Table 8.1.[3] When the GDP per capita is adjusted for inflation, it is called the **real GDP per capita**.

Economists often cite the GDP per capita to compare the relative well-being of people living in different countries. While this may be one broad-stroke way to compare people's well-being across national borders, there are limitations to this measure. For instance, GDP

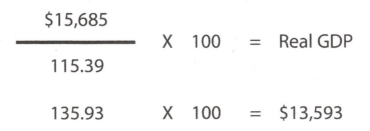

Figure 8.1   Calculating the Real GDP, 2012 ($ billions)
Source: Bureau of Economic Analysis, "Table 3" and "Table 6," *News Release*, June 26, 2013, 8, 11.

Table 8.1   Top 5 Advanced Countries Ranked by GDP Per Capita, 2011

World Rank	Country	GDP per Capita ($ US)
1	Luxembourg	114,232
2	Norway	98,081
3	Switzerland	83,326
4	Australia	61,789
5	Denmark	59,889

Source: World Bank, *World Development Indicators* (data), 2013.

per capita states the average income of people but does not account for the distribution of income within economies. In virtually all economies the poorest segment of society subsists on a tiny fraction of the national income and wealth, while the richest segment of the population is far more prosperous. Another limitation is that the GDP per capita deals only with reported business activity. It therefore excludes barter and the unreported productive enterprise that takes place in the informal economy. Third, GDP per capita may not adjust data to reflect the actual purchasing power of money within an economy. One U.S. dollar, for example, buys more goods in a poorer country such as Haiti than it does in the United States. Finally, GDP per capita does not consider the size or power of economies. None of the seven "major advanced countries," for example, are included in the top five ranking. The major advanced economies, often called the G-7 countries, include Canada, France, Germany, Italy, Japan, the United Kingdom, and the United States.[4]

Calculating the GDP

The most commonly used method of calculating GDP is the *expenditures approach*, which tallies the total spending on final goods and services in four areas: consumption (C), investment (I), government (G), and net exports (Xn). The expenditures approach to calculating the GDP can be stated as an equation: C + I + G + Xn = GDP.

ECONOMICS IN HISTORY: The Birth of the Gross National Product

Simon Kuznets (1901–1985), a twentieth-century American economist, is widely hailed as the father of the gross national product (GNP). Born in Kharkiv, Russia, Kuznets immigrated to the United States in 1922. The following year he entered Columbia University, where he earned a doctorate degree in 1926. He joined the staff of the National Bureau of Economic Research (NBER) in 1927. His professional career included prestigious teaching positions at the University of Pennsylvania, Johns Hopkins University, and Harvard.

Kuznets is best known for his meticulous collection of macroeconomic data related to national output and national income, and the application of this data to economic growth, business cycles, and economic development. In *National Income and Its Composition, 1919–1938* (1941), Kuznets identified key features of national income and product accounts. He stressed the need to determine national income with "consistency and explicitness" yet recognized that limitations existed in estimating aggregate output—the gross national product (GNP). For example, excluded from GNP were goods and services provided "outside of the market system,"[5] such as the services of homemakers and unreported business activity in the informal sector of the economy. Still, the pioneering work of Kuznets provided the foundation of GNP calculations, the primary framework for measuring economic performance in the United States during the post–World War II era.

Table 8.2   Calculating the Nominal Gross Domestic Product, 2012

Components of the GDP	Dollar Value ($ billions)
Consumption spending	11,120
Investment spending	2,062
Government spending	3,063
Net exports	−560
Gross domestic product	15,685

Source: Bureau of Economic Analysis, "Table 3," *News Release*, June 26, 2013, 8–9.

In this equation, "C" represents spending by individuals on consumer goods and services. Consumer goods include items such as automobiles and other motor vehicles, clothing and footwear, food and beverages, furnishings, and gasoline and other forms of energy. Services include people's productive activities in fields such as health care, banking and finance, insurance, real estate, and recreation. In 2012 American consumers spent $11.1 trillion on consumer goods and services, as shown in Table 8.2.[6] "I" represents investment spending by firms and households on new capital, including factories, office buildings, equipment, inventories of products, and houses or apartment buildings. Investment goods accounted for $2.1 trillion in spending. "G" represents government spending at the federal, state, and local levels. Government goods include school buildings, submarines, and libraries, while services are often expressed as salaries of teachers, airport security guards, public officials, and so on. In 2012 about $3.1 trillion was spent on government goods and services.

"Xn" represents net exports, the difference between the dollar value of the nation's imports and exports. Note in Table 8.2 that net exports is a negative number. This occurs when the value of U.S. imports is greater than the value of its exports—about $560 billion more in this case. This $560 billion is called the trade deficit and is subtracted from the U.S. GDP because it represents spending by Americans on foreign-produced goods rather than American-made goods.

MEASURING ECONOMIC GROWTH

Unprecedented government involvement in the national economy during the Great Depression (1930s) and World War II (1941–1945) marked the end of laissez-faire capitalism in the United States. Just one year after the close of World War II, Congress passed the historic Employment Act of 1946, an act that established three main macroeconomic goals for the U.S. economy—full employment, economic growth, and price stability.

Economic Growth Defined

Economic growth occurs when a country's real gross domestic product (GDP) increases over time. Perspectives on economic growth have shifted in recent years, however. Some economists believe that economic growth occurs only when national output increases per person, as measured by real GDP per capita. Others view economic growth qualitatively as well as quantitatively and insist that rising real GDP per capita be accompanied by measurable improvements in people's quality of life.

One way to illustrate economic growth is by an outward, or positive, shift in a nation's production possibilities frontier (PPF). Such a shift is shown in Figure 8.2. The positive

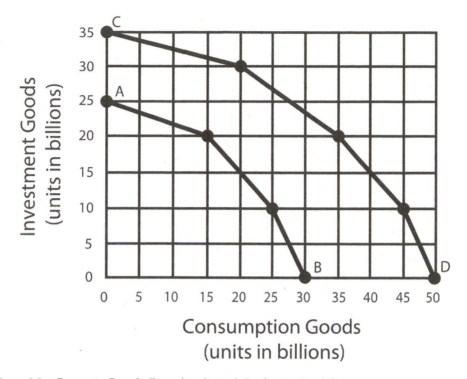

Figure 8.2 Economic Growth: Expanding Society's Production Possibilities

shift of the country's PPF from curve AB to curve CD in Figure 8.2 indicates that more consumption goods *and* investment goods are produced along the outer curve CD than along the original inner curve AB. The positive shift of the country's PPF is the result positive economic or political forces that affect the supply side of markets. That is, these forces enable an economy to produce more goods and services than was originally possible. Important determinants of economic growth, such as expanded national savings and investment and the efficient use of resources, are discussed in the next section of this chapter.

Tracking Economic Growth with the Business Cycle

The **business cycle** illustrates the short-term ups and downs in the real gross domestic product (GDP) over time. The business cycle is comprised of two phases, an expansion and a contraction, as shown in Figure 8.3. During an *expansion* the real GDP rises. Improvements in job creation, business investment, real income, consumer confidence, and consumer spending often accompany expansions. During a *contraction* the real GDP falls. A contraction of at least two consecutive quarters, or six months, is normally considered a **recession**. Today economists at the National Bureau of Economic Research (NBER) consider a variety of other factors before they declare that the U.S. economy is in recession, however. Other benchmarks of a recession are negative changes in the unemployment rate, investment levels, incomes, and retail sales figures. A **depression** is a severe, prolonged recession.

The business cycle also has two points: a peak and a trough. The *peak* represents the highest point on a business cycle, while the *trough* is the lowest point. These points are also

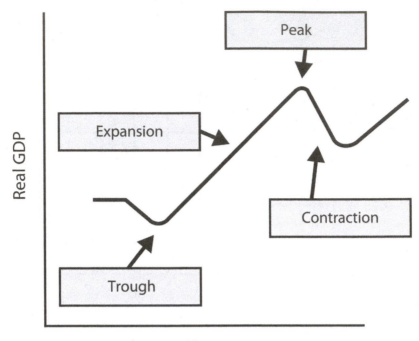

Figure 8.3   The Business Cycle Model

shown in Figure 8.3. Technically, an expansion in the business cycle occurs between the trough and the peak. A contraction, on the other hand, occurs between the peak and the trough.[7] Business cycles illustrate short-term changes in national output. But a series of business cycles can also illustrate long-term growth trends over 20, 50, or even 100 years.

Economists use three types of **economic indicators** to predict and assess the duration of business cycles in the U.S. economy. The *leading economic indicators* are indicators that predict the direction of a business cycle. Leading economic indicators might signal an expansion or a contraction. Leading indicators that point to an expansion include increases in business start-ups, applications for building permits, the average manufacturing workweek, new orders for producer and consumer goods, and the Dow Jones Industrial Average (Dow). Declines in the leading indicators suggest the economy is headed for a contraction. *Coincident economic indicators* occur in conjunction with a change in the business cycle. As an economy enters an expansion, for example, personal income, sales volume, and production levels rise. Conversely, when an economy enters a contraction, personal income, sales, and production tend to decline. *Lagging economic indicators* occur months after a change in the business cycle has occurred and often persist even into the next phase of the business cycle. Unemployment is an example of a lagging indicator. Unemployment tends to rise during a contraction and generally carries over for a time into the next phase of the business cycle, the expansion.

Benefits of Economic Growth
Economic growth expands personal and business opportunities and choices. First, economic growth improves people's standard of living. **Standard of living** refers to the

Table 8.3   Real GDP and the Standard of Living, 1960–2010 (measured in constant 2005 $US)

Year	Real GDP ($ billions)	Disposable Personal Income	Personal Consumption Expenditures
1960	$2,829	$10,865	$9,871
1970	$4,266	$15,158	$13,361
1980	$5,834	$17,091	$14,881
1990	$8,027	$23,568	$21,249
2000	$11,216	$28,899	$26,939
2010	$13,063	$33,025	$30,034

Source: U.S. Bureau of the Census, "Table 679," "Table 455," *Statistical Abstract of the United States: 2012* (Washington, DC: U.S. Government Printing Office), 2011, 443; Bureau of Economic Analysis, "Current Dollar and 'Real' Gross Domestic Product," July 27, 2012.

material well-being of people. Economic growth in the United States gained momentum during the twentieth century, and people's standard of living, on average, rose accordingly. Between 1900 and 1950 people's real income—income adjusted for inflation—increased by about 170 percent.[8] As a result, the standard of living improved for the blossoming middle class, which now could afford to buy many of the comforts of life such as a home, a car, consumer durables, and other consumer goods. Similarly, between 1960 and 2010 Americans' real per capita disposable (after-tax) income tripled, as did their spending on consumer items, as shown in Table 8.3.[9]

A second benefit of economic growth is an improved quality of life for people. **Quality of life** implies a higher standard of living plus other improvements in the human condition. Economic growth helps create the wealth necessary for public investments in education, health care, infrastructure, social programs, and so on. The size of public investments in these programs is dependent on the amount of tax revenues collected from society's private sector, however. The richer advanced economies make significant public investments, which increase people's economic opportunities, expand their choices, and attend to their needs. The wealth derived from economic growth also enables people to enjoy additional leisure pursuits such as personal interests and recreation.

A third benefit of economic growth is its ability to maintain the virtuous cycle of growth and development. Growing, prosperous societies are able to save money, a prerequisite for investments in new technology, private and social capital, human capital, and entrepreneurship. Business investment results in business formation, job creation, and technological advances. Investment is also the wellspring of product innovation, as evidenced by improvements ranging from computers and software, to cell phones and tablets, to hybrid automobiles. Meanwhile, less efficient producers and those that cannot adapt to changing tastes in the marketplace are weeded out—a process colorfully described by economist Joseph A. Schumpeter as "creative destruction."[10]

DETERMINANTS OF ECONOMIC GROWTH AND PRODUCTIVITY

The process of economic growth relies on a number of interrelated economic, political, and social factors that work in concert to increase national output. At the core of economic growth is the need to increase productivity over time. **Productivity** measures the amount of output that is produced per unit of input. On the national level, the amount of output refers to the real GDP, and the inputs are the factors of production—natural resources,

---

PRIMARY DOCUMENT: Joseph A. Schumpeter Explains Creative Destruction

Capitalism, then, is by nature a form or method of economic change and not only never is but never can be stationary. . . . The fundamental impulse that sets and keeps the capitalist engine in motion comes from the new consumers' goods, the new methods of production or transportation, the new markets, the new forms of industrial organization that capitalist enterprise creates. . . .

[This] industrial mutation . . . incessantly revolutionizes the economic structure *from within*, incessantly destroying the old one, incessantly creating a new one. This process of Creative Destruction is the essential fact about capitalism.

Capitalism, Socialism, and Democracy, Joseph A. Schumpeter

---

human resources, and capital goods. When the mix of resources used in production results in greater output per unit of input, productivity rises. When the mix of resources produces lesser output per unit of input, productivity falls.

The most common measurement of productivity is the productivity of labor. The productivity of labor is calculated by dividing the value of national output by the number of workers in the labor force. For instance, from 1975 to 2011 the productivity of U.S. workers more than doubled.[11] This means that workers in 2011, on average, were able to produce twice as much output as workers in 1975. Five main determinants of economic growth and productivity are the use of savings for productive investment, the efficient use of resources, entrepreneurship and new knowledge, a favorable economic environment, and good governance.

Economic growth can enhance people's quality of life, including educational opportunities. (Monkey Business Images/Dreamstime.com)

Saving and Investing: The Virtuous Cycle

Gross saving and investment are the pillars of a virtuous cycle of economic growth and development. This is because people's savings create a pool of money that can be used for productive investments. Significant investment is possible when the pool of savings is deep. Lesser investment possibilities exist when the pool of savings is shallow. The virtuous cycle of growth and development occurs when significant sums of money are saved and invested in an economy. New businesses, jobs, income, and wealth spring from these investments.

Gross saving is the amount of savings by individuals, businesses, and government in an economy. In 2011 gross saving in the United States was about $1.84 trillion, a drop from $2.2 trillion recorded in 2006 just prior to the Great Recession. The personal savings of individuals and business savings, mainly in the form of undistributed corporate profits, accounted for most gross saving in 2011. Government saving, on the other hand, was a negative $1.3 trillion, largely due to the massive federal budget deficit that year.[12] Between 2007 and 2012 the U.S. gross saving rate, or gross saving as a percentage of GDP, hovered in the 11 percent to 15 percent range, among the lowest recorded by the world's major advanced economies, as shown in Table 8.4.[13]

Gross investment consists of private and public sector investments in an economy. Gross investment is financed mainly by gross savings. In 2012 U.S. gross investment was about $2.4 trillion. Nearly $2.1 trillion of U.S. gross investment was made by businesses and individuals in the private sector of the economy, and the remaining $368 billion was made by the federal and state governments in the public sector of the economy. Businesses invested $1.6 trillion in 2012, mainly on computers and other information processing equipment ($555 billion), industrial and transportation equipment ($394 billion), and nonresidential production facilities such as factories, retail outlets, and mines ($463 billion). Hundreds of billions of dollars were also invested in private sector residential structures such single-family houses.[14]

Gross investment in the global economy varies by world region, and by countries' income level and stage of economic development. One international measure of gross investment is **gross capital formation**, which deals mainly with investments to expand a country's fixed assets. This measure includes spending on land improvements, roads, railways, schools, hospitals, machinery and equipment, factories and office buildings, and residences. The World Bank reported that gross capital formation, expressed as a percentage of GDP, is relatively low in Europe and central Asia, Latin America, and sub-Saharan

Table 8.4   Saving and Investment by Major Advanced Economies, 2012

Major Advanced Economies	Savings (percentage of GDP)	Investment (percentage of GDP)
Canada	20.8	24.5
France	17.6	19.9
Germany	24.4	17.2
Italy	17.1	17.6
Japan	21.6	20.6
United Kingdom	10.8	14.3
United States	13.1	16.2

Source: International Monetary Fund, "Table A15," *World Economic Outlook, April 2013*, 172–173.

Africa. The gross capital formation rates for the richer countries, including the United States, were also low. Higher rates of capital formation occurred in East Asia and the Pacific, and South Asia.[15]

Efficient Use of the Factors of Production

Economic growth is based on an economy's ability to produce goods and services. **Production** occurs when people use the factors of production, or productive resources, to produce these products. The three main factors of production are natural resources, human resources, and capital goods. These resources are unevenly distributed in the world. Yet to achieve economic growth societies must acquire and use resources in efficient and innovative ways.

Natural resources, or gifts of nature, are things present in the natural environment that are used in production. Natural resources include minerals, oil, natural gas, rivers, oceans, fish, animals, soil, forests, plants, and sunlight. Natural resources provide many of the raw materials needed to produce goods and services. At times a variety of natural resources are available within a region or a country. The United States, for example, has abundant fertile land, forests, navigable rivers, deep-water harbors, and minerals. In other countries economic activity sometimes centers on a single resource such as crude oil in the Persian Gulf nations of Kuwait, Saudi Arabia, and the United Arab Emirates. Still other countries lack domestic supplies of key resources but are able to acquire them through trade or foreign investment. For example, Japan's meteoric economic growth during the post–World War II era relied on the import of petroleum, minerals, timber, and other natural resources not readily available within its borders. Similar trade and investment opportunities have promoted rapid economic growth in China and in the Newly Industrialized Asian Economies (NIEs), including Hong Kong SAR, Korea, Singapore, and the Taiwan Province of China.

Human resources are the people engaged in production. Human resources include assembly line workers, miners, contractors, and farmers in the goods-producing sector and teachers, doctors, and engineers in the services-producing sector. Investments in human resources create human capital. **Human capital** represents the expanded abilities and skills workers acquire through education, apprenticeships, or other training. Skilled, healthy workers are generally more productive and contribute more to a country's economic growth than poorly trained workers. The advanced economies make significant investments in human capital. The United Nations found that students in countries with "very high human development" averaged 11.5 years of education, compared to just 4.2 years of education for students in "low human development" countries. Predictably, the countries with high levels of education were among the most advanced and prosperous in the global economy, while countries with low levels of education were among the poorest.[16]

Capital goods are items that are used to produce other products. Capital goods include construction equipment, mine shafts, factory buildings, and tractors in the goods-producing sector and television cameras, surgical instruments, and information processing equipment in the services-producing sector. Investment in new capital goods increases a nation's **capital stock**, the total amount of capital available to produce goods and services. Expanding the nation's capital stock supports the goal of **capital deepening**, which occurs when a nation's capital stock *per worker* increases over time. Capital deepening is essential to economic growth. Heavy investments in new capital goods by the NIEs over the past few decades, for example, enabled these economies to rise into the ranks of the advanced economies.

A nation's capital stock supports growth only if this capital is employed in production. In the U.S. economy the **capacity utilization rate** measures how much of its productive capital is employed at any moment in time. During periods of economic expansion the capacity utilization rate typically exceeds 80 percent. During economic downturns the capacity utilization rate drops. The capacity utilization rate dipped as low as 68.6 percent during the Great Recession in 2009, when nearly one-third of the country's productive capital sat idle for a period of time. A tepid economic recovery pushed the U.S. capacity utilization rate to 78.7 percent by 2012.[17]

Entrepreneurship and Knowledge

Entrepreneurship represents the actions of entrepreneurs who develop new products, production methods, or businesses. Entrepreneurship is sometimes considered a factor of production, joining natural resources, human resources, and capital goods. Entrepreneurs are innovators and risk-takers who transform ideas into commercial enterprises. The founding of Apple Computer by Steven Jobs, Microsoft by Bill Gates, and Walmart by Sam Walton testify to the importance of entrepreneurial activity in the U.S. economy. The annual *Global Entrepreneurship Monitor* (*GEM*) has made compelling links between entrepreneurship and economic growth and development. The *GEM 2011 Global Report* investigated entrepreneurial activity in 52 economies. One conclusion from this study was that "an economy's prosperity is highly dependent on a dynamic entrepreneurship sector."[18]

Closely related to the topic of entrepreneurship is knowledge. Knowledge promotes **innovation**, the process of converting scientific discoveries and technological advances into profitable products or improved methods of production. Knowledge and innovation often ripple through an economy, sparking additional business formation, job creation, and national output. Under the banner of new growth theory, economist Paul M. Romer argued that economic growth is mainly the result of new knowledge. For example, new knowledge created through investments in education, research and development, and other means supported economic growth in the United States and Japan after World War II. New growth theorists also argue that knowledge is not subject to the law of diminishing returns. The **law of diminishing returns** states that as additional inputs are used in production, progressively smaller amounts of output are created. Instead, these new growth theorists contend that knowledge spawns increasing returns, as the boundless applications and adaptations of new ideas create limitless commercial possibilities.

During the twentieth century the benefits of knowledge gained through research and development (R&D) became more apparent to businesses and to the government. Businesses, especially large corporations, created R&D departments to remain competitive in domestic and global markets. In 2009 total spending on R&D in the United States was $400 billion. Of this total, private industries supplied $247 billion in R&D funding, about three-fifths of all money spent on R&D, as shown in Table 8.5. The top private sector R&D spenders were found in six industry groups: chemicals, computer and electronic products, aerospace and defense manufacturing, automotive manufacturing, software and computer-related products, and R&D services. Another major source of R&D funding was the federal government ($124 billion). Finally, state governments, colleges and universities, and nonprofit organizations spent $29 billion on R&D. Historically, nations with

Thomas Alva Edison at his New Jersey research laboratory, 1901. (Library of Congress)

relatively high spending on R&D include the United States, Japan, Germany, and South Korea.[19]

Favorable Economic Environment

The process of economic growth is enhanced by a favorable economic environment, which includes a sophisticated infrastructure, supportive economic institutions, and macroeconomic stability. A country's infrastructure includes public sector facilities and services such as roads and bridges, airports and seaports, water and sanitation systems, hospitals, schools, courts and prisons, and other public goods that support an orderly living environment and predictable business climate. The government finances most of its spending on infrastructure—sometimes called social capital—with tax dollars. A country's infrastructure also includes private sector features such as information and communications systems, electric power networks, and other energy systems. Infrastructure construction and maintenance is a high priority item in the advanced countries but often is underfunded in the developing world.

Table 8.5 U.S. Funding for Research and Development, 2009

Source of Funding for R&D	R&D Funding ($ billions)	R&D Funding (% of total)
Private industries	247	61.8
Federal government	124	31.1
Other	29	7.1
Total R&D Funding	400	100.0

Source: National Science Foundation, "Table 4.1," *Science and Engineering Indicators, 2012.*

Supportive market-oriented economic institutions, formal and informal, are also crucial to economic growth. Some market institutions are abstract, such as private property rights, voluntary exchange, economic freedom, and profit incentives. Yet these institutions motivate people to work, save, invest, and take financial and business risks in domestic and foreign markets. Other institutions are more tangible. For example, banks and other depository institutions channel savings into productive investments. Stock and bond markets provide a mechanism to raise funds for business start-ups, expansions, or mergers and acquisitions. Public institutions, such as the Federal Reserve System (Fed) and the Securities and Exchange Commission (SEC), provide oversight of financial markets.

Finally, macroeconomic stability supports economic growth. The federal government promotes macroeconomic stability—stable prices and full employment—through responsible monetary and fiscal policies. In the U.S. economy the Federal Reserve System (Fed), the nation's central bank, implements monetary policy. During times of inflation the Fed uses its monetary tools to tighten credit and withdraw money from the economy. These actions reduce the primary cause of inflation—too much money chasing too few goods. If the economy slumps into a recession, however, the Fed loosens credit and

ECONOMICS IN HISTORY: General Purpose Technology and the Birth of the Internet

Government support for R&D takes many forms, including grants to colleges and universities, financial aid to private firms, and funding for general purpose technologies. A **general purpose technology** (GPT) is a technology that could, over time, have many possible uses depending on the creativity of entrepreneurs and other innovators in the economy. Government funding of GPTs is sometimes necessary to defray prohibitive research costs. The selection of research projects for such funding is based mainly on the likelihood of spillover benefits for the economy and society. Perhaps the best-known GPT is the Internet.

The Internet, originally called ARPANET, was a GPT financed through the U.S. Department of Defense. Its main goal was to facilitate communication and information sharing by linking computers located at different sites. As the linkages grew, the project was taken over by the National Science Foundation.[20] Since its invention (1969), the Internet's commercial value increased with the introduction of complementary technologies such as email in 1972 and the World Wide Web (WWW) in 1989. By 2012 about 2.3 billion people worldwide were Internet users, according to the International Telecommunications Union (ITU).[21] The value of U.S. ecommerce, which is conducted over the Internet, accounted for $3.4 trillion in 2009. Most of this $3.4 trillion in ecommerce was for business-to-business (B2B) transactions ($3,073 billion) rather than business-to-consumer (B2C) transactions ($298 billion).[22]

expands the money supply. These actions stimulate business activity. Congress stabilizes the economy through fiscal policy. Congress fights inflation by withdrawing money from the economy by raising taxes or lowering government spending. Congress fights recession by pumping money into the economy by lowering taxes or increasing government spending.

Good Governance

Good governance occurs when the government is honest and competent in the discharge of its responsibilities. At the core of good governance is the rule of law, an understanding that all participants in the nation's economic and political life must abide by the same rules. Good governance promotes economic growth by encouraging people's participation in the formal economy and by creating equal opportunities for success.

The advanced economies of the world have long traditions of good governance. Specific indicators of good governance include a fair system of taxation, enforceable patent and copyright laws, legal protections for private property and private profits, effective antitrust laws, transparency in public and private sector business transactions, the absence of corruption and political cronyism, and a host of rules and regulations to protect the rights of marketplace participants, including workers, investors, savers, and consumers. Combined, these features of good governance provide incentives for people to develop and apply their talents in the formal economy. On a broader level, good governance supports human rights, gender equity, tolerance, and democracy.

Democracy and freedom support market-oriented economic institutions and economic growth. **Democracy** is a type of political system that relies on broad-based citizen participation, free elections, and the rule of law. The political freedoms inherent in democracies are compatible with the economic freedoms of capitalism. That is, democracy and capitalism embrace freedom of choice and informed decision making by the people. Studies by the Freedom House, the world's most recognized authority on global political trends and the status of freedom, established a direct relationship between freedom and economic growth. This conclusion applies to countries at all levels of economic development.[23] Not all countries with growing economies are democratic, however. China, one of the fastest growing economies in the world in recent decades, maintains an undemocratic, one-party political system. Similarly, the growing economies of some oil-rich Persian Gulf countries such as the United Arab Emirates and Saudi Arabia are monarchies.

Corrupt political institutions, on the other hand, undermine economic growth and development. **Corruption** is the abuse of public trust for personal gain. Corruption occurs when public officials or private sector business people intentionally circumvent existing laws and ethical standards to improve their own wellbeing. The activities commonly associated with corruption are manifest in a tangled web of improprieties among public officials, government agencies, private businesses, or other special interest groups. Corruption reduces a country's growth potential. Rampant bribery, intimidation, and cronyism stifle legitimate business start-ups, investment, research and development, and innovation. Corruption also weakens entrepreneurship, retards capital formation, and discourages long-term global connections such as foreign direct investment (FDI), international trade, and foreign aid. This type of unstable business environment also encourages the hasty exodus of skilled workers and financial resources from the country.

LIMITATIONS OF ECONOMIC GROWTH

People may simply assume that higher national output and progrowth policies are good for the economy and all groups of people. Yet there are costs as well as benefits to economic growth. For example, production and consumption decisions involve trade-offs. A **trade-off** occurs when people choose to use resources one way rather than another way. At times trade-offs associated with economic growth result in certain benefits going to one group of people at the expense of another.

Poverty and the Distribution of Income and Wealth

One problem often associated with a dynamic, growing economy is a widening income gap and wealth gap between groups of people. Historically economic growth has been the norm in the United States. President John F. Kennedy's famous statement that "a rising tide raises all boats" suggests that sustained economic growth will improve all people's well-being. Measurable income and wealth data in the United States challenge this assumption, however.

The income gap between America's richest and poorest citizens has increased steadily in recent decades, as shown in Table 8.6. Between 1970 and 2010 the percentage of money income received by the richest 20 percent of the population, identified in the table as the highest quintile, climbed from 43.3 percent to 50.2 percent. To put it another way, the richest 20 percent of the U.S. population earned half of all income in 2010. Conversely, the percentage of money income received by each of the four lower quintiles—the lower 80 percent of the population—declined during this 40-year period.[24]

The distribution of income in any given year can be illustrated on a Lorenz curve, as shown in Figure 8.4. The vertical axis of the graph shows the percentage of income divided into segments of 20 percent each. The horizontal axis shows the U.S. population, by the lowest 20 percent, then the lowest 40 percent, the lowest 60 percent, and so on. The points on the Lorenz curve, labeled A–E, shows the percentage of income each segment of the population receives. At point A, for example, the lowest (poorest) 20 percent of the population received just 3.3 percent of income in 2010. Point B shows that the lower 40 percent of the population received 11.8 percent of the income (3.3% + 8.5%). Point C shows that the lower 60 percent of the population received 26.4 percent of the income (3.3% + 8.5% + 14.6%). Point D shows that the lower 80 percent of the population received 49.8 percent of the income (3.3% + 8.5% + 14.6% + 23.4%). The remaining 50.2 percent of income is earned by the richest 20 percent of the people, as shown at point E.

Table 8.6   Distribution of Money Income in the U.S. by Quintile, 1970–2010 (% earned by each quintile)

Income Quintile	1970	1980	1990	2000	2010
Lowest quintile	4.1	4.2	3.8	3.6	3.3
Second quintile	10.8	10.2	9.6	8.9	8.5
Third quintile	17.4	16.8	15.9	14.8	14.6
Fourth quintile	24.5	24.7	24.0	23.3	23.4
Highest quintile	43.3	44.1	46.6	49.8	50.2

Source: U.S. Bureau of the Census, "Table 694," *Statistical Abstract of the United States: 2012*, 454; U.S. Bureau of the Census, "Table 3," *Current Population Reports*, September 2011, 11.

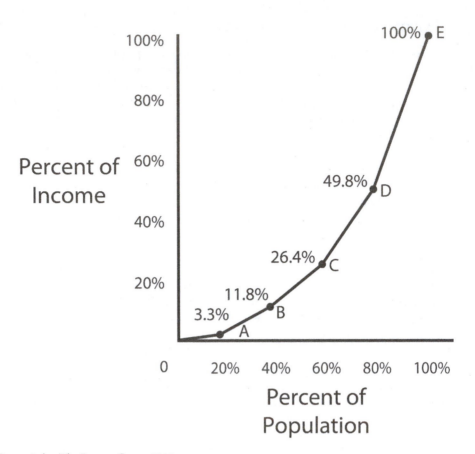

Figure 8.4   The Lorenz Curve, 2010

The distribution of income has a major impact on who is considered poor or not poor in the United States. Even with detailed income data, poverty is difficult to measure, however. The U.S. Census Bureau says that **poverty** occurs when a family's income falls below the official poverty line. The **poverty line**, which the Census Bureau calls the poverty threshold, is the income level that separates the poor from the nonpoor. The government calculates the poverty line by multiplying a typical family's annual food budget times three, a formula that has changed little over the past half-century. The poverty line inches upward each year as price levels rise. In 2012 the Census Bureau determined that a family of two was poor if its annual money income dipped below $14,960; a family of four was poor if its annual income fell below $23,497; and a family of nine or more persons was poor if its annual income fell below $47,536. These numbers vary some depending on the actual composition of the household, such as the number of dependent children, grandparents, or other relatives.[25] The U.S. Department of Health and Human Services (HHS) uses a slightly different measure of poverty called poverty guidelines to determine eligibility for government assistance programs. A comparison of recent U.S. poverty thresholds (2012) and poverty guidelines (2013) is shown in Table 8.7.[26]

The **poverty rate** measures the percentage of Americans living in poverty. Over the past several decades the U.S. poverty rate has generally fluctuated between 12 percent and

Table 8.7   U.S. Poverty Thresholds and Guidelines, 2012–2013

Size of Family	Poverty Thresholds (Census) 2012	Poverty Guidelines (HHS) 2013	Size of Family	Poverty Thresholds (Census) 2012	Poverty Guidelines (HHS) 2013
1	$11,722	$11,490	6	$31,485	$31,590
2	$14,960	$15,510	7	$35,811	$35,610
3	$18,287	$19,530	8	$39,872	$39,630
4	$23,497	$23,550	9	$47,536	add $4,020 per person
5	$27,815	$27,570			

Source: U.S. Department of Health and Human Services, "2013 Poverty Guidelines," *Federal Register*, January 24, 2013; U.S. Bureau of the Census, "Preliminary Estimates of Weighted Average Poverty Thresholds for 2012," January 18, 2013.

15 percent of the U.S. population. In the most recent 10-year period, the poverty rate climbed steadily from 12.1 percent in 2002 to 15 percent in 2011. During this same 10-year period, the number of Americans falling below the poverty line climbed from 34.6 million people to 46.2 million people. Much of this dramatic rise in poverty was attributed to the negative effects of the Great Recession (2007–2009) on people's incomes. Historically the U.S. poverty rate has been higher for minorities than for the white, non-Hispanic population. In 2011, for example, the poverty rate for whites was 9.8 percent, while the poverty rates for blacks (27.6 percent) and Hispanics (25.3 percent) were significantly higher.[27]

In the United States the wealth gap between the rich and the poor is even greater than the income gap. A common measure of wealth in the United States is a household's net worth. **Net worth** is the difference between a household's gross assets and its liabilities. Assets are usually divided into two categories: financial assets and nonfinancial assets. *Financial assets* include stocks, bonds, retirement accounts, certificates of deposit, and a host of transaction accounts such as checking accounts, savings accounts, and money market deposit accounts. *Nonfinancial assets* include the value of items owned such as a house, a business, or even a car. A household's *liabilities* are its debts—the amount of money owed to others. For most households the largest liability is the amount owed on a home mortgage. In 2010 the net worth for many households plummeted due to falling housing prices (a drop in the value of a nonfinancial asset) and a drop in the value of securities such as stock and bonds (a drop in the value of financial assets). In 2010, the top 1 percent of Americans owned 34.5 percent of all wealth. The top 10 percent owned about 75 percent of all wealth. Conversely, in 2010 the bottom 50 percent of the American people owned just 1.1 percent of all wealth.[28]

Since the 1960s a comprehensive social welfare system has redistributed some of society's income and wealth to the needy, including those living in poverty. A major expansion of the nation's social programs, often called the Great Society programs, began during the presidency of Lyndon B. Johnson (1963–1969). Great Society programs expanded civil rights protections, educational opportunities, and the safety net of social programs. Several Great Society programs enacted or expanded during the 1960s included the food stamp program, Medicare, and Medicaid. Today's most important public assistance programs for the poor are Temporary Assistance for Needy Families (TANF), Supplemental

Despite the expansion of social programs since the 1960s, poverty remains a persistent economic problem in the United States. (Shutterstock.com)

Security Income (SSI), Medicaid, and the Supplemental Nutrition Assistance Program (SNAP)—formerly the food stamp program.

Environmental Stresses

For decades economists, sociologists, and scientists have warned that unbridled economic growth is unsustainable. In *Small is Beautiful: Economics as if People Mattered* (1973), E. F. Schumacher warned that the planet was on a "collision course" with economic collapse and that humanity must "begin to see the possibility of evolving a new life-style, with new methods of production and new patterns of consumption: a life-style designed for permanence."[29] Schumacher, Rachel Carson (*Silent Spring*, 1962), Paul R. Ehrlich (*The Population Bomb*, 1968), Barry Commoner (*The Closing Circle*, 1971), and others challenged people to consider the costs *and* benefits of their economic choices. The environmental costs of economic growth generally concern environmental degradation, climate change, and resource depletion.

Some environmental degradation is an inevitable result of production. On the one hand, production creates the wide variety of goods and services needed to sustain life and provide for people's comforts. On the other hand, unbridled production fouled the air, water, and land with pollutants; created wastelands with strip mining, aggressive timbering, overgrazing, and overplanting; and destroyed natural habitats with urban sprawl. Critics of growth also point to mounting evidence that inefficient production methods and unsustainable consumption have contributed to global warming. The 2009 UN conference on climate change in Copenhagen, Denmark, underscored the need to reduce toxic emissions into the atmosphere—a sentiment echoed by many world leaders who attended the Copenhagen Summit soon thereafter.

Another environmental cost of economic growth is resource depletion. Resource depletion occurs when resources are used in production but not replaced. **Nonrenewable resources**, including petroleum and natural gas, are consumed in the production process and cannot be reclaimed for further use. Further, nonrenewable resources are in finite supply. **Renewable resources**, such as forests, fish, and animals, can be replenished. Critics of economic growth have traditionally focused on the inevitable depletion of the world's finite supply of nonrenewable resources. Major international organizations, including the United Nations, have documented that resource depletion is taking place. Particularly troubling is the depletion of basic resources such as fresh water, arable soil, forests, and oceans. The *World Resources Report: 2012–2013* focused on ways countries with limited resources could best meet the needs of growing populations, especially in the developing world.

CHAPTER 8 SUMMARY

The Gross Domestic Product
- The gross domestic product (GDP) states the value of national output each year.
- The expenditures approach to calculating GDP tallies spending by consumers, businesses, and the government.

Measuring Economic Growth
- Economic growth occurs when the real GDP or real GDP per capita increases over time.
- Trends in a country's business cycle can illustrate periods of positive economic growth or negative growth.
- The main benefits of economic growth are an improved standard of living and quality of life for people.

Determinants of Economic Growth and Productivity
- The virtuous cycle of savings and investment is the wellspring of business formation, job creation, and economic prosperity.
- The efficient use of natural, human, and capital resources expands an economy's ability to produce goods and services.
- Entrepreneurship and new knowledge jump-start innovation and new business activity.
- A favorable economic environment includes a well-developed infrastructure, supportive economic institutions, and macroeconomic stability.
- Good governance improves incentives for people to participate in the formal economy by leveling the playing field.

Limitations of Economic Growth
- Economic growth can widen the income gap and wealth gap between society's richest and poorest people.
- Economic growth can intensify environmental stresses associated with ecosystem decay, climate change, and resource depletion.

NOTES

1. U.S. Department of Commerce (DOC), Bureau of Economic Analysis (BEA), "Table 3: Gross Domestic Product and Related Measures; Level Changes From Preceding Period," *News Release*, June 26, 2013, 8-9.

2. Ibid.; DOC/BEA, "Table 6: Price Indexes for Gross Domestic Product," *News Release*, June 26, 2013, 11.

3. World Bank, "GDP per Capita (Current US$)," *World Development Indicators, 2013*, 1-11, http://data.worldbank.org/indicator/NY.GDP.PCAP.CD

4. Ibid.; International Monetary Fund (IMF), "Table B: Advanced Economies by Subgroup," *World Economic Outlook, April 2013* (Washington, DC: IMF Publication Services, 2013), 139-140.

5. Simon Kuznets, *National Income and Its Composition, 1919–1938* (New York: National Bureau of Economic Research, Inc., 1941), 9.

6. DOC/BEA, "Table 3: Gross Domestic Product and Related Measures; Level Changes From Preceding Period," *News Release*, June 26, 2013, 8-9.

7. National Bureau of Economic Research (NBER), "The NBER's Business Cycle Dating Committee," September 20, 2010, www.nber.org/cycles/recessions.html

8. U.S. Bureau of the Census, "Series D 722-727: Average Annual Earnings of Employees, 1900 to 1970," "Series 683-688: Indexes of Employee Output (NBER), 1869 to 1969," *Statistical History of the United States: From Colonial Times to the Present* (New York: Basic Books, Inc., 1976), 162, 164.

9. U.S. Bureau of the Census, "Table 679: Selected per Capita Income and Product Measures in Current and Chained (2005) Dollars, 1960 to 2010," *Statistical Abstract of the United States: 2011* (Washington, DC: U.S. Government Printing Office, 2012), 443; Bureau of Economic Analysis, "Current-Dollar and 'Real' Gross Domestic Product," July 27, 2012, www.bea.gov/national/xls/gdplev.xls

10. Joseph A. Schumpeter, *Capitalism, Socialism, and Democracy*, 3rd ed. (New York: Harper & Row Publishers, 1950), 82-83.

11. Council of Economic Advisors, "Table B-49: Productivity and Related Data, Business and Nonfarm Business Sectors, 1963–2012, Appendix B," *Economic Report of the President: 2013* (Washington, DC: U.S. Government Printing Office, 2013), 382.

12. Council of Economic Advisors, "Table B-32: Gross Saving and Investment, 1964–2012," *Economic Report of the President: 2013*, 362.

13. IMF, "Table A15: Summary of Sources and Uses of World Savings," *World Economic Outlook, April 2013*, 2013, 172-175. World Bank, "Table 4.8: Structure of Demand," "Table 4.9: Growth of consumption and investment," *2012 World Development Indicators* (Washington, DC: World Bank, 2012), 242-244, 245-249.

14. DOC/BEA, "Table 3: Gross Domestic Product and Related Measures; Level Changes From Preceding Period," *News Release*, June 26, 2013, 8-9.

15. World Bank, "Table 4.8: Structure of Demand," "Table 4.9: Growth of Consumption and Investment," *2012 World Development Indicators* (Washington DC: World Bank Publications, 2012), 242-244, 245-249.

16. United Nations Development Program (UNDP), "Table 1: Human Development Index and Its Components," *Human Development Report, 2013* (New York: UNDP, 2013), 144-147.

17. Council of Economic Advisors, "Table B-54: Capacity Utilization Rates, 1965–2012," *Economic Report of the President: 2013*, 2013, 387.

18. Niels Bosma, Sander Wennekers, and Jose Ernesto Amoros, *Global Entrepreneurship Monitor 2011 Extended Report: Entrepreneurs and Entrepreneurial Employees across the Globe* (Babson Park, MA: Babson College, 2012), 8.

19. National Science Foundation (NSF), "Table 4.1: U.S. R&D Expenditures, by Performing Sector and Source of Funding, 2004–2009"; U.S. Bureau of the Census, "Table 779: Research and Development (R&D) Expenditures by Sources and Objective, 1980–2008," "Table 800: National Research and Development (R&D) Expenditures as a Percent of Gross Domestic Product by Country, 1990–2009," "Table 806: Funds for Domestic Performance of Business Research and Development

(R&D) in Current and Constant (2005) Dollars by Source of Funds and Selected Industries, 2005–2008," *Statistical Abstract of the United States: 2012*, 522, 525.

20. Council of Economic Advisors, "Support for Research and Development," *Economic Report of the President: 2000* (Washington, DC: U.S. Government Printing Office, 2000), 123-124.

21. International Telecommunications Union (ITU), World Telecommunications, "Key Statistical Highlights: ITU Data Release June 2012," *ICT Indicators Database*, 2012.

22. U.S. Bureau of the Census, "U.S. Shipments, Sales, Revenues and E-Commerce: 2009 and 2008," *E-Stats*, www.census.gov/estats

23. Freedom House, "Freedom and Economic Growth," *Freedom in the World: 2000-2001* (New York: Freedom House, Inc., 2000), www.freedomhouse.org/research/freeworld/2001/essay1g.htm

24. Carmen DeNavas-Walt, Bernadette D. Proctor, and Jessica C. Smith, U.S. Bureau of the Census, "Table 3. Income Distribution Measures Using Money Income and Equivalence-Adjusted Income: 2009 and 2010," (*Current Population Reports*, P60-239), *Income, Poverty, and Health Insurance Coverage in the United States: 2010*, (Washington, DC: U.S. Government Printing Office), 2011, 11; and U.S. Bureau of the Census, "Table 694. Share of Aggregate Income Received by Each Fifth and Top 5 Percent of Households: 1970 to 2009," *Statistical Abstract of the United States: 2012*, 454.

25. DOC/U.S. Bureau of the Census, "Preliminary Estimates of Weighted Average Poverty Thresholds for 2012," January 18, 2013.

26. U.S. Bureau of the Census, "Preliminary Estimate of Weighted Average Poverty Thresholds for 2012, January 18, 2013; and U.S. Department of Health and Human Services, "2013 Poverty Guidelines," *Federal Register* (Washington, DC: HHS), January 24, 2013.

27. Council of Economic Advisors, "Table B-33: Median Money Income (in 2011 Dollars) and Poverty Status of Families And People, By Race, 2002-2011," *Economic Report of the President: 2013*, 364; U.S. Bureau of the Census, "Table 2. Poverty Status of People by Family Relationship, Race, and Hispanic Origin, 1959–2010," *Current Population Survey: Annual Social and Economic Supplements*; Thomas Gabe, *Poverty in the United States: 2010* (Congressional Research Service, CRS Report for Congress), March 9, 2012, 1-3.

28. Linda Levin, "Table 2: Share of Total Net Worth by Percentile of Wealth Owners, 1989–2010," *An Analysis of the Distribution of Wealth Across Households, 1989–2010* (Congressional Research Service: CRS Report for Congress), July 17, 2012, 4; Jesse Bricker, et. al., "Changes in U.S. Family Finances from 2007 to 2010: Evidence from the Survey of Consumer Finances," *Federal Reserve Bulletin* 98, no. 2 (June 2012): 1, 17, 77.

29. E. F. Schumacher, *Small Is Beautiful: Economics as if People Mattered* (New York: Harper & Row, 1973), 21.

9

The Financial System Promotes Economic Activity

Modern economies rely on money and a variety of financial institutions to support business activity. Some financial institutions such as banks, thrifts, and credit unions accept deposits and pool savings for productive investments and consumer loans. Other financial institutions such as stock and bond markets, mutual funds, and futures markets also help raise money for business start-ups and other productive purposes. Globalization has integrated financial institutions around the world, which has created opportunities for productive investment but has also laid the groundwork for financial contagion.

MONEY AND THE MONEY SUPPLY

Money is any item that is commonly accepted in payment for goods or services, or in payment of debts. Money has been used for thousands of years to facilitate business and financial transactions. The use of money is a far more efficient mechanism of exchange than **barter**, the direct exchange of one good for another. Barter requires a double coincidence of wants, and tedious negotiations to determine the relative value of goods in the marketplace.

Functions and Characteristics of Money

Money has three primary functions in an economy. First, money serves as a medium of exchange. That is, the item that is used as money is commonly accepted in payment for products. Second, money serves as a unit of account. In the United States monetary units are stated in dollars and cents, and prices enable people to easily compare the value of products. Third, money serves as a store of value because it holds its worth over time. The ability of money to retain its purchasing power over time increases people's confidence in the economy and their willingness to save, invest, work, and produce.

Throughout history societies have struggled to create and maintain a monetary system that could satisfy these three interrelated functions. Three characteristics help distinguish "good" money from "bad" money. First, good money is commonly accepted in payment for products. The acceptability of money is derived mainly from its scarcity, durability,

---

PRIMARY DOCUMENT: Alan Greenspan Calls Money the Lubricant of Economic Progress

[A]t root, money—serving as a store of value and medium of exchange—is the lubricant that enables a society to organize itself to achieve economic progress. The ability to store the fruits of one's labor for future consumption is necessary for the accumulation of capital, the spread of technological advances and, as a consequence, rising standards of living ...

So long as individuals make contractual arrangements for future payments valued in dollars, there must be a presumption on the part of those involved in the transaction about the future purchasing power of money. No matter how complex individual products become, there will always be some general sense of the purchasing power of money both across time and across goods and services. Hence, we must assume that embodied in all products is some unit of output and hence of price that is recognizable to producers and consumers and upon which they will base their decisions.

Speech to the American Enterprise Institute (December 5, 1996), Alan Greenspan

---

and stability in value. These qualities help explain why gold and silver coins have been accepted as money for millennia.

Second, good money is easily divisible. The divisibility of money into precise monetary units facilitates business and financial transactions. U.S. money is highly divisible, with several denominations of coin and paper currency. Coins are measured in units of cents, with 1, 5, 10, 25, 50, and 100 cent pieces. Paper currency, called Federal Reserve Notes, is subdivided into denominations of $1, $2, $5, $10, $20, $50, and $100. The government discontinued the use of larger denominations of $500; $1,000; $5,000; and $10,000 in 1969.[1]

Third, good money is portable. The portability of money enables it to be transported easily from place to place. Historically the use of paper currency and checks expanded the portability of money in modern economies. Today, electronic funds transfer (EFT) technology has eased many types of transactions through the use of debit cards, automated teller machines, computer banking, and other e-transfers. Alan Greenspan, who served as Chairman of the Federal Reserve System under four presidents, described money as the financial lubricant of economic progress.[2]

Types of Money

Economists generally identify three types of money: commodity money, representative money, and fiat money. **Commodity money** is an item that is used to buy other products or settle debts, and also has value in itself. Bails of tobacco were often used as a type of commodity money in colonial Virginia and Maryland during the 1600s and early 1700s. Commodity money is not a particularly effective type of money because it lacks divisibility and portability, and its value changes with the supply or demand for the crop, mineral, or other item that serves as money.

Representative money is a type of money that has no inherent value but represents something of value. During the early twentieth century the U.S. government issued Gold Certificates, a type of representative money that could be redeemed for gold. Gold redemption ended in 1934, however, and Gold Certificates were removed from circulation. U.S. Silver Certificates, another type of representative money, were issued until 1957 and were redeemable for silver bullion until 1968.[3] Over time the redemption of these paper notes

The Bureau of Engraving and Printing in Washington, D.C. produces U.S. paper currency. (Bureau of Engraving and Printing/U.S. Department of the Treasury)

for gold and silver depleted U.S. supplies of these precious metals, and the government discontinued their use. Federal Reserve Notes was another form of representative money in the early twentieth century, and could be redeemed for gold until 1934.

Fiat money is a type of money that derives its value by government decree, or fiat. That is, the government declares its currency to be valuable without backing it with gold, silver, or other precious item. Federal Reserve Notes, today's paper currency, represent "legal tender for all debts" and thus must be accepted in all types of transactions in the United States. The stability of the U.S. government and its money supply are vital to maintaining the purchasing power of fiat money.

Measurements of the Money Supply

The **money supply**, or money stock, consists of the total amount of money in circulation in an economy. To be counted in the nation's money supply, money must be available for use in a variety of transactions and investments. Thus, the U.S. money supply does not

Table 9.1   U.S. Money Supply (M1), May 2013

Components of M1	Dollar Value ($ billions)	Percentage of M1
Coin and paper currency	1,116.3	44.1
Demand deposits	959.0	37.8
Other checkable deposits	455.7	18.0
Traveler's checks	3.7	0.1
Total M1	2,534.7	100.0

Source: Federal Reserve System, *Federal Reserve Statistical Release*, June 27, 2013.

include money stored away by the Federal Reserve System (Fed), the Treasury Department, or other federal agencies. Today economists use two main measures to determine the size of the money supply, the M1 and M2. In 2006 the Fed discontinued use of a third measure of the money supply, the M3.

M1 is often called transactions money because it can readily be spent. M1 is the narrowest measurement of the nation's money supply. The four main components of M1 are coin and paper currency, demand deposits, other checkable deposits, and traveler's checks. In May 2013 the M1 topped $2.5 trillion, as shown in Table 9.1. Coin and paper currency was the single largest category of M1. The second largest component was demand deposits, which represents the money held in individual checking accounts in banks. Another significant component of M1 was other checkable deposits (OCDs) such as negotiable order of withdrawal (NOW) accounts, credit union share draft accounts, and automated transfer service (ATS) balances at banks, thrifts, and credit unions. Traveler's checks accounted for less than 1 percent of M1.[4]

M2 is a broader, more inclusive measure of the nation's money supply than M1. M2 consists of M1 plus near monies such as savings deposits (including money market deposit accounts, or MMDAs); small-denomination time deposits of less than $100,000; and retail money market mutual funds (MMMFs). *Near monies* are highly liquid assets that are easily converted into money. In May 2013 the nation's M2 topped $10.5 trillion, as shown in Table 9.2. The largest category of near monies in M2 was savings deposits, which were held in depository institutions. These near monies of M2 totaled $8 trillion and represent the non-M1 portion of the M2. Thus, the M2 totaled $10.5 trillion in 2013 ($2.5 trillion + $8 trillion = 10.5 trillion).[5]

Table 9.2   U.S. Money Supply (M2), May 2013

Money Supply	Components	Dollar Amount ($ billions)	Measurements (M1 and M2) ($ billions)
M1	Currency	1,116.3	M1 = $2,534.7
	Demand deposits OCDs	959.0	
	Traveler's checks	455.7	
		3.7	
Non-M1, M2	Savings deposits	6,803.4	Non-M1,
	Small time deposits	580.6	M2 = $8,017.9
	Retail money funds	633.9	
Total M2	All components	M1 + Non-M1, M2	Equals $10,552.6

Source: Federal Serve System, "Tables 1, 3, 4," *Federal Reserve Statistical Release*, June 27, 2013.

BANKS AND OTHER DEPOSITORY INSTITUTIONS

The **banking system** of the United States consists of a central bank, commercial banks, thrift institutions (savings and loan associations and savings banks), and credit unions. Commercial banks, thrifts, and credit unions accept deposits from savers and extend loans to borrowers and are thus referred to as depository institutions. The banking system provides a variety of financial services to individuals, businesses, and the government, which stimulates both the supply side and the demand side of markets. In recent years new information technology, such as electronic banking, has increased the efficiency of the U.S. banking system. You will read more about America's central bank, the Federal Reserve System, in Chapter 10.

Commercial Banks

Commercial banks are private financial corporations owned by stockholders and operated by professional management for profit. Commercial banks pool money by accepting savers' deposits, collecting interest payments on loans, or earning profits from other investments such as the bank's holdings of U.S. government securities. Commercial banks are the largest type of depository institution. In March 2013 commercial banks accounted for $13.4 trillion in industry assets, or 86.3 percent of all assets held by depository institution, as shown in Table 9.3. In 2013 commercial banks also had deposits of $10 trillion, had loans and leases of $6.9 trillion, and employed about 2 million workers.[6] Savers' deposits in commercial banks are insured by the Federal Deposit Insurance Corporation (FDIC) up to $250,000.

Commercial banks were originally established to attend to the financial needs of businesses. Over time they expanded their services to meet the needs of businesses *and* consumers. Today commercial banks offer a safe haven for people's savings, personal and business checking accounts, credit cards, easy access to cash at ATMs, and a variety of financial services. They also extend loans to consumers and businesses. Consumer loans, also called personal loans, enable people to purchase expensive items such as automobiles and furnishings in the present and repay the amount of the loan plus interest in the future. The largest personal loan for many households is the home mortgage loan. In mid-2012 outstanding mortgage debt hit $13.1 trillion, $3.6 trillion of which was owed to commercial banks.[7] Business loans, on the other hand, are made to producers of goods and services. Business loans enable firms to upgrade or expand plant and equipment, finance mergers or acquisitions, or satisfy other business needs.

Table 9.3   U.S. Depository Institutions, 2013

Type of Depository Institution	Number of Institutions	Total Assets ($ billions)	Industry Assets (% of total)
Commercial banks	6,048	13,363	86.3
Savings institutions (S&Ls, savings banks)	971	1,062	6.9
Credit unions	6,753	1,055	6.8
All depository institutions	13,772	15,480	100.0

Source: Federal Deposit Insurance Corporation, *Statistics on Depository Institutions*, March 31, 2013; National Credit Union Administration, "Federally Insured Credit Unions," March, 2013.

Commercial banking has become more consolidated in recent years. During much of the 1970s and 1980s, for example, more than 14,000 commercial banks operated in the United States. By 2013 just 6,048 remained as FDIC-assisted and voluntary mergers of commercial banks, and some bank failures, reduced their number. Another sign of consolidation in the banking industry is the dominance of the top four commercial banks within the industry. Ranked by total assets, each of the top four U.S. commercial banks controlled more than $1 trillion in assets in 2013. These four megabanks are JP Morgan Chase ($1.95 trillion), Bank of America ($1.46 trillion), Citibank ($1.31 trillion), and Wells Fargo ($1.27 trillion).[8]

Thrift Institutions

The two main types of thrift institutions are savings and loan associations and savings banks. Thrift institutions are also called thrifts or saving institutions. In 2013 thrifts accounted for $1.1 trillion in industry assets, or 6.9 percent of all assets held by depository institutions, as shown in Table 9.3. They also granted $624 billion in loans to borrowers.[9] Over the past few decades banking deregulation has enabled thrifts to provide many of the same financial services as commercial banks, which has blurred some traditional distinctions between these financial institutions. Most thrifts are federally chartered rather than state chartered.[10]

Savings and loan associations (S&Ls) are savings institutions designed to meet the financial needs of households rather than businesses. The first S&L was founded in 1831 and as time passed, many S&Ls popped up in the Northeast. S&Ls pooled members' money so that they could extend home mortgage loans to members. In the early years most S&Ls were organized as *mutual institutions*, which are owned by depositors. Later other S&Ls were organized as *stock institutions*, which were owned by stockholders. Today S&Ls continue to grant loans for home mortgages, repair, and construction. S&Ls also provide a variety of personal and commercial loans. The Depository Institutions Deregulation and Monetary Control Act of 1980 enabled S&Ls to provide checking accounts, retirement accounts, and other financial services. Since 2005 the Deposit Insurance Fund (DIF) has insured S&L deposits. In 2008 this deposit insurance was increased from $100,000 to $250,000. For years the Office of Thrift Supervision (OTS) and the FDIC regulated S&Ls. In 2011 the OTS became part of the Office of the Comptroller of the Currency (OCC), which today regulates federally chartered S&Ls.[11]

Savings banks are savings institutions that focus on providing home mortgages and personal loans. Savings banks have existed in the United States for about two centuries and, like S&Ls, are concentrated in the Northeast. Most savings banks were originally organized as mutual institutions. *Mutual savings banks* are owned by depositors, called members, and operated as nonprofit institutions. Any profits earned by mutual savings banks are distributed to members. Since the 1980s many savings banks have either been organized as or converted to stock savings banks. *Stock savings banks* are owned by stockholders and are operated for profit. Savings deposits in savings banks are insured by the FDIC up to $250,000 per account.

Credit Unions

Credit unions are nonprofit financial cooperatives that are owned and operated by their members. The first U.S. credit union was founded in Manchester, New Hampshire, in 1909. During the early twentieth century credit unions grew in popularity mainly because they met the basic financial needs of their members. That is, they accepted deposits, paid competitive interest rates on these deposits, and offered small personal loans to members. Membership in a credit union was typically limited to those who belonged to the organizing group—a corporation, a labor union, or other group. In recent decades credit union membership has expanded, rising from 55.7 million members in 1990 to 94.6 million members in 2013. During this same period of time, industry consolidation reduced the number of credit unions from 12,860 to 6,753, while credit union assets grew from $200 billion to $1.1 trillion, and outstanding loans increased from $127 billion to $600 billion.[12] Nearly two-thirds of all credit unions are chartered by the federal government and the remainder by state governments.[13]

Deregulation in financial markets enabled credit unions to offer a wider array of deposit accounts and financial services. In addition to the original savings accounts, credit unions now offer share drafts (check-like accounts), money market shares, share certificates, and retirement accounts. Credit union lending has also changed significantly in recent decades. In 2013 home mortgage loans accounted for 41 percent of all lending. Other major categories of loans included loans for new and used cars (30 percent), and other real estate (12 percent).[14] The National Credit Union Administration (NCUA) charters and supervises the nation's 6,753 credit unions and manages the National Credit Union Share Insurance Fund (NCUSIF), which insures members' deposits up to $250,000.[15] Ranked by total assets, the largest credit union in 2013 was Navy Federal, with $54 billion in total assets, $36 billion in outstanding loans, and 4.3 million members. Other major credit unions were State Employees, Pentagon Federal, and Boeing Employees.[16]

Types of Savings Accounts

Depository institutions offer a wide variety of deposit accounts, but most fall into one of four categories: savings accounts, money market deposit accounts, certificates of deposit, or checking accounts. Deposit accounts offer security, as depositors' money is protected from theft or other loss and is insured by the FDIC, DIF, or NCUSIF. Still, there are differences among deposit accounts in terms of yield, liquidity, check writing privileges, associated fees, and minimum deposits.

A *regular savings account* is one common deposit account. The two types of regular savings accounts are the passbook account and the statement account. The passbook savings account requires the depositor to present a passbook when transactions are made. In a statement savings account, however, the depositor receives a monthly transactions statement from the bank. The interest payment on regular accounts is usually the lowest of any deposit account. Liquidity is high because withdrawals from the account can be made quickly. Savings accounts do not offer check writing privileges. Some banks and thrifts assess a monthly fee if the minimum monthly balance falls beneath a certain dollar amount. Credit unions call their savings accounts *share accounts*.

A *money market deposit account* (MMDA) typically pays a higher rate of interest than does a regular savings account. Interest rates on MMDAs are variable, fluctuating with the interest the depository institution receives on its own investments. Liquidity is relatively high because MMDAs offer limited check writing privileges. Depository institutions may impose monthly fees on MMDAs, and a minimum balance of $250 or more is often required to maintain the account. Credit unions sometimes call MMDAs *money market shares*.

A *certificate of deposit* (CD), also called a time deposit, requires that a deposit remain in an account for a specified period of time. There are two types of CDs. Fixed-rate CDs, also called traditional CDs, offer a relatively high and fixed rate of interest to depositors. Recently, some depository institutions have offered variable-rate CDs that in today's market go by many names such as index-linked, market-linked, equity-linked, or structured CDs.[17] Liquidity for CDs is relatively low compared to other deposit accounts mainly because all CDs have a fixed maturity date, and checks cannot be written against CD accounts. Financial institutions often assess financial penalties for early withdrawals from CD accounts. The minimum deposit for CDs ranges from a few hundred dollars to more than $100,000. Credit unions call CDs *share certificates*.

A *checking account* is a fourth type of deposit account. Regular checking accounts typically offer no interest and often require that a small minimum balance be maintained in the account. Special checking accounts, called negotiable order of withdrawal accounts (NOW accounts), pay interest to depositors but also require a larger minimum balance. Because checking accounts offer instant access to a depositor's money, they are highly liquid. Liquidity is further enhanced by electronic funds transfer technology, which permits depositors to gain access to their funds through ATMs, the use of debit cards, and home computer banking. Depository institutions often levy fees on checking accounts, the use of ATMs, and other checking transactions. Credit unions call checking accounts *share draft accounts*.

Types of Retirement Accounts

Saving money is essential for people's future financial security. Some saving, such as mandatory Social Security deductions from workers' wages, is required by law. Social Security contributions are stored in a general fund rather than in a personal account, however. Financial experts advise prudent saving and investing during people's working years to support their future financial security. Popular retirement accounts include the traditional individual retirement account (IRA), Keogh plan, Simplified Employee Pension (SEP) plan, and traditional 401(k) plan. All of these plans offer tax advantages, but none are federally insured.

A *traditional IRA* is a tax-deferred retirement account for employees. Taxes are not paid on the amount contributed to the traditional IRA, or on the interest that accrues, until the money is withdrawn during retirement. There are limits on the annual contribution to an IRA, and there are penalties for early withdrawal. In 2012 the maximum contribution for most people was $5,000 per year. Contributors can start withdrawing money from the IRA without penalty at age 59.5. The Employee Retirement Income Security Act (1974) created the first IRAs. A *Roth IRA* is a retirement account in which a worker contributes after-tax money to the account. The main benefit of a Roth IRA is that the principal, plus all interest earned during the life of the account, is tax free when withdrawn during retirement. Some upper-income people are not eligible to purchase Roth IRAs.[18] The Taxpayer Relief Act (1997) created the Roth IRA.

A *Keogh plan* is a retirement plan for the self-employed and small businesses. Income contributed to a Keogh plan is tax deferred until it is withdrawn from the account during retirement. Self-employed workers, often sole proprietors, can contribute up to 25 percent of their self-employment income to a Keogh plan as long as the sum does not exceed $49,000. In addition, employees of these small businesses can participate as long as the employer pays the entire contribution.[19] The Self-Employed Individuals Tax Retirement Act (1962) established the Keogh plan.

A *Simplified Employee Pension (SEP) plan* is another retirement plan for small businesses. SEP plans allow the employer to make tax-deductible retirement contributions directly into an individual retirement account (IRA) for each employee and are usually called SEP-IRAs. The amount of the contribution varies depending on the workers' wage and on market conditions—in good times the employer is free to contribute more money into the individual employee's SEP-IRA, and when business is slow the employer is free to cancel contributions completely. In 2012 the maximum contribution to a SEP-IRA was 25 percent of the worker's wage, with an upper limit of $50,000. SEP-IRAs have become more popular in recent years because they are easy to set up and offer employers some payment flexibility. SEPs were authorized by Congress in 1978.[20]

A *traditional 401(k) plan* is a retirement plan set up by an employer. Under 401(k) plans, the employer may match all or a portion of the employee's contribution to the retirement plan. The employee's contribution is tax deferred; thus, neither the contribution nor accrued interest payments are taxed until withdrawals are made during retirement. In 2011 the maximum annual employee contribution to a traditional 401(k) plan was $16,500 for employees under 50 years of age, and $22,000 for employees 50 or over—limits that were significantly higher than traditional IRAs or Roth IRAs. For sole proprietorships with no employees, the *individual 401(k) plan* offers even greater benefits because the proprietor is both employer and employee; hence, a larger contribution is possible each year. The risks involved in traditional 401(k) plans became painfully obvious in the early 2000s when the collapse of Enron and other large corporations wiped out several large 401(k) plans. The wave of business failures during the Great Recession of 2007–2009 also cut deeply into some traditional 401(k) accounts. The Internal Revenue Code of 1978, Section 401(k), created 401(k) plans.[21]

OTHER FINANCIAL INSTITUTIONS

Trillions of dollars flow through the U.S. banking system each year, providing security and interest income for savers, and a pool of loanable funds for borrowers. Thus, the banking system is an important feature within the larger financial system of the country. There are other important components of the U.S. financial system, however. Some of the key institutions include stock markets, bond markets, mutual funds, and futures exchanges.

Stock Markets

A **stock market**, or stock exchange, is a mechanism by which stocks are traded. That is, a stock market links buyers and sellers of stocks. Stocks of publicly traded companies are listed on a stock exchange. Some stock markets such as the New York Stock Exchange (NYSE Euronext) still conduct some of their business on a trading floor. Others, such as the Nasdaq Stock Market (Nasdaq OMX), are decentralized networks of investors and stock dealers that communicate and trade stocks through electronic trading systems. Today these exchanges are globally networked.

Recent consolidations of stock markets have resulted in some major changes in the financial services industry. One major change was the merger of the NYSE Group and Euronext N.V. in 2007. The NYSE Group was formed by a merger between the NYSE and the Archipelago exchange. Euronext was the operator of five major European securities exchanges, including stock exchanges in Amsterdam (Netherlands), Brussels (Belgium),

Lisbon (Portugal), and Paris (France), and a derivatives exchange in London (United Kingdom). The 2007 "merger of equals" between the NYSE Group and Euronext N.V. created NYSE Euronext. NYSE Euronext was hailed as the world's first global stock exchange. In 2008 NYSE Euronext also purchased the American Stock Exchange (AMEX), thus integrating AMEX into this global securities market. In 2013 NYSE Euronext was purchased by Intercontinental Exchange (ICE).[22] During this same time period Nasdaq purchased several foreign and domestic stock exchanges, including the Boston Stock Exchange (2006) and the Philadelphia Stock Exchange (2007), and exchanges in Sweden, Finland, Denmark, and other countries. Now called Nasdaq OMX, it remains a major player in global securities markets.[23]

On the eve of its takeover by ICE, NYSE Euronext was the largest stock exchange in the world based on its market capitalization. **Market capitalization** simply refers to the dollar value of stocks listed on a stock exchange at any moment in time. Market capitalization can change when the value of stocks increases during a bull market or decreases during a bear market. It can also change when corporations either leave or join a certain stock exchange. By the close of 2012 market capitalization for the NYSE Euronext (U.S.) was $14.1 trillion, followed by Nasdaq OMX ($4.6 trillion), Tokyo Stock Exchange ($3.5 trillion), London Stock Exchange ($3.4 trillion), and the NYSE Euronext (Europe, $2.8 trillion). The NYSE Euronext (Europe) data covers four stock exchanges: Amsterdam, Brussels, Lisbon, and Paris. Global market capitalization for the world's stock exchanges in 2012 was $54.6 trillion—a $7 trillion jump over the 2011 totals of $47.4 trillion. Rounding out the top 10 stock exchanges in the world were exchanges in Hong Kong (China SAR), Shanghai (China), Toronto (Canada), Frankfurt (Germany), and Sydney (Australia). Trillions of dollars in stock trades take place each year on stock exchanges.[24]

Stock markets are an important type of financial market. First, stock markets raise investment capital for corporations in primary markets. Stock trading in a *primary market* occurs when a business issues new stocks for sale to investors. The proceeds from the sale of new issues in primary markets enable corporations to build plants, purchase real capital, and attend to other business expenses. A corporation's first issue of stock to investors is called an *initial public offering* (IPO). Recent IPOs have raised billions of dollars for Facebook ($16.6 billion in 2012), General Motors ($20 billion in 2010), and Visa ($19.7 billion in 2008).[25]

Second, stock markets provide a way for investors to earn profits, called capital gains, in secondary markets. Stock trading in a *secondary market* involves the purchase and sale of previously issued stocks. The investor earns capital gains when the stock sells for more than its original purchase price. Of course, all investments involve some risk, and an investor can also incur losses, which occur when the selling price of the stock is less than its original purchase price.

Third, stock markets send financial signals to investors, businesses, consumers, and others throughout the economy. The performance of the stock market indicates the level of confidence investors have in specific firms, in specific industries, in different economic sectors, or in the direction of the overall U.S. economy. In fact, economists consider positive or negative trends in the stock market to be a key *leading economic indicator*, or predictor of future economic activity in the overall economy. The Dow Jones Industrial Average (DJIA), more commonly called the Dow, is one important measurement of stock performance on the New York Stock Exchange. The Dow achieved a series of record-breaking performances during the summer and fall of 2013, and surpassed 16,000 in November

Table 9.4   Composition of the Dow Jones Industrial Average, 1896 and 2013

The DJIA over Time	*Number of Companies*	*Composition of the DJIA*
DJIA in 1896	12	American Cotton Oil, American Sugar, American Tobacco, Chicago Gas, Distilling & Cattle Feeding, General Electric, Laclede Gas, National Lead, North American Utility, Tennessee Coal & Iron, U.S. Leather, U.S. Rubber
DJIA in 2013	30	3M, Alcoa, American Express, AT&T, Bank of America, Boeing, Caterpillar, Chevron, Cisco Systems, Coca-Cola, DuPont, Exxon Mobil, General Electric, Hewlett-Packard, Home Depot, Intel, IBM, Johnson & Johnson, JPMorgan Chase, McDonald's, Merck, Microsoft, Pfizer, Procter & Gamble, Travelers, United Technologies, United Health Group, Walmart Stores, Walt Disney

Source: Dow Jones Indexes, "Dow Jones Industrial Average"; CNN Money, "Dow Jones Industrial Average."

of that year. The dramatic increase in the Dow signaled investor confidence in the ongoing U.S. economic recovery.[26] Positive or negative trends can be determined by looking at certain indices of stock performance such as the Dow Jones Industrial Average, or broader indices such as the Standard & Poor's 500. Table 9.4 contrasts the composition of the DJIA in 2013 and 1896.[27] The creation of the Dow is chronicled in the following passage.

ECONOMICS IN HISTORY: Charles H. Dow and the Founding of Two Financial Icons

The Dow Jones Industrial Average is the most recognized stock index in the world. Its founder, Charles H. Dow, was born in Sterling, Connecticut, in 1851. During the 1870s Dow worked as a reporter for several New England newspapers and by the early 1880s had joined a financial news service in New York City. In 1882 Dow and fellow reporter Edward D. Jones formed Dow Jones & Company, which was located on Wall Street. Dow and Jones researched financial news and wrote daily financial bulletins, called flimsies, mainly for financial institutions in the city. The firm's size and reputation grew during the 1880s. In 1889 its respected bulletins, originally published as the *Customer's Afternoon Letter*, were transformed into a financial newspaper called the *Wall Street Journal*.

Dow was editor of the *Wall Street Journal*, and thus his articles reached a wide audience. In 1896 Dow developed the Dow Jones Industrial Average (DJIA), an index comprised of 12 prominent manufacturing companies, to track the performance of stocks on the New York Stock Exchange (NYSE). The DJIA followed on the heels of Dow's first stock index, which tracked mainly railroad companies from 1884 to 1896. Since 1896 the composition and number of companies included in the DJIA has changed significantly. By 1929 the DJIA had grown to 30 companies, the same number as today. Over time additional Dow Jones indexes, including the Dow Jones Transportation Average and the Dow Jones Utility Average, were created to measure the ups and downs of stocks in other industries. The most inclusive of the indexes is the Dow Jones Composite Average.[28]

Bond Markets

A **bond market** is a mechanism by which bonds issued by corporations, the U.S. Treasury, federal agencies, and state and municipal governments are bought and sold. Hence, the bond market is comprised of many types of buyers and sellers of bonds. A **bond** is a type of loan, or IOU. Corporations and governments borrow money by issuing bonds and pledge to repay the borrowed money, called the principle, plus interest in the future.

The money generated by the sale of bonds is used in many productive ways. Corporations issue bonds to finance the construction of productive facilities, purchase new equipment, expand research, or attend to other business expenses. In 2003 General Motors issued $17.6 billion in corporate bonds mainly to firm up its pension plan. The federal government issues bonds to finance the public debt. That is, the money generated through the sale of government bonds is used to make up the difference when government spending exceeds tax receipts. Similarly, state and local governments issue bonds to finance the construction of roads and bridges, schools, hospitals, parks, and other public facilities.

The bond market in the United States is largely electronic, and most trades are made over the counter (OTC). Limited bond trading takes place on a formal bond exchange. Securities firms hire bond dealers, called underwriters, to buy large quantities of bonds directly from bond issuers—corporations or governments—in *primary markets*. Later these underwriters resell some of these bonds to investors in *secondary markets*. Institutional investors such as insurance companies, mutual funds, pension funds, financial institutions, and foreign and domestic governments dominate bond purchases in U.S. bond markets.[29] Individual investors account for a small portion of bond purchases. By 2012 the total outstanding bond market debt in the United States was $38.7 trillion, as shown in Table 9.5.[30]

Corporate bonds, also called corporates, are debt obligations of issuing companies. Bondholders receive a fixed rate of interest, often semiannually. The entire principal is also repaid to the bondholder at the bond's maturity. Interest rates on corporates are usually higher than most government securities because the risk associated with corporates is higher. Interest paid on corporates is also taxable income for the bondholder. Investment-grade corporates are less risky than the high yield bonds, often called *junk bonds*.

Treasury securities are the debt obligations of the U.S. Treasury. Treasury *bills* (T-bills) mature in one year or less, and interest is paid at maturity. Treasury *notes* mature in two to

Table 9.5   U.S. Outstanding Bond Market Debt, 2013

Type of Bond	Amount of Bond Debt ($ trillions)	Percentage of Bond Debt
Corporate bonds	9.3	23.9
U.S. Treasury securities	11.3	29.2
Municipal securities	3.7	9.6
Federal agency securities	2.1	5.4
Mortgage-related securities	8.1	21.1
Money market instruments and asset-backed securities	4.2	10.8
Total U.S. bond debt	38.7	100.0

Source: Securities Industry and Financial Markets Association, "Outstanding Bond Market Debt," March 7, 2013.

10 years and often offer slightly higher interest than T-bills. Treasury *bonds* mature in 10 to 30 years and offer higher interest than Treasury bills or notes. Interest income derived from Treasury securities is exempt from state and local taxes.

Municipal bonds, called *munis*, are debt obligations of cities, counties, states, or other public entities. Maturities vary. Investors buy munis despite the relatively low interest rate mainly because they are less risky than some corporate bonds and because the interest income gained from munis is exempt from most state and local taxes.

Federal agency securities are debt obligations of federal agencies and government-sponsored enterprises (GSEs). These federal securities support mortgages (Fannie Mae, Freddie Mac), energy production (Tennessee Valley Authority), small businesses, and other programs. Maturities vary. Interest is relatively low but is higher than most U.S. Treasury securities. Interest income from federal agency securities is exempt from state and local taxes.

Mortgage securities are created by institutions that buy loans from mortgage lenders and then issue securities that represent this pool of mortgages, a process called securitization. The payments people make on their home mortgages raise the capital needed to repay investors the principle plus interest over time. The interest rate on mortgage securities is often higher than U.S. Treasury securities because the risk on mortgage securities is higher. Interest income from mortgage securities is subject to federal and state income taxes.

Money market instruments are types of short-term loans mainly in the form of certificates of deposit (CDs) and commercial paper. Governments and corporations often use money market instruments to satisfy financial obligations until additional tax receipts are collected or longer-term bills, notes, or bonds can be issued. Maturities vary, but virtually all money market securities mature in less than one year. The interest paid to investors is usually higher than prevailing interest rates on bank savings accounts.

Asset-backed securities are created by institutions that buy loans from lenders and then issue securities that represent the pool of loans—such as home mortgage loans, credit card debt, automobile loans, and student loans. The payments people make on their loans raise capital to repay the principle and make interest payments to investors over time.[31]

Mutual Funds

A **mutual fund** is a company that creates a diversified pool investment portfolio and sells shares in this fund to investors. The four main categories of mutual funds are domestic and world equity funds, bond funds, money market funds, and hybrid funds—funds that invest in a combination of stocks and bonds. An equity fund invests in shares of U.S. and foreign corporations. Equity funds are the largest type of fund and account for about 45 percent of all mutual fund assets, as shown in Table 9.6.[32]

Table 9.6   U.S. Mutual Fund Assets, 2012

Categories of Mutual Funds	*Amount Invested ($ billions)*	*Percentage of All U.S. Funds*
Equity funds	5,934.3	45.5
Bond funds	3,426.4	26.3
Money market funds	2,693.5	20.6
Hybrid funds	991.0	7.6
Total U.S. mutual funds	13,045.2	100.0

Source: Investment Company Institute, "Table 3," *2013 Investment Company Fact Book*, 144.

The amount of risk and the potential for financial gain varies from fund to fund. Investors purchase stock in a mutual fund in much the same way as they purchase stock in a corporation. In other words, each investor, called a shareholder, is a part owner of the mutual fund. The main asset of a mutual fund is its diversified portfolio of securities. When the value of individual securities within the fund's portfolio rises, investors are typically awarded dividends. In addition, the value of the entire mutual fund can rise over time. This enables investors to earn capital gains. In many cases, the dividends and capital gains earned by shareholders are ploughed directly back into the fund.

Mutual funds have become a popular investment option for investors in recent decades. In 1980 the total U.S. assets of mutual funds were just $135 billion spread across 564 funds. By 2012 total U.S. mutual fund assets exceeded $13 trillion spread across 7,596 funds. These funds were often managed by financial firms called sponsors. The $13 trillion in U.S. mutual fund assets accounted for about half of all mutual fund assets worldwide ($26.8 trillion). Large institutional investors in mutual funds included pension funds, state and local governments, and businesses. In addition, 92.4 million individuals in the United States owned mutual funds. To put it another way, nearly half of all U.S. households owned shares of at least one mutual fund. Globally in 2012 there were 73,243 mutual funds in the world, including 21,103 in the Americas; 34,470 in Europe; 16,703 in Asia and the Pacific; and 967 in Africa.[33]

Futures Markets

A **futures market**, or futures exchange, is a mechanism by which *contracts* for items are bought and sold. Thus, the operation of a futures market is similar to the operation of a stock market or bond market. In a futures market, however, investors buy and sell *futures contracts*, which are formal agreements to take a delivery of an item (buy the item) or make a delivery of an item (sell the item) at a specific date in the future. Also listed on the contract is the agreed upon price for the item, the quantity, and the location for the delivery. Items traded in futures markets generally fall into one of two categories: commodities or financial instruments. Popular commodities include agricultural products such as corn or wheat, energy sources such as crude oil or natural gas, and precious metals such as gold or silver. Two important financial instruments traded in futures markets are government securities such as Treasury notes or bonds, and world currencies.[34]

As early as the 1860s futures contracts were used at the Chicago Board of Trade (CBOT) for agricultural products. Under the contract investors agreed to buy quantities of grain from producers for a set price and to take delivery later in the year. This system provided some price stability in agricultural markets, as market participants knew in advance the terms of the transaction. A locked-in price enabled the grain producer to calculate with precision the firm's revenues and enabled the buyer to anticipate the costs of grain in the production of bread or other finished good. Over time this system also sparked a lively trade in futures contracts. For example, if investors were confident that grain would fetch a higher price than was stated in the futures contract, the contract became more valuable—and a good investment for a speculator who wanted to buy the contract for a low price today and sell it for a higher price in the future.

Today's futures markets operate under many of the same basic principles that guided futures markets more than a century ago. Naturally, technological advances and the types of items traded have brought the process into the twenty-first century. On the floor of futures exchanges, contracts are negotiated through sophisticated electronic communications, which are often used in conjunction with the time-honored shouting and hand signaling of traders in the "pit." Floor-based and electronic trading is fast paced and efficient, which adds to the liquidity of futures contracts. This trading is also highly speculative, which contributes to the volatility of contract prices.

Recent consolidations in the futures industry have brought several major futures exchanges under one roof. The merger of two venerable exchanges, the Chicago Mercantile Exchange (CME) and the Chicago Board of Trade (CBOT) in 2007 created the CME Group, Inc. A year later the CME Group acquired the New York Mercantile Exchange (NYMEX) and its affiliated Commodities Exchange (COMEX). Today the CME Group is the world's largest futures exchange, with offices in several major U.S. cities and in other financial hubs such as London, Tokyo, Calgary, Hong Kong, Singapore, Sao Paulo, Belfast, and Seoul. The opening of the CME Group's Global Command Center in 2010 illustrates the industry's commitment to global connectivity in futures trading.[35]

ISSUES IN THE GLOBAL FINANCIAL SYSTEM

Financial contagion refers to the spread of a financial crisis from one country or region to other countries or regions. Economic interdependence, an underpinning of globalization, increases the danger of financial contagion. Economic interdependence is generally viewed favorably because it creates a mutually supportive web of economic opportunities. But interdependence can also create financial instability. Advanced technologies capable of instantaneous cross-border transfers of assets, such as stocks or bonds, have created greater volatility in global financial markets. Financial crises originating in Mexico,

The global financial system facilitates cross-border financial and business activity. (Andreblais/Dreamstime.com)

Brazil, Russia, and Thailand destabilized global financial markets in the 1990s, as did the financial crisis of 2007–2008. These crises accented the need for meaningful financial reform at the national and global levels.

Financial Contagion and the East Asian Financial Crisis of 1997–1998

The East Asian financial crisis of 1997–1998 was the world's most serious bout with financial contagion during the 1990s. The seeds of the East Asian crisis were sown in Thailand. In the early 1990s investment opportunities in Thailand caught the eye of foreign investors. Foreign and domestic investors speculated in Thai stocks and other securities, developed and undeveloped real estate, and other assets. Soon asset prices soared to unreasonably high levels.

Beneath the glitter of the investment boom were serious weaknesses in the Thai financial system, however. Inadequate banking supervision, poor assessment models for credit risk, and excessive borrowing in global capital markets spelled disaster for Thailand's financial sector. Complicating the country's financial picture were governance problems, including public corruption, a lack of transparency, and inadequate economic data for informed policy decisions.

Short-term, speculative investments invite periods of boom and bust. In Thailand the bottom fell out of the speculative boom in 1997. Shaken investors stampeded to sell their holdings of Thai securities, properties, and other assets. The panicked sell-off of Thai assets, a type of herd behavior, is characteristic of speculative investment. The financial meltdown weakened Thailand's currency, the baht, and threw the overextended banking system and securities market into chaos. Fears of a regional financial meltdown caused similar asset sell-offs in other East Asian countries, resulting in severe economic downturns, as shown in Table 9.7.[36]

The financial contagion was soon knocking at the doors of Tokyo, New York City, and London. The financial crisis, which slowed business activity and dimmed consumer confidence in East Asia, also reduced Japanese, American, and European exports to Asian markets. Global securities markets, such as the New York Stock Exchange, dipped under the weight of the East Asian financial collapse. Global economic growth slowed.

International financial institutions and governments were forced to intervene. The International Monetary Fund (IMF), Asian Development Bank (ADB), World Bank, and United States orchestrated a $125 billion financial bailout to prevent a total collapse of major East Asian economies. Calls for financial reform centered on stricter supervision

Table 9.7   East Asian Financial Crisis and Real GDP, 1996–2000

| Countries | *Real Gross Domestic Product (percentage change)* | | | | |
	1996	*1997*	*1998*	*1999*	*2000*
Hong Kong SAR	4.5	5.0	−5.3	3.0	10.5
Indonesia	8.0	4.5	−13.1	0.8	4.8
Korea	6.8	5.0	−6.7	10.9	9.3
Malaysia	10.0	7.3	−7.4	6.1	8.3
Philippines	5.8	5.2	−0.6	3.4	4.0
Thailand	5.9	−1.4	−10.5	4.4	4.6

Source: International Monetary Fund, "Table 2" and "Table 6," *World Economic Outlook, April 2002*, 158, 165.

of banks and securities markets, heightened surveillance of countries' macroeconomic policies and performance, and technical support for good governance.[37]

The Financial Crisis of 2007–2008

The financial crisis of 2007–2008 was the greatest threat to the U.S. financial system since the Great Depression. How could a financial crisis of this magnitude occur? Economists still debate this question. Yet many conclude that the financial crisis of 2007–2008 resulted from a perfect storm of ill-advised legislation, speculative investments, and the misuse of complex financial instruments by financial institutions.

The repeal of the Glass-Steagall Act was one contributor to this perfect storm. Glass-Steagall, which was born during the financial chaos of the 1930s, had separated commercial banking from the more risky investment banking since its inception in 1934. While the formal repeal of Glass-Steagall occurred in 1999, pieces of this act had already been discarded beginning in the 1980s. The 1999 repeal removed the final barriers to financial mega-mergers and encouraged the creation of a vast array of entangling, secretive investments among major financial institutions, including commercial banks, investment banks, and insurance companies. These entanglements set the stage for the rapid spread of financial failure from one troubled institution to others.

Second, by 2005 and 2006 a dramatic drop in residential home prices shook the U.S. real estate and construction industries. The drop in real estate and construction had an immediate impact on the U.S. and global financial systems. This is because banks had bundled home mortgages into securities, a process called the securitization of mortgages. These mortgage-based securities were sold to investors in the United States and around the world. When the U.S. housing boom burst in 2005 and 2006, the value of physical properties and mortgage-based securities plummeted. Individuals, businesses, financial institutions, and governments lost trillions of dollars on these investments.

Third, banks had also jumped into a number of complex and risky financial instruments during the 1990s and early 2000s. Financial institutions invested trillions of dollars in derivatives and in credit default swap contracts—a type of insurance policy to cover losses on securities. These largely unregulated secret investments faltered during the financial crisis. Major financial institutions such as Lehman Brothers (an investment bank) and Washington Mutual (a savings bank) failed and were bought by other financial institutions. Further mergers and acquisitions of shaky financial institutions staved off a broader financial collapse. In the financial chaos that followed, banks hastily tightened credit and refused to loan to the public or to each other. This paralyzed the financial system and created a serious credit crunch.

The financial crisis of 2007–2008 not only brought the global financial system to its knees, but also weakened overall economic performance in the United States and in most other parts of the world. In the United States the financial panic quickly spread to other areas of the economy and directly affected producers, workers, and consumers. Anticipating an economic downturn, and crippled by the credit crunch, producers reduced production, fired workers, and postponed new investment in plant and equipment. As a result, the unemployment rate soared to over 10 percent, and real gross domestic product declined. At the same time terrified investors pulled money from the stock market, causing the Dow Jones Industrial Average to fall from a record high of 14,165 in October 2007 to just 6,547 in March 2009. This plunge in the Dow index mirrored the decline in the overall value of stocks, as the equity in many investors' portfolios dropped by about half. Consumer confidence and spending plummeted. In December 2007 the U.S. economy had officially sunk into a recession, now called the Great Recession, which lasted until June 2009—the longest recession of the post–World War II era. The perfect storm of financial and economic troubles had knocked the wind out of most advanced economies.

The U.S. economy eventually limped out of the financial crisis of 2007–2008 and the Great Recession of 2007–2009. Many negative economic indicators such as high unemployment and home foreclosure rates, and sluggish GPD growth persisted for years thereafter. Many economists believe that a number of short-term and long-term government efforts helped avert a catastrophic financial and economic meltdown.

Emergency policies, such as tax rebates and stimulus spending, pumped about a trillion dollars of federal money into the hands of individuals and businesses. The Troubled Asset Relief Program (TARP) brought hundreds of billions of dollars in federal loans to shaky financial institutions such as Bank of America, City Group, and AIG. Deposit insurance was raised from $100,000 to $250,000 by the Federal Deposit Insurance Corporation to discourage panic runs on banks. Corporate bailouts helped save jobs and supported auto giants General Motors and Chrysler as they climbed out of bankruptcy. Government incentive programs such as Cash for Clunkers (Car Allowance Rebate System) and tax credits for new home buyers stimulated consumer spending on major items. Lower interest rates, largely due to the action of the Federal Reserve System, eased the credit crunch and stimulated private sector borrowing and spending.

The Dodd-Frank Wall Street Reform Act (2010) also created a series of long-term reforms to strengthen the U.S. financial system. Key elements in this reform package included greater government oversight of financial institutions, regulation of investment instruments, and scrutiny of credit rating agencies that assess risk in the securities industry.[38]

CHAPTER 9 SUMMARY

Money and the Money Supply
- Money serves as a medium of exchange, a unit of account, and a store of value. Good money is acceptable, divisible, and portable.
- The three types of money are commodity money, representative money, and fiat money.
- The U.S. money supply consists of the total amount of money in circulation. Two measurements of the money supply are the M1 and M2.

Banks and Other Depository Institutions
- Commercial banks are for-profit financial corporations that accept deposits, extend loans, and offer a wide variety of financial services to individuals and businesses.
- Thrift institutions, such as savings and loan associations and savings banks, are depository institutions that mainly grant personal and home mortgage loans.
- Credit unions are member-owned nonprofit financial cooperatives that accept deposits and make personal and home mortgage loans.
- Depository institutions offer four main types of savings accounts: regular savings account, money market deposit account, certificate of deposit, and checking account.
- Retirement accounts such as the individual retirement account, Keogh plan, Simplified Employee Pension, and 401(k) offer tax advantages to savers.

Other Financial Institutions
- A stock market is a mechanism by which shares of corporations are traded in primary and secondary markets.

- A bond market is a mechanism by which corporate and government bonds are traded in primary and secondary markets.
- A mutual fund is a company that creates a diversified investment portfolio and sells shares in the fund to investors.
- A futures market is a mechanism by which contracts for items, such as commodities and financial instruments, are traded.

Issues in the Global Financial System

- The East Asian financial crisis of 1997–1998 illustrated the dangers of financial contagion in the highly interdependent global financial system.
- The financial crisis of 2007–2008 illustrated the dangers of highly speculative investments in largely unregulated financial markets.

NOTES

1. U.S. Department of the Treasury, Bureau of Engraving and Printing, "Currency Facts," www.moneyfactory.gov/uscurrency/largedenominations.html

2. Alan Greenspan, "The Challenge of Central Banking in a Democratic Society," speech delivered to the American Enterprise Institute for Public Policy, Washington, DC, December 5, 1996, www.federalreserve.gov/BOARDDOCS/SPEECHES/19961205.htm

3. Federal Reserve Bank of Boston, *Currency Points: Understanding Our Money* (Boston: Federal Reserve Bank of Boston), 6.

4. Federal Reserve System (Fed), "Table 1: Money Stock Measures," "Table 3: Seasonally Adjusted Components of M1," *Federal Reserve Statistical Release*, June 27, 2013, 1, 3, www.federalreserve.gov/releases/h6/current

5. Fed, "Table 1: Money Stock Measures," "Table 3: Seasonally Adjusted Components of M1," and "Table 4: Seasonally Adjusted Components of Non-M1 M2," *Federal Reserve Statistical Release*, June 27, 2013, 1, 3, 4, www.federalreserve.gov/releases/h6/current

6. Federal Deposit Insurance Corporation (FDIC), *Statistics on Depository Institutions*, March 31, 2013, www.2.fdic.gov/sdi/main?asp; National Credit Union Administration, "Federally Insured Credit Unions," March, 2013, www.ncua.gov/DataApps/Documents/CRS2013-03.pdf

7. Council of Economic Advisors, "Table B-76: Mortgage Debt Outstanding by Holder, 1973–2012," *Economic Report of the President: 2013*, (Washington, DC: U.S. Government Printing Office, 2013), 404.

8. Federal Reserve System, "Large Commercial Banks," *Federal Reserve Statistical Release*, March 31, 2013, www.federalreserve.gov/releases/lbr/current/lrg_bnk_1st.pdf

9. Federal Deposit Insurance Corporation (FDIC), *Statistics on Depository Institutions*, March 31, 2013, www.2.fdic.gov/SDI/SOB; FDIC, "Historical Statistics on Banking," November 15, 2012, www.fdic.gov

10. Office of Thrift Supervision (OTS), "Table 2.1: Federally Insured Thrift Institutions, 1958–2010 and OTS-Regulated Institutions by Charter Type, 1978–2010," *2010 Fact Book: A Statistical Profile of the Thrift Industry* (OTS), June 2011, 5.

11. U.S. Department of the Treasury, Office of the Comptroller of the Currency (COC), "Answers about the OTS/OCC Merger on July 21, 2011," www.helpwithmybank.gov/get-answers/answers-about-the-ots-occ-merger.html

12. National Credit Union Administration (NCUA), "Federally Insured Credit Unions," March 2013, www.ncua.gov/DataApps/Documents/CRS2013-03.pdf; U.S. Census Bureau, "Table 1183: Federal and State-Chartered Credit Unions: Summary, 1990 to 2010," *Statistical Abstract of the United States: 2012*, 2011, 738; NCUA, "History of Credit Unions," www.ncua.gov/about/history/Pages/CUHistory.aspx

13. NCUA, "Overall Trends," Federal Trends in Federally Insured Credit Unions, March 31, 2013, www.ncua.gov/Legal/Documents/Reports/FT20130331.pdf

14. NCUA, "Loan Distribution," *Financial Trends in Federally Insured Credit Unions*, March 31, 2013, 4, www.ncua.gov/Legal/Documents/Reports/FT20130331.pdf

15. NCUA, *How Your Accounts Are Federally Insured*, (Alexandria, VA: NCUA), October 2011, 1-2.

16. Navy Federal Credit Union, "About Navy Federal," 2013, www.navyfederal/about/about.asp; Credit Unions Online, "Top 100 U.S. Credit Unions," www.creditunionsonline.com/top100 creditunions.html

17. FDIC, "Certificates of Deposit: Tips for Savers," www.fdic.gov/deposit/deposits/certificate

18. IRS, *Individual Retirement Arrangements (IRAs)*, Publication 590, December 16, 2011, 6–10, www.IRS.gov;IRS, "Amount of Roth IRA Contributions That You Can Make for 2012," www.irs.gov/retirement/participant/article/0,,id=188238,00.html; IRS, "IRS Contribution Limits," www.irs.gov/retirement/participant/article/0,,id=211358,00,htm; CNN Money, "Ultimate Guide to Retirement (IRAs)," http://money.cnn.com/retirement/guide/IRA_Basics.moneymag/index.htm

19. CNN Money, "Ultimate Guide to Retirement (Keogh Plan)," http://money.cnn.com/retirement/guide/selfemployment_keoghs.moneymag/index.htm

20. IRS, *Retirement Plans for Small Business*, Publication 560 (for use in preparing 2011 returns), February 7, 2012, 2-3, 5, www.IRS.gov; IRS, "Chapter 15: Simplified Employee Pensions (SEPS)," prepared by George Drosehn and Al Reich; Department of Labor (DOL), "SEP Retirement Plans for Small Businesses," www.dol.gov/ebsa/publications/SEPPlans.html

21. IRS, "401(k) Resource Guide: Plan Sponsors, 401(k) Plan Overview," www.irs.gov/retirement/sponsor/article/0,,id=151800,00.html; IRS, "401(k) Plans," www.irs.gov/retirement/article/0,,id=120298,00.html; Stuart Robertson, "The Top Three Retirement Plans for Small Business," *Forbes*, March 29, 2011, www.forbes.com/sites/stuartrobertson/2011/03/29/the-top-three-retirement-plans; CNN Money, "Ultimate Guide to Retirement (401(k) plans)," http://money.cnn.com/retirement/guide/selfemployment_individual401k.moneymag/index

22. NYSE Euronext, "NYX Statement Regarding EU Decision to Approve Proposed Combination with Intercontinental Exchange," *News Release*, June 24, 2013, www.nyse.com/press/13720736 32961.html; NYSE Euronext, "NYSE Group and Euronext Announce Merger," *NYSE Group Newsletter* 13, no. 3 (June 2006), www.nyse.com/about/publication/1145959806931.html; NYSE Euronext, "New York Stock Exchange," www.nyx.com/en/who-we-are/history/newyork; "NYSE Euronext," *Hoovers*, www.hoovers.com/company/NYSE_Euronext/crtxji-1.html

23. NASDAQ OMX, "NASDAQ OMX Corporate Timeline," www.nasdaqomx.com/aboutus/timeline

24. World Federation of Exchanges (WFE), "Table 1: Domestic Market Capitalization, and Largest Domestic Equity Market Capitalizations at Year-End 2012 and 2011," *2012 WFE Market Highlights*, January 23, 2013, www.worldexchanges.org/statistics/2012%20WFE%20Market%20Highlights

25. Evelyn M. Rusli and Peter Eavis, "Facebook Raises $16 Billion in I.P.O.," *New York Times*, May 17, 2012, http://dealbook.nytimes.com/2012/05/17/facebook; David Welch, Lee Spears, and Craig Trudell, "GM IPO Raises $20 Billion Selling Common. Preferred," *Bloomberg*, November 17, 2010, www.bloomberg.com/news/2010-11-16/gm; Katie Benner, "Visa IPO Prices at Record $17.9B," *CNN Money*, March 19, 2008, http://money.cnn.com/2008/03/18/news/companies/visa_ipo.fortune

26. CNN, "Dow Jones Industrial Average Fast Facts: Records," November 27, 2013, www.cnn.com/2013/05/31/us/dow-jones-industrial-average-fast-facts

27. Dow Jones Indexes, "Dow Jones Industrial Average," www.djindexes.com/mdsidx/downloads/brochure_info/DOW_Jones_Industrial_Ave; CNN Money, "Dow Jones Industrial Average," http://money.cnn.com/data/dow30

28. "Dow Jones Timeline," *Wall Street Journal*, 2007, http://online.wsj.com/public/resources/documents/info-DJTimeline0706.html"DJIA Historical Timeline," Dow Jones Industrial Average Learning Center, 2013, www.djaverages.com

29. Securities Industry and Financial Markets Association (SIFMA), "What You Should Know: The Role of Bonds in America," www.investinginbonds.com/learnmore.asp?catid=3&id=50

30. SIFMA, "Outstanding U.S. Bond Market Debt, 1980 to 2013," 2013, . . .www.sifma.org/. . ./cm-us-bond-market-outstanding-sifma.xls

31. SIFMA, "What You Should Know: The Role of Bonds in America," www.investinginbonds.com/learnmore.asp?catid=3&id=50

32. Investment Company Institute (ICI), "Table 3: Total Net Assets of the Mutual Fund Industry," *2013 Investment Company Fact Book*, 53rd ed. (Washington, DC: ICI, 2013), 144.

33. Investment Company Institute (ICI), " 2012 Facts at a Glance," "Table 60: Worldwide Net Assets of Mutual Funds," "Table 61: Worldwide Number of Mutual Funds," *2013 Investment Company Fact Book*, 53rd ed. (Washington, DC: ICI, 2013), 2, 201-202.

34. NYSE Euronext, "Futures," http://nyse.nyx.com/learningcenter/allaboutinvesting/futures

35. CME Group, "Spirit of Innovation: Timeline of Achievements," www.cmegroup.com/company/history/timeline-of-achievements.html; CME Group, "Global Offices," www.cmegroup.com/company/history/global-offices.html

36. International Monetary Fund Staff, "Table 2: Advanced Economies: Real GDP and Total Domestic Demand," "Table 6: Developing Countries; By Country, Real GDP," *World Economic Outlook April 2002: Recessions and Recoveries, April 2002* (Washington, DC: IMF Publication Services, 2002), 158, 165.

37. IMF Staff, "Recovery from the Asian Crisis and the Role of the IMF," *IMF Issues Brief,* June 2000, www.imf.org/external/np/exr/ib/2000/06300,htm#II

38. U.S. Senate, "Brief Summary of the Dodd-Frank Wall Street Reform and Consumer Protection Act," http://banking.senate.gov/public_files/070110_Dodd_Frank_Wall_Street_Reform

10

Promoting Economic Stability

The three main types of economic instability are unemployment, sluggish or negative economic growth, and inflation. Over time the government has increased its role in promoting economic stability. Today the government's main stabilization policies are monetary policy, which is formed by the Federal Reserve System, and fiscal policy, which is determined mainly by Congress. There are limitations to these stabilization policies. Since the Great Depression of the 1930s, a number of different approaches to economic stabilization have been implemented with varying degrees of success.

PRICE INSTABILITY

Laissez-faire capitalism dominated the U.S. economic landscape for much the nineteenth and early twentieth centuries. Under laissez-faire capitalism America shunned most types of government intervention in economic activity, including interventions to stabilize prices in the economy. The severity of the Great Depression of the 1930s and the sacrifices necessary to mobilize the nation during World War II (1941–1945) irrevocably altered people's perceptions of "limited government," however. Immediately after World War II, Congress passed the Employment Act of 1946. This historic act helped define economic stability by making "maximum employment, production, and purchasing power"[1] central economic goals of the U.S. economy. Protecting the purchasing power of the U.S. dollar is directly linked to price stability, namely, preventing inflation and deflation in the economy.

Types of Inflation

Inflation is an increase in the overall price level for goods and services in an economy. The two main types of inflation are demand-pull and cost-push inflation. **Demand-pull inflation** occurs when excess demand in the economy causes people to bid up the prices of products. That is, aggregate (total) demand is greater than the aggregate (total) supply in the overall economy. Economists often describe demand-pull inflation as "too much money chasing too few goods."

The main culprit for most demand-pull inflation is irresponsible government policies that flood the economy with paper currency. When the government injects too much money into an economy, the currency loses value. This forces producers to increase the prices of many products. In extreme cases the resulting inflation races out of control, a situation called hyperinflation. Hyperinflation renders a currency virtually worthless, as was the case in post–World War I Germany. More recently hyperinflation in Zimbabwe during the early 2000s caused this nation to formally abandon its currency in 2009. Since 2009 business activity in Zimbabwe has been conducted in foreign currencies, including the U.S. dollar.

Cost-push inflation occurs when the costs of production increase, forcing businesses to increase the price of their output. The costs of production are payments that businesses make in exchange for the factors of production. A wage, for example, is the cost businesses incur when they employ workers. Businesses also pay for other factors of production such as capital goods and natural resources. The oil price shocks of the mid-1970s and late 1970s showed how higher resource costs, in this case a higher price for crude oil, pushed prices higher for many products in the United States. In 1972 the annual inflation rate stood at just 3.2 percent. During the first oil price shock, the U.S. inflation rate hit 6.2 percent in 1973, 11 percent in 1974, and 9.1 percent in 1975. Similarly, the second oil price shock contributed to double-digit inflation rates of 11.3 percent in 1979, 13.5 percent in 1980, and 10.3 percent in 1981.[2]

Measuring Inflation

The U.S. government's most basic measurement of price stability is the inflation rate. The **inflation rate** is the percentage increase in the overall price level of goods and services in an economy. The government uses the consumer price index (CPI) to calculate the inflation rate. CPI data is collected each month to determine whether the prices of commonly consumed items have increased or decreased. This bundle of items is often referred to as the *market basket* of commonly consumed products. The market basket consists of products in eight main categories: food and beverages, housing, apparel, transportation, medical care, recreation, education and communication, and other products.[3] A similar index, called the **producer price index** (PPI), measures price changes for raw materials, intermediate goods, and other items used to produce products.

A reference point called the base year enables price comparisons over time. The CPI is set at 100 at a base year. The most commonly used base year is 1982–1984, a spread of three years. At the base year the government says $1 equals 100 percent of its value. If the price of the market basket of goods increases, the CPI rises. When the price of the market basket decreases, the CPI falls. The CPI increased from 100 in 1982–1984 (the base year) to 229.6 in 2012. This means that it would have taken about $2.30 in 2012 to purchase the same amount of goods that $1.00 purchased 30 years earlier.

The annual inflation rate is calculated by dividing the net change in CPI from year 1 to year 2, by the CPI in year 1, as shown in Figure 10.1. In this example the net change in the CPI from 2011 to 2012 was 4.7 index points. Thus, the inflation rate for 2012 was 2.1 percent (4.7/224.9 = 0.021). An inflation rate of 2 percent or so is generally viewed as normal, even healthy, in a growing economy. Since the early 1990s the United States has achieved price stability, with an inflation rate generally ranging from 1.5 percent to 3 percent.[4] The inflation rate in other advanced economies, on average, was in sync with that of the United States during the 2000s. The inflation rate in the emerging market and developing economies generally ranged from 6 percent to 9 percent during the same period.[5]

Some economists question the accuracy of the CPI in measuring price changes in the U.S. economy. One concern is that the CPI may overstate price increases. This is because

$$\frac{\text{2012 CPI} - \text{2011 CPI}}{\text{2011 CPI}} = \text{Inflation Rate for 2012}$$

$$\frac{229.6 - 224.9}{224.9} = \frac{4.7}{224.9} = 2.1\%$$

Figure 10.1   Calculating the Inflation Rate, 2012
Source: Department of Labor/Bureau of Labor Statistics, "Consumer Price Index," June 18, 2013.

CPI data charts changes in the regular prices of products in a fixed market basket. Many consumers avoid regular-price items by purchasing lower-priced substitute goods or by purchasing goods at discount retail outlets. These buying habits of price-conscious consumers expand the purchasing power of their dollars. Thus, these savvy consumers do not feel the full impact of higher-price items recorded in the CPI data. Another concern is the problem of maintaining a fixed market basket of products. This is because the market basket of goods necessarily changes when producers stop making certain products or when the quality of products in the market basket improves over time. For example, changes in product quality are the norm with information and communications technologies such as computers, laptops, tablets, and cell phones. The U.S. Bureau of Labor Statistics makes periodic adjustments in the CPI to address some of these concerns.[6]

Inflation erodes the purchasing power of money in an economy. (Photographerlondon/Dreamstime.com)

Costs and Benefits of Inflation

Inflation reduces the purchasing power of money and imposes costs on different groups. Unanticipated inflation erodes the real value of workers' wages, savers' deposits, and consumers' disposable income. Inflation is especially severe for people on fixed incomes, including those who rely on public assistance programs such as Temporary Assistance for Needy Families, a federal transfer program not indexed to the inflation rate. Uncertainty caused by unanticipated inflation also sours business investment in new capital, retards job creation, and dims prospects for economic growth. Figure 10.2 shows the impact of inflation on the value of the U.S. dollar from 1950 to 2010.[7] Note that the value of the U.S. dollar dropped in each decade. During the inflation-ridden 1970s the real value of the dollar dipped by more than 50 percent. The reference point for dollar values is the base year of 1982–1984, where the government established that $1 equaled $1.

Inflation also benefits some people. The main beneficiary of unanticipated inflation is debtors. Debtors benefit if they have taken out long-term loans that have a low fixed interest rate. In 2012 many banks offered 30-year fixed rate mortgages at historically low annual interest rates of about 4 percent. If inflation increases significantly in 2013 or thereafter these borrowers will benefit because they will repay their mortgage debt with cheaper, less valuable dollars in the future.

Deflation

Deflation, sometimes called negative inflation, occurs when the general price level in an economy decreases. Deflation is most often the result of insufficient aggregate demand in

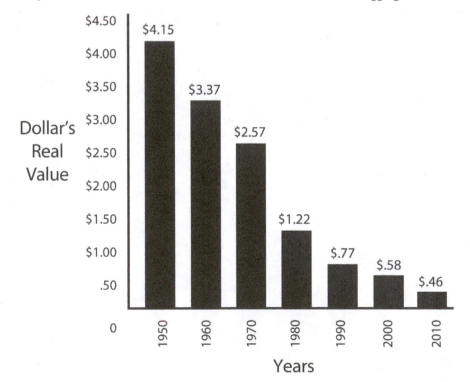

Figure 10.2   Impact of Inflation on the Value of the U.S. Dollar, 1950–2010
Source: U.S. Census Bureau, *Statistical Abstract of the United States: 2012*, "Table 724," 473.

an economy and is most likely to occur when large numbers of people are unemployed during a recession or depression. The United States suffered from severe deflation during the post–World War I economic downturn in 1921 (−10.5 percent) and 1922 (−6.1 percent), and during the early years of the Great Depression in 1931 (−9.0 percent), 1932 (−9.9 percent), and 1933 (−5.1 percent).[8] More recently many advanced economies around the world experienced a brief period of deflation during the global recession of 2007–2009. In 2009 deflation occurred in the United States (−0.3 percent), Ireland (−1.7 percent), Japan (−1.3 percent), Spain (−0.2 percent), Sweden (−0.5 percent), Switzerland (−0.5 percent), the Taiwan Province of China (−0.9 percent), and other countries.[9]

Deflation sends signals to producers and consumers that hinder economic growth. For instance, many businesses respond to deflation by reducing production, a predictable response to the expectation of lower prices for their output. Production cutbacks ripple through the economy, causing worker lay-offs and lower business investment. Deflation also discourages consumer spending on big-ticket items such as automobiles, consumer durables, and home renovations or repair. One reason for this drop in consumer spending is the specter of job loss during economic slowdowns. In addition, some consumers postpone major purchases with the expectation of still lower prices in the future. Persistent deflation in the Japanese economy during the 1990s and early 2000s stunted economic growth in the world's third largest economy.[10]

UNEMPLOYMENT AND UNDEREMPLOYMENT

Unemployment refers to the number of people in the labor force that do not have a job. The **unemployment rate** is the percentage of the labor force that is without work. Unemployment is another type of economic instability. The unemployment rate rises when the economy sinks into a recession or depression. At the height of the Great Depression in 1933, for example, the U.S. unemployment rate hit 25 percent of the labor force.

Types of Unemployment

There are three main types of unemployment. *Frictional unemployment* is the temporary joblessness that occurs naturally in a dynamic economy. It includes workers who are in-between jobs, who are re-entering the job market, or who are new entrants. Economists view frictional unemployment as normal, even healthy, in a fast-changing economy. The frictionally unemployed simply need time to find the best match between their job skills and available jobs. *Structural unemployment* is a longer-term type of unemployment that results from a mismatch between workers' skills and job opportunities. Structural unemployment often occurs when workers' skills become obsolete. The recent loss of certain manufacturing jobs in America's "sunset" industries illustrates this process. *Cyclical unemployment* is job loss that stems from a downturn in the business cycle, as occurs during a recession or depression. Consumer confidence and spending slow during economic downturns, which cause businesses to cut production and jobs. The Great Recession of 2007–2009, for example, resulted in a severe unemployment problem in the United States.

Economists generally agree that full employment is achieved when the economy hits its natural rate of unemployment. The **natural rate of unemployment** is often equated with the percentage of the labor force that is frictionally and structurally unemployed.

The natural functioning of dynamic economies is bound to displace some workers while creating opportunities for others. Cyclical unemployment, on the other hand, results from a change in the business cycle rather than the structure of the economy. Today many economists say that the natural rate of unemployment in the U.S. economy is between 5 and 6 percent of the civilian labor force. Government stabilization policies are most concerned with reducing cyclical unemployment.

Measuring Unemployment

The government's most basic measurement of the U.S. employment situation is the unemployment rate. The **unemployment rate** is the percentage of the U.S. labor force without a paid job. The unemployment rate is calculated by dividing the number of workers not currently employed by the number of workers in the entire labor force. In June 2013, for example, the U.S. unemployment rate was 7.6 percent because 11.8 million U.S. workers were officially unemployed out of a labor force of 155.8 million (11.8 million/155.8 million = 0.076, or 7.6 percent). The **employment rate**, on the other hand, is the percentage of the labor force with a paid job. In June 2013 the U.S. employment rate was 92.4 percent (100 percent −7.6 percent = 92.4 percent).[11]

The U.S. unemployment rate tends to rise during recessions and fall during periods of economic expansion. Since World War II the United States has experienced 11 recessions. The most severe of these recessions occurred in 1973–1975, 1981–1982, and 2007–2009, when annual unemployment rates rose to 8.5 percent, 9.7 percent, and 9.3 percent respectively.[12] Economists call unemployment a lagging economic indicator mainly because job loss continues to plague the economy even after a recession has ended. Figure 10.3 shows the U.S. employment rate from 2000 to 2012.[13] Note that the unemployment rate continued to increase even after a mild recession ended in 2001. Unemployment was also a serious economic problem after of the Great Recession ended in 2009.

The U.S. unemployment rate shows the percentage of the labor force without a job but does not show how different groups within the economy are affected by joblessness. For example, unemployment tends to be more severe for minorities, the youth, and those with lower levels of education. In June 2013 the unemployment rate for whites in the United States was 6.6 percent but was significantly higher for African Americans (13.7 percent) and Hispanics (9.1 percent). At the same time 7.6 percent of the entire U.S. labor force was without work, but the rate was triple for teen workers (24 percent). Level of educational attainment also influences the employment picture. Workers with a lower level of education not only have a higher unemployment rate, but also have a lower participation rate in the U.S. labor force, as shown in Table 10.1. The **labor force participation rate** shows the percentage of work-age individuals who are part of the labor force.[14] Note that in 2013 the unemployment rate for workers with less than a high school diploma was more than double that of college graduates.

Many economists believe that the U.S. employment situation requires a broader unemployment measure than the official unemployment rate. In other words, they argue that the real rate of unemployment should include other jobless groups that are not presently counted as unemployed. The largest group that is not counted in the government's unemployment figures is marginally attached workers. **Marginally attached workers** are persons who are willing and able to work but who could not find employment during the previous 12 months and who did not look for a job for four or more weeks prior to the government's employment survey. In June 2013 there were 2.6 million marginally attached

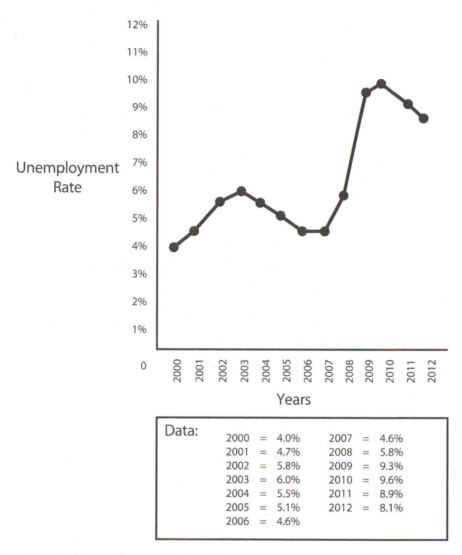

Figure 10.3 U.S. Unemployment Rate, 2000–2012
Source: U.S. Census Bureau, "Table B-42," *Statistical Abstract of the United States: 2013*, 374.

workers in the U.S. economy. If marginally attached workers were counted as unemployed, the unemployment rate for June 2013 would have jumped from 7.6 percent to 9.1 percent.[15]

The U.S. employment situation is further complicated by the presence of underemployment. **Underemployment** is the underutilization of employed workers in the economy. Thus, the underemployed are a subset of employed workers in the labor force. Underemployment occurs when workers are obliged to take a job beneath their skill level or work fewer hours than desired. According to the International Labor Organization (ILO), underemployment exists when employed workers are "willing and available to work 'more adequately.' "[16] The government keeps track of just one type of underemployment—involuntary part-time workers. Involuntary part-time workers prefer to work additional hours but are prevented by the lack of full-time job opportunities. In 2013 there were

Table 10.1   Unemployment, Labor Force Participation, and Educational Attainment, June 2013

Educational Attainment	Number in Civilian Labor Force (1000s)	Labor Force Participation Rate	Number of Unemployed Workers	Unemployment Rate
Less than high school diploma	11,161	44.5	1,192	10.7
High school graduate, no college	36,320	59.1	2,757	7.6
Some college or associate degree	37,297	68.1	2,372	6.4
Bachelor's degree and higher	49,466	75.6	1,929	3.9

Source: U.S. Department of Labor, Bureau of Labor Statistics, "Table A-4: Educational Status of the Civilian Population 25 Years and over by Educational Attainment," *News Release*, July 5, 2013. Data seasonally adjusted.

8.2 million involuntary part-time workers in the U.S. economy. The ILO describes involuntary part-time work as *time-related underemployment*.[17]

THE FEDERAL RESERVE SYSTEM AND MONETARY POLICY

The role of the federal government in promoting price stability, full employment, and economic growth has grown dramatically since the Great Depression. The two main types of stabilization policies are monetary policy and fiscal policy. In the United States monetary policy is conducted by the Federal Reserve System. The nation's fiscal policy, on the other hand, is conducted by Congress.

The Federal Reserve System: A Unique Central Bank

The **Federal Reserve System**, also called the Fed, is America's central bank. The Fed serves two categories of clients: banks and the U.S. government. The Fed was established by the Federal Reserve Act in 1913, and by 1914 the Fed was up and running. Congressional debates over the need for a central bank, as well as its structure, were conducted in the shadow of two devastating economic downturns—the panic of 1893 and the panic of 1907. In the nineteenth and early twentieth centuries, the term "panic" was often used to describe a severe economic downturn such as a depression or recession.[18] Two institutions, the Board of Governors and the 12 regional Federal Reserve Banks, coordinate most Fed functions. The Fed's overall mission is "to foster the stability, integrity, and efficiency of the nation's monetary, financial, and payment systems so as to promote optimal macroeconomic performance."[19]

A central bank is a nation's single most important monetary authority. Today virtually all countries have a national financial institution that serves as a central bank. Examples include the Deutsche Bundesbank (Germany), Banque de France, Banco Central do Brazil, the Bank of England, and the Federal Reserve System (United States). Since the late 1990s some functions of the central banks in Europe, including the Bundesbank and Banque de France, have been delegated to the European Central Bank (ECB)—an institution of the European Union (EU).

Most central banks share some common features. For instance, central banks hold member banks' cash reserves. These reserves enable central banks to respond to economic crises in a timely manner. Central banks typically issue currency, regulate and supervise the banking system, and devise a national monetary policy. In addition, most central banks are nonprofit institutions that are owned and operated by the federal government to promote economic stability and growth.

The U.S. Federal Reserve System is among the world's most unique central banks. First, the Fed operates through 12 regional Federal Reserve Banks located in cities across the nation, rather than through a single national bank. Second, as an "independent entity within the government," the Fed is largely insulated from the everyday political maneuverings of elected officials.[20] Third, only nationally chartered banks are required to join the Fed. Fourth, member banks rather than the federal government own the 12 regional Federal Reserve Banks. Finally, the Fed is a self-supporting, nonprofit institution. The Fed's net earnings derived from the purchase or sale of government securities, interest from loans, or fees for financial services are handed over to the U.S. Treasury.[21] In 2012 the Fed's net earnings totaled $88.4 billion.[22]

Organizational Structure of the Fed

The Board of Governors (BOG) sits at the top of the Fed's organizational structure. The BOG is organized as a federal agency and consists of seven members, each appointed to a 14-year term by the president of the United States and subject to confirmation by the Senate. The president also appoints the chairman of the board, who is selected from among the seven board members to serve a four-year term of office. Ben Bernanke was appointed to the board's top spot first by Republican president George W. Bush, to serve as chairman from 2006 to 2010. Bernanke was reappointed by Democratic president Barack Obama for a second term from 2010 to 2014. In February 2014, another Obama appointee, Janet Yellen, began a four-year term as Fed chair. Yellen became the first woman to head the Federal Reserve System.

The BOG has broad responsibilities in the realm of promoting a sound banking system and economic stability—stable prices, full employment, and economic growth. It supervises and regulates banks, collects and shares economic information with policy makers, participates in multilateral organizations, and is a powerful voice in the formulation of the nation's monetary policy. The board also meets regularly with three advisory committees: the Federal Advisory Council, which deals with general economic and banking issues; the Consumer Advisory Council, which deals with consumer credit and related issues; and the Thrift Institutions Advisory Council, which deals with financial concerns of savings and loan associations, savings banks, and credit unions. The Board of Governors and its 2,540 staff workers operate from its headquarters in Washington, DC.[23]

The 12 regional Federal Reserve Banks and the 24 Branch Reserve Banks represent a second tier in the Fed. Each of the 12 Reserve Banks serves a specific district in the United States: (1) Boston, (2) New York, (3) Philadelphia, (4) Cleveland, (5) Richmond, (6) Atlanta, (7) Chicago, (8) St. Louis, (9) Minneapolis, (10) Kansas City, (11) Dallas, and (12) San Francisco. A nine-member Board of Directors administers each Reserve Bank. Three directors represent the interests of commercial banks in the region, while the six remaining directors represent the interest of the public—consumers, labor, industry, agriculture, and so on. The nine directors, in turn, select the Reserve Bank's president, a selection that requires the approval of the Board of Governors in Washington, DC. Similarly, a board of directors governs each of the 24 Branch Reserve Banks. The Federal Reserve Banks are often referred to as "the operating arms of the central banking system" because of their role in bank supervision, currency distribution, and the implementation of monetary policy.[24]

A third tier in the Federal Reserve System consists of the member banks. All nationally chartered commercial banks and bank trust companies must belong to the Fed.

Membership is optional for state-chartered banks. Member banks are required to purchase stock in the regional Federal Reserve Bank, for which they receive an annual dividend. In 2012 there were 6,063 commercial banks operating in the U.S. economy. Of this total 2,051 were member banks, of which 1,222 were nationally chartered commercial banks and 829 were state-chartered commercial banks. The remaining 4,012 banks were state nonmember commercial banks. While only one-third of all commercial banks in the United States were members of the Fed in 2012, member banks accounted for 81 percent of all commercial bank loans and investments in U.S. government securities.[25] Savings and loan associations, savings banks, and credit unions are not eligible to become member banks. The Depository Institutions Deregulation and Monetary Control Act of 1980 extended most of the requirements and benefits of membership to the thrift institutions, however.

Functions of the Fed

The Fed has several major functions in the U.S. economy, all of which are related to its mission of creating a stronger and more stable monetary and financial system. First, the Fed formulates and implements the nation's monetary policy. The Fed's **monetary policy** is used to alter the money supply and the cost of credit in pursuit of national economic goals such as economic growth, full employment, and price stability. The primary tools

---

ECONOMICS IN HISTORY: U.S. Central Banks in the Early Republic

Shortly after the U.S. Constitution was ratified in 1788, disagreements erupted over the proper role of government in the economy. One divisive issue was whether the United States should create a central bank. Alexander Hamilton, the first secretary of the treasury, supported the creation of a central bank. Hamilton insisted that Congress had the power to create a central bank under the necessary and proper clause of the Constitution (Article I, Section 8, Clause 18). Hamilton believed that a central bank would strengthen the nation's monetary system and credit.

Thomas Jefferson, the nation's first secretary of state, opposed the creation of a central bank. He argued that because the Constitution made no mention of a national bank, Congress had no authority to create one. Jefferson, a champion of rural and agricultural interests, also feared that a powerful central bank would trample the rights of states and hinder the natural development of local economies.

Hamilton's views prevailed, and Congress created the First Bank of the United States in 1791. Under the provisions of its 20-year charter, the First Bank (1791–1811) served as a commercial bank. It accepted deposits, made consumer and business loans, and provided other financial services. The First Bank also served as the fiscal authority for the federal government. It collected taxes, paid the government's bills, issued bank notes, and handled the purchase and sale of government securities. The First Bank did not have the power to supervise or regulate state banks, however. From its headquarters in Philadelphia and branch banks in Baltimore, Boston, Charleston, and New York City, the First Bank brought order and stability to America's financial system during the early republic. Its charter expired in 1811.

The Second Bank of the United States was established after the young republic suffered through five years of financial disorder from 1811 to 1816. The Second Bank's (1816–1836) 20-year charter gave it many of the same functions as the First Bank. It also inherited the distrust of many common people and animosity of powerful political leaders. In 1832, four years before the Second Bank's charter was to expire, Congress approved a bill to recharter the Second Bank for an additional 20 years. President Andrew Jackson vetoed this bill, however. The Second Bank's charter quietly expired in 1836. The United States waited nearly 80 years to create its next central bank, the Federal Reserve System.

of monetary policy are open market operations, the discount rate, and the reserve requirement. During economic downturns, or recessions, these monetary tools are used to increase the money supply and lower interest rates, thereby stimulating business activity. Conversely, to slow inflation the Fed's monetary tools are used to decrease the money supply and increase interest rates. By withdrawing money from the economy and making credit more expensive, the Fed reduces inflationary pressures that result from too much money chasing too few goods.

A second function of the Fed is the supervision and regulation of banking institutions. This function is designed to ensure the stability of financial institutions and the security of depositors' savings. Supervision deals with the Fed's oversight of business practices employed by member and nonmember financial institutions and their compliance with existing banking laws. The Fed's supervisory role is sometimes performed in conjunction with other federal agencies such as the Federal Deposit Insurance Corporation (FDIC), the Office of the Comptroller of the Currency (which absorbed the Office of Thrift Supervision in 2011), and the National Credit Union Administration (NCUA). The Fed's regulatory role is to create rules and guidelines by which U.S. financial institutions and foreign institutions that operate in the United States are organized and run. Recently the Fed also assumed a leading role in implementing the historic Dodd-Frank Wall Street Reform and Consumer Protection Act of 2010, landmark legislation that addressed financial security and fairness issues in the U.S. financial system. Since 1978 the Federal Financial Institutions Examinations Council (FFIEC) has brought representatives from federal and state regulatory agencies together to coordinate regulations in the banking industry.[26]

A third function of the Fed is to supply important financial services to banks, the U.S. government, and the American people. One financial service is the Fed's electronic payments systems, which include the Automated Clearing House (ACH) and the Federal Reserve Communications System (Fedwire), which speed transactions among financial institutions, government agencies, and citizens. ACH processes payments electronically. ACH was designed to reduce the use of cumbersome paper checks for recurring payments, such as the direct deposit of payroll, direct payment of mortgages and other bills, interest and dividend payments, tax refunds, and Social Security and other government transfer payments. In 2012 the Fed's ACH system processed 12 billion commercial and government ACH transactions valued at $24 trillion.[27] Fedwire links the Federal Reserve Banks and depository institutions, enabling larger transfers of money and securities within the financial system. In 2012 the Fedwire Funds Service accounted for 132 million transfers valued at $599 trillion—an average of $2.4 trillion per day.[28]

The Fed's other major financial services include check clearing, making seasonal adjustments in the money stock, and acting as the government's fiscal agent. The Fed operates check clearing centers across the country to sort and process checks. In 2012 the Fed processed about 6.6 billion checks, a number that continues to fall as people substitute electronic payments for paper checks. The Fed adjusts the nation's money stock to accommodate shifts in business activity at different times of the year, such as holiday shopping seasons and planting seasons in the agricultural sector. The Fed also replaces damaged or "unfit" money. It distributed $37 billion in new bills into circulation in 2012.[29] Finally, as the federal government's fiscal agent, the Fed collects and deposits federal tax receipts, issues and redeems government securities, manages government agencies' accounts, and processes government checks to business vendors and citizens. Today the Fed conducts the great majority of these services electronically.[30]

Monetary Policy Tools

Monetary policy represents the actions of the Federal Reserve System, America's central bank, to regulate the nation's money supply and the cost of credit. Monetary policy promotes the economic goals of maximum production, full employment, and stable prices. The two types of monetary policy are easy money and tight money policies. An **easy money policy** uses Fed tools to expand the nation's money supply and use of credit to increase aggregate demand in the economy. This stimulates business activity and jobs creation to counter the effects of economic downturns. A **tight money policy**, on the other hand, contracts the nation's money supply and access to credit decrease aggregate demand in the economy. This decrease in aggregate demand reduces inflationary pressures caused by too much money chasing too few goods. Tight money policy is typically used during overheated expansions. The Fed's three main monetary policy tools are open market operations, the discount rate, and the reserve requirement.

The Fed's most important monetary policy tool is open market operations, which involves the government's purchase and sale of government securities. The Federal Open Market Committee (FOMC), the Fed's top decision-making body, decides when to buy or sell government securities such as Treasury bills and notes on the open market. The FOMC is comprised of all seven governors who serve on the Fed's Board of Governors,

The Federal Reserve Bank of New York conducts open market operations for the Federal Reserve System. (Federal Reserve Bank of New York)

plus five regional Reserve Bank presidents. The purchase or sale of government securities is conducted through the trading desk at the Federal Reserve Bank of New York.

The Fed's open market operations can be used to jump-start a sluggish economy or to slow an overheated economy. The FOMC *buys* securities from dealers in the banking system to increase aggregate demand and jump-start business activity during economic downturns. By purchasing U.S. government securities, the Fed increases banks' cash reserves, which enables banks to make additional loans and other investments. A larger pool of loanable funds also tends to reduce interest rates, which encourages individuals and businesses to borrow and spend money. Conversely, the FOMC *sells* U.S. government securities to dealers in the banking system to slow economic activity, reduce inflation, or both during the expansion phase of the business cycle. By selling U.S. government securities, the Fed soaks up money from the banking system. This reduces banks' ability to make loans and investments. The sale of these securities also tends to increase interest rates charged by banks, which further discourages borrowing by individuals and businesses.

The **discount rate**, a second Fed tool, is the interest rate charged by the Fed for short-term loans made to member and nonmember banks. The discount rate is set by the board of directors at each of the 12 regional Federal Reserve Banks, subject to the approval of the Board of Governors in Washington, DC. A change in the discount rate sends signals to the banking system about the health of the economy and the economic challenges facing the nation.

The regional Federal Reserve Banks lower the discount rate to increase aggregate demand during economic downturns. A lower discount rate encourages banks to borrow from the Fed and thus increases banks' ability to make loans to individuals and firms. Conversely, the regional Federal Reserve Banks raise the discount rate to decrease aggregate demand, mainly to fight inflation. A higher discount rate discourages banks from borrowing from the Fed and reduces banks' ability to extend loans. Recently the Fed reduced the discount rate 12 times to stimulate borrowing and spending during and after the Great Recession (2007–2009). These reductions brought the discount rate down from 6.25 percent during the summer of 2007 to just 0.50 percent in December 2008. During this same period the Fed reduced the federal funds rate 10 times, from 5.25 percent to 0.25 percent or less.[31] The **federal funds rate** is the interest rate banks charge to other banks for short-term loans.

The **reserve requirement**, a third Fed tool, is the percentage of transactions deposits that depository institutions must hold as reserves either in their own vaults or at their regional Federal Reserve Bank. Transactions accounts include checking or share draft accounts, automatic transfer service (ATS) accounts, negotiable order of withdrawal (NOW) accounts, and others. The Board of Governors establishes and periodically adjusts the reserve requirement. At the close of 2012, for example, the reserve requirement was set at 0 percent on transaction accounts of $0 to $12.4 million; 3 percent on transaction accounts between $12.4 and $79.5 million; and 10 percent on transaction accounts of more than $79.5 million.[32]

The Fed lowers the reserve requirement to increase the amount of money banks can loan to people. This increases aggregate demand and business activity to combat economic downturns. Conversely, the Fed raises the reserve requirement to reduce the amount of money banks can loan to people. This action decreases aggregate demand and slows business activity mainly to fight inflation. The reserve requirement is the least used monetary tool mainly because frequent changes in required reserves disrupt banks' long-term loan and investment strategies. In addition, changes in the reserve requirement have a relatively small impact on economic activity because reserves are restricted to transactions deposits.

Quantitative Easing

Quantitative easing is a Fed tool that injects money into the economy through the banking system to promote economic growth and jobs creation. Under quantitative easing (QE), the Fed purchases large quantities of financial assets such as Treasury notes or mortgage-backed securities (MBS) from banks. Fed payments for these assets are sent electronically to the banks. These electronic transfers of cash to the banks represent newly created money which, in effect, increases the nation's money supply and enables banks to make additional loans. QE injections also tend to reduce interest rates, which encourages people to borrow money. The Fed uses quantitative easing when the traditional Fed tools alone cannot stimulate economic growth. Until recently quantitative easing was a rarely used Fed tool.

Quantitative easing was used extensively during the Great Recession of 2007–2009 and immediately thereafter. Three rounds of quantitative easing called QE1, QE2, and QE3 pumped trillions of dollars into the economy. The government purchased a total of $1.75 trillion in financial assets from the banking system under QE1 (2008–2010) and QE2 (2010–2011). These assets consisted mainly of U.S. government securities and MBS. QE3, which began in September 2012, enabled the Fed to purchase $40 billion in MBS each month, with no certain ending date for these purchases.[33] In December 2012 the Fed agreed to purchase an additional $45 billion per month in longer-term U.S.

PRIMARY DOCUMENT: Ben Bernanke Announces a Third Phase of Quantitative Easing (QE3)

As you know, the Federal Reserve System conducts monetary policy under a dual mandate from Congress to promote maximum employment and price stability. The United States has enjoyed broad price stability since the mid-1990s and continues to do so today. The employment situation, however, remains a grave concern. . . .

The weak job market should be a concern for every American. High unemployment imposes hardships on millions of people, and it entails a tremendous waste of human skills and talents. Five million Americans have been unemployed for more than six months, and millions more have left the labor force—many of them doubtless because they have given up on finding suitable work. . . .

[T]he FOMC decided today on new actions. . . . Specifically, the Committee decided to purchase additional agency mortgage-backed securities, or MBS, at a pace of $40 billion per month. . . . The program of MBS purchases should increase the downward pressure on long-term interest rates more generally, but also on mortgage rates, specifically, which should provide further support for the housing sector by encouraging home purchases and refinancing.

[T]he Committee will closely monitor incoming information on economic and financial developments in coming months, and if we do not see substantial improvement in the outlook for the labor market, we will continue the MBS purchase program, undertake additional asset purchases, and employ our policy tools as appropriate until we do. We will be looking for the sort of broad-based growth in jobs and economic activity that generally signal sustained improvement in labor market conditions and declining unemployment. Of course, in determining the size, pace, and composition of any additional asset purchases, we will, as always, take appropriate account of the inflation outlook and their efficacy and costs.

Federal Reserve System Press Release (September 13, 2012), Ben Bernanke government securities. Hence, by 2013 the Fed was infusing $85 billion per month into the U.S. economy through its purchase of securities.[34]

Quantitative easing is a controversial stabilization policy. It became a political hot potato during the presidential campaign of 2012. Supporters of the QEs argued that the Great Recession and lackluster recovery that followed justified the massive infusion of money into the economy. Supporters noted that the QEs contributed to the fall of interest rates, including interest rates on home mortgages, and encouraged borrowers to take out loans and spend more freely. Supporters also pointed to a rise in investor confidence as evidenced by a dramatic improvement in corporate stock performance during this period. Opponents of the QEs maintained that the wave of government purchases of assets was little more than printing money, which they feared would eventually cause inflation. Further, they noted that economic growth and job creation remained weak during the period despite the massive infusion of newly created money into the economy.

In December 2013 Fed Chair Ben Bernanke announced that the Fed would begin to "taper" its monthly bond-buying spree from $85 billion to just $75 billion starting in January 2014. This tapering, or scale-back of QE, was a Fed response to improving economic conditions in the United States, such as a decline in unemployment rate and positive GDP growth.

FISCAL POLICY

Fiscal policy represents the actions of Congress to promote economic growth and stability. Since the Great Depression the federal government has used fiscal policy to achieve these goals. Fiscal policy is often divided into two strands: discretionary fiscal policy and nondiscretionary fiscal policy. The two main tools of fiscal policy are taxation and government spending.

Fiscal Policy Tools

Discretionary fiscal policy refers to the conscious actions by Congress to achieve economic growth and stability, mainly through changes in tax policy and government spending. These actions typically require Congress to pass new legislation. There are two types of discretionary fiscal policy: expansionary and restrictive. An **expansionary fiscal policy** uses tax cuts and additional government spending to inject money into the economy and thereby increase aggregate demand. Economists refer to these money injections as priming the pump so that the economy can move forward. Higher aggregate demand gives producers the incentive to produce more goods and hire more workers. Expansionary fiscal policy is used to fight recessions and depressions. A **restrictive fiscal policy**, on the other hand, requires tax hikes and lower government spending to decrease aggregate demand. Restrictive policies withdraw money from the economy to slow inflation or curb the exuberant growth that may accompany an economic expansion.

The use of discretionary fiscal policies to restore the economic health of the U.S. economy gained momentum during the Great Depression of the 1930s. British economist John Maynard Keynes popularized the use of discretionary fiscal policy in his landmark book *The General Theory of Employment, Interest, and Money* (1936). Since that time Keynesians and non-Keynesian policy makers have used taxes and government spending to promote the goals of growth, full employment, and price stability. For example, Congress and the president supported more than $1 trillion in additional discretionary spending to jump-start the sputtering U.S. economy during the Great Recession (2007–2009). This burst of discretionary spending, called stimulus spending, occurred during the presidencies of George W. Bush and Barack Obama. During the same time period the government extended certain tax breaks and offered a tax rebate to put more money into the hands of individuals and firms.

Nondiscretionary fiscal policy refers to the built-in or *automatic stabilizers* that exist within the tax system and federal spending programs—especially government transfer payments. Automatic stabilizers tend to inject money into the economy when the economy dips into recessions. These cash injections increase aggregate demand, and motivate businesses to increase production and hiring. Automatic stabilizers also withdraw money from the economy when prosperity returns. The two main automatic stabilizers in the U.S. economy are the progressive income tax and public transfer payments.

The progressive income tax is a tax on people's income, mainly income from wages. During recessions, when some workers lose their jobs or are underemployed, wage income declines. As a result, these workers automatically pay less in taxes to the government. During expansions, on the other hand, workers' wages rise. A higher wage automatically increases these workers' tax obligations, which helps prevent the economy from overheating. In a similar way public transfer payments inject additional money into the economy during downturns and withdraw money during expansions. One type of transfer payment is unemployment insurance (UI), a major public transfer payment offered to the temporarily unemployed. UI payments increase during recessions when the unemployment rate is high and decrease during expansions when unemployment subsides. For example the number of unemployed workers collecting UI payments was just 2.6 million in 2007, before the start of the Great Recession. By 2010 the number of workers receiving UI payments had jumped to 9.7 million. During this same period of time, UI payments increased from $31 billion to $150 billion, nearly a fivefold increase.[35] Other transfer payments, such as Temporary Assistance for Needy Families (TANF) and the Supplemental Nutrition Assistance Program (SNAP), also inject additional money into a depressed economy.

Limitations of Stabilization Policies

It is tempting to conclude that economists and informed policy makers have their thumb on the pulse of the economy and that they can diagnose and cure any economic malady that might occur. But even with advancements in economic modeling and forecasting, and the many lessons learned from earlier bouts with similar economic problems, economic science lacks the precision of the physical sciences. After all, economic science deals with the behaviors of people, which are often unpredictable. As a result, there are certain limitations to society's ability to achieve macroeconomic goals such as economic growth and stability through monetary or fiscal policies.

One limitation of monetary and fiscal policies concerns the timeliness of the government's response to changing economic conditions. Time lags occur between the recognition of an economic problem, and the creation and implementation of appropriate stabilization policies to deal with the problem. For example, it was not until December 2008 that the National Bureau of Economic Research (NBER) announced that the U.S. economy had entered into a recession in December 2007. Thus, the NBER announcement came a year after the change in the business cycle had occurred. Time lags are inevitable considering the complexity of modern economies. Time lags are especially troublesome when formulating fiscal policy because a greater number of elected representatives in Congress must agree on a suitable set of tax policies and spending programs.

A second limitation is the politicization of economic problems. Political pressure on elected officials has risen dramatically in recent years. The architects of fiscal policy in Congress feel these pressures. Political gridlock has thwarted the spirit of compromise on sensitive issues related to taxation and government spending—the two main tools of fiscal policy. From 2009 to 2012 this gridlock even prevented the federal government from passing a federal budget. Political gridlock associated mainly with the funding of the Affordable Care Act also resulted in a partial federal government shutdown in October 2013. Appointed governors of the Federal Reserve System, on the other hand, are more sheltered from political pressures as they form the nation's monetary policy.

A third limitation is the uncertainty of policy coordination. There is sometimes disagreement between the Fed and the nation's highest elected officials about what constitutes an appropriate stabilization policy. In the early 1980s, for example, the United States faced two economic problems: rising inflation and recession. Fed chairman Paul Volcker implemented a tight money policy, which decreased aggregate demand, to fight skyrocketing inflation. Meanwhile, President Ronald Reagan and Congress pursued aggressive tax cuts—an expansionary fiscal policy—to reverse the economic downturn and revive the sputtering economy. These conflicting policies sent mixed messages to the economy.

Different Approaches to Stabilization

The **classical school** of economic thought opposed most government intervention in the economy. In his book *An Inquiry into the Nature and Causes of the Wealth of Nations* (1776), British economist Adam Smith created the intellectual foundations for the classical school. In the United States, classical school economists supported laissez-faire capitalism during the 1800s and early 1900s. Laissez-faire capitalism relied on free and competitive markets to allocate resources in a fair and efficient manner. Government intervention, on the other hand, was viewed as an obstacle to economic progress. The government's main function was to provide for the nation's security against foreign and domestic threats and provide a sound business environment, not to regulate businesses, provide a social safety net, or tinker with business cycles. The severity of the Great Depression of the 1930s caused many people to reject the classical school's laissez-faire views and, instead, turn toward additional government involvement in the economy.

The **Keynesian school** of thought championed demand-management economics. In *The General Theory of Employment, Interest, and Money* (1936), John Maynard Keynes rejected classical economics and supported a more activist role for government to promote growth and stability. Soon the followers of Keynes were referred to as Keynesians. Keynesians supported aggressive monetary and fiscal policies to influence aggregate demand in the economy—to increase aggregate demand during times of recession and reduce aggregate demand during times of inflation. During the Great Depression of the 1930s, the most serious economic downturn of the twentieth century, the Keynesians urged the Fed to adopt an easy money policy and urged Congress and the president to adopt an expansionary fiscal policy. Keynesians influenced government stabilization policies for decades after the Great Depression ended. The introduction of a new type of instability—stagflation—during the 1970s, rained on the Keynesians' parade, however. **Stagflation** is the simultaneous occurrence of recession and high inflation. The Keynesian approach to stabilization was ill equipped to fight recession and inflation at the same time. Despite this

Many people supported a larger role for government in the U.S. economy during the Great Depression (1930s). (Library of Congress)

setback, some economists and policy makers still hold fast to Keynesian ideas, as evidenced by the easy money policies and expansionary fiscal policies used to address the Great Recession of 2007–2009.

Monetarism, another approach to stabilization, gained momentum during the 1970s. **Monetarism** favored a fixed, predictable rate of growth in the nation's money supply as the surest road to long-term prosperity. Monetarists, led by economist Milton Friedman, also believed that free markets and a resilient private sector should guide economic activity. Monetarists cheered when Fed chairman Paul Volcker instituted strict guidelines on the growth of the nation's money supply to quell spiraling inflation during the late 1970s. This policy reigned in inflation but also contributed to a severe recession by the early 1980s.

Supply-side economics, a stabilization approach that gained popularity during the presidency of Ronald Reagan in the 1980s, stressed the role of incentives to stimulate productivity and economic growth. Supply siders stressed the role of incentives to instigate higher productivity and national output. The supply-side approach to stabilization relied on policies to increase aggregate supply, rather than to manipulate aggregate demand in the economy. **Aggregate supply** represents the total output of goods and services in an economy. President Ronald Reagan (1981–1989) staunchly supported the supply-side approach to stabilization during his presidency. Reagan believed that proper supply-side incentives must include tax cuts as well as reductions in business regulations and wasteful government spending. The centerpiece of Reagan's supply-side agenda was the Economic Recovery Act of 1981, which cut personal and corporate income taxes by 25 percent between 1982 and 1984. Economist Arthur Laffer, through the Laffer curve, explained that lower tax *rates* would generate greater tax *revenues* by expanding the tax base. Economists still debate the impact of supply-side policies on the prolonged expansion of the 1980s and on the massive federal deficits of the period.

In recent years new classical economics has become an influential school of thought in the stabilization debate. **New classical economics** assumes that both wages and prices are flexible and that people have sufficient economic information to anticipate government economic policies. Much of what is "new" in the new classical economics centers on the rational expectations hypothesis, a theory developed by Nobel Laureate Robert E. Lucas Jr. and other economists at the University of Chicago. According to the *rational expectations hypothesis*, people are privy to an immense body of economic information and by using "all available information" they will, on average, accurately predict future economic events, including monetary policy and fiscal policy. People's expectations, in turn, influence their present economic behaviors such as saving, investing, and spending, which limit the effectiveness of future stabilization policies. Critics of the rational expectations hypothesis argue that people have neither the time nor the inclination to collect and analyze the economic data needed to anticipate government policies or predict future economic outcomes.

CHAPTER 10 SUMMARY

Price Instability
- Inflation occurs when the overall price level in an economy rises.
- The Consumer Price Index is used to calculate the inflation rate.
- Inflation erodes the purchasing power of money, which hurts certain groups and helps others.
- Deflation occurs when the overall price level in an economy falls.

Unemployment and Underemployment
- Unemployment occurs when workers in the labor force do not have a paid job.
- The unemployment rate measures the percentage of the labor force currently without work.
- Measurements of unemployment are complicated by factors such as underemployment and the exclusion of marginally attached workers from government employment data.

The Federal Reserve System and Monetary Policy
- The Federal Reserve System, or Fed, is the central bank for the United States.
- The Fed's organizational structure is unique, balancing decision making between a Board of Governors and 12 regional Federal Reserve Banks.
- The Fed's most important function is the implementation of the nation's monetary policy.
- The Fed's three main monetary policy tools are open market operations, discount rate, and reserve requirement.
- Quantitative easing increases the amount of loanable funds and reduces the cost of credit.

Fiscal Policy
- Discretionary and nondiscretionary fiscal policies supports the goals of growth and stability.
- Time lags, political pressures, and policy coordination limit the effectiveness of government stabilization policies.
- Different schools of economic thought offer different prescriptions for economic stability.

NOTES

1. Henry S. Commager, Ed., "The Employment Act of 1946," in *Documents in American History*, 7th ed. (New York: Appleton-Century-Crofts, 1963), 514–15.

2. U.S. Department of Labor (DOL), Bureau of Labor Statistics (BOL), "Consumer Price Index," Washington, DC, June 18, 2013, ftp://ftp.bls.gov/pub/special.requests/cpi/cpiai.txt

3. DOL/BLS, "Consumer Price Index, June 2013," *News Release*, July 16, 2013, www.bls.gov/news.release/pdf/cpi.pdf

4. DOL/BLS, "Consumer Price Index," June 18, 2013.

5. International Monetary Fund (IMF), "Table A5:. Summary of Inflation," *World Economic Outlook, April 2013* (Washington, DC: IMF, 2013), 156.

6. Bureau of Labor Statistics, Division of Consumer Prices and Price Indexes, "Hedonic Quality Adjustment in the CPI," February 23, 2012, www.bls.gov/cpi/cpihqaitem.htm

7. U.S. Census Bureau, "Table 724: Purchasing Power of the Dollar, 1950 to 2010," *Statistical Abstract of the United States: 2012* (Washington, DC: U.S. Government Printing Office, 2011), 473.

8. Ibid.

9. IMF, "Table A6: Advanced Economies, Consumer Prices," *World Economic Outlook, April 2013* (Washington, DC: IMF, 2013), 157.

10. World Bank, "Gross Domestic Product, 2012," *World Development Indicators* (database), July 1, 2013, http://databank.worldbank.org/data/download/GDP.pdf

11. DOL/BLS, "Table A-1: Employment Status of the Civilian Population by Sex and Age," The Employment Situation, June 2013, *News Release*, July 5, 2013, www.bls.gov/news.release/pdf/empsit.pdf

12. Council of Economic Advisors, "Table B-42: Civilian Unemployment Rate, 1966–2012, *Economic Report of the President: 2013* (Washington, DC: U.S. Government Printing Office, 2013), 379; National Bureau of Economic Research (NBER), "US Business Cycle Expansions and Contractions," www.nber.org/cycles.html

13. Ibid.

14. DOL/BLS, "Table A-1: Employment Status of the Civilian Population by Sex and Age," "Table A-2: Employment Status of the Civilian Population by Race, Sex and Age," "Table A-3: Employment Status of the Hispanic or Latino population by Sex and Age," "Table A-4: Employment Status of the Civilian Population 25 Years and over by Educational Attainment," The Employment Situation, June 2013, *News Release*, July 5, 2013, www.bls.gov/news.release/pdf/empsit.pdf

15. DOL/BLS, "Table A-15: Alternative Measures of Labor Underutilization," "Table A-16: Persons Not in the Labor Force and Multiple Job Holders by Sex, Not Seasonally Adjusted," The Employment Situation, June 2013, *News Release*, July 5, 2013, www.bls.gov/news.release/pdf/empsit.pdf

16. International Labor Organization (ILO), "Underemployment Statistics," 2012, www.ilo.org/global/statistics-and-databases/statistics-overview-and-topics/underemployment

17. DOL/BLS, "Table A-8: Employed Persons by Class of Worker and Part-Time Status," The Employment Situation, June 2013, *News Release*, July 5, 2013, 1; Organization for Economic Cooperation and Development, "Time Related Underemployment," http://stats.oecd.org/glossary/details.asp?ID=3542

18. Board of Governors of the Federal Reserve System, *The Federal Reserve System: Purposes & Functions* (Washington, DC: Board of Governors, 2005), 1–3.

19. Board of Governors of the Federal Reserve System. *Government Performance and Results Act Annual Performance Report 2011* (Washington, DC: Board of Governors, 2012), 5.

20. Board of Governors of the Federal Reserve System, *The Federal Reserve System: Purposes & Functions*, 2005, 3.

21. Ibid., 3–13.

22. Board of Governors of the Federal Reserve System, *Annual Report Budget Review, 2013* (Washington, DC: Publications, BOG, 2013), 2.

23. Board of Governors of the Federal Reserve System, *99th Annual Report: 2012* (Washington, DC: Board of Governors, 2013), 1–2.

24. Board of Governors, *The Federal Reserve System: Purposes & Functions*, 10.

25. Board of Governors, "Table 7: Principal Assets and Liabilities of Insured Commercial Banks, by Class of Bank, June 30, 2012 and 2011," *99th Annual Report: 2012*, 2013, 302.

26. Board of Governors, *The Federal Reserve System: Purposes & Functions*, 1–5; Board of Governors of the Federal Reserve System, "Implementing the Dodd-Frank Act: The Federal Reserve Board's Role," 2012, www.fedealreserve.gov/newsevents/reform_miletones.htm

27. Board of Governors of the Federal Reserve System, "Table 12: Operations in Principal Departments of the Federal Reserve Banks, 2009–2012," *99th Annual Report: 2012*, 2013, 315.

28. Board of Governors of the Federal Reserve System, *99th Annual Report: 2012*, 2013, 93; Board of Governors, "Fedwire Funds Service: Annual Data, 1987–2012," www.federalreserve.gov/paymentsystems/fedfunds_ann.htm

29. Board of Governors of the Federal Reserve System, "Table 6A: Reserves of Depository Institutions, Federal Reserve Bank Credit, and Related Items, Year-End 1984–2012 and Month-End 2012," *99th Annual Report: 2012*, 2013, 94, 294.

30. Federal Reserve Board, "Federal Reserve Banks," "The Structure of the Federal Reserve System," www.federalreserve.gov/pubs/frseries/freri3.htm; Federal Reserve Bank of St. Louis, "Providing Financial Services," *In Plain English*, http://stlouisfed.org/publications/pleng/payment_services.htm; Board of Governors, *The Federal Reserve System: Purposes & Functions*, 2005, 83–99.

31. Federal Reserve Bank of New York, "Historical Changes of the Target Federal Funds and Discount Rate, 1971 to Present," www.newyorkfed.org/markets/statistics/dlyrates/fedrate.html; Board of Governors, "H.15: Selected Interest Rates," July 1, 2013, www.federalreserve.gov/releases/h15/current

32. Board of Governors of the Federal Reserve System, "Reserve Requirement," June 10, 2013, www.federalreserve.gov/monetarypolicy/reservereq.htm

33. Michael D. Bauer, "Fed Asset Buying and Private Borrowing Rates," *FRBSF Economics Letter* (San Francisco: Federal Reserve Bank of San Francisco, May 21, 2012), 1-2, www.frbsf.org/publications/economics/letter/2012/e12012-16.html; Ben Bernanke, "Transcript of Chairman Bernanke's Press Conference," September 13, 2012, www.federalreserve.gov/mediacenter/files/FOMCpresconf2012913.pdf

34. Board of Governors, *99th Annual Report 2012*, 2013, 6; Joshua Zumbrun and Jeff Kearns, "Bernanke Says Fed on Course to End Asset Buying in 2014," *Bloomberg*, June 19, 2013, www.bloomberg.com/news/print/2013-06-19

35. Council of Economic Advisors, "Table B-45: Unemployment Insurance Programs, Selected Data, 1980-2012," *Economic Report of the President: 2013*, 2013, 377.

Part IV

INTERNATIONAL TOPICS

11

International Trade and the Global Trading System

International trade involves cross-border exchanges of products. These voluntary exchanges are based on the principle of mutual benefit. That is, both parties expect to benefit from the exchange. Governments sometimes erect trade barriers, such as tariffs and import quotas, to protect domestic producers from foreign competition. Since the close of World War II, however, a number of trade agreements have reduced trade barriers and created a more open global trading system. Trade liberalization has benefitted many peoples. These benefits are uneven, however, which creates additional challenges for countries in the less connected corners of the global economy.

TRADE BASICS

International trade is the cross-border exchange of merchandise and commercial services. International trade occurs when an individual, business, government, or other entity imports or exports products. An **import** is a product that is purchased from another country. An **export** is a product that is sold to another country. The items that are traded between countries are divided into two broad categories: merchandise and commercial services. In 2012 the value of global trade, measured by global exports, was $22.7 trillion. Trade in merchandise accounted for about 81 percent of global trade ($18.3 trillion), and trade in commercial services accounted for the remaining 19 percent ($4.4 trillion). In 2012 U.S. exports hit $2,161 billion, which made the United States the world's second largest exporter behind China. U.S. exports included merchandise valued at $1,547 billion and commercial services valued at $614 billion.[1]

Growth in International Trade

International trade is viewed as a pillar of globalization. The benefits of international trade are built on the principle of mutual benefit and the theory of comparative advantage. The principle of mutual benefit emphasizes the benefits received by both parties in a voluntary exchange. For instance, international trade expands the range of consumer choice

---

PRIMARY DOCUMENT: WTO Director-General Pascal Lamy Explains Global Value Chains

One reason for deep [economic] integration has been the emergence of global value chains. Until not long ago, we thought of products in terms of a single national origin, bearing a label saying "made in China" or "made in Germany." The expansion over the last two decades or so of global value chains means that most products are assembled with inputs from many countries. In other words, today's goods are increasingly "made in the world." Trade in intermediate goods—a proxy for global value chains—now comprises close to 60 percent of total trade in goods, and continues to be a dynamic sector in international trade.

Speech at the University of International Business and Economics, Beijing (September 20, 2012), Pascal Lamy

---

and sparks technological advances, innovations, and entrepreneurial opportunities in competitive global markets. The theory of comparative advantage, which was popularized by David Ricardo about two centuries ago, argues that international trade promotes regional specialization, production efficiency, and economic growth. In recent decades trade agreements such as such as the General Agreement on Tariffs and Trade (1947–1994) and the World Trade Organization (1995–present) have helped create a rules-based global trading system.

The global trading system represents the sum total of international trade, as well as the institutions and practices that influence cross-border exchanges of merchandise and commercial services. Exchanges within the global trading system have increased dramatically in recent years. The World Trade Organization (WTO) reported that global exports nearly tripled from 2001 to 2012, climbing from $7.7 trillion to $22.7 trillion during the period.[2] In addition, international trade supported economic integration in recent years. In the above passage Pascal Lamy, director-general of the WTO, explains the growing interdependence among trading partners as semifinished goods pass through global value chains.[3]

The top three world regions in the global trading system accounted for 82 percent of all global exports in 2012. The top three exporting regions are Europe (37.8 percent of global exports), Asia (30.6 percent), and North America (13.9 percent). The remaining 18 percent of global exports came from Africa, the Commonwealth of Independent States (CIS), the Middle East, and South and Central America.[4] The world's top five exporting and importing nations are shown in Table 11.1.[5]

Table 11.1   Top Exporting and Importing Nations, 2012

	Top Exporters			*Top Importers*	
Rank	*Country*	*Value ($ bil.)*	*Rank*	*Country*	*Value ($ bil.)*
1	China	2,239	1	United States	2,741
2	United States	2,161	2	China	2,099
3	Germany	1,662	3	Germany	1,452
4	Japan	939	4	Japan	1,060
5	Netherlands	782	5	United Kingdom	856

Source: World Trade Organization, "Appendix Tables 3 and 5," *Press Release*, April 10, 2013, 21, 23.

Balance of Trade: Deficits and Surpluses

The **balance of trade** is the difference between the value of a nation's total imports and total exports in a given year. The balance of trade, sometimes called the trade balance, measures trade in merchandise and commercial services. It is unusual for a nation's balance of trade to settle at a breakeven point where the value of its imports and exports are equal. Instead, nations typically incur a trade imbalance. One type of trade imbalance is a trade deficit, sometimes called a negative balance of trade. A **trade deficit** occurs when the value of a country's imports is greater than the value of its exports. The second type of trade imbalance is a trade surplus, sometimes called a favorable balance of trade. A **trade surplus** occurs when the value of a nation's exports is greater than the value of its imports.

U.S. trade imbalances have shifted from consistent trade surpluses during the 1950s and 1960s, to consistent trade deficits since the 1970s. Annual trade surpluses during the 1960s averaged $3 billion per year. During the 1970s the trend toward trade deficits was established as the United States recorded seven trade deficits during the decade. The U.S. economy recorded its last trade surplus in 1975. U.S. trade deficits continued to grow during the decade of the 1980s (averaging $85 billion per year) and the 1990s (averaging $105 billion per year). From 2000 to 2012 the average U.S. trade deficit hit $544 billion per year.[6]

In recent decades the United States has recorded trade deficits in merchandise trade, and surpluses in commercial services trade. Trade in merchandise is the import or export of physical items such as capital goods, industrial supplies and materials, consumer goods, automotive goods and parts, foods and beverages, and animal feeds. In 2012 the United States exported $1,547 billion in merchandise to other countries and imported $2,335 in merchandise from other countries, according to the WTO. Thus, the United States incurred a $788 billion *merchandise* trade deficit. The United States fared better in its global exchanges of commercial services such as travel, passenger fares, other transportation, royalties and fees, wholesale and retail trade, financial services, and a host of professional services. In 2012 the United States exported $614 billion in commercial services to other countries and imported just $406 billion in services. Thus, the United States had a trade surplus in *services* of $208 billion. The overall U.S. trade deficit totaled $580 billion because the large merchandise trade deficit ($788 billion) was only partially offset by the more modest trade surplus in services ($208 billion).[7]

Economists debate the main causes for the persistent and growing U.S. trade deficits. One explanation is that America's prosperity fuels an insatiable appetite for consumer goods—both foreign and domestic. Second, irregular or sluggish economic growth in other world regions has hurt U.S. exports to foreign markets, as occurred in the wake of global economic and financial crises since 2007. Third, foreign producers have become more competitive in recent decades. Producers in the Newly Industrialized Asian Economies (NIEs) of East Asia, China, India, and elsewhere have competed favorably for consumers' dollar votes. Fourth, certain government interventions in foreign exchange markets, including currency manipulation, have created an unlevel playing field for trade. China, for example, has held the value of its currency, the yuan, artificially low. This enabled Chinese producers to sell their output at lower prices worldwide. Finally, external factors such as the rising price of petroleum have contributed to short-term U.S. trade deficits. The value of petroleum imports to the United States increased from $324 billion in 2010 to $421 billion in 2011—nearly a $100 billion increase during a single year.[8]

Balance of Payments

The **balance of payments** (BOP) is a record of one country's transactions with the rest of the world in a given year. These transactions involve individuals, business firms, the government, and other groups. When a transaction causes money to enter a country, this money is called an inflow. Inflows appear on the country's BOP as a positive number, or credit. When a transaction causes money to exit a country, this is called an outflow. Outflows appear on the country's BOP as a negative number, or debit.

The combined credits and debits shown on a country's BOP statement should be equal during each reporting period. International transactions are counted twice, once as an outflow from a country and once as in inflow to a second country—a process referred to as the double-entry accounting system. The main categories of transactions include the country's current account, capital account, and financial account. Often the data for the capital and financial accounts are combined. Table 11.2 summarizes the BOP for the United States in 2012.[9]

The current account deals with a country's international trade in merchandise and services, net investment income, and unilateral transfers. In 2012, for example, U.S. Bureau of Economic Analysis (BEA) reported a U.S. *merchandise* trade deficit of $741.5 billion. Thus, it is recorded as a debit because it represents an outflow of U.S. dollars to other countries. In that same year, however, the United States recorded a trade surplus in *services* totaling $206.8 billion, which is recorded as a credit because it represents an inflow of foreign currencies into the U.S. economy. Note that the BEA trade data shown in Table 11.2 is slightly different from the World Trade Organization's data shown earlier in this chapter. Net investment income, which consists of interest and dividends payments that cross national borders, was also a credit as money inflows into the United States outweighed outflows by $223.9 billion. Net unilateral transfers, such as U.S. foreign aid and gifts by Americans to foreigners, were recorded as a $129.7 billion debit in 2012. The U.S. current account deficit of $440.4 billion in 2012 is shown in Table 11.2.

The capital account includes a variety of capital transfers between countries. For example, money or other property that migrant or temporary workers carry across a national border represents a capital outflow from the country of departure and an inflow to the country the worker is entering. Inflows and outflows of capital can also result from cross-border sales or purchases of patents, copyrights, and undeveloped properties. In 2012 the

Table 11.2   U.S. Balance of Payments, 2012 ($ billions)

Categories of Transactions	*Debt (−) or Credit (+)*
Current Account	
Merchandise trade balance	−741.5
Services trade balance	+206.8
Net investment income	+223.9
Net unilateral transfers	−129.7
Summary of current account	−440.4
Capital account	+7.0
Financial account	+439.4
Statistical discrepancy	−5.9
Sum of the U.S. balance of payments	0

Source: Bureau of Economic Analysis, "Table 1," *News Release*, June 14, 2013; BEA and WTO trade data differ slightly; some rounding.

capital account in the United States recorded a $7 billion surplus, which shows as a credit of $7 billion.

The financial account records the cross-border sale or purchase of assets. Some of the main categories of traded assets include corporate stocks and bonds, government securities, and long-term foreign direct investment (FDI) in other countries—including money spent on mergers and acquisitions (M&As) and on the construction of new production facilities by transnational corporations. In 2012 the United States had a $439.4 billion surplus in its financial account. Finally, a statistical discrepancy (−$5.9 billion) is figured into the BOP statement. A statistical discrepancy results mainly from unreported cross-border transactions and inconsistencies in accounting procedures in the global economy.

The BOP receives significant media attention in the United States mainly because of the growing current account deficits. From 1960 to 2012 the U.S. current account has been in surplus 18 times, mainly during the 1960s and 1970s. It has been in deficit 34 times, mainly since the 1980s. In fact, the U.S. current account has been in surplus just three times since 1980. Massive merchandise trade deficits have accounted for the lion's share of recent current account deficits. From 2000 to 2012 the average current account deficit was $545 billion per year.[10]

Absolute and Comparative Advantage

An **absolute advantage** exists when a nation or other economic region is able to produce a good or service more efficiently than a second nation or region. Adam Smith, who penned *An Inquiry into the Nature and Causes of the Wealth of Nations* (1776), used the principle of absolute advantage to defend regional specialization and free trade in global markets. There are two main ways to measure a region's absolute advantage. First, a region has an absolute advantage if it can produce the same quantity of a product as another region while using fewer resources in the process. Second, a region has an absolute advantage if it can produce a greater quantity of a product than another region using the same amount of resources.

Nations or other regions achieve an absolute advantage in the production of a good in different ways. In some cases, absolute advantage stems from conscious policies or business practices that develop and use resources efficiently. For example, heavy investments in education create a skilled labor force. Similarly, investments in capital goods, research and development (R&D), and an economic infrastructure contribute to more efficient and productive business enterprises. A nation's absolute advantage might also be derived from its supply of natural resources, such as large tracts of arable land, plentiful rainfall and sunlight, expansive forests, or generous mineral deposits. For example, Saudi Arabia, Kuwait, and the United Arab Emirates have large reserves of crude oil. Not surprisingly, these oil-producing nations have an absolute advantage in the production of oil over countries such as Japan, France, and Germany, which have scant oil reserves.

A **comparative advantage** exists when a nation or economic region is able to produce a product at a lower opportunity cost compared to another nation or region. Key to understanding comparative advantage is that mutually beneficial trade between two nations can take place even if one country enjoys an absolute advantage in the production of both traded products. The theory of comparative advantage has been used to justify free trade policies since the early 1800s. Robert Torrens introduced the theory of comparative advantage in his *Essay on the External Corn Trade* (1815). But it was David Ricardo who popularized the theory in his book *The Principles of Political Economy and Taxation* (1817).

Sophisticated capital resources, such as a robotized assembly plant, influence a country's absolute and comparative advantage. (Rainer Plendl/Dreamstime.com)

The theory of comparative advantage is a natural complement to the earlier theory of absolute advantage.

There are different ways to measure one country's comparative advantage over a second country. One way is to compare different rates of output generated by the two countries. Suppose the United States is able to produce 100 flashlights (compared to just 50 flashlights in Mexico), or 100 disposable cameras (compared to just 20 in Mexico). In this situation the United States has an advantage in both products, but it is still mutually beneficial for each nation to specialize in the production of the product that it produces most efficiently. That is, each country should produce the product in which it has the greatest advantage, or at least the lesser disadvantage. Note that the United States is able to produce twice as many flashlights as Mexico, a two to one advantage, and five times as many disposable cameras as Mexico, a five to one advantage. Hence, from an economic perspective the United States should specialize in the production of disposable cameras because it enjoys the greatest advantage. Mexico should specialize in the production of flashlights because it has the lesser disadvantage.

Another way to illustrate the theory of comparative advantage is to compare the relative input costs, often measured in labor hours, needed to produce two goods from different countries. This second measurement is concerned with the amount of inputs (labor hours) needed to produce a good, rather than with the quantity of output generated by each nation. Suppose Ghana can produce one unit of cocoa or one unit of soybeans using just two hours of labor, as shown in Table 11.3. Sierra Leone, on the other hand, needs four

Table 11.3   Comparative Advantage: Labor Inputs in the Production of Cocoa and Soybeans

	1 Unit of Cocoa	1 Unit of Soybeans
Ghana	2 hours of labor	2 hours of labor
Sierra Leone	4 hours of labor	10 hours of labor

hours of labor to produce one unit of cocoa and or 10 hours of labor to produce one unit of soybeans. In this situation Ghana can produce each product more efficiently than Sierra Leone, but Ghana's comparative advantage is in the production of soybeans, where it is five times as productive as Sierra Leone. Sierra Leone's comparative advantage is in the production of cocoa because this is where it has the lesser disadvantage.

The theory of comparative advantage supports national or regional specialization and efficiency. Yet there are practical concerns with the application comparative advantage in today's global trading system. First, comparative advantage assumes that resources within nations are easily transferable from a less efficient industry to a more efficient industry—which may or may not be the case. Second, the added costs of transporting traded items may reduce or eliminate the cost advantage gained through specialization. Third, trade barriers such as tariffs or import quotas might upset cross-border exchanges. Finally, specialization discourages diversification in an economy. If specialization is taken to an extreme the result is a one-crop economy. A one-crop economy revolves around a single product or service such as a certain agricultural output, mineral, or other resource. One-crop economies place a nation at the mercy of sudden global shifts in demand or catastrophic losses in supply through drought, infestation, or other circumstance.

Foreign Exchange Market

The **foreign exchange market**, also called the forex market, is a network of commercial banks, investment banks, brokerage houses, and other financial institutions that buy and sell currencies for profit. The currencies that are traded are called foreign exchange or, more simply, forex. The process of trading foreign exchange is called forex trading. In 2010 the daily turnover in the forex market was $4 trillion, a significant jump from daily trading of $1.2 trillion in 2001.[11] Most forex trading is short term and highly speculative. The foreign exchange market operates worldwide, but in 2010 more than half of all forex trading took place in just two countries—the United Kingdom (36.7 percent) and the United States (18 percent). Other major countries in the global forex market were Japan, Singapore, Switzerland, Hong Kong SAR, and Australia.[12]

The forex market represents the institutions and practices of banks, brokerage firms, securities dealers, and other participants in forex trading. Commercial banks assume a central role in forex trading through interbank or direct dealing transactions. Many large commercial banks operate globally and keep at least one forex trading station open at all times. Forex markets operate nonstop, 24 hours per day during a typical five-day business week. A global electronic transfer cooperative called SWIFT (Society for Worldwide Interbank Financial Telecommunication) processes and posts financial transactions.[13]

The modern foreign exchange market has changed significantly since its inception in 1946. Under the Bretton Woods System from 1946 to 1973, the main role of the foreign exchange market was currency conversion for purposes of trade. During this period the **fixed exchange rate system** pegged the value of national currencies to the U.S. dollar or to gold. The U.S. dollar was also fixed to gold, with $1US equal to 1/35th of an ounce

Table 11.4   Exchange Rates, July 11, 2013

Country	Currency	U.S. Equivalent	Currency per U.S. Dollar
Canada	dollar	$0.9648	1.0466
China	yuan	$0.1630	6.1352
Japan	yen	$0.0101	99.6600
United Kingdom	pound	$1.5182	0.6664
Euro Area*	euro	$1.3097	0.7706

*Euro Area consists of the 17 European nations of the Eurozone.
Source: "Exchange Rates," *Wall Street Journal*, July 12, 2013.

of gold. Most international trade was conducted with major currencies, often called hard currencies. Pegging currencies to the U.S. dollar and to gold stabilized the postwar global financial system.

During the 1970s a flexible exchange rate system replaced the fixed rate system. Under the **flexible exchange rate system,** the forces of supply and demand determine the value of national currencies. When the demand for a country's currency increases, the currency appreciates or gains strength compared to other currencies. When the demand for a currency decreases, however, the currency depreciates or weakens relative to other currencies. In the flexible exchange rate system, the primary mission of the forex market changed from the traditional currency conversion to the buying and selling of national currencies for profit. Over the past several decades governments, mainly through their central banks, have also intervened in the forex market to stabilize national currencies.

Exchange rates state the value of one currency compared to a second currency. Four pieces of information are included in published exchange rates: the country, the name of the currency, the U.S. equivalent, and the currency per U.S. dollar, as shown in Table 11.4.[14] The U.S. equivalent expresses the value of a foreign currency in terms of the U.S. dollar. For instance, on July 11, 2013, the Chinese yuan was worth about 16 cents compared to the U.S. dollar, while one United Kingdom's pound was worth $1.52 in U.S. currency. The currency per U.S. dollar states how many units of a foreign currency it would take to equal $1. Note that it would take about 100 Japanese yen to equal $1, but it would take just 77 euro cents to equal $1. Exchange rates are published daily in major newspapers such as the *Wall Street Journal* and the *New York Times*.

TRADE BARRIERS

Trade barriers are government-imposed restrictions on trade, mainly on the import of goods from other countries. The main types of trade barriers are tariffs and import quotas, but other trade barriers also exist. The use of trade barriers to restrict imports is often referred to as protectionism. Free trade, the opposite of protectionism, favors the elimination of tariffs and other nontariff barriers to trade. Since World War II many trade barriers have been dismantled.

Tariffs

A **tariff**, or customs duty, is a federal tax on an imported good or service. Tariffs are imposed by the government for three main reasons. First, tariffs raise revenue for the government. This type of tariff, called a *revenue tariff*, was popular in the United States during the 1800s. In fact, revenue tariffs were a main source of U.S. government receipts during much of the nineteenth century. Second, tariffs protect domestic industries from foreign competition. A *protective tariff* increases the price of an imported product and thereby discourages people from buying the imported product. Third, tariffs are used to retaliate against another country's unfair trade practices. *Retaliatory tariffs* discourage unfair trading practices such as dumping or excessive business subsidies, each of which create an unlevel playing field within the global trading system.

Tariffs are levied in one of two ways. First, a tariff or duty can be levied on a specific quantity of an imported good. Weight, volume, size, and number are common types of quantity measurements. For instance, a country could assign a $1 duty on each gallon of imported wine or a $100 duty on each ton of imported sugar. Second, an ad valorem duty is levied as a percentage of the imported good's market price. Ad valorem duties are more complex because a change in the price of the imported good changes the amount of the duty.

Governments have reduced or eliminated many tariffs in recent years mainly to comply with international trade agreements. Membership in regional trade agreements (RTAs) such as the Southern Common Market (MERCOSUR) and the North American Free Trade Agreement (NAFTA) has required tariff reductions among member nations. On a broader scale the World Trade Organization (WTO) has also overseen the dismantling of trade barriers, including tariffs, in the global trading system.

Import Quotas

An **import quota** is a type of trade barrier that limits the quantity of a product a government will allow into a country during a specified time period. An import quota specifies a quantity limit by number of items, weight, volume, or other measurement. In the United States an import quota can be established by congressional action or a presidential decree, such as an executive order. Over the past several decades the United States has used import quotas to restrict the amount of sugar imported from the Caribbean, lamb from New Zealand and Australia, and clothing from China. Historically the three main types of import quotas used by the United States have been absolute quotas, tariff rate quotas (TRQs), and tariff preference levels.

An **absolute quota** establishes a specific quantity of an imported good that is allowed into a country during a period of time, typically one year. An absolute quota can be bilateral or global. A *bilateral* quota limits the amount of an import from one trading partner. In 1999 the United States imposed a bilateral quota on lamb from Australia, a quota that remained in effect until 2001. A *global* quota sets a limit on the import of a good from all foreign producers. In the early 1980s the United States imposed a global quota on sugar imports from the Caribbean and other low-wage nations. Recently the United States stopped using absolute quotas to limit imports.[15]

A **tariff rate quota** (TRQ) permits the import of a specific quantity of a product at a reduced tariff rate during a period of time. Unlike the absolute quota, however, the TRQ allows the import of additional quantities items beyond the quota limit as long as the producer is willing to pay a higher tariff on these additional items.[16] The United States' absolute quota on sugar evolved into a TRQ during the 1980s largely to comply with trade rules negotiated under the General Agreement on Tariffs and Trade (GATT), a multilateral agreement that established international trade rules from 1947 to 1994.[17]

A **tariff preference level** is an import quota established through a regional trade agreement. Like TRQs, a tariff preference level establishes a fixed amount of a good that can enter a country at a low tariff rate but permits additional quantities to enter the country if the importer is willing to pay a higher duty. Tariff preference levels apply to a variety of goods that are traded in the global economy, including many textile and apparel products, dairy products, agricultural products, and animal feeds. As the number of RTAs has grown, numerous preferential trade agreements have been negotiated around the world.[18]

Other Trade Barriers

Other types of trade barriers have restricted trade between nations. For example, a **voluntary quota** is a bilateral trade agreement that either limits the import of a specific good into a country or expands the export of a certain good to a trading partner. A voluntary quota is an alternative to imposing an import quota by law or government decree. Once a voluntary quota is negotiated, the terms are binding. Voluntary quotas were often viewed as a type of backdoor protectionism. That is, for decades voluntary quotas sidestepped free trade pledges made under the General Agreement on Tariffs and Trade and the World Trade Organization. The two types of voluntary quotas are voluntary export restraint agreements and voluntary import expansion agreements. A **voluntary export restraint** (VER) agreement restricts the quantity of a product that can be exported from one country to another. In the past U.S. VERs set specific limits on the number of auto exports the United States would allow from Japan and on the amount of clothing and footwear it would accept from East Asian countries. VERs were phased out by 2005 under the watchful eye of the WTO. A **voluntary import expansion** (VIE) agreement requires a trading partner to accept additional imports from a country. U.S. VIEs, for example, required Japan to open its doors to additional American-made products such as semiconductors and auto parts during the 1990s.[19]

Many trade restrictions on textiles and other products have been eased or eliminated in recent years. (Bloomberg via Getty Images)

ECONOMICS IN HISTORY: The OPEC Oil Embargo of 1973–1974

The sting of an economic embargo was felt by the United States and other advanced economies during the early 1970s. In 1973 the Arab members of the Organization of Petroleum Exporting Countries (OPEC) imposed an oil embargo on the United States, Japan, and several western European countries to punish these countries for their support for Israel during the 1973 Arab-Israeli War. The United States, a staunch supporter of Israel, bore the brunt of the oil embargo. Shortages of gasoline, home heating oil, and other petroleum-based products caused hardships for consumers and businesses.

The embargo was lifted in March 1974, largely in response to negotiations that removed Israeli troops from certain conquered territories. But the oil embargo of 1973–1974 had demonstrated the power of the OPEC cartel to cut global oil production and raise oil prices, as well as influence foreign policy decisions by major industrialized countries.[20]

An **embargo** is a type of economic restriction that stops trade and other commercial contacts with another country. A comprehensive economic embargo halts all trade, investment, and other commercial contacts with the targeted country. A selective embargo, on the other hand, stops trade in a specific good or type of technology. Over the past few decades embargoes have been initiated by countries, such as the United States; multilateral organizations, such as the United Nations (UN); producer cartels, such as the Organization of Petroleum Exporting Countries (OPEC); and regional trade blocs, such as the European Union (EU). The comprehensive U.S. embargo on Cuba, which began in 1962, stopped virtually all trade, investment, and other business dealings between the United States and Cuba for decades. This embargo was still in force in 2012, with some relaxation of restrictions.[21] The United Nations (UN) has used embargoes to support the organization's peacekeeping and humanitarian functions. For example, the United Nations slapped a comprehensive trade embargo on Iraq in 1990 to pressure Iraq to withdraw its troops from neighboring Kuwait. The failure of this UN embargo prompted a military response early in 1991, which history records as the First Gulf War.[22]

TRADE AGREEMENTS

Trade agreements liberalize international trade. Some trade agreements create and enforce uniform trade rules for countries operating within the global trading system. Examples include the General Agreement on Tariffs and Trade and the World Trade Organization. Regional trade agreements focus on trade liberalization among a select group of nations. Examples include the European Union (EU) and North American Free Trade Agreement (NAFTA). Bilateral trade agreements between just two countries have also become more popular in recent years.

General Agreement on Tariffs and Trade

The **General Agreement on Tariffs and Trade** (GATT) was a multilateral agreement that established rules for international trade from 1947 to 1994. GATT's overriding goal was to promote free trade among nations. In 1947, twenty-three countries met in Geneva, Switzerland to negotiate the original set of GATT trade rules and tariff reductions for the post–World War II global trading system.[23]

The original GATT agreement became a rallying point for noncommunist countries that supported trade expansion as a way to promote economic growth and development. Under the auspices of GATT a series of eight multilateral trade negotiations took place from 1947 to 1994. These multilateral trade negotiations were called *trade rounds*. Early trade rounds concentrated on reducing tariffs on merchandise trade. Later trade rounds, especially the Tokyo Round (1973–1979) and the Uruguay Round (1986–1994) expanded negotiations to include trade in services and deal with issues such as unfair subsidies, dumping, and protections for intellectual property rights.[24]

GATT principles provided an anchor for the orderly expansion of international trade during the post–World War II period. One important GATT principle was most favored nation (MFN), which required that if a trade concession was granted to one trading partner, it would be automatically applied to all GATT members. A second principle, national treatment, required that foreign and domestic output be treated in a fair and equal manner within nations. In practice this meant that imported goods, once appropriate tariffs had been paid, could not be penalized through the imposition of additional taxes or regulations. A third principle, the reporting of trade barriers, supported transparency by requiring members to justify the imposition of tariffs, import quotas, or other trade restrictions.

World Trade Organization

The **World Trade Organization** (WTO) is an international organization that oversees the operation of the current rules-based multilateral trading system. The Treaty of Marrakesh established the WTO at the close of the Uruguay Round of trade negotiations in 1994. The WTO began operations on January 1, 1995. In July 2013 the WTO consisted of 159 member nations. The WTO's headquarters is located in Geneva, Switzerland. Its director-general is Pascal Lamy.[25]

The WTO's main function is to monitor and enforce trade rules in the global economy. The WTO administers the complex trade agreements listed in the WTO agreement. Article 1 of the WTO charter, the General Agreement on Tariffs and Trade, deals with rules of merchandise trade. Article 1 is often called GATT 1994 to distinguish it from the original GATT agreement of 1947. Article 2, the General Agreement on Trade in Services (GATS), deals with trade in commercial services. Article 4, the Agreement on Trade-Related Aspect of Intellectual Property (TRIPS), provides uniform legal protections for scientific, technological, and artistic achievements. In addition, the WTO is a forum for trade negotiations, a dispute-settlement mechanism, and a source of technical expertise on trade and development for the world's poorer countries.[26]

WTO operations are guided by six core principles. The first principle is nondiscrimination. Nondiscrimination means that all member nations enjoy most favored nation (MFN) status and that all products—foreign and domestic—receive equal treatment in nations' markets. The second principle is freer trade through the reduction of trade barriers. The third principle is predictability in trade. Predictability is enhanced by the transparency of trade rules. The fourth principle is fair competition. Fair competition reduces market distortions such as export subsidies and dumping. The fifth principle is economic development through trade, which includes certain trade preferences and trade assistance to the world's poorer countries. The sixth principle is environmental protection, which includes protections for the health and safety of life on the planet.[27]

The WTO's dispute settlement process represents the enforcement arm of the organization. This process enables member nations to bring formal trade grievances against one

Multilateral and bilateral trade agreements encourage regional specialization and international trade. (Byvalet/Dreamstime.com)

another in a global forum. Trade complaints are heard by small panels of experts. A member country found guilty breaking WTO trade rules is required to correct the violation with due speed or face retaliatory tariffs or other penalties. From 1995 to 2012 a total of 452 trade disputes were brought before the WTO, the great majority of which were settled through discussion and consultation rather than through formal panel proceedings.[28]

Regional Trade Agreements

A **regional trade agreement** (RTA) is an agreement that creates reciprocal trade concessions, such as the elimination of tariffs, among member nations. Some RTAs also promote regional economic integration by establishing common standards for labor rights, environmental protection, foreign investment, and fair competition. RTAs include multilateral and bilateral agreements. In 2012 there were 546 RTAs in the global economy, 354 of which were active.[29] RTAs are controversial mainly because trade and investment concessions listed in RTAs are inherently discriminatory against nonmember countries. Yet Article 24 of the WTO's charter permits trade concessions among members as long as RTAs do not impose additional trade restrictions on nonmember nations.[30] RTAs are categorized by level of economic integration.

A **free trade area** (FTA) is a type of RTA that eliminates trade barriers among member nations but permits individual members to devise their own restrictions on imports from nonmember nations. Examples of free trade areas include the North American Free Trade Agreement (NAFTA), the ASEAN Free Trade Area (AFTA), the European Free Trade Association (EFTA), and the Dominican Republic–Central America–United States Free Trade Agreement (CAFTA-DR). NAFTA is the world's largest FTA. It is comprised of Canada, Mexico, and the United States. The three NAFTA nations' combined gross domestic product (GDP) was about $19 trillion in 2012.[31] Trade among the NAFTA nations grew from $288 billion in 1993 to $1 trillion in 2011.[32]

A **customs union** creates free trade among member nations and a common external trade policy with nonmember nations. The common external tariff (CET) is a custom union's most visible external trade policy. A CET requires RTA members to levy the same import tariffs on goods entering the customs union. An example of a customs union is the Southern Common Market (MERCOSUR), which evolved from a free trade area to a customs union in the early 2000s. MERCOSUR is comprised of five full members (Argentina, Brazil, Paraguay, Uruguay, and Venezuela), along with several associate and ascending members.[33]

A **common market** eliminates all trade barriers among member nations, has a common external trade policy, and opens national borders to other resource flows from member nations such as cross-border flows of labor and capital. Today the Caribbean Community (CARICOM) is a common market. Revisions in the treaty binding member nations together over the past few decades increased the level of economic integration among member nations. In addition to meeting the requirements for a common market, CARICOM members also coordinate their macroeconomic policies.[34]

An **economic and monetary union** is the most thoroughly integrated form of RTA. An economic and monetary union includes all of the features of a common market and adds other forms of economic integration such as common currency, a unified economic and political policy, and common institutions to make and enforce the organization's rules. The European Union (EU) is the world's most highly integrated economic and monetary union. With the addition of Croatia in 2013, EU membership increased to 28 nations. The European Central Bank (ECB) coordinates the EU's monetary policy to promote price stability, economic growth, and jobs. EU institutions also develop common policies related to cross-border investment, labor standards and mobility, agriculture, energy, the environment, tourism, foreign aid, and other economic activity. By 2013 the EU's single currency, the euro, had replaced the national currencies of 17 of the 28 EU members. These 17 nations comprise the *Eurozone* within the larger EU. In 2012 the combined GDPs of EU nations was larger than the GDP of the United States.[35]

CHALLENGES TO TRADE LIBERALIZATION

Trade liberalization occurs when governments and other institutions reduce trade barriers and support free trade. Challenges to free and fair global trade remain, however. Unfair pricing, government subsidies to domestic industries, and other concerns continue to distort free market outcomes and skew the benefits of free trade in the global economy.

Dumping and Government Subsidies
Dumping is an illegal trade practice that occurs when a producer from one country sells a product in a second country at a price lower than its production costs or lower than the price charged in the producer's home market. In addition, dumping must cause material damage to producers in the second country. Material damage takes many forms, including negative effects on industry output, employment, market share, sales, or profits. The difference between the foreign product's price in its home market and the lower price in the second country is called the dumping margin. U.S. firms, labor unions, or other injured parties can initiate a dumping complaint.[36] The World Trade Organization's

Anti-Dumping Agreement established strict guidelines about how member nations should investigate and respond to dumping or unfair subsidization.

Another unfair trade practice occurs when government subsidies to export industries give certain firms a competitive advantage in global markets. Unfair financial assistance to businesses include tax breaks, low-interest government loans, or direct cash payments to firms. Subsidies are viewed as unfair because they lower the price of subsidized products, which makes these products more attractive to buyers in home and foreign markets.

Dumping and unfair subsidization are viewed as harmful to the global trading system mainly because they disrupt normal pricing mechanisms, encourage production inefficiencies, threaten domestic producers, and invite retaliation by foreign governments. In the United States the Import Administration (IA) and U.S. International Trade Commission (USITC) rule on dumping and unfair subsidization complaints.[37] An affirmative ruling means that a foreign producer has engaged in unfair trade practices and that retaliatory measures are warranted. A negative ruling means that there is insufficient cause to retaliate against the foreign producer. From 1980 to 2008, U.S. agencies ruled on 1,632 unfair trade petitions against foreign producers, of which 637 received an affirmative ruling and 995 received a negative ruling or were dismissed.[38] In 2012 the United States had 283 antidumping and countervailing duty orders in effect, more than half with just five countries: China (114 orders), India (23), Taiwan Province of China (16), South Korea (14), and Japan (13).[39] A **countervailing duty** is a retaliatory tariff designed to offset the financial advantage gained through dumping or subsidization.

Terms of Trade

Terms of trade measures the relative unit prices of a country's exports and imports. The terms of trade is expressed as a ratio of a country's export price index to its import price index. Today these price indexes are linked to a 2000 base year, at which time the terms of trade index was set at 100. A favorable movement in a country's terms of trade occurs when the terms of trade index rises above 100. A favorable movement indicates the unit price of goods exported by a country has increased relative to the unit price goods imported by that country. A country's terms of trade deteriorates when the index falls below 100. This occurs when the unit price of goods exported by a country has decreased relative to the unit price of goods imported by the country.

Historically the terms of trade has been a contentious trade issue, particularly when the terms of trade turned against commodity-producing poorer countries in their trade dealings with the richer industrialized countries. In the past developing countries were encouraged by some multilateral development organizations to specialize in commodities such as cocoa, coffee, cotton, rubber, sugar, or tobacco. The result was sometimes unbalanced development and an overreliance on a single crop. One-crop economies left some poorer economies more vulnerable to changes in global market conditions and the resulting periods of economic boom and bust.

From 2000 to 2011 the terms of trade shifted with market conditions. For example, during this period of time there was a dramatic increase in the price of oil and certain mineral and mining products, which improved the terms of trade for oil-producing and mineral-producing nations in Africa, Latin America, and the Middle East. At the same time the terms of trade worsened for some manufacturers in East Asia and Southeast Asia due to fierce price competition with manufacturers from the advanced economies.[40]

Fair Trade

Fair trade occurs when importers purchase quality goods produced in a manner that is socially responsible and environmentally friendly. Fair trade is sometimes confused with free trade, but they are not the same. Fair trade is based on the goal of economic equity. This is because fair trade promotes long-term sustainable trade relationships mainly between small agricultural producer organizations and the buyers of agricultural output in global markets. Free trade, on the other hand, is based on the goal of economic efficiency. This is because free trade seeks to maximize production and minimize costs by using society's resources in the most productive ways.[41] In 2011 there were 1,030 fair trade producer organizations, mainly producer cooperatives, operating in the global economy. Most producer organization were located in Latin America (557 producer organizations), followed by Africa (320) and Asia (153). The leading products produced by these producer organizations were coffee, fruits and vegetables, cocoa, and tea.[42]

Fair trade benefits the producers of agricultural products as well as the buyers of these goods in global markets. Local producer groups benefit from a higher standard of living and quality of life. Under fair trade guidelines farmers and other producers receive a guaranteed minimum price for their output. Efforts are also made to improve workplace safety and to end child labor. In addition, business profits, called *premiums*, fund community-improvement projects in education, health care, infrastructure, and the environment.[43]

Firms that buy fair trade items also benefit from these special trade relationships. By nurturing trade relationships with local producer groups, these buyers receive a reliable flow of quality products for global distribution. Global buyers also demonstrate corporate social responsibility (CSR) by supporting a living wage for workers, workers' rights, and a healthier natural environment in some of the world's poorest regions. By 2011 more than 11,000 different Fair Trade Certified products were being sold in 70,000 retail stores throughout the United States.[44] The demand for fair trade items grew steadily during the 2000s, topping $1 billion by 2010.[45]

Localization

Localization is a system of economic and political activity that emphasizes local decision making. Economically, localization favors small-scale production, the use of local resources, and consumption by self-reliant communities or regions. Politically, localization favors full citizen participation by individuals, elements of civil society, and other local stakeholders. Supporters of economic localization include think tanks and a variety of non-governmental organizations and other groups. Economic localization is the antithesis of globalization, which strives to create a more integrated and interdependent global economy.

Economic localization is based on satisfying local needs with local resources. A community, nation, or even a regional cluster of nations could be viewed as local decision makers. At the community level localization supports policies that provide a favorable business environment for small-scale enterprises, including self-sustaining family farms. It also favors the creation and enforcement of legal protections for labor and the environment in local, competitive markets. It supports the conservation of resources, use of renewable energy, consumption of local output, and conditions supportive of microenterprise. At the national level localization favors the **new protectionism**, which stresses heavy government restrictions on the three pillars of globalization—international trade, foreign direct investment (FDI), and cross-border financial flows.

CHAPTER 11 SUMMARY

Trade Basics
- International trade occurs when producers engage in cross-border exchanges of goods or services.
- A trade deficit occurs when the value of a nation's imports is greater than its exports, and a trade surplus occurs when the value of a nation's exports is greater than its imports.
- The balance of payments is a broad measure of one country's transactions with the rest of the world.
- Producing and trading products in which a nation has a comparative advantage promotes economic efficiency and regional specialization.
- The foreign exchange market has evolved significantly since the adoption of the flexible exchange rate system.

Trade Barriers
- A tariff is a customs duty that raises the price of certain imports.
- An import quota limits the quantity of certain imports.
- Other trade restrictions have been used to correct trade imbalances.
- An embargo limits some or all trade with a targeted country.

Trade Agreements
- The General Agreement on Tariffs and Trade (GATT) promoted free trade in the global economy from 1947 to 1994.
- The World Trade Organization has expanded on GATT's free trade mission since its founding in 1995.
- The four main types of regional trade agreements have achieved different levels of economic integration for member nations.

Challenges to Trade Liberalization
- Dumping and certain government subsidies are viewed as unfair trade practices.
- Shifts in global market conditions affect a country's terms of trade.
- Fair trade addresses equity concerns in the global trading system.
- Localization opposes most aspects of economic globalization.

NOTES

1. World Trade Organization (WTO), "Appendix Table 3: Merchandise Trade: Leading Exporters And Importers, 2012," "Appendix Table 5: Leading Exporters and Importers in World Trade in Commercial Services, 2012," World Trade 2012, Prospects for 2013, *Press Release/688*, April 10, 2013, 21, 23.

2. Ibid.; WTO, "Table A6: World Merchandise Exports by Region and Selected Economy, 2001–2011," "Table A8: World Exports of Commercial Services by Region and Selected Economy, 2001–2011," *International Trade Statistics: 2012*, 211–214, 220–223.

3. Pascal Lamy, WTO director-general, "Lamy Warns Rise of Regional Trade Agreements Could Lead to 'Policy Fragmentation,'" September 20, 2012, www.wto.org/english/news_e/sppl_espp1246_e.htm

4. WTO, "Appendix Table 1: World Merchandise Exports by Region and Selected Economies, 2012," "Appendix Table 2: World Trade of Commercial Services by Region and Selected Country, 2012," World Trade 2012, Prospects of 2013, *Press Release/688*, April 10, 2013, 19–20.

5. WTO, "Appendix Table 3: Merchandise Trade: Leading Exporters and Importers, 2012," "Appendix Table 5: Leading Exporters and Importers in World Trade in Commercial Services, 2012," World Trade 2012, Prospects for 2013, *Press Release/688*, April 10, 2013, 21, 23.

6. Council of Economic Advisors, "Table B-103: U.S. International Transactions, 1953–2012," *Economic Report of the President, 2013*, 442; U.S. Department of Commerce (DOC), Bureau of Economic Analysis (BEA), "U.S. International Transactions (2012)," *News Release*, June 14, 2013, www.bea.gov/newsreleases/international/transactions/2013/pdf/trans113.pdf

7. WTO, "Appendix Table 3: Merchandise Trade: Leading Exporters and Importers, 2012," "Appendix Table 5: Leading Exporters and Importers in World Trade in Commercial Services, 2012," World Trade 2012, Prospects for 2013, *Press Release/688*, April 10, 2013, 21, 23.

8. James K. Jackson, "U.S. Trade Deficit and the Impact of Changing Oil Prices," Congressional Research Service (RS22204), June 18, 2012, 3–4.

9. DOC/BEA, "U.S. International Transactions (2012)," *News Release*, June 14, 2013, www.bea.gov/newsreleases/international/transactions/2013/pdf/trans113.pdf

10. Ibid.; and Council of Economic Advisors, "Table B-103: U. S. International Transactions, 1953–2012," *Economic Report of the President, 2013*, 442.

11. Bank for International Settlements (BIS), "Table 1: Global Foreign Exchange Market Turnover by Instrument," *Triennial Central Bank Survey: Foreign Exchange and Derivatives Market Activity in 2010*, November 2012 (Annex Tables).

12. BIS, "Triennial Central Bank Survey of Foreign Exchange and Derivatives Market Activity in April 2010," www.bis.org/publ/rpfx10.htm

13. Society for Worldwide Interbank Financial Communication (SWIFT), "[Response to] 'Principles for Financial Market Infrastructures,' " July 28, 2011, 1.

14. "Exchange Rates: New York Closing Snapshot," *Wall Street Journal*, July 12, 2013, http://wsj.com/mdc/public/page/2_3021-forex.html

15. U.S. Customs and Border Protection (CBP), Department of Homeland Security, "Trade: Types of Quotas," July 20, 2012, www.cbp.gov/xp/cgov/trade/trade_programs/textiles_and_quotas/quota_frq/types/

16. Ibid.

17. Ibid.

18. Ibid.

19. Amelia Porges, "U.S.-Japan Trade Negotiations: Paradigms Lost," *Trade with Japan: Has the Door Opened Wider?* ed. Paul Krugman (Chicago: University of Chicago Press, 1991), 319–20.

20. Office of the Historian, U.S. Department of State, "OPEC Oil Embargo, 1973–1974," www.history.state.gov/milestones/1969-1976/OPEC

21. Damien Cave, "Easing of Restraints in Cuba Renews Debate on U.S. Embargo," *New York Times*, November 19, 2012, www.nytimes.com/2012/11/20/world/americas/changes-in-cuba-create-support-for-easing-embargo.html

22. "Confrontations in the Gulf: Text of U.N. Resolution on the Iraq Air Embargo," *New York Times*, September 26, 1990, www.nytimes.com/1990/09/26/world/confrontation-in-the-gulf-text-of-un-resolution-on-the-iraq-air-embargo.html

23. WTO, "The GATT Years: From Havana to Marrakesh," *Understanding the WTO: Basics*, 2012. www.wto.org/english/thewto_e/whatis_e/tif_e/fac4_e.htm

24. Ibid.

25. WTO, *WTO Annual Report 2013* (Geneva: WTO, 2013), 8-9; WTO, "Who We Are," *Understanding the WTO*, www.wto.org/english/thewto_e/whatis_e/who_we_are_e.htm; WTO, "The GATT Years: From Havana to Marrakesh," *Understanding the WTO: Basics*, 2012, www.wto.org/english/thewto_e/whatis_e/tif_e/fac4_e.htm

26. WTO, "What We Stand For," *Understanding the WTO*, www.wto.org/english/thewto_e/whatis_e/what_stand_for-e.htm

27. WTO, *WTO Annual Report, 2013* (Geneva: WTO, 2013), 3.

28. WTO, "Settling Disputes: A Unique Contribution," *Understanding the WTO*, www.wto.org/english/thewto_e/whatis/tif_e/disp1_e.htm; WTO, "Dispute Settlement: Current Status of Disputes," www.wto.org/english/tratop_e/dispu_e/dispu_current_status_e.htm; Yonov Frederisk Agah, "WTO Dispute Settlement Body Developments in 2010," www.wto.org/english/tratop_e/dispu_e/speech_agah_4mar10_e.htm

29. WTO, *WTO Annual Report, 2013* (Geneva: WTO, 2013), 17, 60.

30. WTO, "General Agreement on Tariffs and Trade 1994," www.wto.org/english/res_e/books_e/analytic_index_e/gatt1994_09_e.htm

31. World Bank, "Gross Domestic Product 2012," *World Development Indicators* (database), July 1, 2013, http://databank.worldbank.org/data/download/GDP.pdf

32. Office of the U.S. Trade Representative, "Joint Statement from 2012 NAFTA Commission Meeting," April 2012, www.ustr.gov/about-us/press-office/pressreleases/2012/april/joint-statement-2012

33. Europa, "Mercosur: Common Market of the South," http://eeas.europa.eu/mercosur/index_en.htm

34. CARICOM Secretariat, "The CARICOM Single Market and Economy (CSME)," www.caricom.org/jsp/single_market/single_market_index.jsp?menu+csme&prnf=1; CARICOM Secretariat, "The Caribbean Community," 2011, www.caricom.org/jsp/community/community_index.jsp?menu+community&prnf=1

35. European Commission, "What Is the Euro Area?" http://ec.europa.eu/economy_finance/euro/adoption/euro_area/index_en.htm; Europa, "European Union: The Economy," http://europa.eu/about_eu/facts-figures/economy/index_en.htm

36. U.S. International Trade Commission (USITC), Department of Commerce (DOC), "Antidumping and Countervailing Duty Laws under the Tariff Act of 1930," www.usita.gov/press_room/usad.htm; International Trade Administration, DOC, "An Introduction to U.S. Trade Remedies," http://ia.ita.doc.gov/intro/index.html

37. Ibid.

38. U.S. International Trade Commission, "Table 1: Title VII Case Summary," *Import Injury Investigations Case Statistics, FY 1980–2008*, (Washington, DC: Office of Investigations/ITC, February, 2010), 1.

39. U.S. Government Accountability Office (GAO), "Antidumping and Countervailing Duties, Table 1: Top 5 Countries with Most U.S. AD/CV Duty Orders in Place, as of March 2012," *Antidumping and Countervailing Duties: Report to Congressional Requesters* (Washington, DC: GAO, May 2012), 9.

40. UN Conference on Trade and Development (UNCTAD), *Trade and Development Report, 2012* (New York: United Nations, 2012), 8-9; World Bank, "Net Barter Terms of Trade Index," http://data.worldbank,org/indicator/TT.PRI.MRCH.XD.WD

41. Fair Trade USA, "Introduction and Highlights," *Fair Trade USA 2011 Almanac* (Oakland, CA: Fair Trade USA, 2011), 5.

42. Fair Trade USA, "Total Number of Fair Trade Certified Producer Organizations by Product," "Total Number of Fair Trade Certified Producer Organizations by Country," *Fair Trade USA 2011 Almanac*, 8–9.

43. Fair Trade USA, "Premium Payments to Producer Organizations by Product, 1998–2011," *Fair Trade USA Almanac 2011*, 14; Fair Trade USA, "Fair Trade Principles," www.FairTradeCertified.org

44. Fair Trade USA, "Look for the Label," www.FairTradeCertified.org

45. William Neuman, "A Question of Fairness," *New York Times*, November 23, 2011, www.nytimes,com/2011/11/24/business/as-fair-trade-movement-grows

12

The Global Economy and Globalization

For more than a century the global economy has become more integrated and interdependent. This process has accelerated since World War II. The term "globalization" is often used to describe this process of economic integration. Core elements of globalization are international trade, foreign direct investment, and cross-border financial flows. Over time globalization has been fueled by new technologies, transnational corporations, national governments, and multilateral organizations such as the United Nations, World Bank, International Monetary Fund, and World Trade Organization. The costs and benefits of globalization are hotly debated. Proponents credit globalization for the rising prosperity seen around the world. Critics believe globalization widens income gaps and threatens people's quality of life.

THE GLOBAL ECONOMY

The concept of a global economy dates back thousands of years. Ancient civilizations in Egypt, China, Greece, Rome, and elsewhere conducted cross-border business activity by land and sea. Thus, these societies participated in a global economy. The world known to the ancients was much smaller, however. The lack of certain technologies limited these civilizations' ability to produce and exchange products or communicate with distant peoples. More recently new technologies have helped stitch the fabric of the global economy more tightly than ever before. Successive waves of globalization have encouraged cross-border movements of goods and services, labor, technology, real capital, and financial capital to create today's integrated and interdependent global economy.

Global Economy Basics

The **global economy** is the international network of individuals, businesses, governments, and multilateral organizations that make decisions about the production, consumption, and distribution of goods and services. Capitalism, an economic system that relies on decentralized private sector decision making, guides the use of most resources in today's global economy. Global capitalism has created unprecedented prosperity in some countries, especially in the world's 35 advanced economies. The benefits of global capitalism have eluded others, especially people in the world's least developed countries (LDCs).

The International Monetary Fund (IMF) reported that the world's real gross domestic product (GDP) more than doubled from 2002 ($32.3 trillion) to 2012 ($71.7 trillion).[1] Global GDP measures the value of all final goods and services produced in the world economy. Today much of the business and financial activity in the global economy is related to international trade, foreign direct investment, and cross-border financial investments. Several key components of the global economy are shown in Table 12.1.[2]

A number of multilateral organizations, governments, and businesses actively support today's highly integrated global economy. Among the key supporters of global integration are international financial institutions (IFIs) such as the World Bank and the regional development banks. Other supporters are the IMF, the World Trade Organization (WTO), and the family of specialized agencies, programs, and funds associated with United Nations System. These multilateral organizations help establish and enforce common rules to facilitate international trade, investment, and other cross-border exchanges. Similarly, national governments and groups of governments such as the Organization for Economic Cooperation and Development (OECD) support the liberalization of trade and investment, coordinate foreign aid, and otherwise encourage economic cooperation. Transnational corporations (TNCs) and a wide variety of import and export firms rely on cross-border transactions and global supply chains to earn profits. Thousands of nongovernmental organizations (NGOs) and civil society organizations (CSOs) scrutinize the business practices and participate in multilateral organizations. In a sense, NGOs and CSOs are the conscience of the global economy.

New technologies also support cross-border business activity and global integration. During the 1800s the application of steam power to railroads and ships sped the transport

Table 12.1   The Global Economy at a Glance, 2012

Global Economic Indicators*	Economic Performance
World output	
Real GDP (exchange rates)	$71.7 trillion
Real GDP (purchasing power parity)	$83.1 trillion
World output (PPP)	
Advanced economies	50.1%
Emerging market and developing economies	49.9%
Country classifications (number)	
Advanced economies	35 countries
Emerging market and developing economies	153 countries
World trade	
World merchandise trade (exports)	$18.3 trillion
World trade in services (exports)	$4.4 trillion
Total world trade (exports)	$22.7 trillion
Foreign direct investment	
Foreign direct investment (inflows)	$1.35 trillion
Foreign direct investment (outflows)	$1.39 trillion
Foreign exchange market	
Forex trading (daily volume)	$4 trillion

*Includes only the 188 IMF member nations.

Source: International Monetary Fund, World Trade Organization, United Nations Conference on Trade and Development, Bank for International Settlements (2010 data for forex trading).

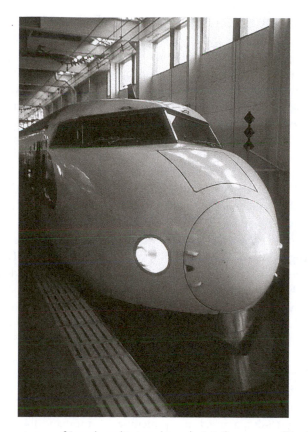

The bullet train system is part of Japan's sophisticated economic infrastructure. (Corel)

of resources, goods, real capital, and people to distant locations. Early communications systems, such as the telegraph and telephone, also prompted cross-border transactions. Today innovative information and communications technologies (ICTs) create a more integrated world that is linked by computers, the Internet, communications satellites, cell phones, and so on. ICTs permit people to store, process, and transmit enormous quantities of information. Similarly, transportation technologies such as supersonic airlines, super tankers, high-speed rail transport, and motor vehicles advance the economic connectivity of peoples in ways unimagined just a few decades ago.

Institutions of the Global Economy

Since World War II a number of multilateral organizations have been founded to promote growth and stability within a more integrated global economy. These institutions include the United Nations, World Trade Organization, International Monetary Fund, and World Bank Group.

The **United Nations System** consists of the six main branches of the United Nations (UN) and an extended family of 26 largely autonomous specialized agencies, programs, and funds. The United Nations was founded in 1945 when 51 countries formally adopted the UN Charter at the San Francisco Conference. By 2013 membership had swelled to 193 nations. The United Nations System promotes world peace, sustainable economic development, and human rights. In 2000, the United Nations adopted eight Millennium

Development Goals (MDGs) to coordinate global efforts to reduce poverty and hunger in the world, and to improve education, health care, the environment, and economic connectivity in the global economy. By 2013 progress had been made in achieving many of the MDGs.[3]

The United Nations' specialized agencies, programs, and funds are largely autonomous, self-financing bodies. Yet these members of the UN family are linked through formal agreements and a shared mission to improve the human condition as defined by the MDGs. Of the 15 specialized agencies within the UN System, those that most directly influence the global economy are the World Bank Group; International Monetary Fund (IMF); World Health Organization (WHO); International Labor Organization (ILO); United Nations Educational, Scientific and Cultural Organization (UNESCO); Food and Agriculture Organization (FAO); and World Intellectual Property Organization (WIPO). Of the 11 UN programs and funds, those most vital to the operation of the global economy are the United Nations Development Program (UNDP), United Nations Environment Program (UNEP), United Nations Children's Fund (UNICEF), World Food Program (WFP), United Nations Population Fund (UNFPA), United Nations Conference on Trade and Development (UNCTAD), and the Office of the United Nations High Commissioner for Refugees (UNHCR).[4]

The **World Trade Organization** (WTO) is an international organization that oversees the operation of a rules-based multilateral trading system. The WTO began operations on January 1, 1995. In July 2013 the WTO consisted of 159 member nations.[5] The WTO, like its predecessor the General Agreement on Tariffs and Trade (GATT), is guided by core principles that support free trade. For instance, the WTO works to reduce trade barriers such as tariffs and import quotas. It also supports the principle of nondiscrimination. This means that member nations enjoy most favored nation (MFN) status, which guarantees that a trade concession granted to one member is automatically granted to all WTO member nations. Nondiscrimination also supports the equal treatment of all products, foreign and domestic, in nations' markets. In short, the WTO seeks to build a global trading system that is accessible, predictable, fair, and sustainable.[6]

The WTO's main function is to promote and protect the smooth flow of trade in the global economy. Its four main areas of operations are trade negotiations, the implementation and monitoring of agreements, dispute settlement among members, and building trade capacity. First, trade negotiations bring all WTO member nations together to establish a common set of trade rules. These negotiations, often called trade rounds, are conducted over a span of years. The most recent trade round, the Doha Round, began in 2001 and was still active a dozen years later. Second, the WTO's monitoring and implementation functions concern members' compliance with trade rules. Third, the dispute settlement function offers a precise and timely process to hear formal trade complaints by one WTO member against another. The WTO's Dispute Settlement Body (DSB) renders a judgment on the trade dispute and can prescribe certain punishments, such as retaliatory tariffs, against offending nations. Fourth, building trade capacity assists poorer economies enter the global economy as full partners. To this end, the WTO offers poorer countries technical assistance and time extensions to comply with WTO trade rules.[7]

The **International Monetary Fund** (IMF), also called the Fund, is a multilateral organization that promotes international monetary cooperation, financial stability, and growth in the global economy. Since its founding in the 1940s the Fund's mission has expanded, as has its collaboration with other institutions such as the World Bank. The Fund's assistance to countries is generally short term, and is focused on promoting financial and banking stability to facilitate international trade, sustainable economic growth, and poverty reduction. In 2013 IMF membership stood at 188 countries.[8]

All members of the Fund are required to contribute to IMF coffers through quota subscriptions, or quotas, in rough proportion to the size of their economies. Historically five countries have contributed about 40 percent of all quotas—the United States (17.4 percent of all quota subscriptions), Japan (6.2 percent), Germany (6.1 percent), France (5 percent), and the United Kingdom (5 percent). Because voting power in the Fund is allotted in rough proportion to each country's financial contribution, these five donor nations hold considerable sway in the policies of the Fund. Major reforms in the Fund in 2008 and 2010 expanded the quotas for the emerging market and developing countries. Under these reforms China's quota, for example, became the third largest, and three other emerging economies cracked the top 10—India, the Russian Federation, and Brazil. At the same time, the Fund doubled total quota commitments from the member nations. When fully implemented the Fund's total quotas will increase from SDR 238.5 billion to SDR 477 billion, which is equivalent to $715 billion in U.S. currency. The SDR is the Fund's unit of accounting.[9]

The cash reserves generated through quota subscriptions finance the Fund's main functions, which include surveillance, technical assistance, and financial assistance. Surveillance involves active monitoring of and consultation with member countries to encourage sound domestic economic policies. Technical assistance provides the financial know-how to create and maintain effective economic institutions, such as a central bank and a treasury. Technical assistance also helps countries develop policies related to taxation, accounting practices, exchange rates, and financial regulations. Finally, the Fund's financial assistance consists mainly of loans to help member countries stabilize currencies, honor foreign debt obligations, pay for imports, or increase foreign reserves. The IMF does not extend loans for major development projects, however.

The Fund has initiated a number of policies and programs to address global economic and financial crises since 2007. For instance, the Fund took steps to increase its lending power to support economic and financial stability in struggling economies. It raised additional money by doubling its quota subscriptions for member countries and by borrowing hundreds of billions of dollars from member nations. These additional resources have enabled the Fund to commit more than $300 billion in new loans since these crises began. In addition, the Fund has simplified the lending process and tailored its assistance to meet the individual needs of countries. In past years the Fund had been roundly criticized for setting rigid, burdensome conditions on loan recipients. Finally, in recent years the Fund has expanded the flow of concessional loans to low-income countries. Concessional loans typically carry lower interest rates and longer repayment periods than the regular nonconcessional loans.[10]

The Fund's loans are granted in a unit of account called Special Drawing Rights (SDRs). The SDR is not a currency. Rather, it is an "international reserve asset," which all member nations receive as a benefit of membership. Fund members can exchange their SDRs for sound currencies of other member nations. In most cases these exchanges are voluntary, but the Fund can mandate an SDR exchange for a "freely usable currency" such as the British pound, the European Union's euro, or the U.S. dollar. Among the Fund's largest borrowers in 2012 were Greece, Portugal, and Ireland.[11]

The **World Bank Group** is a multilateral development organization. Like the IMF, the World Bank was founded as a specialized agency within the United Nations System during

---

ECONOMICS IN HISTORY: The Bretton Woods Conference of 1944

The Bretton Woods Conference took place in July 1944, during World War II. Its overall goal was to establish a basic framework for economic cooperation, financial stability, and economic growth for the postwar period. The conference was held in the United States at Bretton Woods, New Hampshire. Representatives from 44 countries attended the conference.

Delegates to the conference agreed to create the two Bretton Woods Institutions—the International Bank for Reconstruction and Development (IBRD) and the International Monetary Fund (IMF). IBRD, also called the World Bank, was designed to extend longer-term loans to help reconstruct Europe after World War II. The first IBRD loan was made to France in 1947. The IMF, also called the Fund, was designed to provide shorter-term loans to assist countries stabilize currencies and exchange rates, and thus facilitate international trade. Both the World Bank and the IMF were founded as specialized agencies within the United Nations System.[12]

---

the 1940s. In its early years the World Bank consisted of a single organization, the International Bank for Reconstruction and Development (IBRD). IBRD's initial goal was to help rebuild war-torn Europe. Over time the World Bank's composition and mission expanded. Today the World Bank Group consists of five mutually supporting development institutions. Its financial resources come from the sale of securities in global financial markets, interest payments on past loans, and contributions from donor countries. Today the World Bank Group's overarching goals are poverty reduction and economic development through "inclusive and sustainable globalization."[13]

IBRD and its closest partner, the International Development Association (IDA), provide significant financial and technical development assistance to the world's emerging market and developing countries. IBRD extends low-interest development loans to the more creditworthy high-income and middle-income developing countries. Development loans are used to build schools, health facilities, and other infrastructure projects. Loans also target disease prevention, environmental protection, and resource management. In 2012 IBRD committed $20.6 billion to new development projects. In this same year IBRD's outstanding loans totaled $134 billion. Meanwhile, the IDA extends concessional loans and grants to less creditworthy low-income developing countries. Most concessional loans are made interest free, and the repayment period often extends from 25 to 40 years or more. In 2012 the IDA granted about $15 billion to finance over 160 projects in the world's poorest countries. Its outstanding loans in 2012 totaled $124 billion.[14]

Complementing the work of IBRD and the IDA are three other partner organizations within the World Bank Group: the International Finance Corporation (IFC), the International Center for Settlement of Investment Disputes (ICSID), and the Multilateral Investment Guarantee Agency (MIGA). The IFC was founded in 1956 to encourage private sector investment. IFC financial and technical assistance is granted to private firms rather than to governments. ICSID was created in 1966 to reconcile disputes between foreign investors and host governments. Since the 1960s the dispute resolution mechanisms of ICSID have promoted FDI and have influenced numerous investment laws and bilateral investment treaties (BITs). MIGA was established in 1988 to provide investment insurance to foreign companies. MIGA protects these companies from nonfinancial commercial losses such as government expropriations of property, civil war, or other adverse changes to the business environment. From 1988 to 2012 MIGA issued more than $24 billion in political risk insurance for projects in the developing world.[15]

Waves of Globalization

Globalization, in an economics context, refers to the freer cross-border movements of goods and services, labor, technology, real capital, and financial capital to create an integrated and interdependent global economy. The pillars of economic globalization are international trade, foreign direct investment, and cross-border financial flows. Broadly speaking, globalization also deals with cross-border flows of ideas, political and social values, language, and other components of culture. Today globalization is often associated with the flow of Western economic, political, and social beliefs and institutions to other world regions.

Over time economic globalization has had peaks and valleys. One mainstream analysis divides modern globalization into three great waves. The first of these waves spanned from 1870 to 1914. During the first wave international trade and foreign investment expanded as some trade barriers declined and new transportation and communications technologies were developed. It was during this first age that steamships joined steam-powered locomotives to speed the transport of goods and people, while the telegraph and telephone increased the convenience of global communication. These technological advances, along with new economic opportunities, also sparked a mass migration of labor from densely populated regions such as Europe and China to less populated regions such as North America.[16] The first age of globalization crumbled under the destructive weight of World

Great Britain spearheaded the first age of globalization from 1870 to the outbreak of World War I in 1914. (PhotoDisc, Inc.)

War I (1914–1918), the isolationism and protectionism of the 1920s, the global depression of the 1930s, and the carnage of World War II (1939–1945).

The second great wave of globalization rose out of the ashes of World War II, extending from 1945 to 1980. This second wave also benefitted from international agreements and new technologies. Global trade and investment were supported by new organizations such as the World Bank and the International Monetary Fund. Successive trade negotiations, called trade rounds, were conducted under the guidance of the General Agreement on Tariffs and Trade (GATT). Postwar technologies in transportation and communications strengthened global business and financial linkages. Technological advances in high-speed railways, supertankers, supersonic aircraft, and motorized vehicles expanded opportunities for long-distance business enterprise. The new economic connectivity proved especially fruitful to advanced economies such as the United States, Japan, and the nations of western Europe. Most developing countries, on the other hand, tended to lag behind mainly as suppliers of low-cost primary commodities.[17]

The third great wave of globalization, from 1980s to the present, expanded on earlier efforts to liberalize international trade and investment. The third wave continued to harness new technologies as a means to integrate global economic activity. During the third wave the World Trade Organization (WTO) was founded to strengthen the rules of the global trading system. Rapid advances in information and communications technologies (ICTs) such as the Internet, World Wide Web, cell phones, and other wireless technologies accelerated global connectivity. Business-to-business (B2B) and business-to-consumer (B2C) electronic transactions, or ecommerce, expanded into the trillions of dollars. In addition, the third wave was marked by a greater inclusion and influence of developing countries—the so-called new globalizers—such as Brazil, China, India, and South Africa.[18]

The Globalization Debate in Brief

Proponents of globalization argue that open global markets enhance business efficiencies and profits, broaden consumer choice, and improve people's quality of life. Business efficiencies stem mainly from regional specialization. That is, businesses in open global markets are able to use resources based on their comparative advantage. These efficiencies increase production and enable producers to export surpluses to other countries. The increased flow of goods and services across national borders, in turn, expands consumers' access to a greater variety of products and at reasonable prices. Similarly, freer cross-border flows of real and financial capital efficiently allocate resources to regions with high profit potential. Proponents conclude that new global business activity creates jobs and prosperity. A rising global gross domestic product and a falling percentage of people living in extreme poverty bear witness to globalization's success.[19]

Opponents of globalization believe that globalization is neither desirable nor inevitable. Key concerns of the antiglobalization movement include the negative impact of globalization on human and worker rights, the growing income gap between globally connected and disconnected nations, the fragility of the current global financial architecture, and the negative environmental impacts of unbridled economic growth. Expressions of discontent with economic globalization have surfaced in recent years. In the vanguard of the antiglobalization movement are some nongovernmental organizations (NGOs) and civil society organizations (CSOs). In 1999 a loose coalition of NGOs, CSOs, and others disrupted the WTO's ministerial conference in Seattle, Washington. The success of the Seattle protest against the WTO encouraged similar outbursts against the World Bank,

IMF, World Economic Forum, and other proglobalization institutions during the 2000s. Since the early 2000s social forums, sponsored mainly by CSOs and NGOs, have also voiced concerns about global economic topics such as poverty, health care, foreign debt, and migrations of workers.

PILLARS OF GLOBALIZATION

Economic globalization rests on three main pillars, including international trade, foreign direct investment (FDI), and cross-border financial flows. Combined, these three forces create trillions of dollars in global commerce and other financial exchanges every year.

International Trade

The global trading system represents the sum total of international trade, and the institutions and practices that influence exchanges of products across national borders. **International trade** occurs when an individual, business, government, or other entity imports or exports products. An import is a product that is purchased from another country. An export is a product that is sold to another country. Trade in merchandise and commercial services increased dramatically during the 2000s. Global exports jumped from $7.7 trillion 2001 to $22.7 trillion in 2012. Merchandise trade accounted for 81 percent of all global trade ($18.3 trillion), and trade in commercial services accounted for the remaining 19 percent of global trade ($4.4 trillion). In 2012 the top five exporting nations in the world were China, the United States, Germany, Japan, and the Netherlands respectively.[20]

International trade is a pillar of globalization because it tightens commercial connections among nations. The primary benefit of international trade is that it encourages regional specialization. That is, cross-border trade enables producers in different countries to make products best suited to local resources—natural, human, or capital—and then trade their surpluses with other nations. Economists identify this benefit as the principle of comparative advantage. By considering their comparative advantage, firms maximize production efficiency and global output. Economists acknowledge, however, that overspecialization in the production of a single good is inherently unstable. A one-crop economy is ill prepared for shifts in global demand or for supply disruptions caused by blight, drought, natural disasters, or other events.

The United States is among the world's largest participants in the global trading system. In 2012 the United States was the world's top importing nation, purchasing $2,741 billion in merchandise and services from other countries. In addition, the United States was the world's second largest exporter, selling $2,161 billion in merchandise and services to buyers in other nations. Table 12.2 shows several important categories of the U.S. merchandise trade in 2012. Note that the United States imported about twice the automotive vehicles and parts as it was able to export and imported nearly three times the amount of consumer goods than it was able to sell abroad. U.S. merchandise exports were stronger in certain industrial and capital products such as machinery, chemicals, and transportation equipment, as well as in industries that produced foods, beverages, and animal feeds.[21]

The United States has recorded consistent trade deficits in recent decades. In fact, the last U.S. trade surplus occurred during the administration of President Gerald Ford in 1975. Historically, the overall U.S. trade deficits have resulted from significant deficits in merchandise trade, which have been only partially offset by trade surpluses in commercial

Table 12.2   Categories of U.S. Merchandise Imports and Exports, 2012

Merchandise Categories	U.S. Imports		U.S. Exports	
	($ billions)	(%)	($ billions)	(%)
Foods, feeds and beverages	110.3	4.8	132.8	8.6
Industrial supplies	730.4	32.1	501.1	32.4
Capital goods	548.6	24.1	527.4	34.1
Auto vehicles and parts	297.8	13.1	146.1	9.4
Consumer goods	516.3	22.7	181.7	11.8
Other goods	71.9	3.2	56.6	3.7
All merchandise	2,275.3	100.0	1,545.7	100.0

Source: U.S. Department of Commerce, Bureau of the Census and Bureau of Economic Analysis, "Exhibit 6," *News*, July 3, 2013, 6 (WTO and Department of Commerce data differ slightly).

services.[22] In 2012, for example, the U.S. merchandise trade deficit of $788 billion was coupled with a trade surplus in services of $208 billion, resulting in an overall trade deficit of $580 billion.[23] The United States recorded merchandise trade deficits with all of its top trading partners in 2012, as shown in Table 12.3. The ranking for top trading partners is determined by the combined value of all imports and exports between the United States and another country. By this standard Canada was the top trading partner of the United States in 2012 with total trade in imports and exports hitting $617 billion. Others in the top five included China ($536 billion), Mexico ($494 billion), Japan ($216 billion), and Germany ($157 billion). Note that about 40 percent of the entire U.S. merchandise trade deficit in 2012 was with just one country—China. The United States recorded more modest merchandise trade surpluses with other trading partners, also shown in Table 12.3.[24]

Despite the decades-long string of U.S. trade deficits, the benefits of international trade to the United States are compelling. First, trade expands the range of consumer choice by increasing the availability of goods that cannot be produced, or at least cannot be produced efficiently by domestic firms. Many commonly consumed items such as foods and beverages, clothing, electronic products, and fuels are imported from abroad. Second, trade benefits the overall economy. The U.S. Department of Commerce reported that U.S. exports supported nearly 10 million jobs in 2012 and provided business opportunities for 300,000 U.S. companies. Some of these firms produced the types of merchandise shown in Table 12.2. Others supported the fast-growing services sector, which includes royalties and license fees, and services related to management and consulting, research and development, computers and information, and the installation and repair of equipment. In all, about

Table 12.3   Largest U.S. Merchandise Trade Deficits and Surpluses, 2012

Country	Trade Deficits ($ billions)	Country	Trade Surpluses ($ billions)
China	−315.1	Hong Kong SAR	+32.0
Japan	−76.3	Australia	+21.7
Mexico	−61.3	United Arab Emirates	+20.3
Germany	−59.7	Netherlands	+18.4
Saudi Arabia	−37.5	Belgium	+12.1

Source: U.S. Bureau of the Census, *Foreign Trade Data*, February 8, 2013.

30 percent of all U.S. exports in 2012 consisted of services. In that same year total U.S. exports of merchandise and services accounted for 13.9 percent of the nation's gross domestic product (GDP).[25]

Foreign Direct Investment

A second pillar of globalization is foreign direct investment. **Foreign direct investment** (FDI) occurs when an investor from one country gains ownership or control of a business in another country. The investor is often a transnational corporation, but other investors such as individuals, investment funds, and even state-owned enterprises (SOEs) can also be involved in FDI. FDI creates a long-term relationship between the parent company and its overseas affiliate. It is assumed that the investor will take an active role in running its foreign affiliate. In 2012 the developing countries received 52 percent of all FDI inflows, followed by inflows to the advanced countries (41.5 percent) and transition countries (6.5 percent). Most FDI outflows came from the richer advanced countries (65 percent), followed by developing countries (31 percent) and transition countries (4 percent).[26]

The main types of FDI are cross-border mergers and acquisitions, and greenfield investments. Cross-border mergers and acquisitions (M&As) represent a legal joining of two existing companies under a single ownership. A relatively small number of M&As are true "mergers of equals," as occurred in the 1999 merger of U.S. oil giants Exxon and Mobil into ExxonMobil. Instead, most M&As are acquisitions. Cross-border acquisitions occur when an investor simply buys controlling interests in a foreign firm. Often, the purchase of as little as 10 percent of the acquired firm's stock constitutes ownership in the foreign firm. The benefits of purchasing a foreign firm include access to the acquired firm's markets, resources, technology and patents, intellectual property, brand name, or other assets. Of course, the acquired firm can receive these same rewards through the acquisition. The second type of FDI, greenfield investment, occurs when a new production facility is built. Thus, greenfield investments might involve the building of factories, mines, plantations, or shopping malls in a foreign country. In recent years greenfield investments have accounted for a greater percentage of FDI than have M&As.[27]

The ebb and flow of FDI during the 2000s generally mirrored the larger ups and downs in economic activity in the global economy. FDI increased steadily during much of the 2000s and peaked in 2007 just prior to the global recession and other financial crises. The global economic slump of the late 2000s and the sputtering recovery of the early 2010s dampened enthusiasm for FDI, however. FDI outflows, for example, dipped from their peak of $2.3 trillion in 2007 to just $1.2 trillion in 2009. Even the FDI rebound in 2011 ($1.7 trillion) could not be sustained in 2012 when FDI outflows again dipped to just $1.4 trillion. Likewise, FDI inflows peaked at $2 trillion in 2007 but dipped to just $1.2 trillion in 2009. The FDI inflow rebound in 2011 ($1.5 trillion) was also fleeting as inflows again retreated to $1.4 trillion a year later. The main culprits in the 2012 FDI collapse were sluggish global growth and the especially weak economic performance by many European Union (EU) countries.[28]

Foreign direct investment, like international trade, strengthens economic integration and interdependence in the global economy. Several aspects of this economic integration are shown in Table 12.4. For example, the ties between parent company and foreign affiliates in 2012 were strengthened by the ownership of $87 trillion in foreign assets by TNCs and other investors. Other ties that bound economies together were $26 trillion in sales by the foreign affiliates of TNCs and the 72 million jobs that were dependent on profitable

Table 12.4   Transnational Corporations: Selected Indicators, 1982–2012 ($ billions)

Global Indicators	Dollar Values are at Current Prices			
	1982	1990	2000	2012
FDI inflows	$59	$203	$1,271	$1,351
FDI outflows	$28	$233	$1,150	$1,391
Sales of foreign affiliates	$2,541	$5,479	$15,680	$25,980
Total assets of foreign affiliates	$1,959	$5,759	$21,102	$86,574
Number of employees of foreign affiliates (1000s)	17,987	23,858	45,587	71,695

Source: UNCTAD, *World Investment Reports, 2001, 2003, 2013.*

business connections between parent companies and their foreign affiliates. The output of foreign affiliates added trillions of dollars to the global gross domestic product.[29]

Transnational corporations play an important role in national economies and in the global economy. TNCs own trillions of dollars in assets, earn trillions of dollars in revenues, and employ tens of millions of workers. There are different ways to rank order these business giants, as shown in Table 12.5.[30] Ranked by foreign assets, the largest TNC in 2012 was General Electric with $338 billion in foreign assets. Ranked by total revenues the largest corporation was Royal Dutch Shell with $484 billion in total revenues. Ranked by number of employees Walmart Stores topped the list with 2.2 million workers. Ranked by total revenues more than half of the world's top 500 corporations were headquartered in just three countries—the United States (132), China (89), and Japan (61).[31]

Many TNCs rely on production sharing to coordinate the productive efforts of foreign affiliates, subcontractors, and independent producers. **Production sharing** occurs when a good is produced in stages and in different production facilities. Often these production facilities are located in different countries. Production sharing has expanded alongside the liberalization of trade and investment. Today the term "global value chains (GVCs)" is often used to describe production sharing. Experts estimate that 60 percent of international trade involves exchanges of intermediate goods, sometimes called semifinished goods. Intermediate goods require further processing or assembly and then are re-exported to the next phase of production along a GVC. Production sharing is more suited to goods that can easily be made in stages such as clothing, electronic devices, and automotive

Table 12.5   Rankings of the World's Largest Nonfinancial Corporations, 2012

Rank	Ownership of Foreign Assets	Total Revenues	Total Number of Employees	Total Profits
1	General Electric	Royal Dutch Shell	Walmart Stores	ExxonMobil
2	Royal Dutch Shell	Walmart Stores	China National Petroleum	Apple
3	BP	ExxonMobil	State Grid	Gazprom
4	Toyota Motor	Sinopec Group	Hon Hai Precision Ind.	Volkswagon
5	Total SA	China National Petroleum	Sinopec Group	Royal Dutch Shell

Source: UNCTAD, "Web Table 28," *World Investment Report: 2013*; "Global 500: The World's Largest Corporations," *Fortune*, July 22, 2013, F1–F7; CNN Money, "Global 500," 2013.

products.[32] Production sharing benefits businesses by reducing production costs. It also stimulates cross-border cooperation and the sharing of technology, management techniques, and standardized accounting and other business practices.

The expansion of FDI during the 1990s and much of the 2000s was fueled by new telecommunications technologies, changes in financial regulations, and trade and investment liberalization. Advanced telecommunications allowed TNCs to tap a broader pool of financial resources in global financial markets. These funds were used to fund M&As and greenfield investments. In addition, during the early 2000s many countries relaxed rules and regulations that governed lending and investment practices of banks and other financial institutions. These regulatory changes reduced restrictions on cross-border financial transactions. Finally, the trend toward liberalization of trade and investment allowed market forces, including the profit motive, to drive business activity. As a result, FDI peaked in 2007 with FDI inflows and outflows topping $2 trillion.

The most visible sign of investment liberalization was the many investment treaties negotiated during the past two decades. In 2012 there were 3,196 international investment agreements in the global economy. An **international investment agreement** (IIA) is a bilateral or multilateral treaty that establishes the rules, procedures, or responsibilities of parties involved in a cross-border investment. Most IIAs are bilateral investment treaties (BITS) between just two countries. Of the 3,196 IIAs in force in 2012, there were 2,857 BITS and 339 other IIAs named within other free trade agreements.[33] The first BIT was negotiated between Germany and Pakistan in 1959. Most BITs have common provisions. First, BITs require equal treatment of foreign firms in host countries, which protects foreign firms from discriminatory taxes or regulations. Second, BITs guarantee the security of foreign investments from some noncommercial losses such as expropriations of property or the ruinous effects of civil unrest. Third, BITs protect the right of TNCs to transfer corporate funds, including business profits, from the host country to the home country. Fourth, BITs include dispute-settlement provisions, which often rely on the services of the World Bank's International Center for Settlement of Investment Disputes (ICSID).[34]

In more recent years countries have imposed stricter regulations on FDI, and have negotiated fewer IIAs than in the past. Stricter regulation of FDI has been especially noticeable in extractive industries such as timbering and mining. In fact, there were four times as many regulations on FDI in 2012 as there were in the early 2000s. The gradual expansion of FDI-related restrictions during the 2000s awakened concerns about investment protectionism. Generally speaking, **investment protectionism** refers to government regulatory restrictions on FDI for a host of economic or political reasons. A related concern, the slowdown in new IIAs, also hinted that enthusiasm for FDI was waning in some nations. In fact, just 20 new BITs and 10 other IIAs were negotiated in 2012. The 20 newly negotiated BITs represented the lowest number in a generation.[35]

Cross-Border Financial Flows

The third pillar of globalization is the flow of financial capital across national borders. The main types of financial flows between nations include foreign direct investment (FDI), portfolio investments, and bank borrowing. The common thread that underlies each type of financial flow is that assets from one country are acquired by someone from another country. FDI flows represent long-term cross-border investments by investors such as TNCs. Portfolio investments, on the other hand, are typically short-term purchases of bonds, stocks, other securities, or other assets. National currencies are even bought and sold for profit. Bank borrowing involves cross-border transfers of money from creditors to borrowers.[36]

Economists have coined the term "financial globalization" to describe the integration of global financial markets. Financial globalization is encouraged by many of the same forces that stimulate international trade, such as sophisticated information and communications technologies (ICTs), supportive financial regulatory regimes, and market-oriented liberalization of trade and investment. Combined, these forces create a global financial system that is larger, more integrated, more complex, and often more efficient. But there are also risks embedded in this largely unregulated global financial system, including the rapid and unpredictable cross-border inflows or outflows of financial capital. In recent years some countries have devised policies, called **capital flow management** measures (CFMs) to restrict or better regulate the flow of financial capital between nations.[37]

The traditional benefits of cross-border financial flows center on the efficient and profitable allocation of funds in the global economy. Ideally, cross-border financial flows channel investments and loans from countries with excess money to cash-starved countries. By linking investment money with promising business or investment options in another country, both parties stand to win. That is, lenders and investors earn a healthy return on their money, while recipients grow their businesses and, indirectly, grow their economies. Most cross-border flows originate in the advanced economies.[38] During the early 2000s these financial flows mushroomed from less than 10 percent of global gross domestic product (GDP) to 20 percent of global GDP. The global financial crisis of 2008–2009 resulted in a free-fall in global financial flows, however. By 2010–2012 global financial flows were on the mend but still had not recovered to precrisis levels.[39]

Changes in the exchange rate system during the early 1970s also expanded another type of cross-border investment option in the global economy—foreign exchange trading. **Foreign exchange trading**, also called forex or fx trading, is the buying and selling of currencies by currency dealers for profit. The transition from a fixed exchange rate system to a flexible exchange rate system opened the door to forex trading. Today a highly integrated foreign exchange market provides a mechanism for forex trading. The main participants in forex trading are banks, brokerage firms, and securities dealers. In 2010 over one-half of global turnover in foreign exchange took place in just two countries, the United Kingdom (36.7 percent of foreign exchange turnover) and the United States (18 percent). The Bank for International Settlements (BIS) reported that *daily* foreign exchange and derivative trading hit $4 trillion in 2010.[40]

Forex and derivative trading is short term, highly speculative, and potentially destabilizing to the global financial system. Sophisticated communications technologies, deregulated financial markets, and the absence of globally recognized investment rules enable speculators to quickly alter money inflows and outflows between countries. Coupled with the volatility of traditional capital flows, the largely unregulated trading of currency and derivatives raises the danger of financial crises, including financial contagion, as occurred during the East Asian financial crisis of the late 1990s.[41]

CHALLENGES TO GLOBALIZATION

Globalization has helped improve people's lives in many regions of the world. The benefits of globalization are not universal, however. In some instances globalization has deepened income inequalities between economies and among people within an economy. As a result, some people grow more prosperous while others fall further behind. The main

Since 1919 the International Labor Organization, headquartered in Geneva, has supported worker rights in the global economy. (International Labour Organization)

challenge of globalization is to create a global economy in which all people have a fair chance to succeed.

Race to the Bottom Theory

The **race to the bottom theory** contends that globalization undermines the standard of living for workers, disrupts local economies and cultures, and threatens the integrity of the natural environment. The term "race to the bottom" came into common usage during the 1990s. It accompanied the liberalization of international trade, FDI, and other cross-border business and financial activity. The race to the bottom theory is hotly debated.

Race to the bottom theorists argue that international trade, FDI, and cross-border financial flows create uneven economic opportunities in the global economy. They contend that large corporations are able to pressure host governments to offer highly favorable labor and environmental concessions in exchange for trade and investment deals. The result is the exploitation of workers in sweatshops, depletion of natural resources, and deterioration of ecosystems. Harsh working conditions in Mexico's maquiladora companies and in China's emerging industrial sector are often used to illustrate this exploitation. Past excesses by foreign extractive industries, such as mining and lumbering, illustrate the pillage of the natural environment, especially in the world's poorer regions. Developing countries that are unwilling or unable to play by these rules are further marginalized and, in effect, are unplugged from any possible benefits of global connectivity. Some nongovernmental organizations (NGOs) and civil society organizations (CSOs) subscribe to this theory.

Other economists believe the race to the bottom theory is a myth and that the benefits of globalization far outweigh the costs. They note that globalization continues to create jobs that elevate millions of people into a growing global middle class.[42] They contend that

Strip mining degrades local ecosystems and is a type of unsustainable production. (David Davis/ Dreamstime.com)

corporate codes of conduct and internationally recognized labor standards such as the International Labor Organization's (ILO) *Declaration on Fundamental Principles and Rights at Work* protect workers' rights. In addition, they argue that FDI has spillover benefits for host economies such as technology transfers, the infusion of management skills, global connectivity, and the introduction of best practices in the world of business. They conclude that trade and investment decisions in the global economy are based mainly on the sophistication of an economy's infrastructure, the stability of its economic and political institutions, and its commitment to private property rights, rather than on the exploitation of low-cost human or natural resources. Supporters of globalization, such as multilateral organizations and most governments, argue that globalization has increased average incomes and reduced extreme poverty in the developing world.[43]

Global Environmental Stresses

Environmental degradation refers to a wide variety of human-induced and naturally occurring stresses on the natural environment. Environmental degradation disrupts the balance of nature in all types of ecosystems—grasslands, forests, agrosystems (areas used for agriculture), freshwater systems, and coastal systems. Environmental degradation also affects the global commons such as the atmosphere and the oceans. While ecosystems are dynamic, abrupt changes caused by humans have tested the limits of ecosystems to adapt and survive. Rising populations, industrialization, urbanization, permanent agriculture and animal domestication, aquaculture and commercial fishing, and mass consumption have contributed to environmental degradation. In its landmark *World Resources 2000–2001* the World Resources Institute proposed an "ecosystem approach" to support a sensible and sustainable use of the world's resources, as shown in the following passage.[44]

PRIMARY DOCUMENT: The World Resources Institute Proposes an Ecosystem Approach

An ecosystem approach broadly evaluates how people's use of an ecosystem affects its functioning and productivity.

An ecosystem approach is an integrated approach. Currently, we tend to manage ecosystems for one dominant good or service such as fish, timber, or hydropower without fully realizing the tradeoffs we are making. In doing so, we may be sacrificing goods or services more valuable than those we receive—often those goods and services that are not yet valued in the marketplace such as biodiversity and flood control. An ecosystem approach considers the entire range of possible goods and services and attempts to optimize the mix of benefits for a given ecosystem. Its purpose is to make tradeoffs efficient, transparent, and sustainable.

World Resources 2000–2001, World Resources Institute

The degradation that affects the land, the atmosphere, and the seas is often the result of poor choices by people. Unwise uses of the land include overfarming, overgrazing, and deforestation—the process of stripping timber from regions to satisfy business or household needs. Land degradation also results from abusive acts such as strip mining and the creation of toxic waste dumps. Reckless uses of land accelerate other destructive natural processes such as desertification—the transformation of fertile land to desert. The degradation of the atmosphere stems mainly from toxic emissions from businesses, motor vehicles, and aircraft. For example, destructive chlorofluorocarbons (CFCs) emissions depleted large areas of the earth's ozone layer, creating "ozone holes" that by the 1970s and 1980s were exposing people to the sun's dangerous ultraviolet (UV) radiation. In addition, fossil fuels emissions spewed carbon dioxide, methane, and nitrous oxide into the atmosphere. Many scientists believe that heavy concentrations of these gases trap the Earth's heat, a process that causes climate change.[45] The degradation of the seas is caused by industrial effluent, human sewage, and toxic run-off of pesticides, fertilizers, and other chemicals. Overharvesting of the seas by highly mechanized deep sea fishing techniques and by intensive small-scale coastal fishing also degrade these water environments.[46]

A number of major **multilateral environmental agreements** (MEAs) have been negotiated by nations since the 1980s to combat environmental degradation. In fact, by 2012 more than 250 MEAs were in force in the global economy. MEAs deal with a variety of environmental concerns such as pollution control, biological diversity, climate change, ozone depletion, desertification, hazardous waste disposal, and environmental accidents.[47] The most successful MEA is the Montreal Protocol on Substances that Deplete the Ozone Layer (1987), which banned CFCs and other substances harmful to the Earth's ozone. Compliance with the original ban and with the five adjustments to the protocol has aided the ozone's recovery—a process the National Aeronautics and Space Administration (NASA) expects to be completed by 2065.[48] Less successful was the 1992 United Nations Framework Convention on Climate Change, which called for reductions in greenhouse gases, the main villain in climate change. A follow-up agreement, the Kyoto Protocol of 1997, established specific targets for the reduction of gaseous emissions from the advanced economies. Developing countries, including emerging giants such as China and India, were largely exempted from these targets, however. In the early 2000s the United States withdrew from the Kyoto Protocol. By 2012 other advanced economies such as Japan, Canada, New Zealand, and Russia also opted out of the accord.[49]

CHAPTER 12 SUMMARY

The Global Economy
- The global economy is an international network of businesses, governments, and organizations that make production and consumption decisions.
- A number of multilateral organizations were created during the post–World War II period to promote global growth and stability.
- Modern globalization has progressed in irregular waves to create today's highly integrated global economy.
- The benefits and costs of globalization are hotly debated.

Pillars of Globalization
- Trade liberalization has expanded international trade in merchandise and commercial services in recent decades.
- Foreign direct investment creates long-term cross-border investment opportunities.
- Cross-border financial flows transfer ownership of people's assets.

Challenges to Globalization
- The race to the bottom theory warns of globalization's negative effects on people.
- Environmental degradation has been only partially addressed by multilateral environmental agreements.

NOTES

1. International Monetary Fund (IMF), "Table A1: Summary of World Output," *World Economic Outlook: April 2013* (Washington, DC: IMF, 2013), 149; IMF, "Table 1: Summary of World Output," *World Economic Outlook: April 2004* (Washington, DC: IMF, 2004), 187.

2. IMF, "Table A1," *World Economic Outlook: October 2013*, 149; World Trade Organization (WTO), "Appendix Table 3: Merchandise Trade: Leading Exporters and Importers, 2012," "Appendix Table 5: Leading Exporters and Importers in World Trade in Commercial Services, 2012," *Press Release*, April 10, 2013, 21, 23; United Nations Conference on Trade and Development (UNCTAD), "Annex Table 1: FDI Flows, by Region and Economy, 2007–2012," *World Investment Report: 2013* (New York: United Nations, 2013), 213; Bank for International Settlements, "Table 1: Global Foreign Exchange Market Turnover by Instrument," *Triennial Central Bank Survey: Foreign Exchange and Derivatives Market Activity in 2010*, November 2012 (Annex Tables).

3. United Nations (UN), *The Millennium Development Goals Report: 2013* (New York: United Nations, 2013), 4-5; UN, "Growth in United Nations Membership, 1945–Present," www.un.org/en/members/growth.shtml; UN, "Structure and Organization," www.un.org/en/aboutun/index.shtml #Others; UN Department of Public Information, "United Nations Development Goals, Factsheets 1–8," September, 2010, www.un.org/millenniumgoals

4. UN, "Structure and Organization," www.un.org/en/aboutun/structure/index.shtml#Others

5. WTO, *WTO Annual Report 2013* (Geneva: WTO, 2013), 8-9; WTO, "Who We Are," *Understanding the WTO*, www.wto.org/english/thewto_e/whatis_e/who_we_are_e.htm; World Trade Organization (WTO), "The GATT Years: From Havana to Marrakesh," *Understanding the WTO: Basics*, 2012, www.wto.org/english/thewto_e/whatis_e/tif_e/fac4_e.htm

6. Ibid.

7. WTO, "Explore our Areas of Activity," www.wto.org

8. IMF, "The IMF and the World Bank: Factsheet," August 22, 2012, www.imf.org/external/np/exr/facts/imfwb.htm; IMF, "Cooperation and Reconstruction (1944–71)," www.imf.org/external/about/histcoop.htm; IMF, "Factsheet: The IMF at a Glance," August 22, 2012, www.imf.org/external/np/exr/facts/glance.htm

9. IMF, "IMF Members' Quotas and Voting Power, and IMF Board of Governors," July 16, 2013; IMF, "Quota and Voting Shares before and after Implementation of Reforms Agreed in 2008 and 2010," www.imf.org/external/np/sec/pr/2011/pdfs/quota_tbl.pdf; IMF, "Factsheet: IMF Quotas," August 24, 2012, www.imf.org/external/np/exr/facts/quotas.htm; IMF, "Factsheet: Where the IMF Gets Its Money," August 24, 2012, www.imf.org/external/np/exr/facts/finfac.htm

10. IMF, "Factsheet: IMF's Response to the Global Economic Crisis," March 29, 2013, www.imf.org/external/np/exr/facts/changing.htm

11. IMF, "IMF Lending Arrangements as of December 31, 2012," www.imf.org/external/np/fin/tad/extarr11.aspx; IMF, "Factsheet: Special Drawing Rights (SDRs)," August 24, 2012, www.imf.org/external/np/exr/facts/sdr.htm

12. IMF, "The IMF and the World Bank: Factsheet," August 22, 2012, www.imf.org/external/np/exr/facts/imfwb.htm; World Bank Group, "World Bank History," 2013, www.worldbank.org/WBSITE/EXTERNAL/EXTABOUTUS/EXTARCHIVES

13. The World Bank, "History," January 31, 2012, www.worldbank.org/WBSITE/EXTERNAL/EXTABOUTUS

14. Ibid.; World Bank, "What We Do," March 8, 2012, http://web.worldbank.org; IBRD, *Management's Discussion & Analysis and Financial Statements*, June 30, 2012, 2-3; IDA, *Management's Discussion & Analysis and Financial Statements*, June 30, 2012, 3.

15. IFC, "About IFC," www.ifc.org; MIGA, "Overview," www.miga.org/whoweare/index.cfm; ICSID, "About ICSID," https://icsid.worldbank.org

16. The World Bank, *Beyond Economic Growth*, www.worldbank.org/debweb/english/beyond/global/chapter12.html; Paul Collier and David Dollar, eds., *Globalization, Growth and Poverty: Building an Inclusive World Economy*, World Bank Policy Research Report (Washington, DC: World Bank and Oxford University Press, 2002).

17. Ibid.

18. Ibid.

19. IMF Staff, "Globalization: A Brief Overview," May 2008, www.imf.org/external/np/exr/ib/2008/053008.htm

20. World Trade Organization (WTO), "Appendix Table 3: Merchandise Trade: Leading Exporters and Importers, 2012," "Appendix Table 5: Leading Exporters and Importers in World Trade in Commercial Services, 2012," *Press Release*, April 10, 2013, 21, 23; WTO, "Table A4. Merchandise Trade by Selected Groups of Economies, 2001–2011," and "Table A5. Trade in Commercial Services by Selected Groups of Economies, 2001–2011," *International Trade Statistics* (Geneva, Switzerland: WTO, 2012), 209–210.

21. U.S. Department of Commerce (DOC), Bureau of the Census and Bureau of Economic Analysis (BEA), "Exhibit 6: Exports and Imports of Goods by Principal End-Use Category," *News*, July 3, 2013, 6.

22. Council of Economic Advisors, "Table B-103: U.S. International Transactions, 1953–2012," *Economic Report of the President: 2013*, 442.

23. WTO, "Appendix Table 3: Merchandise Trade: Leading Exporters and Importers, 2012," and "Appendix Table 5: Leading Exporters and Importers in World Trade in Commercial Services, 2012," *Press Release*, April 10, 2013, 21, 23.

24. U.S. Bureau of the Census, "Foreign Trade Data," February 8, 2013, www.census.gov/foreign-trade/top/dst/2012/deficit.html

25. DOC/ITA, *U.S. Trade Overview 2012* (Washington, DC: DOC/ITA, 2013), 1-4.

26. UNCTAD, "Table I.3: Selected Indicators of FDI and International Production, 1990–2012," "Annex Table 1: FDI Flows, by Region and Economy, 2007–2012," *World Investment Report: 2013*, 24, 213–216.

27. UNCTAD, "Figure 1.9: FDI Projects by Sector, 2011–2012," *World Investment Report: 2013* (New York: UNCTAD, 2013), 8; UNCTAD, *World Investment Report: 2007* (New York: UNCTAD, 2008), 245–246.

28. UNCTAD, "Table I.3: Selected Indicators of FDI and International Production, 1990–2012," "Annex Table 1: FDI Flows, by Region and Economy, 2007–2012," *World Investment Report: 2013*, 24, 213–214.

29. Ibid.; "Table 1.1: Selected Indicators of FDI and International Production, 1982–2002," "Table 1.2: FDI Inflows to Major Economies, 2001 and 2002," *World Investment Report 2003: FDI Policies for Development; National and International Perspectives* (New York: United Nations, 2003), 3, 7; UNCTAD, "Table 1: Selected Indicators of FDI and International Production, 1982–2000," *World Investment Report 2001,* Overview (New York: United Nations, 2001), 2.

30. Stephanie N. Mehta, "Global 500: The World's Largest Corporations," *Fortune*, July 22, 2013, F1-F7; CNN Money, "Global 500," 2013; UNCTAD, "Web Table 28: The World's Top 100 Non-Financial TNCs, Ranked by Foreign Assets, 2012," www.unctad.org/wir

31. Stephanie N. Mehta, "Global 500: The World's Largest Corporations," *Fortune,* July 22, 2013, F1, F7.

32. UNCTAD, *World Investment Report: 2013*, xxi.

33. Ibid., xix.

34. UNCTAD, *Bilateral Investment Treaties: 1959–1999* (New York: United Nations, 2000), 1, 20, 88; Office of the U.S. Trade Representative, "Bilateral Investment Treaties," www.ustr.gov/trade -agreements/bilateral-investment-treaties

35. UNCTAD, *World Investment Report: 2013*, xix.

36. IMF, "IMF Adopts Institutional View on Capital Flows," *IMF Survey Magazine: Policy*, December 3, 2012, www.imf.org/external/pubs/ft/survey/so/2012/POL120312A.htm

37. IMF, "The Liberalization and Management of Capital Flows: An Institutional View" (Executive Summary), November 14, 2012, 1–2, 6–10.

38. Committee on International Economic Policy and Reform, "Banks and Cross-Border Capital Flows: Policy Challenges and Regulatory Responses," *Brookings*, September 2012, www.brookings.edu/ research/reports/2012/09/ciepr-banks-capital-flows

39. Organization for Economic Cooperation and Development (OECD), *OECD Economic Outlook*. Vol. 2011/1 (2011): 288–292.

40. Bank for International Settlements (BIS), "Table 1: Global Foreign Exchange Turnover by Instrument," *Triennial Central Bank Survey: Foreign Exchange and Derivatives Market Activity in 2010*, November 2012 (Annex Tables); BIS, *Triennial*, www.bis.org/publ/rpfx10.htm

41. The Federal Reserve Bank of San Francisco, "What Caused East Asia's Financial Crisis?" *FRBSF Economic Letter*, August 7, 1998, www.frbsf.org/econrsrch/wkly1tr98/e198-24.html

42. IMF, *World Economic Outlook: October 2012*, xvi.

43. United Nations, *The Millennium Development Goals Report 2013* (New York: UN, 2013); United Nations, "Millennium Development Goals," www.un.org/millenniumgoals/poverty.shtml

44. World Resources Institute (WRI), World Bank, UN Development Program, UN Environment Program, *World Resources 2000–2001: People and Ecosystems, The Fraying Web of Life* (Washington, DC: World Resources Institute, 2000), 226.

45. WRI *et al.*, *World Resources 2010–2011: Decision Making in a Changing Climate* (Washington, DC: WRI, 2011), 2.

46. WRI, *World Resources 2000–2001*, 76, 78.

47. WTO, "The Doha Mandate on Multilateral Environmental Agreements (MEAs)," www.wto.org/ english/tratop_e/envir_e/envir_neg_mea_e.htm; European Commission (EU), "Multilateral Environmental Agreements," http://ec.europa.eu/environment/international_issues/agreements_en.htm

48. National Aeronautics and Space Administration (NASA), "2012 Antarctic Ozone Hole Second Smallest in 20 Years," November 2, 2012, www.nasa.gov/topics/earth/features/ozone-hole-2012.htm; United Nations Environment Program (UNEP), "The Montreal Protocol on Substances That Deplete the Ozone Layer," 2012, http://montreal-protocol.org/new_site/en/montreal_protocol.php

49. United Nations Framework Convention on Climate Change, "Status of Ratification of the Kyoto Protocol," http://unfccc.int/kyoto_protocol/status_of_ratification/items/2613.php; "UN Conference Adopts Extension of Kyoto accord," *USA Today*, December 8, 2012, www.usatoday.com/story/news/ world/2012/12/08un-conference-extends-kyoto-accord

13

Sustainable Economic Development

Sustainable economic development is an important goal in the global economy. The advanced economies have reached this goal. The emerging market and developing countries continue to work toward this goal. The vast majority of the world's population lives in the emerging market and developing countries. Through growth-oriented domestic policies and foreign assistance, the world's poorer economies seek to transform the vicious cycle of poverty into a virtuous cycle of development. Key challenges to sustainable economic development are global poverty, the marginalization of people in the informal sector of economies, and unsustainable external debt.

CLASSIFICATIONS OF ECONOMIES

Major multilateral institutions such as the World Bank and the International Monetary Fund use different classification systems to group the world's economies. The income classification, for example, identifies four categories of countries by gross national income (GNI) per capita. Income classification helps determine a country's eligibility for certain loans, grants, or other assistance. Another classification system distinguishes economies by level of economic development. This system distinguishes between the advanced economies, and the emerging market and developing economies.

Classification by Income Level

The World Bank and many other international institutions classify countries or economies by their gross national income per capita. **Gross national income** (GNI) measures the nation's total income by adding the value of all final goods and services produced in an economy each year with the net receipts of other wage or investment income from abroad. The *GNI per capita* states people's average annual income by dividing the GNI by the country's mid-year population. The World Bank introduced the GNI per capita measurement in 2000. It replaced the gross national product (GNP) per capita as the preferred method of comparing nations' relative well-being.

Economists sometimes speak of countries and economies in the same breath, but they are not always the same thing. In 2012, for example, there were 214 economies but just 195 countries in the world. The main reason for this disparity is that some countries

Table 13.1   Classification of the World's Economies, 2012 (measured in $US)

Country Classification	Number of Economies	GNI per Capita (Atlas Method)	Average GNI per Capita (Atlas)	Average GNI per Capita (PPP)
Low income	36	$1,035 or less	$584	$1,387
Lower middle income	48	$1,036–$4,085	$1,877	$3,912
Upper middle income	55	$4,086–$12,615	$6,987	$10,712
High income	75	$12,616 or more	$37,595	$37,545
World	214		$10,015	$12,079

Source: World Bank, "New Country Classifications," July 2, 2013.

control one or more affiliated regions that report their economic data separately. Economic data for China, for example, is reported separately from its two special administrative regions (SARs), Hong Kong SAR and Macao SAR. Similarly, economic data for the U.S. economy is reported separately from its affiliated economies such as American Samoa, Guam, Puerto Rico, and the U.S. Virgin Islands.[1]

The World Bank classification identifies four categories of economies based on GNI per capita. These categories include low-income economies, lower-middle-income economies, upper-middle-income economies, and high-incomes economies, as shown in Table 13.1.[2] The low-income and middle-income economies are generally called developing economies. The World Bank emphasizes that the term "developing economies" is a term of convenience and "is not intended to imply that all economies in the group are experiencing similar development or that other economies have reached a preferred or final stage of development. Classification by income does not necessarily reflect development status."[3] In fact, of the 75 high-income economies that existed in 2012, less than half were considered advanced economies. A number of high-income economies—such as Liechtenstein, Monaco, Kuwait, Poland, Qatar, the Russian Federation, and the United Arab Emirates—were not considered advanced economies due to the inadequate size or sophistication of their economies.

The GNI per capita offers a basis for national comparisons of economic well-being. Yet there are limitations to using income data alone to compare economies. First, nations' income data is generally confined to reported business activity, which ignores barter transactions and other transactions in the informal sector of the economy. As a result, the government may understate national income. Second, income data, particularly data collected in the developing world, is often unreliable. Third, GNI per capita cannot assess the actual distribution of income within an economy. In many economies much of the income is skewed in favor of the rich over the poor.[4] Fourth, the Atlas method of reporting GNI data, which uses official market exchange rates to convert the value of currencies, fails to account for differences in currencies' purchasing power. To address this issue, some international data is adjusted on a purchasing power parity (PPP) basis. Simply stated, **purchasing power parity** estimates the actual buying power of different currencies, taking into account differences in product prices around the world. The average income comparisons shown in Table 13.1, using either the Atlas or PPP measures, show a significant advantage for people in high-income economies.

Advanced Economies

The **advanced economies** (AEs) are the richer, more industrialized countries of the world. AEs are often referred to as the developed economies or developed countries.

Table 13.2   Advanced Economies by Subgroup, 2012

Major Advanced Economies	Other Advanced Economies		
Canada	Australia	Hong Kong	Norway
France	Austria	SAR*	Portugal
Germany	Belgium	Iceland	San Marino
Italy	Cyprus	Ireland	Singapore*
Japan	Czech Rep.	Israel	Slovak Rep.
United Kingdom	Denmark	Korea*	Slovenia
United States	Estonia	Luxembourg	Spain
	Finland	Malta	Sweden
	Greece	Netherlands	Switzerland
		New Zealand	Taiwan*

*Newly Industrialized Asian Economies (NIEs)

Source: International Monetary Fund, *World Economic Outlook April 2013*, 137, 140.

In 2004 the International Monetary Fund (IMF) revised the global classification of countries from three to two categories. Prior to 2004 the three categories of countries included advanced, developing, and transition. The revised IMF categories include AEs, and emerging market and developing economies.

The classification of economies by multilateral organizations such as World Bank and the IMF is not exactly the same. IMF data, for example, identifies just 188 economies compared to 214 economies reported by the World Bank. IMF data excludes countries that are not members of the IMF as well as countries that have limited or unreliable economic data. Both the World Bank and the IMF agree on the number and composition of the world's 35 advanced economies, as shown in Table 13.2.[5] The IMF reports that these 35 AEs accounted for 15 percent of the world's population in 2012 but produced 50.1 percent of global GDP and 61.2 percent of global trade on a PPP basis.[6]

The advanced economies benefit from a virtuous cycle that supports and strengthens sustainable economic development. The virtuous cycle is based on the use of national savings for productive investment. The result of this investment is **capital deepening**—the increase in real capital per worker over time. Capital deepening increases worker productivity along with sustained economic growth and development.

The advanced economies maintain the virtuous cycle by nurturing a progrowth and pro-development business climate. *Economic* factors conducive to economic development include capital formation, which stems from significant saving and investing in capital goods; human capital development, which is derived from education, training, and other investments in the labor force; and innovation, which is supported by research and development (R&D), economic freedom, and entrepreneurial activity. *Political* factors that favor sustainable development include good governance and significant investment in public infrastructure and social programs.

Most business activity in advanced economies is associated with the production and consumption of services. A lesser amount of output is made by the goods-producing sector. The services-producing sector includes transportation and public utilities, wholesale and retail trade, real estate, banking and other financial services, computer data processing services, government, and others. The goods-producing sector includes basic industries and agriculture. The basic industrial categories are manufacturing, construction, and mining.

Raffles Place, in downtown Singapore, symbolizes successful economic development in the Newly Industrialized Asian Economies. (Amanda Hall/Robert Harding World Imagery/Corbis)

Agriculture consists of farming, dairying, livestock and poultry, forestry, fishing, and shell-fish industries. In 2010 over 75 percent of the gross domestic product (GDP) in the high-income countries consisted of services, with lesser amounts in industry and agriculture, as shown in Figure 13.1. National output in the United States, the world's largest advanced economy, was even more skewed in favor of services (79 percent of GDP) over industry (20 percent) and agriculture (1 percent).[7]

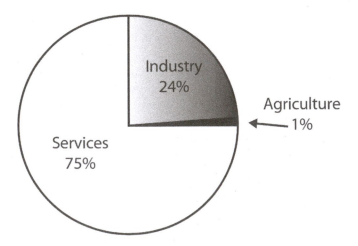

Figure 13.1   Structure of Output: High-Income Economies, 2010
Source: World Bank, *World Development Indicators: 2012*, 218–220.

Table 13.3   Emerging Market and Developing Economies, 2012*

Regional Subgroups	Number of Economies	World Population (%)	Global GDP (%)	Global Exports (%)
Central and Eastern Europe	14	2.6	3.4	3.4
Commonwealth of Independent States	12	4.1	4.3	4.0
Developing Asia	28	49.0	25.1	16.7
Latin America and the Caribbean	32	8.4	8.7	5.6
Middle East and North Africa	22	8.8	5.8	7.1
Sub-Saharan Africa	45	12.3	2.5	2.1
Totals	153	85.1	49.9	38.8

Source: International Monetary Fund, *World Economic Outlook April 2013*, 139.
**Some rounding.

Most people living in the advanced economies enjoy a high standard of living and quality of life. In part, this is a result of a relatively high GNI per capita in the advanced economies. A high GNI per capita expands consumer choice and opportunities to pursue leisure activities. In addition, the wealth of advanced economies enables government to provide essential public goods, including infrastructure and a social safety net to support people's well-being. One internationally recognized measure of quality of life is the Human Development Index (HDI), which is reported annually by the United Nations Development Program (UNDP). The HDI assesses quality of life indicators such as life expectancy, access to education, and GNI per capita. Not surprisingly, the advanced economies consistently dominate the "very high human development" category. Topping the 2012 HDI rankings were Norway, Australia, the United States, the Netherlands, and Germany respectively. The "low human development" category, on the other hand, was dominated by low-income and lower-middle-income countries.[8]

Emerging Market and Developing Economies

The **emerging market and developing economies** represent a broad range of economies that implement market-oriented reforms to promote economic growth and development. The term emerging market and developing *economies* is often used interchangeably with emerging market and developing *countries*. Under the World Bank's classification system, there were 179 emerging market and developing economies and 35 advanced economies operating in the global economy in 2012. Emerging market and developing economies included all of the low-income (36 economies), lower-middle-income (48), and upper-middle economies (55), plus 40 of the 75 high-income economies.[9]

The IMF classification of economies identified 153 emerging market and developing economies as well as 35 advanced economies in 2012. A regional grouping of these economies is shown in Table 13.3. Under the IMF classification the emerging market and developing economies accounted for 85 percent of the world's population, half of global GDP, and nearly 40 percent of global exports. Developing Asia held a leading position among the six regional subgroupings, accounting for about half of the world's total population and a quarter of global GDP. China and India were the dominant producers in Developing Asia.[10]

Strategies for economic development differ widely. Countries often create a formal **development plan** to guide the country's path toward development. A development plan sets targets, or goals, for savings and investment, production, wages and income, international trade, and macroeconomic performance in the realms of price stability, employment, and economic growth. Over time some development plans have employed a command model, which centralized decision making in the hands of government officials. The authoritarian state-planning apparatus of the former Soviet Union from the late 1920s to the early 1990s illustrates this type of planning. In more recent decades most development plans have emphasized the market model, which values private property rights, profit incentives, economic freedoms, and global connectivity. The planning process in the market model also supports inclusion by various stakeholders such as businesses, organized labor, and segments of civil society.

Many emerging market and developing economies have taken steps toward economic development. One significant measure of their progress is the success of many nations in meeting Millennium Development Goal (MDG) targets. In 2000 the United Nations General Assembly adopted the *United Nations Millennium Declaration*, which pledged to reduce global poverty and improve people's quality of life. The accompanying MDGs outlined an agenda for global development, with specific targets to achieve by 2015. Heading the eight MDGs was poverty reduction, which soon became the centerpiece of the global development agenda. The United Nations reported that the number of people living below the international poverty line of $1.25 per day fell by about 700 million people from 1990 to 2010. This means that the UN met its MDG target of halving extreme poverty—a target that was achieved five years ahead of schedule.[11] In addition, between 1990 and 2010 more than 2 billion people in the developing world gained access to improved drinking water, and millions more were saved from diseases such as malaria and tuberculosis. Significant progress was also made in achieving other MDG targets in the realms of public education, gender equity, child mortality, maternal health, environmental protection, and the establishment of global partnerships for development.[12]

Another measure of progress is the growing share of global output and international trade controlled by emerging market and developing economies. For example, in 2001 these countries produced just 43.8 percent of global output. By 2012 this percentage increased to 49.9 percent. During these same years world output increased from $46.7 trillion to $83.1 trillion—a $36.4 trillion increase (PPP). In other words, the emerging market and developing countries commanded a greater piece of global output from a significantly larger global pie. Similarly, the emerging market and developing economies' share of international trade increased dramatically from 2001 to 2012, rising from just 25 percent of global exports in 2001 to 38.8 percent of exports a decade later.[13]

The progress of many emerging market and developing economies is not shared by all countries, however. The least developed countries, for example, have lagged behind. The **least developed countries** (LDCs) are the 49 poorest and most vulnerable countries in the global economy. The United Nations (UN) describes LDCs as "structurally disadvantaged" and the "most likely to experience difficulties in their efforts to come out of poverty."[14] The United Nations identifies an LDC by its low GNI per capita, weak human assets, and high vulnerability to economic shocks such as natural disasters or disruptions in trade. Of the 49 LDCs that existed in 2012, most were located in Africa (34), followed by Asia (9), the Pacific (5), and the Caribbean (1).[15]

Generally speaking, the low-income and middle-income developing economies also lag behind the advanced economies in the structure of national output. In 2010 many low- and middle-income countries continued to rely heavily on traditional agriculture and

Traditional subsistence agriculture in Mozambique, 2002. (Eric Miller/The World Bank)

industry, rather than on the production of services, as shown in Figure 13.2.[16] Recall from Figure 13.1 that the high productivity in the advanced economies enabled a shift away from agriculture and industry in favor of services.

SUSTAINABLE ECONOMIC DEVELOPMENT

Sustainable economic development occurs when an economy creates and maintains economic institutions and practices that enable ongoing economic growth and substantive improvements in people's quality of life. Sustainable economic development requires that people make responsible economic choices in the present so as not to impinge on future generations' ability to meet their economic needs. It is also alert to the interconnectedness of peoples and the effects of production and consumption decisions on the environment, worker and human rights, and local cultures. Finally, it recognizes that neither level of economic development nor poverty is a permanent condition.[17]

The Virtuous Cycle

The **virtuous cycle** refers to the upward spiral of savings, investment, and production in an economy. The virtuous cycle leads to sustainable economic development. A convergence of many mutually supporting economic, political, and social factors is necessary to enable the virtuous cycle of development to replace the vicious cycle of poverty in the world's poorer regions. Broad factors that accelerate the virtuous cycle are higher national savings, the efficient use of resources, and good governance.

National savings provides the fuel for productive business investment. Broadly speaking, savings refers to the pool of financial resources available for people to borrow. In the advanced economies national savings is distributed to borrowers through a sophisticated

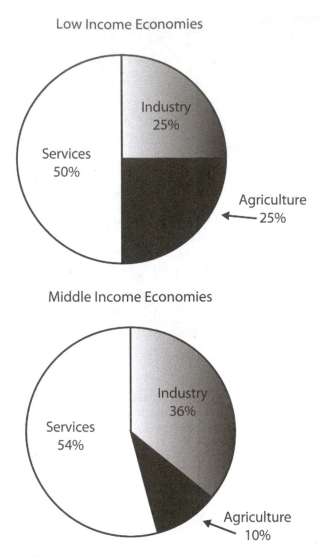

Figure 13.2   Structure of Output: Low-Income and Middle-Income Economies, 2010
Source: World Bank, *World Development Indicators: 2012*, 218–220. Some rounding.

capital market. A **capital market** consists of several types of financial intermediaries such as banks, stock markets, bond markets, venture capital funds, and other institutions that pool money for businesses to borrow. Supplementing domestic savings, especially in the poorer countries, are investments by transnational corporations, foreign banks, and development institutions. The ultimate goal is **capital deepening**, which occurs when consistent investment increases the amount of real capital per worker over time. Real capital, or capital goods, takes many forms such as tools, equipment and machinery, buildings, software, and so on. Capital flight, on the other hand, slows the virtuous cycle. **Capital flight** occurs when wealthy people in poorer countries invest their money, or financial capital, in safer or more profitable ventures abroad. Capital flight is a recurring problem in the developing world.

ECONOMICS IN HISTORY: The Rise of Development Economics

Development economics is a specialized field of study in economics that deals with sustainable economic development. Development economics gained acceptance as a field of study after World War II. The spread of independence movements and the process of nation-building during the postwar era forced government leaders and economists to consider the impact of decolonization on developing countries.

Some early development economists stressed linear development, which outlined uniform, sequential, and predictable stages of economic development. W. W. Rostow was a leading advocate of the linear theory of development. In his book *The Stages of Economic Growth: A Non-Communist Manifesto* (1960), Rostow identified five developmental stages that began with traditional societies and progressed to the modern age of mass consumption and capital-intensive production.

Other early development economists stressed how specific forces promoted growth and development. For example, Sir Arthur Lewis focused on the benefits of investment, including foreign direct investment (FDI), to advance a poor country's transition from subsistence agriculture to modernity. At about the same time, economist Robert M. Solow argued that the main drivers of economic growth were new technologies and knowledge.

In recent decades development economics has embraced a more comprehensive view of human progress. For example, Peruvian economist Hernando de Soto favors the extension of property rights to the poor and the inclusion of the informal sector into the formal economy. De Soto views these reforms as necessary for capital formation, growth, and prosperity. Another current theme in development economics is the need to infuse information and communications technologies (ICTs) into developing economies. These economists believe the use of ICTs bridges the digital divide, fosters connectivity, and enables poorer countries to leapfrog into the twenty-first century.

The efficient use of society's productive resources is a second factor that supports the virtuous cycle. The efficient use of natural resources avoids waste and environmental degradation, and supports the use of renewable resources. The efficient use of human resources is enhanced by improvements in people's health, education, and incentives structures—including entrepreneurial opportunities. These and other policies could mitigate the losses resulting from the **brain drain**—the exodus of well-educated professionals from poorer countries to greener pastures in richer countries. Finally, capital deepening increases the productivity of workers. Investments in information and communications technologies (ICTs), for example, reduce the digital divide between richer and poorer economies. Policies to attract responsible foreign direct investment (FDI) also infuse new physical capital, technology, and management skills into host economies.

Good governance is a third foundation of the virtuous cycle. **Good governance** refers to the work of honest and competent public officials in pursuit of society's goals. Democratic governments in the advanced countries developed principles of good governance over time. These principles were built on the rule of law—the understanding that all participants in the economic or political life of the country must abide by the same rules. The rule of law encourages business activity by guaranteeing equal access to business opportunities and equal protections for private property and profits. Good governance is also concerned with providing other support structures for a progrowth business environment such as a quality economic infrastructure and a safety net of social services. Multilateral development institutions have extended financial and technical assistance to help developing countries achieve good governance. Their assistance works to establish effective tax systems, fair business codes, uniform accounting principles, sound financial institutions, and appropriate regulatory systems.

Multilateral Development Institutions

Foreign aid to developing countries stimulates the virtuous cycle of development. Foreign aid includes a variety of cross-border grants, loans, and technical and other assistance. Governments and multilateral organizations provide significant aid to developing countries. Other sources of aid include transnational corporations, nongovernmental organizations (NGOs), civil society organizations (CSOs), private foundations, and individuals. Four of the most important multilateral development institutions are the World Bank Group, regional development banks, the International Monetary Fund, and a number of specialized agencies, funds, and programs within the United Nations System.

The **World Bank Group** is a member-owned international organization that provides development assistance to emerging market and developing countries. Its headquarters is in Washington, DC, but many of its 10,000 employees are stationed in its 120 offices throughout the world. The World Bank consists of five mutually supporting institutions: the International Bank for Reconstruction and Development (IBRD), the International Development Association (IDA), the International Finance Corporation (IFC), the International Center for Settlement of Investment Disputes (ICSID), and the Multilateral Investment Guarantee Agency (MIGA). Today the World Bank's overriding mission is twofold—to "end extreme poverty" and "promote shared prosperity."[18]

To achieve these goals the World Bank works with local stakeholders such as governments, civil society organizations, and businesses to develop a Country Assistance Strategy (CAS). A CAS is a country-specific plan that addresses the individual country's most pressing development needs. For example, a CAS might focus on improving one or more features of a country's infrastructure such as transportation, sanitation, water supply, energy, or information and communication technologies. A CAS might also support other economic, political, or social needs such as education, health care, agricultural development, resource management, good governance, or banking and finance. World Bank assistance includes loans, interest-free credits, grants, technical assistance, and other services that support poverty reduction and sustainable economic development. Different institutions within the World Bank Group cater to different categories of borrowers. For example, the International Bank for Reconstruction and Development (IBRD) makes loans to the more creditworthy emerging market and developing countries. The International Development Association (IDA), on the other hand, extends concessional loans and grants to the poorest and least creditworthy developing countries.[19]

Regional development banks (RDBs) are member-owned, multilateral lending institutions. Some member nations are located within the geographic region served by the bank, while others are located outside the region. RDBs' loanable funds are derived from financial contributions by member countries, interest payments on past loans, and the sale of securities to foreign investors. RDBs extend loans to support poverty reduction programs and sustainable economic development. In 2012 the four major RDBs operating in the global economy were the African Development Bank Group (AfDB Group), which consisted of 78 member nations; the Asian Development Bank (ADB), which consisted of 67 members; the Inter-American Development Bank (IDB), which consisted of 48 members; and the European Bank for Reconstruction and Development (EBRD), which consisted of 64 members. EBRD is concerned not only with promoting sustainable development, but also with facilitating the economic transition of former communist countries in eastern and central Europe and western Asia toward open market economies. Smaller RDBs promote economic development in the Caribbean, Central America, and the Islamic world.

The **International Monetary Fund** (IMF) is a multilateral organization designed to stabilize the international monetary system. Through surveillance, technical assistance, and financial assistance, the IMF supports programs to strengthen nations' financial institutions, policies, and practices. The IMF, in conjunction with the World Bank, has also supported poverty reduction initiatives, including the Heavily Indebted Poor Countries (HIPC) Initiative. Since 1996 the HIPC Initiative has offered external debt relief to the world's poorest countries. In 2005 the Multilateral Debt Relief Initiative (MDRI) was created to supplement the HIPC Initiative. MDRI funding comes from the IMF, the World Bank, and the African Development Bank. In 2012, thirty-nine of the world's poorest countries were eligible or potentially eligible for debt relief.[20]

The **United Nations** (UN) is the world's leading public forum for discussing issues of global concern. The United Nations' mission centers on preserving peace, promoting economic development, and supporting human rights. Under the umbrella of the United Nations System, a variety of largely autonomous and self-financing specialized agencies, programs, and funds work to improve the human condition. Those most concerned with sustainable development are the International Labor Organization (ILO); the World Health Organization (WHO); the United Nations Educational, Scientific, and Cultural Organization (UNESCO); the United Nations Conference on Trade and Development (UNCTAD); the United Nations Population Fund (UNFPA); the United Nations Development Program (UNDP); and the United Nations Environment Program (UNEP). Technically, the World Bank and the IMF are also specialized agencies within the UN System.[21]

Microfinance Institutions

Microfinance institutions (MFIs) are organizations that provide a range of financial services to clients, mainly the poor in developing countries. MFIs accept savers' deposits, extend loans, transfer money, sell insurance policies, and process remittances. The most important of these financial services is to make microcredit loans. Microcredit loans, or microloans, are small loans of perhaps $100 to $200 that are typically made to small businesses called microenterprises. Microenterprises use microloans to finance business start-ups or to grow existing businesses.[22] Common microenterprises include retail and repair shops, bakeries, farms, and handicraft shops. The growth of microcredit as a means to reduce global poverty inspired the United Nations to proclaimed 2005 as the Year of Microcredit.

MFIs are one leading source of microcredit to the world's poorest citizens. MFIs take many forms, such as rural and agricultural banks, consumer cooperatives, banks for specific industries such as fisheries or livestock, or even traditional institutions such as commercial banks. Many MFIs also partner with other groups, including banks, nongovernmental organizations (NGOs), and private voluntary organizations (PVOs). By the early 2010s thousands of MFIs were providing financial services to millions of low-income entrepreneurs in the global economy. MFIs are an alternative to other traditional sources of loans such as moneylenders, pawnshops, or family or friends. In 2010 there were 3,652 recognized MFIs in the global economy. These MFIs provided microloans and other financial

Table 13.4   Microfinance Institutions, 2010

World Region	MFIs (number)	MFIs (%)	MFI Clients (millions)	MFI Clients (%)
Sub-Saharan Africa	1,009	27.6	12.7	6.2
Asia and the Pacific	1,746	47.8	169.1	82.4
Latin America and the Caribbean	647	17.7	13.8	6.7
Mid-East and North Africa	91	2.5	4.3	2.1
Industrialized countries	159	4.4	5.4	2.6
World totals	3,652	100.0	205.3	100.0

Source: *State of the Microcredit Summit Campaign Report 2012*, "Table 1" and "Table 3," 3, 38.

services to 205 million people, about three-quarters of them women. Nearly half of all MFIs operated in the Asia and the Pacific region, as shown in Table 13.4. Clients in Asia and the Pacific also accounted for more than 80 percent of all microcredit loans.[23]

MFIs generally share certain characteristics. Many MFIs are nonprofit organizations. MFIs generally provide microloans and a variety of microfinance services such as microsavings and microinsurance. MFIs require repayment of microloans, plus interest. High interest rates charged by many MFIs are necessary to cover the high costs of processing large numbers of small loans. Microloans tend to be short term, with repayment expected in less than one year. Microloan repayments of principal and interest are often made in weekly or biweekly installments. Some MFIs use peer pressure rather than collateral to facilitate the repayment of microloans. Most clients are women. MFIs obtain initial start-up funds from a variety of sources, including governments, multilateral donors, and private foundations.

The Grameen Bank in Bangladesh is widely recognized as the world's first MFI and today is among the world's largest MFIs. Muhammad Yunus, who earned his doctorate in economics at Vanderbilt University (1970) in the United States, experimented with microloans in the mid-1970s. In 1983 Yunus established the Grameen Bank, a formal MFI designed to supply financial resources to the poor. He reasoned that microloans could bring millions of marginalized people, who had been shunned by commercial lenders, into the economic mainstream. In June 2013 the Grameen Bank had $1.1 billion in outstanding loans. Since its inception the Grameen Bank has extended $13.9 billion in microloans to millions of borrowers in Bangladesh. Historically the repayment of loans has topped 97 percent. The Grameen Bank provides financial services to 8.4 million members spread across 81,387 villages in Bangladesh. About 96 percent of the Grameen Bank's members are women.[24]

The rapid expansion of microfinance in the global economy has not come without some growing pains. One concern is that MFIs charge high interest rates on microcredit loans, sometimes topping 100 percent on an annual basis. High interest rates, coupled with misperceptions about the cost of borrowing, create a debt trap for borrowers. Excessive debt loads that cannot be repaid are harmful not only to the borrower, but also to the MFI. In 2010 massive credit defaults by borrowers in Andhra Pradesh, a state in southern India, illustrated the negative effects of the debt trap. These defaults undermined the financial stability of millions of households and the operation of many MFIs in the region.[25] A second concern is that microloans are sometimes used to increase borrowers' immediate consumption rather than to initiate long-term productive investments or other entrepreneurial activity. Finally, critics of microfinance lament the evolution of some MFIs from nonprofit organizations that assist the poor to for-profit banks that serve the interests of investors. The conversion of Mexico's top MFI, Compartamos Banco, into a for-profit financial institution in 2007 illustrated this concern.[26]

Foreign Aid

Foreign aid is a cross-border transfer of financial resources, technical advice, real capital, or other assistance. In most cases these transfers originate with donors from richer countries. In its broadest context the term "foreign aid" can be applied to any development assistance, humanitarian or emergency assistance, or military assistance. Foreign aid is derived from a number of sources. Bilateral aid typically travels between two governments. Multilateral aid travels from international organizations to governments, nongovernmental organizations, or businesses. Private foundations, corporations, voluntary organizations, colleges and universities, and other elements of civil society supply foreign aid to the needy. Individuals, through remittances of money to their home countries, also contribute to financial flows between countries.

Members of the Organization for Economic Cooperation and Development (OECD) represent one major source of foreign aid. Within the 34-member OECD is the Development Assistance Committee (DAC), which consists of 26 member nations. DAC coordinates the distribution of members' foreign aid, called official development assistance (ODA), to poorer countries and to multilateral development organizations such as the World Bank and regional development banks. ODA includes aid for the "economic development and welfare of developing countries"[27] but does not include military assistance to recipient countries. Measured in current dollars—that is, dollars not adjusted for inflation—DAC countries committed $125.6 billion in net ODA in 2012 to support projects to improve education, build infrastructure, and attend to humanitarian needs.[28] Net ODA is the amount of aid once various repayments have been made by recipient countries to donor countries. The top recipients of gross ODA in 2011 are shown in Table 13.5.[29] Gross ODA is the total amount of aid before any repayments are made by recipient countries to donor countries.

The largest portion of ODA is committed to the world's poorest countries. Ranked by world region, the top recipient of gross bilateral ODA in 2011 was Sub-Saharan Africa (37 percent of ODA), followed by South and Central Asia (20 percent), Other Asia and

Table 13.5   Top Ten Recipients of ODA, 2011

Rank	Recipient Country	Amount ($ millions)
1	Afghanistan	5,683
2	Congo, Democratic Republic of	4,289
3	India	3,278
4	Indonesia	2,629
5	Pakistan	2,596
6	Vietnam	2,354
7	China	2,280
8	Ethiopia	1,958
9	Iraq	1,909
10	Haiti	1,793
Top 10 Recipients Combined		(27% of ODA)

Source: Organization for Economic Cooperation and Development, Development Assistance Committee, "Total DAC Flows at a Glance."

Table 13.6   Top Donors of ODA, 2012

Largest ODA Donors Total Contributions ($ billions)			Largest ODA Donors Percentage of Country's GNI		
Rank	Country	ODA	Rank	Country	ODA
1	United States	30.5	1	Luxembourg	1.00
2	United Kingdom	13.7	2	Sweden	0.99
3	German	13.1	3	Norway	0.93
4	France	12.0	4	Denmark	0.84
5	Japan	10.5	5	Netherlands	0.71
Total (All DAC Donors)		125.6	DAC Average		0.29

Source: Organization for Economic Cooperation and Development, Development Assistance Committee, "Table 1," *Aid Statistics*, March 4, 2013.

Oceania (17 percent), Latin America and the Caribbean (12 percent), the Middle East and North Africa (10 percent), and Europe (4 percent). Ranked by countries' income classification, the highest percentage of bilateral ODA was allocated to the least developed countries (LDCs) and other low-income developing countries (46 percent), followed by the lower-middle-income countries (36 percent), and upper-middle-income countries (18 percent).[30]

The flow of ODA to poorer regions has generally increased over the past three decades. Measured in *constant* 2010 dollars ODA increased from $59.8 billion in 1981 to $128.4 billion in 2012, more than doubling during the 30-year period. Measuring ODA in constant, inflation-adjusted dollars more accurately reflects the true growth of ODA over time. Despite this increase in ODA, the average ODA granted by DAC member nations in 2012 was just 0.29 percent of their combined GNI—far below the unofficial United Nations ODA guideline of 0.7 percent of GNI. Just five DAC countries met the unofficial target of 0.7 percent of GNI. The largest ODA contributors by dollar amount and percentage of GNI in 2012 are shown in Table 13.6.[31]

The amount of foreign aid entering the world's poorer countries is still debated. The Organization for Economic Cooperation and Development (OECD) has begun to quantify some of the non-ODA sources of foreign assistance. The OECD found that non-ODA sources accounted for more than $400 billion in aid in 2011. Non-ODA sources of aid include groups such as non-DAC countries, various international organizations, and private foundations. Further, the OECD estimated that in 2011 financial remittances added another $345 billion to global foreign aid. **Remittances** are transfers of money sent by people working outside their native country to people, usually family members, in their home country. The OECD estimated that ODA, non-ODA, and remittances combined accounted for more than $900 billion in aid to the developing world.[32]

The effectiveness of foreign aid is debated. One concern is that foreign aid might promote a culture of dependency rather than a helping hand toward sustainable economic development. Another concern is that foreign aid might not reach intended recipients. This concern stems from the absence of good governance in some recipient countries. Corruption, cronyism, and other abuses of the public trust sometimes results in the theft or misuse of foreign aid. A third concern is that some aid efforts are inefficient and poorly coordinated. This is a special concern during crisis relief when humanitarian efforts might be impeded by costly organizational bureaucracies, redundant programs, or ineffective delivery systems. Finally, some question whether aid is "real aid" or "phantom aid." ODA, for example, counts debt relief, administrative costs, and technical cooperation as aid even though these initiatives involve no cross-border monetary flows.[33] This phantom aid may show up as an entry on a financial ledger, but may have a limited impact on people's well-being.

CHALLENGES TO GLOBAL PROSPERITY

In recent decades there have been significant economic gains for many people in the global economy. Challenges to a more generalized global prosperity remain. Major challenges include the growing income gap between richer and poorer peoples, the marginalization of people in the informal sector of economies, and the financial burdens imposed by high external debt. These challenges are especially persistent in the world's poorest and most vulnerable LDCs.

Low Quality of Life

Quality of life refers to the overall conditions under which people live. Quality of life is concerned with people's level of consumption and other factors related to economic well-being. It also deals with the quality of people's social, political, and cultural environment. It is difficult to measure quality of life and to make cross-border quality of life comparisons. Instead, government leaders, development economists, and others tend to examine a broad range of economic, social, and political indicators of human development. These measurable indicators show that people in high-income countries have a higher quality of life than people in middle-income and low-income countries. Improving the quality of life for

Education enhances human development by expanding people's opportunities, nurturing talents, and developing human capital. (Samrat35/Dreamstime.com)

Table 13.7   Human Development: Selected Quality of Life Indicators, 2012

Indicators	Low Human Develop	Middle Human Develop	High Human Develop	Very High Human Develop
Income				
GNI per capita (ave.)	$1,633	$5,428	$11,501	$33,391
Health				
Life expectancy (years)	59.1	69.9	73.4	80.1
Under-5 mortality (per 1,000 births)	110	42	18	6
Population				
Population (millions)	1,281	3,521	1,039	1,134
Urban population	33.6%	43.7%	74.1%	81.2%
Pop. growth rate	2.2%	1.0%	0.8%	0.5%
Fertility rate	4.2%	2.1%	1.9%	1.8%
Education				
Schooling (ave. years)	4.2	6.3	8.8	11.5

Source: United Nations Development Program (UNDP), "Table 1," "Table 7," "Table 14," *Human Development Report: 2013*, 144–147, 166–169, 194–197.

people in the world's poorer regions is a crucial component in achieving sustainable economic development.

Many quality of life issues fall within the purview of the United Nations' Millennium Development Goals (MDGs). The overarching MDG is to "eradicate extreme poverty and hunger." Quality of life indicators such as gross national income (GNI) per capita and access to food and clean water are used to assess progress toward poverty reduction. Quality of life indicators also consider educational opportunities, occupational training, employment, and gender equality; the adequacy of public services in health care, transportation, and personal security; and governance issues related to citizen participation as well as respect for civil and human rights.

Major multilateral institutions, such as the World Bank the United Nations, collect and publish data about people's quality of life. In its annual *Human Development Report*, the United Nations Development Program (UNDP) offers comprehensive data on quality of life indicators. The UNDP ranks countries by level of human development using a Human Development Index (HDI). The HDI considers quality of life indicators such as life expectancy, adult literacy, educational attainment, and gross national income (GNI) per capita. The HDI ranking in 2012 identified 47 *very high human development* countries, 47 *high human development* countries, 47 *medium human development* countries, and 46 *low human development* countries. Table 13.7 compares and contrasts selected quality of life indicators for these categories of countries.[34] Significant inequalities in income and wealth between countries and within countries complicate analyses of people's overall quality of life.

Marginalized Informal Economies

The **informal economy** consists of business activity that is neither reported to the government nor subject to government restrictions or regulations. Thus, the money value of goods or services produced by firms in the informal economy is not included in national economic aggregates such as GDP or GNI. The informal economy is known by many names such as underground economy, shadow economy, gray economy, and informal sector. The International Labor Organization (ILO), an agency within the United Nations System, has identified two main components of the informal economy—informal business enterprises and informal employment.[35] The data collected by most multilateral organizations on the informal economy consider only licit business activity and exclude criminal activities such as drug trafficking and smuggling. In the **formal economy** businesses and workers report business activities, pay taxes, and comply with business regulations or other requirements. These business activities are reported in national data aggregates.

The structure of business enterprises in the informal economy is diverse. One type of business organization is the own-account enterprise, which is owned and operated by self-employed entrepreneurs such as street vendors or domestic workers. A second type of business organization is the microenterprise, which is a small firm that typically employs several laborers at jobs in auto repair, small-scale construction, or other niche occupations. A third type of business organization is the established business that conducts a portion of its business in the formal sector of the economy and a portion "off the books" in the informal economy. In each type of business organization, businesses and workers intentionally avoid reporting output, employment status, wages, and other aspects of production to circumvent taxes and government regulations.[36]

Informal economies operate beneath the layer of formal reported business activity in all countries. The largest informal economies are found in the developing and emerging market economies. The smallest informal economies appear in the advanced economies. A recent study quantified the size of informal economies in 162 countries by estimating the value of unreported business activity as a percent of gross domestic product (GDP) in each country. This study concluded that the largest informal economies existed in three world regions: Latin America and the Caribbean, Sub-Saharan Africa, and Europe and Central Asia, as shown in Table 13.8.[37]

The study also noted a tremendous variation of informal business activity within each world region. In Latin America and the Caribbean, for example, informal sector activity accounted for more than 60 percent of all business activity in Peru and Bolivia but only about 20 percent of business activity in Chile. Similarly, within the high-income OECD countries, the size of the informal economy in Mexico (31.4 percent of GDP) was more than three times that of the United States (8.7 percent of GDP).[38] Key factors that increase

Table 13.8   Informal Economies by World Region

World Region	Informal Economy (% of GDP)
High income	
High income OECD	17.1
Other high income	23.9
Middle East and North Africa	28.5
East Asia and the Pacific	33.3
South Asia	34.0
Europe and Central Asia	40.5
Sub-Saharan Africa	41.3
Latin American and the Caribbean	42.1

Source: Friedrich Schneider et al., *Shadow Economies All over the World*, 33.

Women sell produce at a market in Gualeceo, Ecuador. The majority of Ecuadorians are *mestizo,* a Spanish term meaning mixed Spanish and Amerindian ancestry. (Rafał Cichawa/Dreamstime.com)

informal sector business activity include high business taxes, stifling business regulations, low worker education and skills, and dire poverty. Factors that reduce informal sector business activity include high national income, universal public education, good governance and the rule of law, and property rights.

The size and importance of informal economies around the world have forced economists and policy makers to assess the benefits and costs of the extralegal sector in economies. Experts generally conclude that the existence of informal economies stimulates entrepreneurial activity, business formation, and jobs creation. In fact, the ILO recently reported that between half and three-quarters of all nonagricultural jobs in the developing countries were in the informal sector. One of the main costs of informal economies is the lack of regulatory protections for workers, especially the unskilled, migrants, women, and other vulnerable groups. Sweatshop working conditions, low pay, and irregular work shifts in the informal sector violate ILO mandates for "decent work." Further, unreported business activity deprives countries of tax revenues that are needed to support key social services.[39]

The merger of the informal and formal sectors of developing economies is viewed as an important development goal by some economists, including noted Peruvian development economist Hernando de Soto. To achieve this goal De Soto favors the extension of private property rights and business rights to the poor. He argues that under existing rules and regulations the poor are denied access to credit and legal standing for their businesses. Thus, the extralegal productive assets of the poor represent trillions of dollars in "dead capital" in the global economy. **Dead capital** consists of assets in the informal sector that cannot be used as collateral to gain credit or otherwise be woven into the formal economy.[40] De Soto makes the case for the inclusion of all businesses into the formal economy.[41]

PRIMARY DOCUMENT: Hernando de Soto Proposes an Extension of Property Rights to the Poor

Imagine a country where the law that governs property rights is so deficient that nobody can easily identify who owns what, addresses cannot be systematically verified, and people cannot be made to pay their debts. Consider not being able to use your own house or business to guarantee credit. Imagine a property system where you can't divide your ownership in a business into shares that investors can buy, or where descriptions of assets are not standardized.

Welcome to life in the developing world, home to five-sixths of the world's population. Their plight underlines a paradoxical reality: capitalism is seen by the West as the answer to global underdevelopment, but it hasn't even been tried because in a capitalist economy, all business deals are based on the rules of property and transactions which do not even exist in the Third World. Their property systems exclude the assets and transactions of 80% of the population, cutting off the poor from the global capitalist economy as markedly as apartheid once separated black and white South Africans. . . .

For poor countries to develop, the poor and lower middle classes must be allowed to use their assets in the same way that wealthier citizens do and the political challenge is to bring those assets from the "extralegal" sector into a more inclusive legal property system. There they can become more productive and generate capital for their owners, growth for the nation, and markets for industry.

"The Hidden Architecture of Capital," Hernando de Soto

Unsustainable External Debt

External debt, also called foreign debt, is money owed by one nation to a foreign government, commercial bank, multilateral organization, or other creditor. Nations borrow money from foreigners to finance public goods such as infrastructure projects, schools, and military goods. Borrowed money is also used to support social services in areas such as health care and nutrition. By 2010 the combined foreign debt of emerging market and developing economies was $4.1 trillion, which represented an increase of nearly $2 trillion since 2000. About 97 percent of this external debt was owed by middle-income developing countries, and the remaining 3 percent was owed by low-income developing countries. Figure 13.3 shows the regional distribution of external debt in 2010.[42]

International creditors expect repayment of borrowed money, plus interest, as stated in the terms of the loan. Private lenders, such as commercial banks, extend loans at prevailing market interest rates. Their goal is to earn profits from these loans. As a result, banks and other private lenders are more inclined to extend loans to the more creditworthy developing nations than to the less creditworthy low-income countries. Multilateral institutions such as the World Bank and the regional development banks make development loans to member countries regardless of income status. Loans to the more creditworthy developing countries are made on a nonconcessional basis, that is, at prevailing interest rates. Loans to the poorest countries, or least developed countries (LDCs), are often made on a concessional basis. Concessional loans have a low interest rate, perhaps as low as zero percent, and a lengthy repayment schedule, perhaps 40 years or more. The International Development Association (IDA), one of five institutions within the World Bank Group, extends concessional loans to the poorest countries.

External debt is a pressing economic problem for many of the world's poorest countries. At issue is the impact of debt servicing on the economic health of these economies. **Debt servicing** occurs when debtor nations make scheduled loan repayments to foreign

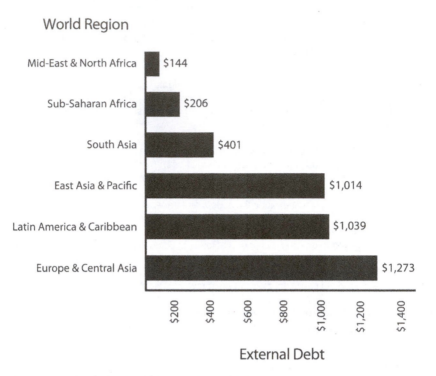

World Region

Mid-East & North Africa	$144
Sub-Saharan Africa	$206
South Asia	$401
East Asia & Pacific	$1,014
Latin America & Caribbean	$1,039
Europe & Central Asia	$1,273

External Debt

Figure 13.3   External Debt by World Region, 2010 ($ billions)
Source: World Bank, *Global Development Finance: External Debt of Developing Countries*, 36.

creditors. Debt repayments consist of a payment on the amount borrowed, called the principal, plus interest. Annual debt servicing obligations for the developing countries climbed from $345 billion in 2000 to $583 billion in 2010, an increase of nearly 70 percent during the decade. Debt servicing drains scarce funds from the public till, which reduces the government's ability to provide basic public goods and services to the people. The IMF and World Bank have identified 39 "heavily indebted" developing countries, most of which are located in sub-Saharan Africa.[43] It is mainly these heavily indebted countries that are burdened with **unsustainable external debt**—debt that cannot be repaid without horrific consequences for the nation and its people.

Multilateral institutions support debt relief programs. In 1996 the IMF and World Bank jointly sponsored the Heavily Indebted Poor Countries (HIPC) Initiative. The HIPC Initiative coordinates bilateral and multilateral debt relief to certain low-income countries. Eligibility for HIPC debt relief assistance is based on a two-step process. The first step, called the decision point, assesses the country's debt level, income classification, and willingness to participate in IMF or World Bank financial reform programs. The second step, called the completion point, requires implementation of financial reforms. In 2005 a second initiative, the Multilateral Debt Relief Initiative (MDRI), began under the auspices of the IMF, the World Bank, and the African Development Bank (AfDB) to expanded debt relief efforts. MDRI also required participating countries to use savings gained from lower debt servicing payments to support social services, education programs, poverty reduction, and other initiatives named in the UN's Millennium Development

Goals (MDGs). By 2010 the total amount of debt relief available to the 39 eligible countries was $76 billion.[44]

CHAPTER 13 SUMMARY

Classifications of Economies
- One classification of economies divides economies into income groups.
- The advanced economies are the most industrialized economies of the world.
- The emerging market and developing economies consist of all economies that have not yet achieved the level of economic development of the advanced economies.

Sustainable Economic Development
- The virtuous cycle is the upward spiral of savings, investment, and production.
- Multilateral development institutions provide financial and technical support to poorer countries.
- Microfinance institutions extend microloans to entrepreneurs.
- Foreign aid assists poorer countries' development efforts.

Challenges to Global Prosperity
- The quality of life for the peoples of the world remains uneven.
- Legal and regulatory protections are lacking in the informal economy.
- Unsustainable external debt is a heavy financial burden on the world's poorest countries.

NOTES

1. World Bank, "Country and Lending Groups," http://data.worldbank.org/about/country-classifications/country-and-lending-groups; Central Intelligence Agency (CIA), *The World Factbook*, www.cia.gov/library/publications/the-world-factbook/rankorder/2119rank.html

2. World Bank, "New Country Classification," July 2, 2013, http://data.worldbank.org/news/new-country-classification; World Bank, "Gross National Income per Capita, 2012: Atlas Method and PPP," "Country and Lending Groups," 2013, http://data.worldbank.org/about/country-classifications/country-and-lending-groups

3. World Bank, "How We Classify Countries," http://data.worldbank.org/about/country-classifications

4. World Bank, "Table 2.9: Distribution of Income or Consumption," *World Development Indicators: 2012* (New York: World Bank, 2012), 74–76.

5. International Monetary Fund (IMF), "Table B: Advanced Economies by Subgroup," *World Economic Outlook: April 2013* (Washington, DC: IMF Publication Services, 2013), 137, 140.

6. IMF, "Table A: Classification by *World Economic Outlook* Groups and Their Shares in Aggregate GDP, Exports of Goods and Services, and Population," *World Economic Outlook: April 2013*, 139.

7. World Bank, "Table 4.2: Structure of Output," *World Development Indicators: 2012*, 218–220.

8. United Nations Development Program (UNDP), "Table 1: Human Development Index and Its Components," *Human Development Report, 2013: The Rise of the South; Human Progress in a Diverse World* (New York: UNDP, 2013), 144–147.

9. World Bank, "Country and Lending Groups," www.worldbank.org/about/country-classifications/country-and-lending-groups

10. IMF, "Table A," *World Economic Report: April 2013*, 139.

11. United Nations, *The Millennium Development Goals Report 2013* (New York: UN, 2013), 2013, 4–5.

12. Ibid.

13. IMF, "Table A," "Table A1: Summary of World Output," *World Economic Outlook: April 2013*, 139, 149; IMF, "Table A," "Table 1," *World Economic Outlook: April 2001* (Washington, DC: IMF, 2002), 158, 167.

14. United Nations Conference on Trade and Development (UNCTAD), "UNCTAD Acknowledges Admission of South Sudan as Forty-Ninth LDC," December 20, 2012, http:// unctad.org/en/pages/newsdetails.aspx?OriginalVersionID=382

15. Ibid.; UNCTAD, *The Least Developed Countries Report: 2012* (New York: UN, 2012), Introduction.

16. World Bank, "Table 4.2: Structure of Output," *World Development Indicators: 2012*, 218-220.

17. UN, "Section 3: Sustainable Development, 27-30," *Report of the World Commission on Environment and Development: Our Common Future*, Brundtland Commission Report (New York: UN, 1987).

18. World Bank, *The World Bank Group Goals: End Extreme Poverty and Promote Shared Prosperity* (Washington, DC: World Bank, 2013), 7.

19. World Bank, "What We Do," July 22, 2013, http://web.worldbank.org; World Bank, "Our Work," January 31, 2012, http://web.worldbank.org; International Bank for Reconstruction and Development, *Management's Discussion & Analysis and Financial Statements*, June 30, 2012, 2-3; International Development Association, *Management's Discussion & Analysis and Financial Statements*, June 30, 2012, 3-4; World Bank, "Country Assistance Strategies," May 24, 2012, http://web.world bank.org

20. IMF, "Debt Relief under the Heavily Indebted Poor Countries (HIPC) Initiative," January 10, 2013, www.imf.org/external/np/exr/facts/hipc.htm

21. United Nations Department of Public Information, "The United Nations System," October, 2011; UN, "Structure and Organization," www.un.org/en/aboutun/structure/index.shtml

22. UN, *Microfinance and Microcredit: How Can $100 Change an Economy?* (New York: UN Department of Public Information, 2004).

23. Jan P. Maes and Larry R. Reed, "Table 1: Figures as of December 31, 2010," "Table 7: Regional Breakdown of Microfinance Data," *State of the Microcredit Summit Campaign Report 2012* (Washington, DC: Microcredit Summit Campaign, 2012), 3, 38.

24. Grameen Bank, *Grameen Monthly Update in US$: June 2013* 402, July 7, 2013, www.grameen -info.org/index; Grameen Bank, "Historical Data Series in USD, 1976–2009," www.grameen-info.org

25. Jan P. Maes and Larry R. Reed, *State of the Microcredit Summit Campaign Report 2012*, 5–7.

26. Neil MacFarquhar, "Banks Making Big Profits from Tiny Loans," *New York Times*, April 13, 2010, www.nytimes.com/2010/04/14/world/14microfinance.html; "Compartamos: From Nonprofit to Profit," *Bloomberg Businessweek*, December 12, 2007, www.businessweek.com/printer/articles/215322 -compartamos-from-nonprofit-to-profit

27. Organization for Economic Cooperation and Development (OECD), "Official Development Assistance: Definition and Coverage," www.oecd.org/dac/stats/officialdevelopmentassistance definitionandcoverage.htm

28. Organization for Economic Cooperation and Development (OECD), "Table 1: Net Official Development Assistance from DAC and Other Donors in 2012," April 3, 2013, www.oecd.org/dac/ stats/aidtopoorcountriesslipsfurtherasgovernmentstightenbudgets;

29. OECD/DAC, "Top Ten Recipients of Gross ODA," www.oecd.org/dac/stats

30. OECD/DAC, "Total DAC Flows at a Glance," www.oecd.org/development/stats

31. OECD/DAC, "Table 1: Net Official Development Assistance from DAC and Other Donors in 2012," "Aid to Poor Countries Slips Further as Governments Tighten Budgets," *Aid Statistics*, March 4, 2013, www.oecd.org/dac/stats/aidtopoorcountriesslipsfurtherasgovernmentstightenbudgets

32. OECD/DAC, "Resource Flows beyond ODA and DAC Statistics," www.oecd.org/dac/stats/ beyond-oda.htm

33. Julia Benn, Andrew Rogerson, and Suzanne Steensen, "Getting Closer to the Core: Measuring Country Programmable Aid," Issue 1, *Development Brief*, OECD, June 2010, 1–2.

34. United Nations Development Program (UNDP), "Table 1: Human Development Index and Its Components," "Table 7: Health," "Table 14: Population Trends," *Human Development Report 2013*, 144–147, 166–169, 194–197.

35. International Labor Organization (ILO), *Statistical Update on Employment in the Informal Economy* (Geneva: ILO Department of Statistics, June 2011), 1–2.

36. ILO, "Informal Economy," www.ilo.org/emppolicy/areas/informal-economy/lang-en/index.htm; World Bank Group, "Concept of Informal Sector," http://Inweb90.Worldbank.org

37. Friedrich Schneider, Andreas Buehn, and Claudio E. Montenegro, "Table 3.3.4: Ranking of 25 OECD Countries According to Size of the Shadow Economy," "Table 3.3.8: Average Informality by World Bank's Regions," *Shadow Economies All over the World: New Estimates for 162 Countries from 1999 to 2007* (Washington, DC: World Bank, July 2010), 25, 33.

38. Ibid.

39. ILO, "Informal Economy," www.ilo.org/emppolicy/areas/informal-economy/lang-en/index.htm; ILO, *Decent Work and the Informal Economy*, Report VI (Geneva: International Labor Office, 2002), 2-4; World Bank Group, "Concept of Informal Sector," http://Inweb90.Worldbank.org

40. Hernando de Soto, *The Mystery of Capital: Why Capitalism Triumphs in the West and Fails Everywhere Else* (New York: Basic Books, 2000), Chapter 3.

41. Hernando de Soto, "The Hidden Architecture of Capital," Institute for Liberty and Democracy, 2001, www.ild.org.pe/publications/articles/677-the-hidden-archietecture-of-capital

42. World Bank, "Summary Table 2: Composition of Total External Debt Stocks for 2010," "All Developing Countries, Summary of External Debt Data," *Global Development Finance: External Debt of Developing Countries 2012* (Washington, DC: World Bank, 2012), 36, 40.

43. IMF, "Factsheet: Debt Relief under the Heavily Indebted Poor Countries (HIPC) Initiative," January 10, 2013, www.imf.org/external/np/exr/facts/hipc.htm

44. Ibid.; IMF, "Factsheet: The Multilateral Debt Relief Initiative," September 30, 2012, www.imf.org/external/np/exr/facts/mdri.htm

Glossary of Selected Terms

Ability-to-pay principle: A principle of taxation stating that people with more income or wealth have a greater capacity to pay taxes than those with lesser income or wealth.

Absolute advantage: Occurs when one country is able to produce a product more efficiently than another country.

Academic economist: An economist employed mainly by colleges and universities to teach, conduct scholarly research, and publish.

Acquisition: Occurs when one firm buys sufficient ownership in a targeted firm to control the purchased firm.

Advanced economies: The richer, more industrialized economies of the world; also called advanced countries, developed economies, and developed countries.

Advertising: A paid announcement by a business or industry to inform consumers about a product and to convince people to purchase the product.

Aggregate demand: The total demand for all goods and services in an economy.

Aggregate supply: The total supply of all goods and services produced in an economy.

Agricultural revolution: The momentous shift from the nomadic lifestyle of the hunters and gatherers to a system based on permanent agriculture.

Appropriated programs: Categories of expenditures in the U.S. federal budget that require annual congressional legislation to fund, such as national defense; contrasted with mandatory programs.

Balanced budget: A budget in which receipts equal expenditures.

Balance of payments: A record of all transactions between people in one country and foreigners, including items such as international trade, foreign direct investment, and foreign aid.

Balance of trade: Measures the difference between the value of a nation's imports and exports.

Banking system: Consists of a central bank, commercial banks, and other depository institutions in a country.

Bankruptcy: The legal recognition that an individual, business, or local government is unable to repay its debts; different chapters of the U.S. bankruptcy code deal with different types of bankruptcy filings.

Barriers to entry: Factors that discourage or prevent firms from entering or exiting an industry.

Barter: A system of exchange in which one good is exchanged for a second good.

Basic economic questions: The universal questions that are answered by economic systems, including what to produce, how to produce, and for whom to produce.

Bear market: A sustained decrease in the value of stocks on a stock exchange.

Benefit-received principle: A principle of taxation that states that people who use certain government goods or services should pay for them.

Bond: A certificate of debt issued by corporations or governments as a means of borrowing money.

Bond market: A mechanism by which corporate bonds and government bonds are traded.

Brain drain: The exodus of skilled workers or other highly educated people from poorer countries to richer countries.

Budget constraint: The limits on consumer choice dictated by people's income and the price of goods.

Budget deficit: Occurs when government expenditures are greater than government receipts.

Budget surplus: Occurs when government receipts are greater than government expenditures.

Bull market: A sustained increase in the value of stocks on a stock exchange.

Business cycle: An illustration of the short-term ups and downs in the real gross domestic product, shown as expansions and contractions in the business cycle model.

Business economist: An economist employed by a firm to analyze economic data and help management make informed business decisions.

Capacity utilization rate: Measures the percentage of a nation's factory capacity that is currently being used in productive enterprise.

Capital deepening: Occurs when a nation's capital stock per worker increases.

Capital flight: Occurs when the wealthy in poorer countries invest their savings in safer, more profitable ventures abroad.

Capital flow management measures: Government policies that restrict or regulate the flow of financial resources between countries.

Capital goods: Items that are used to produce other products; examples include business computers and delivery trucks; one of the three main factors of production.

Capitalism: A type of economic system in which the private sector owns and controls the factors of production.

Capital market: The network of financial institutions that channel savings from households to business firms for the purpose of productive investment.

Capital stock: The total amount of capital goods available to produce products in a nation.

Cartel: An agreement or organization that coordinates the production decisions of independent producers of similar or identical products to influence the product's supply and price; an example is the Organization of Petroleum Exporting Countries.

Ceteris paribus: An assumption made by economists that all factors except the variable being studied can be held constant for a moment in time; the assumption permits economists to study cause-effect relationships by temporarily excluding other variables.

Charge card: a payment card that allows the cardholder to purchase goods at a specific business and repay the borrowed money, typically at the end of each billing cycle.

Circular flow model: An economic model that shows how products and resources are exchanged for money payments in a market economy.

Classical school: A school of economic thought that favors laissez-faire economic principles, including a reliance on free and competitive markets and few government interventions in the economy.

Closed corporation: A type of corporation in which stock ownership is restricted to a small group such as family members.

Closed shop: An arrangement that required employers to hire only labor union members; the Taft-Hartley Act of 1947 banned the closed shop.

Collective bargaining: Empowers union representatives to negotiate with management on behalf of the union membership; increases the market power of union workers.

Collusion: An illegal conspiracy among rival firms designed to fix prices, agree on market share, or otherwise reduce competition.

Command economy: A type of economic system in which the government dictates the answers to the basic economic questions.

Commercial bank: A private for-profit financial corporation owned by stockholders and operated by professional management.

Commodity money: An item that is commonly accepted as a medium of exchange and also has value in itself; an example is tobacco money in colonial Virginia.

Common market: A type of regional trade agreement that eliminates trade barriers among member nations, has a common trade policy, and open national borders to permit other resource flows among members.

Communism: A type of command economy in which the government owns and controls most of the means of production; associated with Marxist doctrine.

Comparable worth: The process of equalizing pay rates between jobs in a workplace that require similar skills; designed mainly to reduce wage inequities based on gender.

Comparative advantage: Exists when a nation or economic region is able to produce a product at a lower opportunity cost compared to another nation; this theory supports regional specialization and free trade.

Competition: The economic rivalry that exists among producers of similar products.

Complementary good: A product that is normally used in conjunction with another product; a battery is a complementary good to a flashlight.

Conglomerate merger: A merger of firms from unrelated industries into a single business.

Constant dollars: The value of the dollar adjusted for inflation; enables fairer comparisons of a currency's value over time; contrasted with current dollars.

Consumerism: The protection of consumer interests.

Consumerists: Individuals or groups that actively support the goals of consumerism.

Consumer movement: The embodiment of the actions, programs, and other forms of activism by individual consumerists and consumerist organizations.

Consumer Price Index: Measures the percentage change in the price of a uniform market basket of products over time; used to calculate the rate of inflation or deflation.

Consumers: People who buy goods and services to satisfy personal wants or needs.

Consumer sovereignty: States that informed consumers exercise freedom of choice and, through their buying decisions, signal producers what to produce.

Consumer surplus: A measure of consumer well-being; the difference between the price a consumer is willing to pay for a product and the actual price of the item.

Consumption goods: The goods and services designed for immediate use by households such as food, electrical appliances, and medical services.

Cooperatives: Independent self-help organizations that are owned and operated by members; types include consumer, producer, and worker co-ops.

Corporate social responsibility: The responsibilities corporations have to their workers and families, consumers, investors, local peoples, governments, and the natural environment.

Corporation: A type of business that is incorporated under state law, owned by stockholders, and typically run by professional managers.

Corporation income tax: A federal tax on corporate profits; also called the corporate income tax.

Correlation-as-cause fallacy: Faulty reasoning that incorrectly assumes that because two events occurred at about the same time, one must have caused the other.

Cost-benefit analysis: A process by which the costs of providing or producing certain public or private goods are weighed against the anticipated benefits of providing or producing these goods; this type of analysis is used to make rational decisions in the public and private sectors.

Costs of production: The payments made by firms in exchange for the factors of production; includes wages, interest, rents, and entrepreneurial profits.

Cost-push inflation: A type of inflation that occurs when an increase in production costs pushes up prices in an economy.

Countervailing duty: A retaliatory tariff designed to offset a financial advantage gained through dumping or subsidization.

Craft union: A labor organization of skilled workers in a single trade such as carpenters or masons.

Credit: A type of voluntary transaction or agreement between a borrower and a lender.

Credit card: A payment card that allows the cardholder to purchase goods from a variety of venues and repay the money in monthly payments.

Credit union: A not-for-profit financial cooperative that is owned and operated by members.

Current dollars: The value of the dollar in the present, not adjusted for inflation; contrasted with constant dollars.

Customs union: A type of regional trade agreement that eliminates trade barriers among member nations and establishes uniform trade policies with nonmember nations.

Dead capital: Assets in the informal economy that cannot be used as collateral, gain credit, or otherwise be woven into the formal economy.

Debt ceiling: A legal limit on the total amount of debt the U.S. Department of the Treasury can issue to the public or to other federal agencies; also called the debt limit.

Debt servicing: The process of repaying debt; often applied to the interest payments on the U.S. national debt, and to the payments by developing countries to foreign creditors.

Deductive approach: A method of forming economic theories which begins with a hypothesis based on observations, followed by data collection and testing.

Default: Occurs when a debtor is not able or not willing to honor existing financial obligations; can apply to an individual, business, or government.

Deflation: An overall decline in the price level in an economy; also called negative inflation.

Demand: The amount of a good, service, or resource that people are willing and able to buy at a series of prices at a moment in time.

Demand-pull inflation: A type of inflation that occurs when excess demand pulls up the prices of products in an economy.

Democracy: A type of political system that relies on broad-based citizen participation, free elections, and the rule of law.

Democratic socialism: A type of economic system in which the government owns and controls some of the means of production and provides extensive social programs; traditionally found in western European countries.

Depression: A severe and prolonged recession.

Derived demand: The demand for a resource, such as labor, is derived from the demand for the product produced by that resource.

Developing countries: The poorer, less industrialized countries; also called developing economies or, more broadly, emerging market and developing countries.

Development plan: A type of economic blueprint that outlines a nation's path toward sustainable economic development.

Differentiated oligopoly: A type of oligopoly in which rival firms produce similar but not identical products; an example is the U.S. breakfast cereal industry.

Diminishing marginal utility, law of: An economic law stating that consumer satisfaction declines as additional units of the same good are consumed in a specified period of time.

Diminishing returns, law of: An economic law stating that as additional inputs (resources) are used in production, they will generate progressively smaller amounts of additional output.

Discount rate: A monetary policy tool used by the Federal Reserve System that involves changes in the interest rate charged by the Fed to banks for short-term loans.

Discretionary fiscal policy: Congressional policies to raise and spend money to achieve macroeconomic goals such as economic growth, full employment, and stable prices.

Division of labor: Specialization applied to labor with the goal of increasing worker productivity; the division of labor becomes more sophisticated as economies become more advanced.

Domestic system: A system of production that relies on small-scale production in people's homes.

Dumping: An illegal trade practice that occurs when a producer from one country sells a product in a second country at a price lower than its production costs or lower than the price in the country of origin.

Easy money policy: The Fed's use of monetary policy tools to expand the nation's money supply to stimulate business activity; contrasted with tight money policy.

Econometrics: The use of sophisticated mathematical models to draw conclusions, explain events, or predict economic behaviors.

Economic and monetary union: The most integrated form of regional trade agreement.

Economic choice: The freedom people have to use their resources or other property as they see fit.

Economic efficiency: The production of products that people are willing to buy and at the lowest possible cost.

Economic growth: A sustained increase in the nation's gross domestic product; sometimes measured by a sustained increase in the real GDP per capita, or real GNI per capita.

Economic indicators: Economic data used to predict and assess the duration of business cycles; the three types of indicators are leading, coincident, and lagging.

Economic law: An economic theory or generalization that has survived repeated testing, such as the law of demand.

Economic model: A simplified version of reality designed to focus on a specific relationship between variables; often shows a cause-effect relationship.

Economics: The study of how people choose to use their scarce resources to satisfy their needs; the study deals with production, distribution, and consumption decisions.

Economic system: The sum total of all economic activity that takes place within a society; economic systems answer the basic economic questions of what, how, and for whom to produce.

Economies of scale: The decline in the average cost of producing a good as the firm's rate of output increases; the concept of economies of scale is used to defend the existence of natural monopolies.

Embargo: The cessation of trade or other commercial contacts with a country for a period of time.

Emerging market and developing economies: A broad range of economies that have not yet entered the ranks of the advanced economies; also called emerging market and developing countries.

Employer firm: A firm that hires employees; contrasted with nonemployer firms.

Employment rate: The percentage of the labor force that has a job.

Entrepreneur: A person who starts a new business, develops a new product, or devises a new way to produce a product; a risk-taker and innovator.

Entrepreneurship: Occurs when a person creates or otherwise advances a business venture independently or within an existing business; the actions of an entrepreneur.

Equilibrium wage: The point of intersection between the labor demand curve and the labor supply curve in a particular labor market.

European Union: The world's most integrated economic and monetary union, consisting of 28 member nations in 2013.

Evidence fallacy: Faulty reasoning that occurs when conclusions are based on insufficient, irrelevant, or inaccurate information.

Exchange rates: States the value of one currency compared to a second currency.

Excise tax: A tax on a specific product such as gasoline, alcohol, or cigarettes.

Expansionary fiscal policy: The use of fiscal policy tools to inject money into a slumping economy to increase business activity; contrasted with restrictive fiscal policy.

Export: A product that is sold to another country.

Expropriation: A government seizure of resources, firms, or other private assets without compensating the previous owner.

External debt: The money owed by one country to foreign governments, banks, multilateral organizations, or other creditors; also called foreign debt.

Factor market: Represents all purchases of resources in an economy; factor market exchanges are illustrated on the circular flow model; also called the resource market.

Factors of production: The resources needed to produce products including natural resources, human resources, and capital goods; entrepreneurship is often considered a fourth factor of production.

Factory system: A system of production that relies on large-scale, capital-intensive production in an industrial setting; a system that relies on specialization and a division of labor.

Fair trade: Involves the purchase of imported goods that were produced in a socially responsible and environmentally friendly manner.

Fallacy: An error in research or reasoning that results in an erroneous conclusion.

Fallacy of composition: Faulty reasoning assuming that what is true for a piece is true for the whole.

Federal budget: A document that outlines how the federal government plans to raise and spend money during a fiscal year.

Federal funds rate: The interest rate that banks charge to other banks for short-term loans.

Federal Reserve System: The U.S. central bank with responsibility for maintaining the stability of the nation's banking and monetary system; also called the Fed.

Fiat money: A type of money that derives its value by government decree; an example is the paper currency used in the United States.

Financial contagion: The spread of a financial crisis from one country to other countries or regions; viewed as a threat to global financial stability.

Firm: A business entity that produces a good or service; also called a business or a business firm.

Fiscal policy: The use of taxes and government spending by Congress to promote economic growth and stability.

Fixed costs: Business costs that do not change with a change in a firm's rate of output; examples include rents, leases, and interest payments on debts; contrasted with variable costs.

Fixed exchange rate system: A system of foreign exchange trading based on a fixed conversion rate among the world's currencies.

Flexible exchange rate system: A system of foreign exchange trading in which market forces determine the relative value of the world's currencies.

Foreign aid: Cross-border transfers to financial resources, technical advice, and other assistance mainly from richer countries to poorer countries.

Foreign direct investment: The long-term cross-border investments by one company to gain ownership or control of production facilities in another country; FDI occurs through mergers and acquisitions, and greenfield investments.

Foreign exchange market: A highly integrated global network of financial institutions that converts currencies and trades currencies for profit.

Foreign exchange trading: The buying and selling of national currencies for profit; forex trading takes place in the foreign exchange market.

Franchise: A business consisting of a parent company called a franchiser and satellite firms called franchisees; examples include Subway and McDonald's.

Free trade: International trade that is not restricted by trade barriers such as import quotas or tariffs.

Free trade area: A type of regional trade agreement that eliminates most trade barriers among member nations but permits members to devise their own trade policies with non-member countries; the FTA is least integrated type of regional trade agreement.

Futures market: A mechanism by which contracts for items are traded; also called a futures exchange.

General Agreement on Tariffs and Trade: A multilateral agreement that established rules for international trade from 1947 to 1994; GATT supported free trade.

General purpose technology: A technology created through government-funded research and development; GPTs create new technologies with potential for further commercial development; an example is the Internet.

Geographic monopoly: Exists when a single firm is the exclusive provider of a product or service to a certain region.

Global economy: The international network of individuals, businesses, governments, multilateral organizations, and others that make or influence production, distribution, and consumption decisions.

Globalization: The process of creating a more integrated and interdependent global economy through expanded international trade, foreign direct investment, cross-border financial flows, and other flows of resources and ideas.

Good governance: Honest and competent government that enforces the rule of law.

Goods-producing sector: Consists of firms that supply tangible items in an economy such as final goods, intermediate goods, and resources.

Government economist: An economist employed by any level of government to collect and analyze data necessary for the operation of government or the formation of public policy.

Government monopoly: Exists when any level of government becomes the sole provider or producer of a good or service; examples include local government control of water and sewage services.

Gross capital formation: Investments that increase the country's fixed assets such as roads, schools, and factories.

Gross domestic product: Measures the total value of all final goods and services produced in a country in a given year; includes the output of domestic and foreign firms within the country.

Gross investment: The sum total of private investment and public investment in an economy in a given year.

Gross national income: Measures people's total income by adding the value of all final goods and services produced in the economy with the net receipts from other wage or investment income from abroad.

Gross national product: Measures the total value of all final goods and services produced by a country's firms operating anywhere in the world; excludes the value of output produced by foreign firms within the country.

Gross saving: The sum total of savings by individuals, businesses, and the government in a country in a given year.

Horizontal merger: A merger of firms that sell similar products in the same market.

Human capital: The expanded abilities and skills of workers in a country due to education or other training.

Human resources: The people engaged in production; examples include teachers, factory workers, and farmers; one of the three main factors of production.

Import: A product that is purchased from another country.

Import quota: A trade barrier that limits the quantity of an imported good.

Incentives: Factors that motivate people to pursue certain actions or behaviors and discourage other actions or behaviors.

Income effect of a price change: States the inverse relationship between the price of good and a household's economic well-being; an increase in a good's price makes a household worse off, while a decrease in a good's price makes the household better off.

Income effect of a wage increase: States that as the wage rate of a worker increases, the worker will work fewer hours and therefore have more leisure time; contrasted with the substitution effect of a wage increase.

Indicative planning: A collaborative, inclusive economic planning process traditionally used by democratic socialist countries.

Inductive approach: A method of forming economic theories, which begins with the identification of a problem, followed by data collection, generalizations, and testing.

Industrialization: The economic transition of an economy from small-scale, labor-intensive production to large-scale, capital-intensive production; historically industrialization occurred in conjunction with the Industrial Revolution.

Industrial union: A labor organization composed of all workers in a firm or industry, regardless of skill level or job description.

Industry: Represents all firms that produce a similar product; an example is the U.S. auto industry.

Inflation: An increase in the overall price level in an economy over time.

Inflation rate: Measures the percentage increase in the overall price level in an economy over time.

Informal economy: Business activity in a country that is neither reported to the government nor subject to government rules or regulations.

Information and communications technologies: The technological advances that radically increase the ability to collect, store, retrieve, and share information; ICTs have transformed business activity and connectivity within the global economy.

Innovation: The process of converting scientific discoveries and technological advances into profitable products or improved methods of production.

Installment credit: Enables consumers to buy goods in the present and repay the dollar amount of the purchase, plus interest, in regular monthly installments.

Interlocking directorate: Occurs when members of one corporate board of directors also sit on a competitor's board of directors; an anticompetitive business practice.

International investment agreement: A bilateral or multilateral treaty that establishes rules and responsibilities of parties involved in a cross-border investment.

International Monetary Fund: A multilateral organization that promotes international cooperation, financial stability, and growth in the global economy; the IMF is a specialized agency within the United Nations system.

International trade: The cross-border exchange of goods or services; trade is conducted by importing and exporting products.

Investment protectionism: Occurs when a government imposes regulations or other restrictions on foreign direct investment.

Joint venture: A business agreement between two or more companies to jointly produce or sell a product; typically a temporary business arrangement.

Keynesian school: A school of economic thought based on the works of John M. Keynes; Keynesians favor government interventions in the economy to influence aggregate demand as a means achieving economic growth and stability.

Labor force: Consists of individuals who are 16 years of age or older and who are employed or actively seeking employment.

Labor force participation rate: The percentage of work-age individuals who are a part of the labor force.

Labor market: A situation in which individuals voluntarily supply their labor in exchange for a wage or salary.

Labor union: A formal association of workers empowered by members to negotiate a labor contract with a firm's management.

Laissez-faire: The belief that market forces, rather than the government, should determine the use of society's resources; often used in conjunction with the term capitalism (laissez-faire capitalism) to denote the importance of marketplace freedoms within a capitalist economic system.

Large business: A firm that satisfies certain criteria in terms of total revenues or number of employees; in common usage a firm with 500 or more employees; contrasted with small business.

Law of demand: An economic law that explains the inverse relationship between the price of a good and the quantity demanded.

Leisure: All uses of time that are not directly related to paid employment.

Limited liability company: A hybrid business organization that combines features from corporations, partnerships, and sole proprietorships.

M1: A narrower measurement of the money supply that includes coin, paper currency, demand deposits, and traveler's checks; also called transactions money.

M2: A broader measurement of the money supply that includes M1, plus near monies such as savings deposits, small time deposits, and money market mutual funds.

Macroeconomics: The branch of economics that deals with economic performance in the overall economy such as the price level, employment, and national output.

Mandatory programs: Categories of expenditures in the U.S. federal budget that do not require annual congressional legislation to fund such as Social Security and Medicare; contrasted with appropriated programs.

Marginalism: An economic analysis that considers the impact of the next or additional unit of consumption or production on an economic decision; most economic decisions are made at the margin.

Marginalist school: A school of economic thought that emphasizes rational decision making at the margin by producers and consumers of products.

Marginally attached worker: A person who is willing to work but who has not been employed during the previous 12 months and who has recently stopped looking for paid employment.

Marginal utility: The additional satisfaction that is derived from the consumption of additional units of the same good during a specific time period.

Market: A situation in which people freely exchange goods, services, financial instruments, or other transferable items.

Market economy: A type of economic system that relies on the private sector to answer the basic economic questions; often used interchangeably with free enterprise system and capitalism.

Market equilibrium: The point at which the demand curve and the supply curve for a product intersect, establishing a market clearing price.

Market structure: The competitive environments under which industries are organized; types include perfect competition, monopolistic competition, oligopoly, and monopoly.

Marxism: A school of economic thought based on the works of Karl Marx; Marxism is grounded in socialist principles and committed to the overthrow of capitalism.

Mercantilism: The belief that a country's wealth is derived from its ability to accumulate gold and silver.

Merger: The union of two firms to form a larger firm; often called a merger of equals such as the 1999 merger of Exxon and Mobil into ExxonMobil.

Microeconomics: The branch of economics that focuses on the interactions among individual decision-making units in an economy such as consumers, workers, or firms.

Microfinance institutions: Organizations that provide microloans and other financial services to the poor, mainly in the developing world.

Minimum wage: A price floor that sets a minimum hourly wage for employees.

Mixed economy: An economy that combines features from the market model and the command model; the term "mixed economy" is often used to describe economies that lean heavily toward the market model, such as the U.S. economy.

Monetarism: A school of economic thought that supports a fixed, predictable rate of growth in the nation's money supply.

Monetary policy: The actions of the Federal Reserve System to alter the money supply and the cost of credit in pursuit of national macroeconomic goals, mainly economic growth and stability.

Money: Any item that is commonly accepted in payment for goods or services, or in payment of debts.

Money supply: The total amount of money in an economy; the two measurements of the money supply are M1 and M2.

Monopolistic competition: A type of market structure in which many firms—perhaps 25, 50, or more—produce similar but differentiated products.

Monopoly: A type of market structure in which one firm dominates the production of a unique product.

Multilateral organization: A group or organization comprised of members from more than one country; often these organizations address global issues.

Mutual fund: A company that creates and manages a diversified portfolio of financial assets; viewed as a more secure investment option than individual stocks.

National debt: The accumulated debt of the federal government over time; also called the federal debt.

Nationalization: A government takeover of a private enterprise with compensation to the previous owner.

Natural monopoly: A single producer of a good or service that exists mainly because the economies of scale reduces the average cost of production as additional units of output are made; natural monopolies, such as local power companies, are regulated by the government.

Natural rate of unemployment: The percentage of the labor force that is frictionally and structurally unemployed.

Natural resources: The gifts of nature used in production; examples include sunlight, natural forests, and rivers; one of the three main factors of production.

Net interest: The amount of money the U.S. government pays in interest on the national debt minus the interest payments and fees it receives from other federal agencies.

Net worth: The difference between a household's gross assets and its liabilities.

Nominal gross domestic product: The gross domestic product not adjusted for inflation; the GDP in current dollars; contrasted with real GDP.

Nondiscretionary fiscal policy: The automatic stabilizers built into the existing tax system and federal spending programs.

Nonemployer firms: Firms that are owned by one person, earn at least $1,000 in revenue in a year, and do not hire employees; contrasted with employer firms.

Nongovernmental organizations: Groups that research issues, share their findings, and advocate for reforms; examples include Oxfam and Amnesty International.

Nonprofit organizations: Organizations designed to provide goods or services to people but not to earn profits for shareholders, employees, or other stakeholders; examples include the Red Cross and Veterans of Foreign Wars.

Nonrenewable resources: Resources that are consumed during production and cannot be replenished, such as natural gas and petroleum.

Normative economics: A type of economics concerned with what ought to be or what ought not be; normative statements are subjective and cannot be objectively tested; also called prescriptive economics. ·

North American Free Trade Agreement: A free trade area comprised of the Canada, Mexico, and the United States.

Offshoring: Occurs when a producer in one country outsources production to another country.

Oligopoly: A type of market structure in which several firms—perhaps three, six, or 10—dominate the output of an industry; economists often say an oligopoly exists when the top four firms in an industry produce at least 40 percent of the industry's output; the two types of oligopolies are differentiated and pure.

Open market operations: A monetary policy tool used by the Federal Reserve System, which involves the sale or purchase of government securities; open market operations is the most used Fed tool.

Opportunity cost: The second best use of limited resources; the good or service that is not produced or consumed; also called the real cost.

Organization for Economic Cooperation and Development: An association of 34 countries that discuss issues of global concern and coordinate official development assistance to poorer countries.

Partnership: A type of business that is owned by two or more people, called partners, each of whom has a financial interest in the firm.

Perfect competition: A type of market structure in which thousands of independently operating firms produce and sell a homogeneous product; an example is the U.S. wheat industry.

Personal income tax: A federal progressive tax on people's taxable income; many states also have a personal income tax; often called the individual income tax.

Physiocratic school: An economic school of thought that stresses the primacy of agriculture and free markets to guide society's use of resources.

Positive economics: A type of economics concerned with what is; positive economic statements can be objectively tested; also called descriptive economics.

Post-hoc fallacy: A type of faulty economic reasoning that assumes a preceding event necessarily causes a subsequent event when, in fact, no causal relationship exists.

Poverty: A condition that exists when a family's income falls below the official government-determined poverty line.

Poverty line: The annual income level set by the government to distinguish the poor from the nonpoor; also called the poverty threshold.

Poverty rate: The percentage of a nation's total population that falls below the official poverty line.

Price ceiling: A government-imposed maximum price that a seller may charge for a good or service; an example is rent control on apartment units.

Price elasticity of demand: Measures the impact of a price change on the quantity demanded of a product.

Price elasticity of supply: Measures the impact of a price change on the quantity supplied of a product.

Price system: The largely invisible price signals that coordinate most production and consumption decisions in a market economy.

Private property: Any good, resource, or other asset that is owned and controlled by an individual or a firm.

Private property rights: Legal codes and other protections that guarantee people's right to own, control, buy, sell, and profit from their private property.

Producer cooperative: A not-for-profit business that is owned and operated collectively by the firm's members mainly to minimize production costs or expand distribution channels.

Producer price index: Measures the percentage change in the prices of raw materials, intermediate goods, and other items used in the production process.

Producers: Firms that make or sell goods and services, mainly to earn profits.

Producer sovereignty: A theory popular in the 1950s and 1960s that consumer choice is manipulated by big business through advertising and marketing campaigns.

Production: The process of converting the factors of production into goods and services.

Production possibilities frontier: An economic model that illustrates the range of possible production choices producers (nations or firms) might make at a specific moment in time; used to show the opportunity cost of production decisions.

Production sharing: The production of a product in stages, often in a number of different countries, to minimize production costs.

Productivity: A measurement of output per unit of input; typically measured in terms of output per unit of labor employed in a production process.

Product market: Represents all purchases of goods and services in an economy; product market exchanges are illustrated on the circular flow model.

Profit: Occurs when a firm's total revenues are greater than its total costs.

Progressive tax: A tax that takes a larger percentage of income from higher-income households than from lower-income households.

Property tax: A local tax on assets such as a house, business, undeveloped property, or car.

Proportional tax: A tax that takes the same percentage of income from all households regardless of income level.

Public corporation: A corporation in which shares of ownership are widely traded.

Public goods: Goods provided by the government that are nonexclusionary and nonrival in consumption; examples include schools and national defense.

Purchasing power parity: A conversion process for nations' currencies that assesses and compares the buying power of money within individual economies.

Pure oligopoly: A type of oligopoly in which rival firms produce an identical product; an example is the U.S. steel industry.

Quality of life: A measure of people's well-being based on income level and other features of the human condition such as access to health services and educational opportunities.

Quantitative easing: A tool of the Federal Reserve System to inject money into the banking system through the purchase of bank assets such as mortgage-backed securities and government securities; designed to increase the availability of loanable funds in an economy.

Race to the bottom theory: A theory critical of transnational corporations and others involved in globalization for the perceived harm that globalization inflicts on workers, the environment, and others in the global economy.

Real GDP per capita: The real GDP divided by a nation's total population; often used as a measure of economic growth.

Real gross domestic product: The gross domestic product that is adjusted for inflation; contrasted with nominal GDP.

Recession: A relatively short-term economic downturn in an economy marked by a decline in real gross domestic product and negative changes in employment, investment, incomes, and retail sales.

Regional development banks: Member-owned, multilateral lending institutions that promote economic development in world regions, including Africa, Asia, Latin America, and Europe.

Regional specialization: Occurs when firms in a geographic region produce one product or a narrow range of products, which are often determined by a country's comparative advantage.

Regional trade agreement: An agreement that creates reciprocal trade concessions for member countries; designed to increase trade among members.

Regressive tax: A tax that takes a larger percentage of income from lower-income households than from upper-income households.

Remittances: Transfers of money sent by people working outside their native country to people living in their native country; viewed today as a major source of foreign aid.

Renewable resources: Resources that can be replenished, such as sunlight and forests.

Representative money: A type of money that has no inherent value but represents something of value; an example was U.S. silver certificates that were redeemable for silver in the past.

Reserve requirement: A monetary policy tool used by the Federal Reserve System; it involves a change in the percentage of transaction accounts that banks must hold as reserves.

Restrictive fiscal policy: The use of fiscal policy tools to withdraw money from an overheated economy to slow business activity or inflation; contrasted with expansionary fiscal policy.

Right-to-work laws: Allows workers at a unionized firm to reject union membership and the payment of union dues but benefit from union-negotiated labor contracts.

Sales tax: A state or local tax on the consumption of certain products.

Savings and loan association: A savings institution designed to meet the needs of households rather than businesses; a type of thrift institution.

Savings bank: A savings institution design to provide home mortgages and other personal loans; a type of thrift institution.

Scarcity: A condition that exists when people have unlimited wants or needs but limited resources to satisfy these material desires; also called the universal economic problem.

School of economic thought: A group of economists who share common ideas about how scarce resources should be used to achieve society's goals.

Services-producing sector: Consists of firms that supply productive activities in areas such as transportation, communications, and retail trade.

Single cause fallacy: Faulty economic reasoning that identifies just one cause of a problem when, in fact, there are multiple causes.

Small business: A firm that satisfies certain criteria in terms of total revenues or number of employees; in common usage a firm with fewer than 500 employees; contrasted with large business.

Social insurance payroll taxes: Federal taxes including the Social Security tax and Medicare tax, which are used mainly provide income and health security for the elderly.

Socialism: A type of economic system based on public ownership and control of key resources and industries; major strands include democratic socialism and authoritarian socialism.

Sole proprietorship: A type of business organization that is owned by one person, the proprietor.

Specialization: Occurs when individuals or firms, economic regions, or nations produce a specific product or narrow range of products (regional specialization); also applies to production processes involving the assembly of interchangeable parts, and specialized use of labor (division of labor).

Stagflation: The simultaneous occurrence of recession and inflation.

Standard of living: A measurement of people's economic well-being based on household income.

Stock: A certificate of ownership in a corporation.

Stock market: A mechanism by which corporate stocks are traded; also called a stock exchange.

Substitute good: A product that can be used in place of a similar product; for example, one brand of energy drink can be substituted for a second brand.

Substitution effect of a price change: States that as the price of a good falls, people will buy more of the good and less of the substitute good; and vice versa.

Substitution effect of a wage increase: States that as the wage rate increases, the worker will work additional hours and therefore will have less leisure; contrasted with the income effect of a wage increase.

Supply: The amount of a product or resource that producers are willing and able to sell at a series of prices at a moment in time.

Supply-side economics: A school of economic thought that stresses the role of incentives, such as tax cuts, to stimulate productive investment and business activity.

Sustainable consumption: Consumption based on the efficient purchase and use of resources and products by consumers, firms, and government so as not to undermine consumption of future generations.

Tariff: A federal tax on an imported product; also called a customs duty.

Tax: A mandatory payment by individuals and businesses to the federal, state, or local government.

Technological monopoly: A single firm that produces a good or service mainly because it alone has access to patented technology used in the good's production.

Third world socialism: A strand of socialism that emphasizes land reform, the elimination of most private property, and central planning.

Tight money policy: The Fed's use of monetary policy tools to contract the nation's money supply to slow business activity and inflation; contrasted with easy money policy.

Total cost: The sum total of a firm's fixed costs and variable costs.

Trade barriers: Government policies mainly designed to discourage or prohibit imports; examples include tariffs and import quotas.

Trade deficit: Occurs when the value of a country's exports is less than the value of its imports; also called an unfavorable balance of trade.

Trade-off: Occurs when people choose to use a resource in one way rather than another way due to the scarcity of the resource.

Trade surplus: Occurs when the value of a country's exports is greater than the value of its imports; also called a favorable balance of trade.

Traditional economy: A type of economic system that relies on custom or tradition to answer the basic economic questions.

Transfer payment: Payment of money, goods, or services by the government to people; the two main categories of transfer payments are social insurance programs and public assistance programs.

Tying agreement: An anticompetitive business arrangement that requires buyers of one good to likewise buy related products, mainly complementary goods, from the same supplier.

Underemployment: The underutilization of employed workers in an economy.

Unemployment: The number of people in the labor force without a job.

Unemployment rate: The percentage of the labor force that is without a job.

Union membership rate: The percentage of workers that belong to a labor union in a country; also used to measure the percentage of workers that belong to a labor union in a sector of an economy, such as the private sector or the public sector.

Union shop: An arrangement that requires workers to join an existing union after they are hired by a firm or other employer.

United Nations System: The world's leading public forum for the discussion of issues of global concern; consists of six main branches and numerous specialized agencies, programs, and funds.

Unsustainable external debt: A foreign debt than cannot be repaid without incurring horrific consequences for the debtor country.

Utility: The amount of satisfaction a person derives from the consumption of a good or service.

Variable costs: Business costs that change along with changes in the firm's rate of output; examples include costs associated with the number of laborers and the amount of materials used in production; contrasted with fixed costs.

Venture initiation: The creation of a new business through entrepreneurial activity.

Vertical merger: A merger of firms that produce different items needed at different phases in the production of a product.

Virtuous cycle: The upward spiral of savings, investment, and production needed for sustainable economic development.

Welfare state: The provision of extensive social programs by the government to provide at least a minimal standard of living for the people; most commonly associated with government welfare policies in democratic socialist economies.

Work: Productive activity in a paid job.

Worker cooperative: A firm owned and operated by its employees.

World Bank Group: A multilateral development organization comprised of five mutually supporting institutions; the main goals of the World Bank Group are to reduce global poverty and promote sustainable economic development; the World Bank is a specialized agency within the United Nations System.

World Trade Organization: A multilateral organization that oversees the operation of the rules-based multilateral trading system; the WTO replaced the General Agreement on Tariffs and Trade in 1995 as the leading proponent of free trade in global markets.

Common Abbreviations in Economics

ACH	Automated Clearing House
ADB	Asian Development Bank
AE	advanced economy
AfDB	African Development Bank (Group)
AFL	American Federation of Labor
AFL-CIO	American Federation of Labor–Congress of Industrial Organizations
ASEAN	Association of Southeast Asian Nations
ATM	automated teller machine
B2B	business-to-business (transaction)
B2C	business-to-consumer (transaction)
BBB	Better Business Bureau
BEA	Bureau of Economic Analysis
BIF	Bank Insurance Fund
BIS	Bank for International Settlements
BIT	bilateral investment treaty
BLS	Bureau of Labor Statistics
BOG	Board of Governors (Fed)
BOP	balance of payments
CARICOM	Caribbean Community
CAS	Country Assistance Strategy
CBOT	Chicago Board of Trade
CCI	Consumer Confidence Index
CD	certificate of deposit
CEA	Council of Economic Advisors
CEO	chief executive office
CET	common external tariff
CFA	Consumer Federation of America
CFM	capital flow management (measures)
CFO	chief financial officer
CI	Consumers International
CIA	Central Intelligence Agency

CIO	Congress of Industrial Organizations
CIS	Commonwealth of Independent States
CME	Chicago Mercantile Exchange (Group)
CPI	Consumer Price Index
CPSC	Consumer Product Safety Commission
CR	Consumers' Research
CR	continuing resolution
CSO	civil society organization
CSR	corporate social responsibility
CU	Consumers Union
DAC	Development Assistance Committee
DJIA	Dow Jones Industrial Average
EBRD	European Bank for Reconstruction and Development
ECB	European Central Bank
ECOWAS	Economic Community of West African States
EEOC	Equal Employment Opportunity Commission
EFW	*Economic Freedom of the World*
EMU	European Monetary Union
EPA	Environmental Protection Agency
EU	European Union
FC	fixed cost
FDA	Food and Drug Administration
FDI	foreign direct investment
FDIC	Federal Deposit Insurance Corporation
FICA	Federal Insurance Contributions Act
FICO	Fair Issac and Company (score)
FLSA	Fair Labor Standards Act
FOMC	Federal Open Market Committee
FTA	free trade area
FTC	Federal Trade Commission
FTZ	free trade zone
FX	foreign exchange
FY	fiscal year
GATS	General Agreement on Trade in Services
GATT	General Agreement on Tariffs and Trade
GDP	gross domestic product
GEM	*Global Entrepreneurship Monitor*
GNI	gross national income
GNP	gross national product
GPT	general purpose technology
GSE	government-sponsored enterprise
GVCs	global value chains
HDI	Human Development Index
HHS	Health and Human Services (Department of)
HIPC	Heavily Indebted Poor Countries (Initiative)
IA	Import Administration

IBRD	International Bank for Reconstruction and Development
ICA	International Co-operative Alliance
ICSID	International Center for Settlement of Investment Disputes
ICTs	information and communication technologies
IDA	International Development Association
IDB	Inter-American Development Bank
IFC	International Finance Corporation
IFI	international financial institution
IIA	international investment agreement
ILD	Institute for Liberty and Democracy
ILO	International Labor Organization
IMF	International Monetary Fund
IPO	initial public offering
IRA	individual retirement account
IRS	Internal Revenue Service
ITA	International Trade Administration
ITUC	International Trade Union Confederation
IWW	Industrial Workers of the World
JV	joint venture
LDCs	least developed countries
LLC	limited liability company
M1	money supply 1
M2	money supply 2
M&As	mergers and acquisitions
MBS	mortgage-backed securities
MDGs	Millennium Development Goals
MDRI	Multilateral Debt Relief Initiative
MEA	multilateral environmental agreement
MERCOSUR	Common Market of the South
MFC	marginal factor cost
MFI	microfinance institution
MFN	most favored nation (status)
MIGA	Multilateral Investment Guarantee Agency
MMDA	money market deposit account
MMMF	money market mutual fund
MRP	marginal revenue product
MSB	marginal social benefit
MSC	marginal social cost
MU	marginal utility
NABE	National Association for Business Economics
NAFTA	North American Free Trade Agreement
NASDAQ	North American Stock Dealers Automated Quotations
NBER	National Bureau of Economic Research
NCL	National Consumers League
NCUA	National Credit Union Administration
NCUSIF	National Credit Union Share Insurance Fund

NGO	nongovernmental organization
NIEs	Newly Industrialized Asian Economies
NLRB	National Labor Relations Board
NLU	National Labor Union
NOW	negotiable order of withdrawal (accounts)
NYSE	New York Stock Exchange
OCDs	other checkable deposits
ODA	official development assistance
OECD	Organization for Economic Cooperation and Development
OMB	Office of Management and Budget
OPEC	Organization of Petroleum Exporting Countries
OTC	over the counter
PPF	production possibilities frontier
PPI	producer price index
PPP	purchasing power parity
PRGF	Poverty Reduction and Growth Facility
PRWORA	Personal Responsibility and Work Opportunity Act
PTO	Patent and Trademark Office
QE	quantitative easing
R&D	research and development
RDB	regional development bank
RTA	regional trade agreement
S&L	savings and loan association
SAR	special administrative region
SBA	Small Business Administration
SDRs	Special Drawing Rights
SEC	Securities and Exchange Commission
SEP	Simplified Employee Pension (plan)
SME	small and medium-sized enterprises
SNAP	Supplemental Nutrition Assistance Program
SOE	state-owned enterprise
SSI	Supplemental Security Income
SWIFT	Society for Worldwide Interbank Financial Telecommunication
TANF	Temporary Assistance for Needy Families
TC	total cost
TNC	transnational corporation
TRIPS	Trade-Related Aspects of Intellectual Property
UI	unemployment insurance
UN	United Nations
UNCTAD	United Nations Conference on Trade and Development
UNDP	United National Development Program
UNEP	United Nations Environmental Program
UNESCO	United Nations Educational, Scientific, and Cultural Organization
USAID	U.S. Agency for International Development
USITC	U.S. International Trade Commission
VC	variable cost

VER	voluntary export restraint
VIE	voluntary import expansion
WHO	World Health Organization
WIPO	World Intellectual Property Organization
WOFE	wholly owned foreign enterprise
WRI	World Resources Institute
WTO	World Trade Organization
WWW	World Wide Web

Selected Bibliography

CLASSIC TEXTS

Drucker, Peter F. *The Essential Drucker: The Best of Sixty Years of Peter Drucker's Essential Writings on Management*. New York: HarperBusiness, 2001.

Ebenstein, Alan O., William Ebenstein, and Edwin Fogelman. *Today's ISMS: Socialism, Capitalism, Fascism, Communism, and Libertarianism*. 11th ed. Upper Saddle River, NJ: Pearson, 2000.

Friedman, Milton, and Rose Friedman. *Capitalism and Freedom*. Chicago: University of Chicago Press, 1962.

Galbraith, John K. *The Affluent Society*. New York: Mentor Books, 1958.

Harrington, Michael. *The Other America: Poverty in the United States*. Baltimore: Penguin, 1962.

Hayek, Friedrich A. *The Road to Serfdom*. 50th Anniversary ed. Chicago: University of Chicago Press, 1994.

Heilbroner, Robert L. *The Worldly Philosophers: The Lives, Times and Ideas of the Great Economic Thinkers*. 7th ed. New York: Touchstone, 1999.

Jones, Mary H. *Mother Jones Speaks*. Ed. Philip S. Foner. Atlanta, GA: Pathfinder, 1983.

Keynes, John Maynard. *The General Theory of Employment, Interest, and Money*. Amherst, NY: Prometheus, 1997.

Kuznets, Simon. *National Income and Its Composition, 1919–1938*. Vol. 1. New York: National Bureau of Economic Research, 1941.

Lewis, W. Arthur. *The Theory of Economic Growth*. London: Unwin Hyman, 1955.

Malthus, Thomas R. *An Essay on the Principle of Population*. Reissue ed. New York: W.W. Norton & Company, 1976.

Marshall, Alfred. *Principles of Economics*. Abridged. Amherst, NY: Prometheus, 1997.

Marx, Karl, and Friedrich Engels. *The Communist Manifesto*. New York: Washington Square Press, 1964.

Mill, John Stuart. *Principles of Political Economy: And Chapters on Socialism*. Ed. Jonathon Riley. New York: Oxford University Press, 1999.

Mun, Thomas. *England's Treasure by Foreign Trade*. New York: Augustus M. Kelly, 1993.

Owen, Robert. *A New View of Society, 1816*. Ed. Jeffrey Stern. New York: Thoemmes, 1996.

Pigou, Arthur C. *The Economics of Welfare*. Piscataway, NJ: Transaction Publishers, 2002.

Ricardo, David. *The Principles of Political Economy and Taxation*. New York: E.P. Dutton & Company, Inc., 1911.

Rostow, W. W. *The Stages of Economic Growth: A Non-Communist Manifesto*. New York: Cambridge University Press, 1960.

Schumacher, Ernst F. *Small Is Beautiful: Economics as if People Mattered*. New York: Harper & Row, 1973.

Schumpeter, Joseph A. *Capitalism, Socialism, and Democracy*. New York: Perennial, 1962.

Smith, Adam. *An Inquiry into the Nature and Causes of the Wealth of Nations*. New York: Oxford University Press, 1976.

Solow, Robert M. *Growth Theory: An Exposition*. New York: Oxford University Press, 1970.

Soto, Hernando de. *The Other Path: The Invisible Revolution in the Third World*. New York: Harper & Row, 1989.

Taylor, Frederick Winslow. *The Principles of Scientific Management*. New York: W.W. Norton & Company, 1947.

United Nations. *Agenda 21 Earth Summit: United Nations Program for Action for Rio*. New York: United Nations, 1992.

Ward, Barbara. *The Rich Nations and the Poor Nations*. New York: W.W. Norton & Company, 1962.

Webb, Sidney, and Beatrice Webb. *The Decay of Capitalist Civilization*. New York: Harcourt, Brace and Company, 1923.

Yergin, Daniel, and Joseph Stanislaw. *The Commanding Heights: The Battle for the World Economy*. Rev. ed. New York: Free Press, 2002.

Yunus, Muhammad, and Alan Jolis. *Banker to the Poor: Micro-Lending and the Battle against World Poverty*. Cambridge, MA: Perseus, 1999.

CURRENT LITERATURE

Bernstein, William J. *A Splendid Exchange: How Trade Shaped the World*. New York: Grove, 2008.

Blinder, Alan S. *After the Music Stopped: The Financial Crisis, the Response, and the Work Ahead*. New York: Penguin, 2013.

Calhoun, Craig, and Georgi Derluguian. *Business as Usual: The Roots of the Global Financial Meltdown*. New York: NYU Press, 2011.

Cavanaugh, John, and Jerry Mander. Eds. *Alternatives to Economic Globalization: A Better World is Possible*. 2nd ed. San Francisco: Berrett-Koehler, 2004.

Clark, Cynthia L. Ed. *The American Economy: A Historical Encyclopedia*. Santa Barbara, CA: ABC-CLIO, 2011.

Davis, Aeron. *Promotional Cultures: The Rise and Spread of Advertising, Public Relations, Marketing and Branding*. Malden, MA: Polity, 2013.

Ehrenreich, Barbara. *Nickel and Dimed: On (Not) Getting By in America* (rev. afterword). New York: Henry Holt and Company, 2001, 2008.

England, Robert S. *Black Box Casino: How Wall Street's Risky Shadow Banking Crashed Global Finance*. Santa Barbara, CA: ABC-CLIO/Praeger, 2011.

Friedman, Thomas L., and Michael Mandelbaum. *That Used to Be Us: How America Fell Behind in the World It Invented and How We Can Come Back*. New York: Picador, 2011.

Helpman, Elhanan. *Understanding Global Trade*. Cambridge, MA: Belknap Press of Harvard University Press, 2011.

Hubbard, Glenn, and Tim Kane. *Balance: The Economics of Great Powers from Ancient Rome to Modern America*. New York: Simon & Schuster, 2013.

Irwin, Neil. *The Alchemists: Three Central Bankers and a World on Fire*. New York: Penguin, 2013.

Issacson, Walter. *Steve Jobs*. New York: Simon & Schuster, 2011.

Johnson, Simon, and James Kwak. *White House Burning: Our National Debt and Why It Matters to You*. New York: Vintage, 2012.

Krugman, Paul R. *End This Depression Now*. New York: W. W. Norton & Company, 2013.

Lawless, Robert E. *The Student's Guide to Financial Literacy*. Westport, CT: Greenwood, 2010.

Noell, Edd S., Stephen L. S. Smith, and Bruce G. Webb. *Economic Growth: Unleashing the Potential of Human Flourishing*. Washington, DC: AEI Press, 2013.

O'Connor, David E. *Encyclopedia of the Global Economy: A Guide for Students and Researchers*. Vols. 1–2. Westport, CT: Greenwood, 2006.

Reich, Robert B. *Beyond Outrage: What Has Gone Wrong with Our Economy and Our Democracy, and How to Fix It*. Expanded ed. New York: Vintage, 2012.

Rycroft, Robert S. Ed. *The Economics of Inequality, Poverty, and Discrimination in the 21st Century*. Santa Barbara, CA: ABC-CLIO/Praeger, 2013.

Schiff, Lewis. *Business Brilliant: Surprising Lessons from the Greatest Self-Made Business Icons*. New York: HarperCollins, 2013.

Schiff, Peter D. *The Real Crash: America's Coming Bankruptcy; How to Save Yourself and Your Country*. New York: St. Martin's, 2012.

Schor, Juliet B. *Plentitude: The New Economics of True Wealth*. New York: Penguin, 2010.

Smith, Hendrick. *Who Stole the American Dream?* New York: Random House, 2012.

Steil, Benn. *The Battle of Bretton Woods: John Maynard Keynes, Harry Dexter White, and the Making of the New World Order*. Princeton, NJ: Princeton University Press, 2013.

Stiglitz, Joseph E. *The Price of Inequality: How Today's Divided Society Endangers Our Future*. New York: W.W. Norton & Company, 2013.

Stiglitz, Joseph E., and Mary Kaldor. *The Quest for Security: Protection without Protectionism and the Challenge of Global Governance*. New York: Columbia University Press, 2013.

Storch, Randi. *Working Hard for the American Dream: Workers and Their Unions, World War I to the Present*. Malden, MA: John Wiley & Sons, 2013.

Timmerman, Kelsey. *Where Am I Wearing: A Global Tour to the Countries, Factories, and People That Make Our Clothes*. 2nd ed. Malden, MA: John Wiley & Sons, 2012.

Wilkinson, Rorden, and David Hulme. Eds. *The Millennium Development Goals and Beyond: Global Development after 2015*. New York: Routledge, 2012.

STATISTICAL REPORTS AND OTHER DATA (MOST ALSO AVAILABLE ONLINE)

Bank for International Settlements. *Triennial Central Bank Survey of Foreign Exchange and Derivatives Market Activity in April 2010*. Basel, Switzerland: BIS, 2010.

Board of Governors of the Federal Reserve System. *The Federal Reserve System: Purposes and Functions*. 9th ed. Washington, DC: Board of Governors, 2005.

Council of Economic Advisors. *Economic Report of the President: 2013*. Washington, DC: U.S. Government Printing Office, 2013 (annual).

Gwartney, James, Robert Lawson, and Joshua Hall. *Economic Freedom of the World: 2012 Annual Report*. Canada: Fraser Institute, 2012 (annual).

Hardoon, Deborah, and Finn Heinrich. *Global Corruption Report, 2013*. Berlin, Germany: Transparency International, 2013 (annual topics).

International Monetary Fund. *World Economic Outlook, April 2013: Hopes, Realities, Risks*. Washington, DC: IMF, 2013 (semiannual).

Schneider, Friedrich, and Dominik H. Enste. *The Shadow Economy: An International Survey*. 2nd ed. New York: Cambridge University Press, 2013.

Schwab, Klaus. Ed. *The Global Competitiveness Report, 2012–2013*. Geneva, Switzerland: World Economic Forum, 2012 (annual).

United National Conference on Trade and Development (UNCTAD). *The Least Developed Countries Report, 2012*. New York: United Nations, 2012 (annual).

United National Conference on Trade and Development (UNCTAD). *Trade and Development Report, 2012*. New York: UNCTAD, 2012 (annual).

United National Conference on Trade and Development (UNCTAD). *World Investment Report, 2013: Global Value Chains; Investment and Trade for Development.* New York: UNCTAD, 2013 (annual).

United Nations Development Program. *Human Development Report, 2013: The Rise of the South; Human Progress in a Diverse World.* New York: UNDP, 2013 (annual).

U.S. Bureau of Labor Statistics. *Occupational Outlook Handbook: 2012–13 Edition.* Washington, DC: U.S. Department of Labor, 2012 (online at www.bls.gov/ooh).

U.S. Bureau of the Census. *Statistical Abstract of the United States: 2012.* 131st ed. Washington, DC: U.S. Government Printing Office, 2011. (In 2013 this statistical abstract changed from a Census Bureau publication to the *ProQuest Statistical Abstract of the United States.*) (annual).

World Bank. *Global Economic Prospects, June 2013.* Vol. 7. Washington, DC: World Bank (semiannual).

World Bank. *World Development Indicators, 2013.* Washington, DC: World Bank, 2013 (annual).

World Bank. *World Development Report, 2013.* Washington, DC: World Bank, 2013 (annual).

World Trade Organization. *International Trade Statistics, 2012.* Geneva, Switzerland: WTO, 2012 (annual).

Worldwatch Institute, and Erik Assadourian. *State of the World, 2013: Is Sustainability Still Possible?* Washington, DC: Island Press, 2013 (annual).

Key Economic Web Sites

This list identifies Web sites that provide timely, authoritative economic information for students, teachers, researchers, and citizens. Included are government departments, agencies, and commissions; nonprofit organizations and advocacy groups; and multilateral organizations.

Administrative Office of the U.S. Courts	www.uscourts.gov
AFL-CIO	www.aflcio.org
African Development Bank	www.afdb.org
American Economic Association	www.aeaweb.org
Asian Development Bank	www.adb.org
Association of Southeast Asian Nations	www.asean.org
Bank of International Settlements	www.bis.org
Bureau of Economic Analysis	www.bea.gov
Bureau of Labor Statistics	www.bls.gov
Bureau of the Census	www.census.gov
Central Intelligence Agency	www.cia.gov
CME Group	www.cmegroup.com
Conference Board	www.conference-board.com
Congressional Budget Office	www.cbo.gov
Consumer Federation of America	www.consumerfed.org
Consumer Product Safety Commission	www.cpsc.gov
Consumers International	www.consumersinternational.org
Department of Agriculture	www.usda.gov
Department of Commerce	www.doc.gov
Department of Energy	www.doe.gov
Department of Health and Human Services	www.hhs.gov
Department of Housing and Urban Development	www.hud.gov
Department of Labor	www.dol.gov
Department of the Treasury	www.ustreas.gov
Economic Freedom Network	www.freetheworld.com
Energy Information Administration	www.eia.gov
Environmental Protection Agency	www.epa.gov
Equal Employment Opportunity Commission	www.eeoc.gov
European Bank for Reconstruction and Development	www.ebrd.com

European Commission to the U.S.	www.euintheus.org
European Free Trade Association	www.efta.int
European Union	http://europa.eu
Eurostat	http://epp.eurostat.ec.europa.eu
Federal Communications Commission	www.fcc.gov
Federal Deposit Insurance Corporation	www.fdic.gov
Federal Reserve System	www.federalreserve.gov
Federal Trade Commission	www.ftc.gov
Fedstats	www.fedstats.gov
Freedom House	www.freedomhouse.org
Government Accountability Office	www.gao.gov
Inter-American Development Bank	www.iadb.org
Internal Revenue Service	www.irs.gov
International Center for Settlement of Investment Disputes	www.icsid.org
International Co-operative Alliance	www.ica.coop.org
International Development Association	www.ida.org
International Finance Corporation	www.ifc.org
International Labor Organization	www.ilo.org
International Monetary Fund	www.imf.org
International Telecommunications Union	www.itu.int
International Trade Administration	www.trade.gov
International Trade Commission	www.usitc.gov
International Trade Union Confederation	www.ituc-csi.org
Multilateral Investment Guarantee Agency	www.miga.org
NASDAQ OMX	www.nasdaqomx.com
National Association for Business Economics	www.nabe.com
National Bureau of Economic Research	www.nber.org
National Cooperative Business Alliance	www.ncba.org
National Credit Union Administration	www.ncua.gov
National Science Foundation	www.nsf.gov
New York Stock Exchange Euronext	www.nyx.com
Office of Management and Budget	www.whitehouse.gov/omb
Office of the United States Trade Representative	www.ustr.gov
Organization for Economic Cooperation and Development	www.oecd.org
Organization of Petroleum Exporting Countries	www.opec.org
Patent and Trademark Office	www.uspto.gov
Population Reference Bureau	www.prb.org
Securities and Exchange Commission	www.sec.gov
Securities Industry and Financial Markets Association	www.sifma.org
Small Business Administration	www.sba.gov
Social Security Administration	www.ssa.gov
Society for Worldwide Interbank Financial Communication	www.swift.com
United Nations	www.un.org
UN Children's Fund	www.unicef.org
UN Conference on Trade and Development	www.unctad.org
UN Development Program	www.undp.org
UN Educational, Scientific, and Cultural Organization	www.unesco.org
UN Environmental Program	www.unep.org
UN Population Fund	www.unfpa.org
World Bank	www.worldbank.org
World Economic Forum	www.weforum.org
World Federation of Exchanges	www.world-exchanges.org

World Health Organization   www.who.org
World Intellectual Property Organization   www.wipo.org
World Resources Institute   www.wri.org
World Trade Organization   www.wto.org
Worldwatch Institute   www.worldwatch.org
World Wide Web Consortium   www.w3.org

Index to Primary Documents

Index to Economics in History

General Index

About the Author

David E. O'Connor is a nationally recognized economics teacher at the Edwin O. Smith High School in Storrs, Connecticut, where he has taught economics since 1975. O'Connor has also served as an Adjunct Professor of Economics since 1993 through the University of Connecticut's Early College Experience program. He has earned many state and national honors in the fields of economic education and social studies, including the Kidger Award (New England History Teachers Association), Connecticut Council on Economic Education's Distinguished Service Award, the Connecticut Council for the Social Studies Honor and Service awards, and the University of Connecticut's Excellence in Teaching Alumni Award. He has served as a College Board Consultant in economics, President of the Connecticut Council for the Social Studies, and Economics instructor at the Taft Summer Institute for Teachers. He has conducted over 100 teacher workshops at state and national conferences, and was named Teacher of the Year for Regional School District #19. He has also worked in assessment with the Educational Testing Service, Psychological Corporation/Harcourt Educational Measurement, and the American Institutes for Research.

Mr. O'Connor has authored or co-authored 19 books or teacher's manuals in the fields of economics, ethnic history, and world history. His more recent books include *Encyclopedia of the Global Economy: A Guide for Students and Researchers* (Greenwood, 2006), *The Basics of Economics* (Greenwood, 2004), *Demystifying the Global Economy* (Greenwood, 2002), and *Basic Economic Principles: A Guide for Students* (Greenwood, 2000). During the early 2000s he authored a series of teacher's manuals and reference materials on the global economy for the University of Connecticut's Center for International Business Education and Research (CIBER). O'Connor also participated in a number of international economics grants. He was an instructor in a two-year U.S. Agency for International Development (USAID) market economics program in Poland during the early 1990s, a participant in a Fulbright scholar program in the Peoples Republic of China in 2002, and co-coordinator for a high school sister schools project with the Linqu Experimental Middle School in Shandong Province, China in 2004.